Introduction to
CORRECTIONS

THIRD EDITION

Richard A. Tewksbury

Administration of Justice
University of Louisville
Louisville, Kentucky

GLENCOE

McGraw-Hill

New York, New York   Columbus, Ohio   Mission Hills, California   Peoria, Illinois

Library of Congress Cataloging-in-Publication Data

Tewksbury, Richard A.
    Introduction to corrections / Richard A. Tewksbury. — 3rd ed.
      p.   cm.
    Rev. ed. of: Introduction to correctional science / Louis P. Carney.
2nd ed. 1979.
    Includes bibliographical references and index.
    ISBN 0-02-800925-8
    1. Corrections.   I. Carney, Louis P.   Introduction to correctional
science.   II. Title.
HV9275.C37   1996
364.6—dc20   96-5356
                                                  CIP

Glencoe/McGraw-Hill
A Division of The McGraw-Hill Companies

Send all inquiries to:
Glencoe/McGraw-Hill
8787 Orion Place
Columbus, OH 43240

ISBN 0-02-800925-8

4 5 6 7 8 9 0 DOC/DOC 0 9 8 7 6 5 4 3

Table of Contents

CHAPTER 5
Administration of the Prison

CHAPTER 8
Prison Unrest

202

APPENDIX B
Selected Amendments to the Constitution of the United States

Preface

Introduction to Corrections is designed to introduce students to the profession, industry, and academic discipline of corrections. The text's goal is to introduce students—whether criminal justice or corrections majors, or simply those interested in knowing how our correctional system *really* works—to the operation of corrections in the United States. This book focuses on the structure of correctional systems, the operations of correctional institutions and programs, the evolutionary and political development of corrections, and the goals of corrections in contemporary society. Additionally, Job Focuses throughout the text introduce students to the vast range of career opportunities available in the ever-growing field of corrections.

The text is designed so that students in a coordinated, sequenced criminal justice program as well as those who take an introductory corrections class as a supplement to a different program of study can understand the basic concepts. After completing this course, students should be able to understand the problems and potential resolutions resulting from both institutional and community correctional efforts.

Content and Features of the Textbook

This text is designed to be accessible to all students, including those with no previous exposure to correctional or criminal justice issues. The author's goal is to present complex issues and subjects in such a way that students new to the field feel comfortable, yet those with more experience can examine issues at a deeper, more analytical level.

The text has been written not only with students' learning in mind, but also has been written to be instructor-friendly. Numerous features incorporated in the book should benefit both students and instructors. The book consists of 14 chapters, and it is recommended that all 14 chapters be included in a semester- or quarter-length course, using the chapters in the order they are presented in the book. The focus of each chapter follows.

Chapter 1 introduces students to the study of crime and social responses to crime. This chapter examines the role of corrections in society's attempt to control crime. The scope of crime in our society and examinations of how crime is measured provide a foundation on which to understand our responses to crime. A variety of forms of punishment philosophies are explored by looking historically at how various cultures have thought about the nature of crime. The first chapter concludes by identifying and defining the goals of corrections.

Chapter 2 explains how corrections functions as one component of an integrated, sequenced criminal justice system. By looking at the concept of law, various forms of laws, and the processes by which laws are created, crime and criminals can be better understood. Chapter 2 ends by explaining how criminal justice operates as a system, and introduces students to the three primary components of the American criminal justice system—law enforcement, judicial processes, and corrections—and explains how the efforts and goals of each component affect the other components.

Chapter 3, "Punishment," draws the student into a more focused assessment of social responses to crime. Students will gain an understanding of how social norms, values, and beliefs guide official responses to crime by looking at how societies have reacted historically against law-breakers. This chapter concludes by explaining how various philosophies of punishment and corrections have guided social reactions to crime. Identifying ideological perspectives sets the stage for the remainder of the text's content: the specific structures and operations of contemporary correctional practices.

"The Prison" is the topic of Chapter 4. The discussion begins with an overview of how correctional institutions have evolved, with special attention to the development of correctional institutions in the United States. The changes in characteristics of prison populations show corrections as a growing industry. Chapter 4 also discusses the two major types of prison systems in our society: state correctional systems and the federal prison system.

In Chapter 5 we explore the "Administration of the Prison." Here, students will discover how prisons operate, what their goals are, and how correctional workers are integral in pursuing and achieving those goals. Throughout Chapter 5, the challenges and stresses of working in a correctional institution are discussed as well as how these factors influence the operations of prisons. Also discussed are how correctional staff are selected, how they are expected to be prepared, and how prison work has changed in recent years.

The focus shifts to the clients of correctional institutions in Chapters 6–8. "The Prisoner" is the topic of Chapter 6. In addition to examining who is in prison and how prison populations have grown in the past two decades, this chapter discusses what prison life is like. By looking at the culture and structure of prison life, students will understand how prison operations are tailored to address the causes of crime while pursuing correctional goals. The section on prison culture explains what incarceration is like and how this culture differs from what most non-inmates experience. Also discussed are the major forms of programming offered in prisons, as attempts to occupy both the inmates' time and energies as well as to change criminals' behaviors. The chapter concludes by explaining how the incarceration experience can have lasting effects on inmates after their release.

Chapter 7 builds on the previous discussions of prison culture by exploring "Prisoners' Rights." As prisons, prison operations, and prison populations have grown and changed, so too have the legal restrictions on correctional systems, institutions, and workers changed. This chapter explores the legal framework that structures the lives of both the prison inmate and the correctional staff person. Beginning with a look at how inmates' rights have developed in the United States, this chapter discusses the major areas of legal concern for both inmates and administrators.

"Prison Unrest" is the topic of Chapter 8. The chapter focuses on how the culture of prisons can lead to violence within the prison. Several forms of violence are identified, which are common to prisons and prison inmates. Why violence is believed to persist in prisons also is explored, with attention paid to both the strengths and weaknesses of these "explanations" for various types of violence. The form of prison violence that receives the most public attention—prison riots—are discussed in depth. Three of the best-known riots in American correctional history are highlighted, showing how the prisons' cultures and operations contributed to the outbreak and control of these riots. Finally, theories for explaining prison riots are reviewed.

Chapter 9 focuses on a rapidly growing segment of the American correctional population: women inmates. In "Corrections for Women," the issues previously addressed regarding male inmates are discussed specifically for women. After examining the extent of women's crime and how to respond to their unique cultural needs, the discussion turns to how corrections for women is structured. The organization and operation of women's correctional facilities is reviewed as are the differences in program offerings and the legal issues that are unique to female inmates.

In Chapters 10–12 the focus moves from prisons to other forms of correctional activities in our society. Chapter 10's "Local Corrections" examines the purpose of jails, how jails differ from prisons, and how the daily operations of jails are carried out. Special attention is given to how jails differ from prisons and how the problems encountered in operating jails are often different and greater than those for prisons. Within these problems, the challenges and stresses for jail staff and administrators are highlighted.

Chapter 11 examines the operations of "Community Corrections." The principles upon which community corrections are based are reviewed first, showing that there are arguments for and against community-based corrections. The historical evolution of community correctional activities shows students how probation—and the modern variations of it—have a solid basis in our cultural heritage. The modern variations in community corrections and how the laws of our society structure those activities are also discussed.

"Parole" is the topic of Chapter 12. Here, the ideas of institutional and community corrections are brought together in an effort to serve both the goals of corrections and address problems in correctional systems. The goals and processes of parole are reviewed as well as the activities of parole officers.

Chapter 13 examines the parallel structure and activities of the "Juvenile Justice" system with the adult system. This chapter provides an overview of the goals, development, and organization of the juvenile justice system with special emphasis on correctional efforts for juveniles.

Chapter 14 concludes the text with an in-depth examination of four major "Contemporary Issues in Corrections." These discussions draw together the issues presented earlier in the text, which explore the two most pressing problems in U.S. corrections today: overcrowding and financial problems. Based on the scope of the administrative problems imposed by these conditions, this chapter looks at two important ways that correctional systems seek to address these problems: privatization of correctional operations and the construction of new prisons. Here, students can complete their understanding of how all components of the correctional system, the criminal justice system, and the larger social and legal institutions of our society are integrated.

Chapter Structure

Chapter Objectives. Each chapter begins with a detailed set of benchmarks to guide students' reading. With these points in mind, students can identify and easily grasp the main points in each chapter.

Key Terms.   The vocabulary for each chapter follows Chapter Objectives. This is a list of the chapter's key terms which, in the chapter, are presented in boldface, with definitions in the margins. Additionally, all key terms are listed and defined in the glossary at the end of the text.

Chapter Outline.   This outline follows the Key Terms and serves as a roadmap indicating where the discussion will progress.

Special Features.   These appear in each chapter and are designed to facilitate the understanding and comprehension of the chapter's major points. Each chapter contains up-to-date information about some of the career opportunities in corrections in the feature called Job Focus. These discussions highlight the responsibilities, necessary preparations, types of daily tasks, and salary requirements that can be expected for particular jobs in the correctional field. Another special feature in each chapter are boxed features, called FYIs, that supplement the main text by showing extended examples or particular applications of ideas. Finally, each chapter contains at least one summary of a relevant and often precedent-setting legal case that has shaped the functions of correctional practice.

Summaries.   Each chapter has an end-of-chapter summary. Here, the major points of the chapter are briefly reiterated for the student's benefit.

Review Questions and Activities.   These questions and activities appear after the summary of each chapter. These questions reiterate the chapter objectives and allow students to assess how well they have understood the major points in the chapter. A list of suggested activities follows the review questions. These challenge students to explore the issues of the chapter in greater depth. They include suggestions for group activities and speakers.

Endnotes.   End-of-chapter notes document the sources of information in the chapter and also serve as sources for additional reading.

About the Author

Richard A. Tewksbury is an Assistant Professor in the Department of Justice Administration at the University of Louisville. Previously, he has taught at a number of colleges and universities, including The Ohio State University, Wilmington College, Columbus State Community College, and Franklin University. He also has worked for the Ohio Department of Rehabilitation and Correction, both as an instructor in prison college programs and as a research analyst. Additionally, he has worked with the Jefferson County, Kentucky Department of Corrections in several inmate education programs, and has conducted extensive research on correctional programming and inmate culture. In 1991 he received his Ph.D. in Sociology from The Ohio State University in Columbus, Ohio. Dr. Tewksbury has published more than 35 scholarly journal articles, books, and professional reports. Currently, he is on the Board of Directors of the Southern Criminal Justice Association, active in the American Correctional Association, Academy of Criminal Justice Sciences, American Society of Criminology, and American Sociological Association, and serves as the editor of the *American Journal of Criminal Justice.*

Acknowledgments

Writing and producing this book has been possible only because of the assistance and support of a number of people. I want to recognize and thank those who have played important roles in assisting me to complete this task. First, to my students and assistants—Monty Stout, Deanna McGaughey, Alexis Miller, and Edith Underwood—I owe a great thanks for their efforts.

Also, my colleagues in Justice Administration at the University of Louisville have provided support and encouragement throughout the long process of producing this book. Also playing important roles in supporting my work have been Patricia Gagné of the University of Louisville and Marty Schwartz of Ohio University. Special thanks are due to my mentor and friend at the University of Louisville, Gennaro Vito, who has always believed in me and supported my work.

Insightful reviewers provided important suggestions and criticisms, and most certainly helped to shape this book. I thank all of the reviewers, including: Carolyn Atkins, Lincoln University, Jefferson City, Missouri; Walter Francis, Central Wyoming College, Riverton, Wyoming; J. M. Howard, Erie Community College, Buffalo, New York; John O'Kane, Adirondack Community College, Queensbury, New York; Hugh O'Rourke, Westchester Community College, Valhalla, New York; Harley Ross, Chaffey College, Rancho Cucamonga, California; Sally Termin, Scottsdale Community College, Scottsdale, Arizona.

Finally, to those who have displayed unending patience and have always been supportive, "thank you" seems like such an understatement. Without the editorial staff at Glencoe/McGraw-Hill Publishing Company, including but not limited to Sue Diehm, this book would be much less than it is today. Extraordinary support, patience, and knowledge have been shown by my editor, Rick Adams. Although we sometimes disagreed, Rick has always been behind me and is the reason this book is a reality. Finally, to my wife, Lisa, who has lived this project with me, I thank you for your love, patience, understanding, and support.

CHAPTER 1

Crime and Corrections

CHAPTER OBJECTIVES

In this chapter we will review the scope of crime in America and examine the different goals that have guided corrections throughout modern history. After reading this chapter, you will be able to:

1. Understand what corrections means in America.

2. Understand the relationship between corrections and the crime problem in modern society.

3. Identify the major sources of crime statistics and their various strengths and weaknesses.

4. Examine the similarities and differences in rates of reported crimes and actual crimes.

5. Discuss the reasons why victims do not report some crimes to law enforcement authorities.

6. Understand the historical development of ways to respond to crime.

7. Discuss the historical social reaction of retaliation to crime.

8. Discuss the historical social reaction of retribution to crime.

9. Discuss the evolution of responding to crime as a reformation of criminal offenders.

10. Identify the guiding goals of current correctional practices.

11. Examine the social responses to crime that seek to prevent crime.

1

KEY TERMS

CHAPTER OUTLINE

Many older prisons are still in operation today.

Corrections and Criminology

Everywhere in today's world we face issues of crime. People in the United States cite crime as one of the most common problems. Even most of our major social problems can be connected to crime. Simply put, crime is everywhere; it is frightening; and our awareness of it is increasing in our country. Since the criminal justice system seems ineffective in stopping crime, many criminals make their careers out of crime. Threats of jail and prison apparently fail to deter criminal activity. In fact, jails and prisons have become temporary stopping-off places for criminals.

Our system of **corrections** is a set of interrelated organizations, agencies, and programs that hold, treat, and sometimes punish those persons known or strongly believed to have committed a crime. One-third of a three-part criminal justice system, corrections is almost entirely dependent on the law enforcement and judiciary components for receiving and assigning of clients. Corrections has very little impact on the law enforcement and judiciary components. However, law enforcement and judiciary activities and decisions control corrections.

Correctional efforts in our country, however, seem to have lost their focus in recent decades. For many years corrections appeared to be exclusively for purposes of punishing lawbreakers. In the twentieth century, changes first emphasized helping (rehabilitating) offenders to change into law-abiding people. The focus of corrections then shifted to working with criminals to better cope with their lives' situations and social environments. Finally, and most recently, the focus appears to be moving toward simply separating criminals from the rest of society and warehousing lawbreakers. These changes in focus mean not only that the actual workings of the correctional system have changed, but it also means that how we view and devote resources to corrections have changed. In the long run, the issue is how effective and efficient our attempts to correct criminals can be. Recent history suggests that we have not been very effective or very efficient.

While corrections is obviously directly connected to studying the criminal justice system functions, we also know that studying corrections is related (but not as obviously) to the study of criminology. **Criminology** is the study of crime. More specifically, as defined by Bartollas and Dinitz, "the objective of criminology is the development of a body of general and verified principles regarding the process of law, crime, and treatment."[1] Through a focus on how laws and lawbreakers are processed and treated, we enter into the overlap with corrections.

Corrections The set of interrelated organizations, agencies, and programs that hold, treat, and sometimes punish people known or strongly believed to have committed a crime.

Criminology The study of crime; the science whose goal is to develop principles to explain the processes of law, crime, and treatment.

In many ways criminology gives us the basic knowledge and understandings of criminal behavior that are used to design and evaluate the workings of correctional systems. Without understanding how criminal events occur and why offenders commit crimes, our efforts in corrections would be without guidance. This would mean we would be even less able to make informed decisions about how to treat offenders and to protect society against criminals who repeat their crimes. **Recidivism,** when criminals repeat their crimes after being convicted and processed through some correctional process, is a major issue of concern for corrections professionals. The criminologist is ultimately interested in reducing crime by understanding the who, what, where, when, and especially the why of crime in general. On the other hand, the correctional professional is concerned with preventing or reducing the likelihood of a known criminal recommitting crime. In these ways the criminologist and the correctionalist are very similar.

Before embarking on a serious and in-depth examination of how the work of corrections is accomplished, we must first review what we know about crime in our society. The remaining portion of this chapter will discuss the size of the crime problem and will review how civilized societies have traditionally responded to the crime problem. We will conclude this chapter by returning to the question, What is the goal of corrections? Finally, we will briefly examine how the structure of our correctional organizations, agencies, and programs works to hold, treat, and sometimes punish lawbreakers, while pursuing these goals.

Recidivism The recurrence of crime by an individual known to have previously committed a crime.

FYI

One popular misconception is that persons of minority races commit a majority of crime in the United States. In fact, more than two-thirds of all persons arrested in the United States are Caucasian.

A Profile of Crime in the United States

One common political issue in the 1990s is the "crime problem" that plagues our society. No doubt, crime is a major problem in our society. However, a close examination of the statistics on crime suggests that not everything we are led to believe is necessarily true. In 1992 the National Crime Victimization Survey reported that there was a total of 33,649,340 incidents of criminal victimization in the United

States. These incidents affected 23 percent of all U.S. households.[2] However, these raw numbers do not really tell us very much about the incidence of crime or about where, to whom, and when crime happens.

As we can see from reviewing Figure 1–1, the level for all crimes has decreased, as has the amount of **household crimes** (offenses against property or one's place of residence) and **personal thefts** (stealing of money or belongings directly from a person). The only type of crime that has increased over the 20-year period has been **violent crime** (offenses that directly bring or directly threaten physical harm to a person). Furthermore, the percentage of

FYI

Crime statistics are often seriously misused. Most notably, crime has *not* increased during the past two decades. Actually, according to reports of crime from crime victims, crime (of all forms) has actually *decreased* since 1973![3]

Household crimes Criminal offenses that victimize people by removing or destroying property.

Personal theft The crime of stealing money or property directly from a person.

Violent crime Criminal offenses that either directly cause or threaten physical harm to a person.

Figure 1–1 The number of victimizations rose from 1973 until the early 1980s and has since declined.

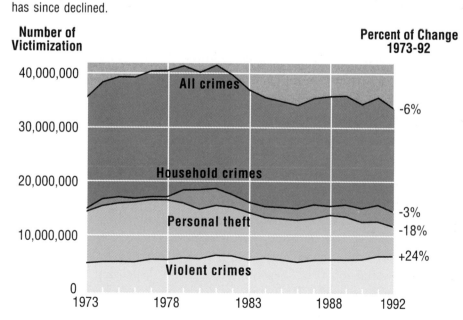

Note: Household crimes include burglary, larceny, and motor vehicle theft. Violent crimes include rape, robbery, and assault.

Source: U.S. Department of Justice, *Highlights from 20 Years of Surveying Crime Victims* (Washington, D.C.: Bureau of Justice Statistics, 1993), p. 7.

U.S. households that were crime victims was lower in 1992 than any year since 1975.[4]

Crime is also one of the most costly social problems in our society. In 1992 crime cost victims more than $17.6 billion dollars.[5] Usually people fear crime because of the possibility of being physically injured. True, many crimes do result in physical injury; but not all crimes, not even violent crimes, result in physical injuries. In fact, only about one-third (31%) of violent crimes lead to physical injuries to victims.[6] Economic losses are more common and, for at least some people, more harmful. Nearly three-fourths (71%) of personal crimes and more than one-fifth (23%) of violent crimes result in economic losses. These losses average (considering all crimes) a cost of $524.[7] However, there are important differences in the degree of economic loss associated with crimes. The average economic loss associated with an assault is $124, compared to the average loss in burglary of $834.[8]

What this suggests is that we must exercise care when discussing the scope of the "crime problem." We must also be careful when we use crime statistics. Not all crime statistics are the same, and you can easily find a statistic to support almost any point of view. This is not to say that crime statistics are not useful or important, for they provide information that guides our planning and working in corrections. Without crime statistics we would not know what to expect today, tomorrow, or next year in our organizations, agencies, and programs. Therefore, we need to examine carefully our sources of statistics and how these statistics are gathered.

Uniform Crime Reports

Uniform Crime Reports (UCR) Official crime statistics that the FBI gathers; the collection of all criminal offenses reported to law enforcement agencies.

The rapid development and population growth in the early 1900s made it clear that all segments of the U.S. criminal justice system needed reliable and consistent data on the occurrences of crime. Whereas local law enforcement agencies and sometimes state agencies kept most crime statistics, there was no organized effort to compile national crime figures until 1930. This is when the Federal Bureau of Investigation (FBI) began collecting and dispensing the **Uniform Crime Reports (UCR).** Representing the reporting of crime by nearly all U.S. law enforcement agencies, the UCR allows the FBI to create a clear picture of where and when and to whom and by whom reported incidents of crime occurred. Those crimes reported to a law enforcement agency (by victims, witnesses, or complainants) or discovered by law enforcement officers are included in the UCR.

Crimes reported to law enforcement officers are included in the UCR.

The most commonly used and referenced portion of the Uniform Crime Reports is Part I. This is reporting on what the FBI has identified as the eight most serious crimes in our society: murder, rape, robbery, assault, burglary, larceny-theft, motor vehicle theft, and arson. The reported incidence of these crimes is combined to create the **crime index.** Therefore, each of these offenses (except arson, due to problems with accurate reporting), because it is a part of the crime index and because each is believed to be an important crime to track, is also referred to as an **index offense.**

As we can see in Table 1–1, more than 14 million serious crimes are reported to law enforcement agencies every year. The majority of these crimes are property crimes, not violent crimes. Figure 1–2 shows the relative size of the number of each index offense compared to the total number of other index offenses. Index rates are calculated to show the number of each type of crime for every 100,000 people.

Crime index The measure of society's most serious crimes; the collection of statistics from the Uniform Crime Reports of the amount of murder, rape, robbery, assault, burglary, larceny-theft, motor vehicle theft, and arson; reported in terms of the number of these offenses per 100,000 people.

Index offense The eight crimes considered the most serious; the eight offenses (murder, rape, robbery, burglary, larceny-theft, motor vehicle theft, and arson) that are combined to create the crime index.

These statistics inform us about the patterns and trends of crime in society. By examining several years' worth of statistics, we can determine whether particular forms of crime are increasing, decreasing, or remaining stable in frequency. We can also use these statistics to learn about the distribution of crime in society.

Victimization Studies

The one set of information that official reporting of crime provides us is certainly not the entire picture. Most people recognize that many incidents of crime in our society are never reported to or discovered by the police. We will discuss some of the reasons for this in the next section. For now it is important to review ways that we can learn about the scope of crime from sources other than official law enforcement records.

The primary alternative form of crime statistics comes from surveys conducted with the general population to identify and count criminal victimizations. The major source for this information is the **National Crime Victimization Survey (NCVS).** The Bureau of the Census conducts this national study every year, and the Bureau of Justice Statistics analyzes and distributes it. Begun in 1972, the NCVS is designed to gather data from a representative sample of almost 100,000 people throughout the United States. This information is used to calculate the extent of criminal victimizations across society.[9] The NCVS estimates *total* crime events, not the number of people

National Crime Victimization Survey (NCVS) The Bureau of the Census' annual national study that gathers data from U.S. citizens about the amount of crime they experienced; the main alternative source of crime statistics to the Uniform Crime Reports.

Table 1–1	Rates of Reported Index Offenses				
Offense	**1990**	**1991**	**1992**	**1993**	**1994**
Murder	23,440	24,700	23,760	24,526	23,305
Forcible rape	102,560	106,590	109,060	104,806	102,096
Robbery	639,270	687,730	672,480	659,757	618,817
Aggravated assault	1,054,860	1,092,740	1,126,970	1,135,099	1,119,950
Burglary	3,073,900	3,157,200	2,979,900	2,834,808	2,712,156
Larceny-theft	7,945,700	8,142,200	7,915,200	7,820,909	7,876,254
Motor vehicle theft	1,635,900	1,661,700	1,610,800	1,561,047	1,539,097
Arson[1]	—	—	—	—	—
Crime index	14,476,630	14,872,883	14,438,191	14,140,952	13,991,675

[1]The UCR reports arson arrest rates and trends, but "sufficient data are not available to estimate totals for this offense."

Sources: Federal Bureau of Investigation, *Crime in the United States* (Washington, D.C.: U.S. Department of Justice, 1991, 1992, 1993, 1994, 1995).

Figure 1–2 Index report rate relative to total number of index offenses.

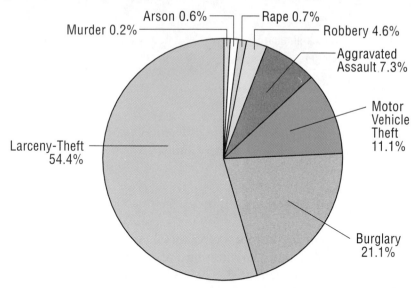

Murder 0.2%
Arson 0.6%
Rape 0.7%
Robbery 4.6%
Aggravated Assault 7.3%
Motor Vehicle Theft 11.1%
Larceny-Theft 54.4%
Burglary 21.1%

Source: Federal Bureau of Investigation, *Crime in the United States* (Washington, D.C.: U.S. Department of Justice, 1993).

out of 100,000 who are victimized as is reported in the UCR. As explained by the U.S. Department of Justice,

> The National Crime Victimization Survey (NCVS) measures the amount and nature of crime in the United States by asking large numbers of people whether they have been crime victims. NCVS provides information about the victims of crime, including the kinds of crimes they have experienced, characteristics of those crimes, impact on the victims, and whether or not the crimes were reported to the police.

In almost all instances, the NCVS reports crime rates higher than those reported in the UCR. This makes sense as the NCVS gathers data directly from victims of crime. There is no "middleman" to act as a filter. This means that the NCVS provides what many criminologists believe to be a more accurate and complete picture of crime in the United States.

However, while the numbers in the NCVS are higher than those in the UCR, the patterns between and within crime categories remain essentially the same across the sources. As can be seen in Table 1–2, while more forcible rapes and robberies are reported by victims in the NCVS

Civilian surveyor asking crime victimization questions of a citizen.

Table 1–2	Number of Forcible Rapes and Robberies, 1993	
	Forcible Rapes	**Robberies**
National Crime Victimization Survey	160,000	1,307,000
Uniform Crime Reports	104,806	659,757

Note: These data are the most recent available.

than in the UCR, the size of the differences between the number of forcible rapes and robberies is very similar.

Nonreporting and Underreporting of Crime

Even with the higher numbers of criminal events reported by victims in the National Crime Victimization Survey, we can still believe that not *all* crime is being counted. The NCVS reveals that many persons who are crime victims, for some reason do not report the crime to law enforcement officers. Victims report many of these incidents to NCVS surveyors, but we would be very naive to believe that victims share all such "hidden crime" with surveyors. This leads to the question, Just how much crime in our society is actually reported to the police? Or, what amount of crime actually enters the criminal justice system?

The NCVS statistics suggest that victims report relatively small percentages of criminal incidents (approximately 35% of all crimes) to law enforcement officials.[10] The severity of the offense and the amount of loss suffered may be victims' primary determining factors for reporting crimes to police. For instance, 50 percent of violent crime victims report the incident to law enforcement authorities, but only 33 percent of household crimes and 25 percent of personal thefts are reported. Among theft offenses, the most likely to be reported are automobile thefts (93% reported).[11] Figure 1–3 shows that among both property crimes and personal crimes (whether including injuries or not), crimes that are most costly and/or that "hit closer to home" are more likely to be reported.

The reporting of crime also appears to be determined, at least in part, by victims' personal characteristics. As shown in Table 1–3, the likelihood of reporting victimization varies by sex and race. Women are more likely to report being a victim of crime, and African-Americans and Hispanics are more likely to report instances when they are victims of violent crimes. The most striking fact about these statistics is: Victims have reported to police less than one-half of the incidents they shared with surveyors. This suggests that perhaps the "crime problem" in our society is much larger than many of our official statistics suggest. This also suggests that there may be some problems with the criminal justice system and how citizens perceive the system, since less than one-half of all crimes are even reported to the police.

Table 1–3	Rates of Reporting Crimes by Sex and Race		
Sex	**Violent Crimes**		**Thefts**
Male	45.0		29.7
Female	56.3		29.4

Source: U.S. Department of Justice, *Criminal Vicitimization in the United States, 1992* (Washington, D.C.: Bureau of Justice Statistics, 1994).

Figure 1–3 Various factors affect whether a crime is reported.

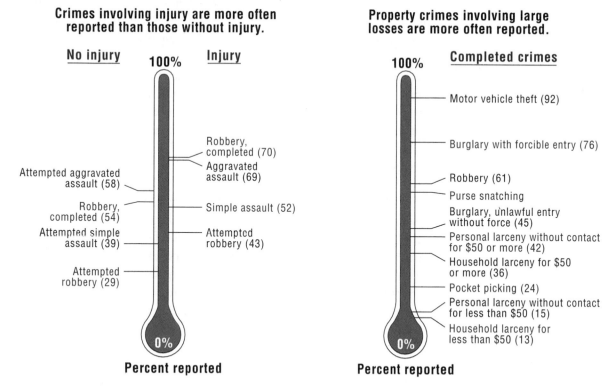

Crimes involving injury are more often reported than those without injury.

No injury   100%   Injury

Robbery, completed (70)
Attempted aggravated assault (58)
Aggravated assault (69)
Robbery, completed (54)
Simple assault (52)
Attempted simple assault (39)
Attempted robbery (43)
Attempted robbery (29)

0%
Percent reported

Property crimes involving large losses are more often reported.

100%   Completed crimes

Motor vehicle theft (92)
Burglary with forcible entry (76)
Robbery (61)
Purse snatching
Burglary, unlawful entry without force (45)
Personal larceny without contact for $50 or more (42)
Household larceny for $50 or more (36)
Pocket picking (24)
Personal larceny without contact for less than $50 (15)
Household larceny for less than $50 (13)

0%
Percent reported

Note: For some types of violent crime, 1992 reporting percentages were not available by whether or not the victim was injured. By definition, attempted assaults are without injury. In 1992, 53 percent of all rapes were reported to the police.

Source: U.S. Department of Justice, *Highlights from 20 Years of Surveying Crime Victims* (Washington, D.C.: Bureau of Justice Statistics, 1993), p. 31.

FYI

One emerging issue of major concern in our society is the extent and severity of crime in our schools. According to the National Crime Victimization Survey,[12] crimes are more common in public schools than in private schools. Younger students (middle school and early high school) are more likely than older high school students to be victims. Schools in major cities are more likely than other schools to have gangs. About three-fourths of high school students report that drugs are available in their schools, and one-half of sixth grade students report knowing where drugs are available in their schools. There appears to be no difference in victimization by race.

We can probably think of many reasons why some people might not call the police to report a crime. For example, they may be involved in crime themselves or may fear "authorities" such as police officers. Consider the case of Mike, who is selling marijuana to his friends. If Paul, who also sells marijuana, hears about Mike's business, comes to Mike's apartment, beats him up, and steals his drugs, how likely is Mike to call the police to report the assault and theft?

However, some of the reasons that actual crime victims give for not reporting may not be quite so obvious. The most common reason that victims say they do not report crimes is that the offender's attempt to harm them or to take something from them was unsuccessful. Other commonly cited reasons include: The victim reported the incident to some other (non–law enforcement) authority; the victim believed there was no evidence or proof; the victim believed that the police would not invest enough time or energy to make the reporting worthwhile; the victim believed that recovering his or her losses was highly unlikely; and the victim believed that the incident was either not important enough to report or simply a private or personal matter. (See Table 1–4).

This lack of reporting suggests that, even with a criminal justice system that has long backlogs and high levels of overcrowding, only a small portion of all "criminals" ever enter the system. However, this is not the only time that a filtering process works in the system. As we will see throughout the text, we need to study crime statistics at several points throughout the system. Only in doing so can we get a complete picture of how the system works and what persons are actually processed through the police and courts to the correctional system.

Society's Historical Reaction to Crime

One age-old axiom that serves us well in corrections is that we should never forget the past and should work to learn from our pasts.

Table 1–4	Reasons for Not Reporting Crimes	
Reason		**Percent of All Nonreporting Victims**
Personal Crimes		
Unsuccessful effort on part of offender		24.2
Reported to a different authority		14.7
Police would be ineffective, inefficient, biased, or not want to be bothered		11.3
Lack of evidence		10.5
Not important enough; private or personal matter		10.4
Believe unable to recover losses		6.8
Not aware crime occurred until much later		4.3
Reporting is too inconvenient or time-consuming		4.1
Other reasons		13.7
Household Crimes		
Unsuccessful effort on part of offender		30.5
Police would be ineffective, inefficient, biased, or not want to be bothered		13.7
Lack of evidence		12.4
Not important enough; private or personal matter		8.9
Believe unable to recover losses		7.9
Not aware crime occurred until much later		7.4
Reported to a different authority		3.5
Reporting is too inconvenient or time-consuming		2.6
Other reasons		13.1

Source: U.S. Department of Justice, *Highlights from 20 Years of Surveying Crime Victims* (Washington, D.C.: Bureau of Justice Statistics, 1993).

Specifically, this means that it is important for us to consider how crime has been viewed historically and to consider these ideas (as well as their practical applications) when we discuss making changes in our present system. The way we view crime in today's world is not the way civilized societies have always viewed crime. In fact, our views today—that crime is a major social problem and criminals need to be either controlled or treated—is a relatively recent way of thinking. As we review the historical evolution of views on crime, we quickly realize that societies have chosen four primary ways to respond to crime. In this section we will briefly study each way of responding to crime and will discuss how some aspects of these response forms are enforced today.

Retaliation

Retaliation Responding to people with actions similar to their crimes because they deserve to suffer similar harms.

Perhaps the earliest response to crime is one that our primitive ancestors brought into civilization. This is the response of revenge. **Retaliation,** the idea of striking back at people who deserve to have done to them what they did to others, was originally used as a way to please the gods. Early civilizations believed that it was necessary to retaliate against wrongdoers so as to avenge the wrongs done against the gods. Retaliation, then, was seen as a responsibility, not simply as a desired response to crime.

Retaliation in early societies did not always mean physical punishment. Instead, it often was carried out in the form of **banishment,** being permanently removed or thrown out of a group or place. Banishment was, however, essentially the same as a death penalty. Being removed from the group meant that one was left to fend alone against nature, roving bands of thieves, murderers, and wild animals. Membership in a group provided security in early societies; removal from the group left one defenseless.

Banishment Being permanently removed from a group or a location.

Retribution

Retribution The idea that a crime (or any wrongdoing) is reacted to with a punishment because the individual who commits a wrong deserves to be punished.

As societies progressed in complexity and grew in size, the emphasis shifted from retaliation to **retribution.** That is, a wrongdoing should be punished because the act deserves punishment. When an individual does wrong, it is society's responsibility to show the wrongdoer that his or her actions will not be tolerated and will result in a negative reaction (a punishment).

Retribution replaced retaliation as society judged that individual criminals were responsible for their actions and that their actions were against other individuals, not against some higher power (gods). Because individuals were held responsible for their actions, society needed to direct a response (or punishment) to the individual. In one way this was a change to thinking that people could be trained. Just as when our ancestors were training animals—by physically punishing them when they misbehaved—so too was it believed that people could be trained. That is, when people misbehaved, they deserved to be punished. In this way society hoped that people could learn from their misbehavior.

Reformation

During the mid-1800s people shifted from a focus on giving punishment so that offenders would learn from their punishment, toward a focus on treating (or changing) offenders. This movement toward **reformation** emphasized change in the individual. We usually think of reforming something as making it better. Thus, if we worked with criminals and understood why they committed crimes, we could change whatever it was that led to their criminality. Reform is treating criminals and making them better (or more law-abiding) people.

In this era we began using the term *corrections* to refer to the activities officials did with convicted criminals. To talk about corrections earlier than this would have been meaningless, as nobody was attempting to "correct" anything. In the mid-1800s, the focus shifted to working with offenders so as to correct their behavior. Corrections, in the modern sense, was born in the nineteenth century, out of efforts to identify what led a person to be a criminal and the accompanying efforts to then alter or remove that cause. Energies were focused on the individual and how changes in the individual could bring about a safer society.

Reformation The idea that when people commit crimes, society should work to change the people so that they do not repeat their crimes.

Prevention

As we move toward the end of the twentieth century, we find that our responses to crime emphasize protection of the community or the prevention of crime. Crime can be prevented in several ways. First, we can protect society by removing those persons who threaten our safety. If we put dangerous people under close supervision or lock them away, then they are unable to victimize others. This is the idea behind public policies that call for long prison terms for repeat offenders.

We can also work to prevent crime by trying to change offenders into law-abiding persons. Treatment

FYI

Preventing crime can also mean making ourselves, as possible victims, less vulnerable. We can prevent the crime that affects us individually by doing things such as making our homes safer, carrying weapons for safety, and avoiding activities that would put us into dangerous places. This is referred to as the practice of *target hardening*. When we make the target of crime harder to access, we can (hopefully) prevent being victims of crime. Logically, we could carry this argument to the point of saying that if *all* possible targets of crime were hardened, then criminals would have little or no opportunity to commit their crimes. In this case crime would be prevented.

programs—such as substance abuse and psychological counseling—are designed to erase the causes of individuals' criminal behavior. If we can remove the reason people commit crimes, then it logically follows that they are less likely to commit crimes and society becomes safer.

Preventing crime comes from several areas, not just corrections. However, corrections and the idea of removing offenders from opportunities to commit crimes are the major ways that our society works to prevent crime.

Goals of Corrections

The purpose of our correctional system is to carry out the sentences criminal courts give in an effective and efficient manner. The correctional worker's goal is to complete a job effectively and efficiently so as to move the system closer to the ultimate goal of controlling crime.

However, this goal can be realized only after several more specific goals are achieved. First, corrections needs to control the amount of crime in society. This means that the number of criminals and criminal events should be reduced. Effectiveness also means that the programs and opportunities presented to offenders need to achieve a goal that is directly related to lessening the likelihood of individual offenders' continuing their criminal actions. Efficiency goals include the idea that programs and opportunities presented to offenders are cost-effective. Correctional activities are not expected to be inexpensive, but they need to be less expensive than the alternative—continued crime by offenders. Concerned not only with the financial costs of programs, efficiency also includes the use of other resources (people, physical facilities, time). Finally, efficiency concerns look not only at what resources corrections uses, but also from where these resources are diverted. To be efficient, a program or opportunity for criminals must make good use of resources. A program should also avoid diverting resources from some other social program, which may use those same resources better.

The goals of corrections are of two types. First is the outcome of the activities of corrections. The goal here is to stop or lower crime among individuals and across society as a whole. Second, the process by which this outcome is pursued should be cost-effective and as minimally disturbing to other social needs as possible. The combination of these two goals—

Crime prevention can come from many sources.

Simply warehousing prisoners may not be the most efficient use of resources.

effectiveness and efficiency—is the key to any assessment of how well corrections works. With this in mind, we will now turn to the how, why, where, and with whom corrections operates. First, though, we must review the first two major components of the criminal justice system. An understanding of law enforcement and the judiciary is important for numerous reasons. Most important for us, however, they must be understood because everything that happens in corrections is directly dependent on what happens in law enforcement and the judiciary.

Summary

The correctional system is the final step in our society's organized, three-step effort to officially catch, judge, and either punish or treat lawbreakers. As the final step in the process, corrections deals with fewer people than do law enforcement and the judiciary components. Only a fraction of the people who commit crimes ever reaches the correctional system.

Crime is a major social problem in our society. However, knowing exactly how much crime exists is a difficult task. We have two basic ways to measure crime: by the number of officially reported incidents and by the number of incidents that citizens discuss when social scientists survey them. Both measures show very high rates of crime.

The manner in which societies have responded to crime has changed in important ways over the centuries. The original responses were based on punishment, either because society viewed punishment as the only moral way to respond or because society believed punishment was necessary to control behavior. From this response to crime, Western civilizations progressed to developing ways to treat or change criminal offenders. Today, this view has been replaced with an emphasis on preventing crime.

Regardless of our individual ideas about what the purpose of corrections should be, the fact remains that our overall goal, as a system, is to achieve a reduction in crime effectively and efficiently.

These are the issues that we will use to conduct our examination of the U.S. correctional system. We will discuss how corrections is done in the United States, who does what jobs in corrections, and who the participants are in these activities. All of these issues will be studied with special attention given to the goal we have seen for corrections: controlling crime in an effective and efficient manner. The issues of effectiveness and efficiency guide public policy and impact how corrections operates in our society. Throughout the remaining chapters, you should ask yourself how what is discussed is related to the ultimate goal of controlling crime.

QUESTIONS FOR REVIEW

1. What does *corrections* mean in American culture?
2. How does corrections work with our law enforcement and judiciary components?
3. How common is crime in the United States?
4. What are the major sources of statistics about crime in our country?
5. What are the strengths and weaknesses of each of our sources of statistics?
6. What are some reasons why victims never report some crimes to the police?
7. What were the earliest ways that societies dealt with lawbreakers?
8. How are today's reactions to crime and criminals different from those of earlier societies?
9. What are the primary goals of our correctional system today?
10. What are the issues that we need to review when we try to determine whether our corrections efforts are effective and efficient?

ACTIVITIES

1. Survey students to find out whether anyone has ever been a victim of a crime and not reported it to the police. What are the crimes most likely not to be reported? Why did these people not report the crimes?
2. Review local newspapers for the past two weeks to find stories reporting on crime. What do these stories suggest are the goals of the criminal justice system?

ENDNOTES

1. Clemens Bartollas and Simon Dinitz, *Introduction to Criminology: Order and Disorder* (New York: Harper & Row, 1989).
2. Patsy Klaus, *The Costs of Crime to Victims* (Washington, D.C.: U.S. Department of Justice, Bureau of Justice Statistics, 1994).
3. U.S. Department of Justice, *Highlights from 20 Years of Surveying Crime Victims* (Washington, D.C.: Bureau of Justice Statistics, 1993).
4. *Ibid.*, p. 8.
5. Klaus, *op. cit.*
6. *Ibid.*

7. *Ibid.*

8. *Ibid.*

9. U.S. Department of Justice, *Criminal Victimization in the United States, 1990* (Washington, D.C.: Bureau of Justice Statistics, 1991), p. iii.

10. *Ibid.,* Table 101.

11. U.S. Department of Justice, *Highlights from 20 Years of Surveying*

Crime Victims (Washington, D.C.: Bureau of Justice Statistics, 1995).

12. Marianne W. Zawitz, Patsy A. Klaus, Ronet Bachman, Lisa D. Bastian, Marshall M. DeBerry, Jr., Michael R. Rand, and Bruce M. Taylor, *Highlights from 20 Years of Surveying Crime Victims* (Washington, D.C.: U.S. Department of Justice, Bureau of Justice Statistics, 1993).

CHAPTER 2

Corrections and Criminal Justice: An Overview

CHAPTER OBJECTIVES

In this chapter we will study how the ideas of criminology, including corrections, are practiced in the criminal justice system to control crime in society. After reading this chapter, you will be able to:

1. Discuss the purposes of the criminal justice system and laws.

2. Explain the various ways that laws are made.

3. Contrast the purposes of procedural and substantive laws.

4. Identify the four sources of law in the United States.

5. Explain the processes by which all four sources of laws are enacted.

6. Identify the three components of the criminal justice system.

7. Explain the purposes and goals of law enforcement.

8. Understand how the judiciary processes criminals into the corrections component.

9. Discuss how corrections depends on the judicial and law enforcement components.

10. Explain how the criminal justice system works as an integrated system.

The Constitution of the United States of America.

Social Functions of Criminal Justice

The criminal justice system was developed to provide society with a way to both enforce the law on lawbreakers and to maintain stability. When asked how they believe criminal justice operates, most people respond: A man commits a violent crime; the police then chase and catch him; the man is sent to court, tried, found guilty, and then sentenced to a number of years in prison. While this scenario certainly does happen sometimes, it is not the usual way our society handles crime. In fact, most depictions of the criminal justice system, especially those in the popular media, are not very accurate.[1] It should not be surprising, then, that American society does not really understand the way that the criminal justice system—and the law—operates.

As we saw in Chapter 1, victims do not report a large proportion of crime to the police. This means that the criminal justice system is often not even involved with crimes. However, when victims report crimes, the criminal justice system operates with the primary purpose of making society safer. That is, we punish (or give treatment to) criminals in the hopes that our actions will prevent future crimes.

The criminal justice system also serves as a symbol of the government's power. Society maintains order by a combination of force and authority. **Force** is the actual use of power to gain physical control over others, whereas **authority** is gaining control over others by implying that force can or may be used. Our system of criminal justice uses both force and authority to ensure that order is maintained in society. For example, force is used when individual offenders are arrested, tried, and sentenced. These actions show what the government actually can do with lawbreakers. Authority, on the other hand, is less concrete; it is how non-lawbreakers view the criminal justice system as a potential user of force to enforce laws. That is, the presence of a criminal justice system gives law-abiding people good reason to stay law-abiding.

Force The use of power to gain physical control over others.

Authority The recognized potential power of a person or an agency to use force.

Everyday reminder of government's authority to regulate behavior.

Role of Law in Society

All societies have rules that regulate citizens' behavior and promote social organization and daily order. Rules of social behavior vary in degrees of complexity and importance. *Folkways,* those "usual ways" of a group of people, are at the most informal level. Because they provide negative reaction from others for unusual ways of doing things, folkways are considered as rules. For example, one unwritten rule in college classrooms is that we dress "appropriately." We assume that we all know what *appropriately* means. However, what if the person sitting next to you came to class one day dressed in a bikini? That person would likely get a few stares; perhaps some classmates would laugh. These are negative reactions that other classmates use to control that student's future behavior. A second type of social rule is called a *more* (pronounced "mor-ay"). Mores are rules that carry moral overtones. What if the person sitting next to you comes to class totally nude? Undoubtedly, some people in class would think this person has some low or loose morals or is a "bad person." Finally, the most formal and strict rules of our society are our laws. Laws serve as the backbone of a civilized society. In simple terms, a law is a rule about what behavior is and is not appropriate for an identifiable group of people.

More formally, **law** is a rule of conduct that an authority recognizes and enforces. In rather direct terms, laws tell people what actions are expected of them and what people may expect from others in society. Our **rights** are what actions we may legitimately expect from others; whereas our **obligations** are the actions that society may legitimately expect from us, based on our specific roles and statuses. Both our rights and obligations are not only expectations, but they can also be compelled by the law's use of force. For any rule to be considered a law, it must meet several criteria:

1. The rule must have *conformity pressures* from an *external source* in the form of *threats* of action.
2. The external pressures for conformity must be *coercive*.
3. Enforcers of the rule need to be *socially authorized* to carry out enforcement activities.
4. Enforcers of the rule need to have *legitimate authority* to use coercive tactics.

Laws exist to structure a society's daily activities. We assume that the law exists to provide citizens with a sense of safety. That is, we feel safe when we believe we can live our lives knowing that we can expect certain things from others and that we must do (or not do) certain things. Feeling safe also means knowing that if and when anyone fails to honor responsibilities, someone in authority will take official action to correct that failure. This is where the criminal justice system enters the picture.

Law A rule of conduct that an authority formally recognizes and enforces; the statements in society that tell people what is expected of them and what they can expect from others.

Rights The actions we may legitimately expect from others in society.

Obligations The actions that society may legitimately expect from us, based on our roles and statuses.

Presence of authority figure as a means to maintain social order.

Substantive and Procedural Law

Law is not only for the purpose of outlining what activities must or must not and may or may not be done. Law is also the basic building block of the systems that make, interpret, and enforce the laws of behavior. This is the basic distinction between substantive and procedural law. **Substantive law** is the set of rules about what behaviors are allowed and required from people. This is what we usually think of when we discuss "law." The substance of the law, the identification of acceptable and unacceptable forms of behavior, comprises the major focus of the law for most people. However, perhaps even more important for a legal system's continued functioning are **procedural laws,** the rules governing how laws are made, interpreted, and enforced. Procedural laws are similar to the written rules of a board game. Procedural laws tell us what people may do to create a new rule, how rules are determined to be "fair," and how people whose job it is to catch rule-breakers may go about that work. Procedural law establishes the structures and ways that substantive laws are made and enforced.

When we think about procedural law, in addition to substantive law, we realize the legal system is actually more complex than most people initially think it is. Procedural laws can oftentimes have more

Substantive law
The set of rules that tell us what behaviors are allowed and required from people; the official rules of society that regulate what people must or must not and may or may not do.

Procedural laws
The rules governing how laws are made, interpreted, and enforced.

influence on maintaining peace and order than can the actual substantive laws of behavior. When we learn that a criminal has not been convicted, or perhaps not even arrested, for crimes that we know were committed, we may complain about the "loopholes" in the law. What we are actually saying is that procedural law was not followed. That is, someone violated the playing rules of the game. When we do not play according to the rules, we essentially lose our turn at the game. Or, we realize that when the rule-enforcers break the rules, the other player (the supposed criminal) gets a "free turn." Therefore, loopholes found in the law do not mean that there is a gap in the law. Instead, loopholes mean that procedural law was violated.

Important to how we structure our society, both substantive and procedural law also exist in several forms. As we will discuss next, American society has four basic sources of law. While each source of law can be and is involved in making both substantive and procedural law, each source is primarily involved in only one form of law.

Sources of Law

Americans have a common misconception that our representatives in state and federal legislatures make all our laws. Thinking ourselves a representative democracy, we believe that the individuals whom we elect to office make and modify all our laws. This is not entirely true.

Yes, legislators make laws and then governors or the President enacts them. However, this is far from the most common method of creating (and removing) laws. While **statutory laws,** those laws that our elected representatives enact, receive the most publicity and public input, they do not comprise the majority of laws that structure our society.

U.S. laws come from four different sources: (1) constitutions, (2) legislatures (statutes), (3) case law, and (4) administrative law. Each type of law tends to focus more or less on either procedural or substantive issues, and each type also has a different degree of involvement in the criminal justice process. Before studying the ways that the criminal justice system (especially corrections) operates, we need first to examine these sources of law.

Constitutions **Constitutions,** or the formal documents creating the structural and procedural parameters of government, are the foundation for all laws within a given jurisdiction. Constitutions create the structure of governments and outline how and what powers are

Statutory laws Laws that elected representatives make; also known as *legislative law.*

Constitutions The formal documents that create the structure and outline the basic procedures of a governmental body; the most powerful forms of law in our society.

given to particular people and governmental agencies. Constitutions, therefore, are primarily concerned with procedural law, not substantive law.

Each state, as well as the federal government, has a constitution. However, the federal Constitution explicitly establishes that any state constitution shall be subordinate to, or less influential than, the federal Constitution. As we see in Figure 2–1, Article VI states that the Constitution is the supreme law of the nation.

Legislatures   Most Americans think "law" is the actions that Congress or their state legislatures or city councils take. These bodies are given authority to make (pass) laws. When potential laws are controversial, they are most likely statutory (legislatively created) laws. Legislative laws are called **statutes** and are organized and maintained in **statutory codes,** which are the cumulative collection of all statutes that govern a particular jurisdiction.

Substantive criminal law is found in the national, state, and local statutes. The majority of laws that define crimes and outline the possible punishments for them are found at the state and local levels. Federal law is rarely involved in criminal cases. Generally speaking, federal law becomes involved in criminal matters only when crimes cross state lines, when the national defense is threatened, or when the offenders or victims are representatives of the national government and are involved in the crimes as a matter of their jobs.

Legislatures are also involved in the creation and modification of procedural laws, although this is less common than their involvement in substantive law. Our nation is based on the political philosophy of

Statutes The laws that legislatures make; most commonly these are substantive laws.

Statutory codes The organized collection of statutes that regulate a particular jurisdiction.

Figure 2–1 Article VI of the United States Constitution.

This Constitution, and the laws of the United States which shall be made in Pursuance thereof; and all treaties made, or which shall be made, under the authority of the United States, shall be the supreme law of the land; and the judges in every State shall be bound thereby, any thing in the Constitution or laws of any State to the contrary notwithstanding.

The Senators and Representatives before mentioned, and the members of the several State Legislatures, and all executive and judicial officers, both of the United States and of the several States, shall be bound by oath or affirmation, to support this Constitution; but no religious test shall ever be required as a qualification to any office or public trust under the United States.

Source: The United States Constitution.

City council enacting legislation to create law.

representative government. This means that we believe in the power of the people, through their elected representatives, to govern themselves. Therefore, the legislative process is central to the principle of government by the people. This is one reason that most Americans believe that the creation of laws is centralized in legislatures.

Many Americans have difficulty understanding the form and language of statutory laws. As shown in Figure 2–2, the three state statutes that define rape all read differently. Clearly, none of the three statutes are as simple as the definitions we know for rape. This means that while our elected representatives create them, statutes are not necessarily written for the "average American" who could quickly and easily grasp their full intent. Therefore, legal experts often need to interpret statutory laws.

Case Law   Interpretations of the law, which occur in appellate courts, are also laws in themselves. The courts in our judicial system interpret the law in two fashions. First, the courts apply the law. When people are suspected to have violated the law, they are brought to court for an official determination of whether the law actually applies to their actions. This is the function of trial courts. Second, courts are responsible for interpreting the legality of our laws. This means that when the passage of a statutory (or administrative) law or the enforcement of such a law is suspected to violate the more powerful

Figure 2–2 Rape statutes of three states.

California[1]

(a) Rape is an act of sexual intercourse accomplished with a person not the spouse of the perpetrator, under any of the following circumstances:

(1) Where a person is incapable, because of a mental disorder or developmental or physical disability, of giving legal consent, and this is known or reasonably should be known to the person committing the act.

(2) Where it is accomplished against a person's will by means of force, violence, duress, menace, or fear of immediate and unlawful bodily injury on the person of another.

(3) Where a person is prevented from resisting by any intoxicating or anesthetic substance, or any controlled substance, administered by or with the privity of the accused.

(4) Where a person is at the time unconscious of the nature of the act, and this is known to the accused. As used in this paragraph, "unconscious of the nature of the act" means incapable of resisting because the victim meets one the following conditions:

(A) Was unconscious or asleep

(B) Was not aware, knowing, perceiving, or cognizant that the act occurred

(C) Was not aware, knowing, perceiving, or cognizant of the essential characteristics of the act due to the perpetrator's fraud in fact.

(5) Where a person submits under the belief that the person committing the act is the victim's spouse, and this belief is induced by any artifice, pretense, or concealment practiced by the accused, with intent to induce the belief.

(6) Where the act is accomplished against the victim's will by threatening to retaliate in the future against the victim or any other person, and there is a reasonable possibility that the perpetrator will execute the threat. As used in this paragraph, "threatening to retaliate" means a threat to kidnap or falsely imprison, or to inflict extreme pain, serious bodily injury or death.

(7) Where the act is accomplished against the victim's will by threatening to use the authority of a public official to incarcerate, arrest, or deport the victim or another, and the victim has a reasonable belief that the perpetrator is a public official. As used in this paragraph, "public official" means a person employed by a governmental agency who has the authority, as part of that position, to incarcerate, arrest, or deport another. The perpetrator does not actually have to be a public official.

Pennsylvania[2]

A person commits a felony (here being "rape") of the first degree when he engages in sexual intercourse with another person not his spouse:

(1) by forcible compulsion;

(2) by threat of forcible compulsion that would prevent resistance by a person of reasonable resolution;

(3) who is unconscious, or

(4) who is so mentally deranged or deficient that such person is incapable of consent.

Tennessee[3]

(a) Aggravated rape is unlawful sexual penetration of a victim by the defendant or the defendant by a victim accompanied by any of the following circumstances:

(1) Force or coercion is used to accomplish the act and the defendant is armed with a weapon or any article used or fashioned in a manner to lead the victim reasonably to believe it to be a weapon;

(2) The defendant causes bodily injury to the victim;

(3) The defendant is aided or abetted by one (1) or more other persons; and

(A) Force or coercion is used to accomplish the act; or

(B) The defendant knows or has reason to know that the victim is mentally defective, mentally incapacitated or physically helpless.

[1] Cal. Penal Code. Section 261 (West, 1994).
[2] 18 Pa. Cons. Stat. Ann. Section 3121 (1984).
[3] Tenn. Code Ann. Section (39-13-502) (1992).

Many inmates appeal their cases, which often result in changes in case law.

Judicial review The process whereby an appellate court reviews a trial court decision and determines whether the decision is within the legal boundaries established by the Constitution.

Case law Court decisions that regulate the outcome of all future, similar cases.

Stare decisis The principle that when courts decide cases, decisions are based on precedents; the idea that laws are accumulated to provide predictability in court decisions.

constitutional law, the judiciary decides the issue. These decisions are the focus of appellate courts.

Together with the principle of government by the people, our founding fathers tried to ensure that our legal system would have a built-in system of checks and balances on power. In part this is accomplished by separating the three branches of government and giving each branch—executive, legislative, and judicial—a different function. Each branch of government is given a method to question and to override the other branches' actions. Executive officers of a state or of the federal government may veto a piece of legislation; the legislature may, in turn, override the veto. The judiciary can decide that a particular piece of legislation or an executive order violates the Constitution and can thereby overturn either action. If the legislature or executive officers wish, they may initiate a movement to amend the Constitution, thereby overriding the judicial decision. Obviously, none of these efforts are easy to accomplish, but this was how our founding fathers structured the checks-and-balances process.

When the judiciary interprets a statute or administrative action, it engages in **judicial review.** This is the process whereby an appellate court hears an appeal of a trial court decision and determines whether the action and the law the trial court's decision is based on are within the legal boundaries established by the Constitution.

Because they are made by legal system representatives and are about the content of the law, these decisions are actually laws themselves. We call this **case law** because it is law made in particular cases. This means that the appellate court's decision is carried forward as the law; this is the legal principle known as *stare decisis.* As defined in *The Law Dictionary, stare decisis* is:

> [t]o follow a precedent. A flexible doctrine of Anglo-American law that when a court expressly decides an issue of law . . . that decision shall constitute a precedent which should be followed by that court and by courts inferior to it, when deciding future disputes, except when the precedent's application . . . is unsuitable to the character or spirit of the people of the state or nation, and their current social, political and economic conditions.[2]

So, even this basic principle of our governmental structure allows for discretion.

Administrative Law Administrative law refers to the rules and regulations that government agencies create. State and federal legislatures give these agencies the power to make "laws." Here, we are talking about laws made by government agencies such as the Internal Revenue Service, the Federal Aviation Administration, the Environmental Protectional Agency, or the Federal Communications Commission.

The greatest number of "laws" in our society is administrative. When we consider the various types of government agencies and the vast range of responsibilities each agency may have, it quickly becomes clear that we can easily be dealing with hundreds of thousands of laws. For this reason, administrative law is a very complex, often very difficult form of law to comprehend.

Apparatus of the Criminal Justice System

The U.S. system of criminal justice has three separate, but overlapping, components. Criminal justice is carried out through the operations of law enforcement, the judiciary, and, finally, the corrections components. Within each component are rules, regulations, and specific roles and functions that must be filled. In the following sections, we will briefly discuss each component and then review how all three components work together to form a system of criminal justice.

Law Enforcement

Law enforcement is the most visible component of our nation's criminal justice system. Those persons and agencies charged with the responsibilities of keeping order in society and making certain that lawbreakers enter the system come to us in several forms. When we think of law enforcement, we usually think of our local police. We also need to include in this category law enforcement agencies from other governmental jurisdictions. Sheriffs represent the law enforcement efforts of county governments, and state police or highway patrols exist in 49 of our 50 states.[3] While the federal government also has a number of law enforcement agencies, there is no national equivalent to the city or state police.

Federal law enforcement agencies enforce only certain areas of the law. For instance, the Secret Service is the law enforcement arm of the Treasury Department; the Bureau of Alcohol, Tobacco, and Firearms devotes itself to enforcing laws about alcohol, tobacco, and firearms; and the Drug Enforcement Administration enforces our laws

JOB FOCUS: DEPUTY SHERIFF

Usually considered a law enforcement job with a county-based agency, a deputy sheriff may also have responsibilities in court and in local corrections. The deputy sheriff is most commonly a uniformed law enforcement officer who performs duties similar to those of local police. Deputies' law enforcement duties include: patrolling the areas to which they are assigned; investigating, apprehending, and arresting criminal suspects; transporting arrestees between jail and court; performing traffic control; and assisting at accident scenes.

Whereas a local or state police department officer is limited to law enforcement duties, the deputy sheriff may also work in the realm of the court by serving legal papers to defendants of both criminal and civil cases, overseeing evictions, and providing security in courtrooms and courthouses. Deputy sheriffs will oftentimes find themselves assigned to work in the local jail. Most jails in the United States are the responsibility of local sheriffs; therefore, the staff in jails is often composed of deputy sheriffs. Some deputies spend a significant portion of their careers working in the jail, although most deputies request transfers to law enforcement duties soon after they have the opportunity.

A high school diploma (or equivalent) and a satisfactory score on a civil service examination are general requirements for the job. Many departments also require a valid driver's license, no criminal record, and the ability to pass physical, psychological, and firearms tests. On a more personal level, the deputy must be willing and able to work a rotating schedule. The work conditions and schedule for almost all law enforcement jobs require a flexible individual. Deputy sheriffs earn between $17,000 and $28,000 per year, depending on locale.

Source: U.S. Department of Labor, Bureau of Labor Statistics, *Occupational Outlook Handbook,* 1994–95 ed., p. 303.

about drugs. There are numerous law enforcement agencies in the federal government; however, none of these agencies have broad, over-arching powers.

The major focus of most law enforcement agencies and officers is to ensure the public's basic security needs. Additionally, law enforcement officers are commonly recognized as one of, if not the only, "24-hour emergency social service agency." When citizens need assistance and no one else is available, they commonly call the police.

Holding a position equivalent to the front lines in a battle against crime, the law enforcement officer makes the critical decision about whether an offender enters the criminal justice system. Without the actions of law enforcement, the judiciary and the corrections components are simply not put into motion.

Judicial Processes

We saw earlier in this chapter that American courts are charged with two primary responsibilities: applying the law and interpreting the law. We have already read about the interpretation process—judicial review—in making case law. More important to the daily functions of the criminal justice system is the first task of our courts: applying the law.

Criminal courts are the places where our society formally decides disputes about whether an individual's actions are within his or her legal rights and obligations. The criminal court's purpose is to hear evidence the government brings against a person (or multiple persons) who is believed to have violated the substantive criminal law. In making this decision, the court applies the law to the specific incidents of a person's behavior. The steps involved in a criminal trial are shown in Figure 2–3. If the individual's actions are found to be within his or her legal rights, that individual will be declared not guilty of the crimes charged him or her. This is known as an **acquittal.** If, however, as is the outcome of the majority of criminal court actions,[4] the individual charged with a crime pleads guilty or is found to be guilty of the charges, the trial ends in a **conviction.**

When acquitted, a person is finished with the criminal justice system. That is, once acquitted, the person is free and has no further processing by the criminal justice system. Also, once acquitted on a particular charge, the person may not be tried again for that specific action. This is the protection against **double jeopardy** as guaranteed by the Fifth Amendment to the Constitution. As stated in the

Acquittal Declaring a defendant not guilty of the charges against him or her.

Conviction Declaring a defendant guilty of, or a defendant pleading guilty to, the charges against him or her.

Double jeopardy Holding a person responsible for a criminal action more than one time; this is prohibited by the Fifth Amendment to the United States Constitution.

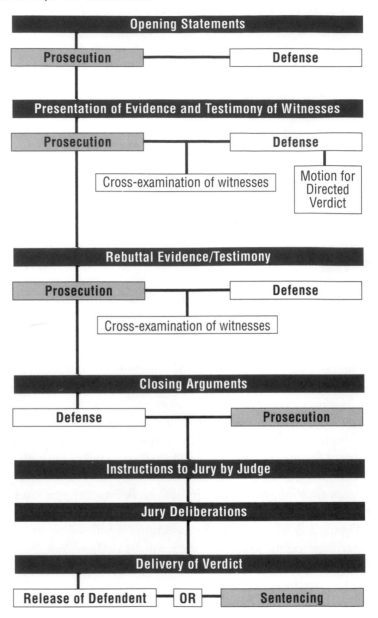

Figure 2–3 Steps in a criminal trial.

Opening Statements

Prosecution — Defense

Presentation of Evidence and Testimony of Witnesses

Prosecution — Defense

Cross-examination of witnesses — Motion for Directed Verdict

Rebuttal Evidence/Testimony

Prosecution — Defense

Cross-examination of witnesses

Closing Arguments

Defense — Prosecution

Instructions to Jury by Judge

Jury Deliberations

Delivery of Verdict

Release of Defendent — OR — Sentencing

Sentence The official, required punishment or course of treatment that a court imposes on a convicted offender.

Constitution, "Nor shall any person be subject for the same offense to be twice put in jeopardy of life or limb."

For offenders who are convicted, the next step is for the court to determine the appropriate **sentence.** A sentence is "the court judgment specifying the penalty imposed upon a person convicted of a

In a criminal trial, the government offers evidence against one or more people who have violated the law.

crime."[5] The procedural law of the court's jurisdiction (either state or federal government) outlines the sentencing process. In this process a number of issues, along with the crime's actual facts, are taken into consideration. Of course, statutory law establishes the possible sentence that may be imposed on the convicted offender. However, in most jurisdictions there is some variance in what exact sentence an individual offender will receive.

The judge determines the appropriate sentence. In most jurisdictions judges are provided information in a **presentence investigation (PSI)** about offenders, their backgrounds, ties to the community, details of the offenses in question, and information about other important life circumstances. Usually prepared by probation departments, PSIs make recommendations to judges about appropriate sentences for individual offenders. Originally developed to provide important information to judges, PSIs also provide some uniformity

Presentence investigation (PSI) A report, usually prepared by a probation department, that informs a sentencing court about the social, criminal, economic, and educational background of a convicted offender; PSIs recommend sentences for offenders, and courts use them as one source of information in deciding sentences.

Apparatus of the Criminal Justice System   **37**

Figure 2–4 Sample presentence investigation report form.

PRE-SENTENCE INVESTIGATION REPORT

FILE #

NAME (Last)   (First)   (Middle)   (Maiden)   DATE COMPLETED

AKA   CAUSE NO.

CURRENT ADDRESS   PERMANENT ADDRESS   CITIZENSHIP

PHONE NUMBER

PLACE OF BIRTH   DOB

MARITAL STATUS

MILITARY SERVICE

SSN   APD

OFFENSE

PENALTY RANGE

CO-DEFENDANT

PLEA

DETAINERS OR CHARGES

PROSECUTING ATTORNEY

SENTENCING JUDGE

PROBATION OFFICER

PRIOR RECORD:
DATE(S)   ARRESTING AUTHORITY   OFFENSE   DISPOSITION

EMPLOYMENT/FINANCIAL STATUS:
DATE(S)   EMPLOYER   POSITION   REASON FOR LEAVING

MEDICAL/MENTAL HEALTH CONCERNS:

SUBSTANCE USE/ABUSE:

VICTIM IMPACT:
VICTIM: LOSS:

TRAVIS COUNTY DISTRICT ATTORNEY'S OFFICE RECOMMENDATION:

ASSESSMENT OF THE DEFENDANT:

RECOMMENDATION:

SOURCES USED TO COMPILE REPORT:

Source: Travis County Community Supervision and Corrections Department, Austin, TX.

to the sentencing process. (See Figure 2–4 for a sample presentence investigation form.) However, practice has shown much inconsistency and disparity in the sentences that are recommended in presentence investigations.[6]

Corrections

Corrections, as we saw in Chapter 1, is a set of interrelated organizations, agencies, and programs that hold, treat, and sometimes punish those people known or strongly believed to have committed a crime. Corrections is, contrary to many assumptions, more than just jails and prisons. In fact, jails and prisons, while the most visible part of corrections, actually involve less than one-half of all people who are processed through the corrections system.

Corrections combines punishing those members of society who commit wrongdoings, working with wrongdoers to effect a change in their behaviors, and keeping track of suspected wrongdoers while the judiciary processes them. However, how corrections achieves these goals is often not what is commonly assumed.

It is important to remember that a wide range of types of correctional programs and institutions exists in the United States. Not only is there a wide range of types of sentences and punishments, but there is also a wide range of differences within each type of sentence. For instance, not all prisons are alike. If we randomly select two prisons from the several thousand U.S. prisons in operation today, we find two facilities that vary in size, structural age, security level and housing, and set of inmates. Most important, these differences mean that the experiences of both staff and inmates of these institutions are also likely to differ. This is commonly overlooked. In fact, as we will see throughout our examination of corrections in the United States, policies and procedures commonly assume that prisons are alike or at least very similar to one another. Our society tends to think that "prison is prison."[7]

Legal requirements strictly guide the operations of corrections in the 1990s. This is the same for law enforcement and the judiciary. However, the major differences between corrections and the other two components of the criminal justice system are the amount of control over and the disposition of cases or people. Both law enforcement and the judiciary have many opportunities to exercise discretion in how they handle individual cases. Although corrections can use some discretion in individual cases, it has more limited opportunities.

JOB FOCUS: COURT BAILIFF

A court bailiff focuses on the task of maintaining order in a state or local jurisdiction courtroom and provides personal protection to the judge and all personnel in the courtroom. The court bailiff is the law enforcement presence in the courtroom.

In maintaining an orderly atmosphere in the courtroom, the court bailiff has the responsibility to make sure courtroom visitors act in nonthreatening ways and that no weapons or other potentially threatening objects are present in the courtroom. This means that a bailiff often conducts searches of courtroom visitors and of the actual courtroom itself.

In addition to the responsibilities of maintaining order, a bailiff also escorts prisoners and jurors in and out of the courtroom and serves as the primary means of communication between the jury and the judge. In many ways the court bailiff is the administrative assistant to the judge, working under a judge's supervision and performing a variety of responsibilities as determined by a judge. Many times a bailiff has responsibilities for writing and keeping a variety of daily reports, screening visitors to the courtroom, keeping the court's appointment calendar, and answering the telephone. A court bailiff's starting salary is between $22,000 and $25,000 annually.

The requirements for a court bailiff include a passing score on a civil service examination and a high school education. In most jurisdictions the applicant with at least some college education will have a distinct advantage. This advantage is more obvious when the applicant has studied some form of law or criminal justice. In addition to these criteria, a court bailiff is expected to have good communication skills (both written and verbal), to have an ability to work well with a variety of people, and to be highly organized and courteous.

Source: U.S. Department of Labor, Bureau of Labor Statistics, *Occupational Outlook Handbook,* 1994–95 ed., p. 303.

People are ordered into the correctional system. This means that not only must people go to corrections, but also that corrections officials must accept them. In contrast, the judiciary and the law enforcement agencies can drop or dismiss a case whenever they believe it is necessary. Corrections officials cannot simply decide to release someone from jail or from probation because they feel like it. Therefore, the position that corrections occupies in the criminal justice system is one with minimal self-control opportunities. Thus, corrections as a component of the U.S. criminal justice system depends on the actions of law enforcement and the judiciary.

Across the United States, one of the most pressing problems affecting the criminal justice system is the increasingly large number of people in our jails and prisons. Overcrowding is a major problem in terms of physical space, finances, and demands on corrections staff. During the 1990s, however, a political movement to "get tough on crime" has dominated the media coverage of criminal justice issues. As we toughen our stance toward crime and criminals, we also simultaneously pack more and more people into our jails and prisons. Some state and local systems have reached the critical point. In several states a second political movement, paralleling the get-tough-on-crime stance, seeks to revise criminal laws to allow, or in some cases give preference to, sentences other than incarceration.

FYI

In 1993 Rhode Island enacted statutory laws to allow alternatives to incarceration or standard probation for a number of criminal offenses. These statutes marked the end of a 17-year effort to overcome overcrowding in the state's prisons. When the final legislation was approved, the Rhode Island Director of Corrections, George A. Vose, Jr., called the new laws "a major redirection in Rhode Island's correctional policy. (This provides) the state with a sound and progressive policy to meet the correctional challenges of the future."

Criminal Justice as a System

We say that our society has a "criminal justice system." What we mean by this is that the three main components—law enforcement, judiciary, and corrections—all work together (although not always cooperatively) in pursuit of a common goal. The goal, of course, is to control and reduce the amount of crime in society.

A systematic approach to criminal justice is based on the idea that each component of the system—and, in fact, each individual job within the criminal justice system—can best be done when one person or one set of people is responsible for one or only a few tasks. This is very similar to the concept of the assembly line. Rather than having one person responsible for finding, apprehending, holding, trying, sentencing, and punishing an offender, each of these tasks is delegated to someone or to some agency. This process becomes a system when clear rules and procedures are established to regulate how the system's goals are pursued.

When we analyze the criminal justice system as a "system," we must remember that we deal not *only* with a system of institutions and agencies, but also with *people*. The way that each component operates affects not only the other agencies in the system, but also the people who work and live in those agencies. One subject that we will continually study is how the experiences of living and working in corrections change people. We also need to remember, though, that the criminal justice system affects a broader range of people, especially those in corrections.

The operation of any system, however, can be only as strong and effective as its weakest part. This means that we must analyze the criminal justice system as a collection of people, as well as of agencies, rules, and procedures. Figure 2–5 shows the distribution of employment within various components of the criminal justice system.

The idea that criminal justice operates as a system in our society suggests ways that the goals of criminal justice are made both easier and more difficult to achieve. All discussions of systems must recognize the five main reasons why systems can fail to achieve their goals:

1. *Flaws in the design of the system.* When the basic plan for how parts work together has errors, the system is doomed to failure or, at least, to poor working conditions.

2. *Failure of the system to keep up with changing social conditions.* Because social systems work with and are staffed by human beings, systems have to constantly modify themselves to meet the needs that society expects of them. If the world changes and we do not change to meet new needs or stop pursuing unnecessary goals, we will eventually not be needed. Thus, we will fail to meet our goals.

3. *Attacks from outside sources.* Social systems compete with other social systems for resources. Other systems, seeking

Figure 2–5 Percentage of total system employees by components of criminal justice system.

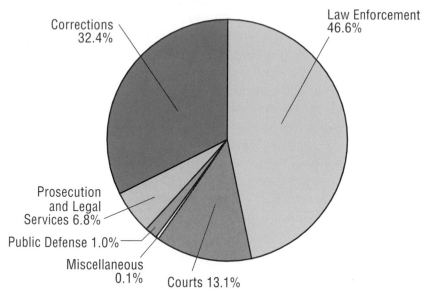

Corrections
32.4%

Law Enforcement
46.6%

Prosecution
and Legal
Services 6.8%

Public Defense 1.0%

Miscellaneous
0.1%

Courts 13.1%

Source: U.S. Department of Justice. *Justice Expenditure and Employment, 1990* (Washington, D.C.: Bureau of Justice Statistics, 1992).

to strengthen themselves, may make political or organizational attacks to defer another system's resources. The attacking system may win; the attacked system may collapse.

4. *Attacks from internal sources.* Not only do different systems compete for resources, but so do the parts of an individual system. These attacks, just like attacks from outside forces, can weaken a part of a system and can lead to the breakdown in the system's functions. Eventually the entire system will collapse.

5. *Poor leadership.* Any system, just like any organization or company, needs a strong, intelligent, forward-looking set of leaders. If the system's leaders cannot or will not have these qualities, the system can be expected to fall victim to the preceding reasons for failure. Also, without leadership to direct its activities, the system could break down on its own.

In the corrections area we know that workers perform their jobs as guided by official procedures and by their personal values and perceptions. This means we must know about the people we assign to different jobs. This way we can predict how they will perform their jobs, and we can develop policies and practices that will guide them in performing their jobs properly. In simple terms, some people are better suited for some jobs than they are for other jobs. As an example, research tells us that correctional officers have a more punitive view of offenders (especially sex offenders) than do case workers and psychologists who work in the system.[8] This is not necessarily a bad thing; it is simply something we need to consider as we develop policies and practices for correctional officers.

If we understand that different persons have different approaches to working (and living) in corrections, we are one step closer to understanding that corrections—and, in fact, all of the criminal justice system—operates in the much larger context of society. The operations of the criminal justice system have wide-ranging effects. The actions of both criminals and our institutionalized means of responding to them have a rippling effect, eventually reaching almost all parts of society.

Placing offenders in jail or in prison affects those persons' families and friends. We call these effects **collateral costs** of corrections.[9] Collateral costs are the disruptions to the personal lives of family members, such as the losses a wife experiences when her husband goes to prison, and the financial problems that involvement in the criminal justice system may cause. (For example, an offender may lose his or her job if that person has to wait several weeks or months in jail before a trial.) Collateral costs also include more abstract consequences such as psychological disturbances for offenders and their friends and family members, disruptions to the family unit, and losses that an employer may encounter when an important worker is lost due to criminal involvement. Consider for just a moment what the full range of effects would be if your professor were arrested and held in jail for the next several months. How would this affect you? How would your college be affected? Who else might suffer collateral costs in this instance?

Collateral costs The disruptions to the lives of those related to offenders and the economic impact on offenders and their families that result from being involved in the criminal justice system.

Summary

The U.S. criminal justice system exists to maintain order in society. It achieves this goal by enforcing the law and by punishing lawbreakers. This goal may seem quite simple and straightforward. However, the idea of "enforcing the law" can be rather complex.

Before talking about *how* we make people obey the law, we have to first clearly define *law*. As we have seen, laws are of several forms: substantive and procedural and as obligations and rights. Also, laws are created in different ways. The criminal justice system's task is not only knowing what the law says, but also knowing how to work within the law (procedural law) to keep society orderly (substantive law). Law, then, is not simply a list of rules that are given to all adults. Law is a constantly changing, sometimes somewhat vague, collection of rules that come in various forms. Regardless of how well we know or do not know what the law is, the fact remains that we all have a responsibility to abide by the law. Those who work in the criminal justice system have the added responsibility of keeping everyone in our community law-abiding.

However, we must remember that criminal justice is not always a completely objective, machine-like set of processes and activities. Rather, the criminal justice system operates within the cultural, legal, and political structure of society. This means there are many possible influences to the system's operation. Some of these outside influences alter how the system is structured and how the system actually carries out its activities. Other influences come from inside the system. This is especially notable when we consider that criminal justice is really a combination of three components: law enforcement, judiciary, and corrections. From within the larger system, influences operate by having one or two smaller components create a client population for another component or by using one component's discretionary decisions to cancel the activities of another component. As we have seen in this chapter, the component of corrections is perhaps the most vulnerable to influences from inside the criminal justice system.

In this chapter we have learned how the criminal justice system and the law operate in an ideal sense. The way we make and enforce laws today, though, is in some ways very different from how our society accomplished these tasks in the past. If we are to completely understand the sometimes complex workings of corrections in the 1990s, we must analyze the sources of these ideas and practices. In the next two chapters, we will examine how our views about criminals have evolved over the past centuries. We will note how some of these ideas have survived today and how some of them have been replaced with "new" ideas.

QUESTIONS FOR REVIEW

1. What are the U.S. criminal justice system's goals?
2. How are laws made in our society?
3. From which source of law do we derive the majority of our laws?
4. Among our sources of law, how are the processes of making laws similar and different?
5. What is the difference between substantive and procedural law?
6. What are the components that form the criminal justice system?
7. What are the goals of law enforcement?
8. What is the role of the judiciary?
9. Explain what is meant by the statement: "Corrections depends on the law enforcement and judiciary components."
10. How do the component systems combine to form a "system" of criminal justice?

ACTIVITIES

1. Attend a session of either your city/county council or state legislature. What actually occurs during the session? How many potential new "laws" are dealt with during the session?
2. Ask an attorney to help you list all of the laws pertaining to a particular type of activity in your community (driving, parking, outdoor decorations, storage at your home, and so on). Go to a place in your community where you can observe whether people obey these laws. If you see many people who do not obey these laws, ask them if they are aware they are breaking the law.

3. Spend a day (or part of a day) with a criminal prosecutor, defense attorney, or police officer to see what exactly is involved in that job.

ENDNOTES

1. Dan Abramson, "Hollywood Goes to Jail: Realistic Depiction of Prison Hard to Find," *Prison Life,* June 1993, pp. 22–24.

2. Wesley Gilmer, *The Law Dictionary* (Cincinnati: Anderson Publishing, 1986), p. 308.

3. Hawaii is the only state without a state-level law enforcement agency.

4. U.S. Department of Justice Statistics, *Sourcebook of Criminal Justice Statistics* (Washington, D.C.: Bureau of Justice Statistics, 1994).

5. George E. Rush, *The Dictionary of Criminal Justice,* 2d ed. (Guilford, CT: Dushkin Publishing Group, 1986), p. 217.

6. Wornie L. Reed and Jonathan D. Thier, "The Presentence Investigation and Discretion in Criminal Sentencing," *California Sociologist,* Vol. 4, No. 2, 1981, pp. 233–245.

7. Gary Beckstrom, "Stress as a Contributor to Crisis in a Correctional Institution," *Emotional First Aid: A Journal of Crisis Intervention,* Vol. 1, No. 2, 1984, pp. 26–36.

8. Wagdy Loza, "Attributions of Blame Toward Incarcerated Rapists Among Correctional Workers: Implications for Staffing," *Canadian Journal of Criminology,* Vol. 35, No. 1, 1993, pp. 59–60.

9. Ralph A. Weisheit and John M. Klofas, "The Impact of Jail: Collateral Costs and Affective Response," *Journal of Offender Counseling, Services and Rehabilitation,* Vol. 14, No. 1, 1989, pp. 51–65.

CHAPTER 3

Punishment

CHAPTER OBJECTIVES

In the last chapter you learned about the overall concepts and structure of corrections and the criminal justice system. After reading this chapter, you will be able to:

1. Distinguish the guiding philosophies of correctional practices of equity and equality.

2. Discuss the evolution of correctional sanctions.

3. Understand the social forces that motivated the evolution of correctional sanctions.

4. Explain the differences between the classical and positivist schools of criminology.

5. Explain the recent theoretical advances responding to the classical-positivist debate in criminology.

6. Differentiate the six major philosophies of corrections.

7. Discuss whether research concludes that deterrence works.

8. Contrast the forms of and identify points of support for deterrence.

9. Trace the history of support and criticism for using rehabilitation in corrections.

10. Identify the current, dominant philosophy for correctional efforts.

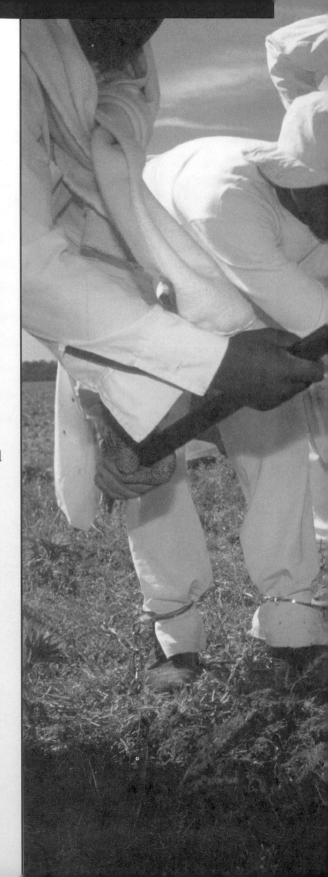

KEY TERMS

CHAPTER OUTLINE

Society imposes punishment on criminals to achieve "justice."

Justice: Equity or Equality?

Crime and deviance are difficult enough to understand. However, what may seem even more difficult to understand is: What constitutes fair and valuable punishment in the context of the criminal justice system?

To understand this question, we must first make an important distinction between easily confused concepts. As Karl Menninger has stated, a difference exists between **punishment,** "pain inflicted over the years for the sake of inflicting pain," and **penalty,** "a predetermined price levied automatically."[1] Penalty should be the goal of the criminal justice system. While causing individuals pain is sadistic and against human nature, it is not inappropriate to impose a penalty to change their behavior. Unfortunately, whenever crime rates significantly increase, the public calls for increased and strong punishments (pain). Little effort is made to determine if increased penalties actually achieve the desired goal of reducing criminal activity. As a result, as we will see in Chapter 4, this typically means an overcrowded correctional system and increased expenses to taxpayers.

Society imposes punishments on criminals supposedly to achieve justice. However, what does "justice" mean? Although most people assume they know what it is, *justice* has several definitions. The simplest definition is that of the Greek philosopher Aristotle, who said that justice means "equality for equals." In contemporary society most people believe that justice means a system that is "fair."

Justice can be viewed as a system of beliefs centered on either equality or equity. As foundations for the pursuit of justice, **equality** means that all similar people and acts receive the same punishments or rewards, whereas **equity** means that all individuals are rewarded or punished according to their contributions to a particular outcome. Therefore, equality-based systems are likely to use legal sanctions such as **determinate sentences** that offer narrow sentencing options. A determinate sentence is a fixed period of time that a convicted offender must serve in prison or on some other form of punishment. On the other hand, equity-based systems rely heavily on discretion and offer **indeterminate sentences.** These are sentences that name a minimum and maximum period of time to serve in a correctional program. Individual variations are possible (and common) depending on the offender's individual circumstances and progress toward change.

Punishment The process of causing others pain for the purpose of making them suffer.

Penalty An imposed cost for the consequences of one's actions; usually considered a negative experience.

Equality Viewing all similar people and acts as deserving the same punishments or rewards.

Equity Rewarding or punishing people for their actions based on their contributions to the outcome of their actions.

Determinate sentences Fixed periods of time that convicted offenders must serve in a correctional program.

Indeterminate sentences Sentences that impose a minimum and maximum period of time that offenders will serve in a correctional program; the actual length of each sentence is determined based on the offender's behavior and rehabilitative progress.

These two competing views of justice become relevant when we consider how a society determines punishments and the goals behind specific punishments. When a society seeks to rehabilitate or change individual offenders, it must have laws and legal procedures based on equity. Similarly, when a society emphasizes protecting citizens from dangerous offenders, equity must guide its decisions. Equality-based systems are usually found in societies that place greater emphasis on ensuring that members know what punishments to expect in response to their criminal acts.

Evolution of Punishment

The Primitive

In many primitive societies, punishment was uncommon and sometimes never used. Life was largely regulated by fear of the unknown. When social norms and rules were broken, primitive societies feared that their gods would be displeased. Therefore, taking actions to soothe the gods, primitive people punished offenders so that their gods would not make everyone suffer. This was not punishment in a modern sense, though. Individuals settled their arguments, and others were not involved unless serious violence or a blood feud developed. If **taboos,** the acts considered so bad that they are essentially unthinkable, were committed, primitive societies could impose death or could banish the offender. **Banishment,** forcing someone to leave a particular society, had the effect of a death sentence, however. Outside their cities and towns, individuals were usually unable to protect, feed, and care for themselves. The goal of banishment, however, was for the security of the society, not to punish the member who had done wrong.

Taboos Actions that are considered unthinkable in a culture.

Banishment The practice of forcing someone to leave a particular location or jurisdiction.

As they advanced culturally, people settled into permanent communities. In time we learned to control the waterways, to build great ships, and to make trips across the oceans from continent to continent. Our means of transportation, our architecture, our weapons, and our tools illustrated our progressive discoveries and increasing mastery of the earth's natural resources. One area in which we failed to progress, however, was in the treatment of criminals. Comforted by a consistent tradition, advancing civilization found no other remedy than severe physical punishment for criminals.

Methods of Vengeance

As late as the nineteenth century in England, more than 200 different offenses carried a potential death penalty. Execution methods displayed incredible imagination, and offenders were put to death in a wide variety of ways. For instance, people were fed to starving animals, torn apart, burned, crushed, mutilated, and crucified. In the eleventh century reign of King Canute in England, preference was shown for execution by skinning victims alive and then impaling them upon stakes. At various points in history, victims were stoned to death, drowned, beheaded by ax or guillotine, poisoned, hanged, suffocated, and boiled in oil. Not until the 1700s and 1800s did punishments shift from imposing pain on the physical body to restricting the offender's liberties and social life.[2]

The need for punishment remains today, but the time for excessive cruelty in punishment has long since passed. The Eighth Amendment to the United States Constitution explicitly forbids "cruel and unusual punishments." However, according to many critics of American death penalty laws, we do impose cruel and unusual punishments. Robert Johnson's examinations of life on death row and working on death row[3] show the chilling emotional impacts that our most extreme form of punishment have on the individual involved and on society as a whole. However, is this "cruel and unusual"? Legally no; morally and ethically, this is still being debated.

Whether explicitly stated or simply unconsciously felt, there are several competing philosophical bases for punishment. We shall examine the broader meanings of these bases in the next section. At this point, we will review the central and important dilemma that punishment theorists face.

FYI

The following is a description of death row at Holman Prison in Alabama:

The physical setting of death row is intimidating. To get there, one must pass through four locked gates. . . . On death row one feels embedded in the prison—lodged figuratively, in its bowels—shut off from light and liberty. The setting is like a tomb, a symbol of the psychological experience of death row confinement. . . . You never really lose the feeling that you have pushed your way as deep down into the prison as you can go. Even guards are noticeably anxious to escape the atmosphere of death row. The living area of death row is divided into four tiers of cells arranged in two cell blocks. . . . In a sense, each tier is a miniature death row, with its own prisoner population, social climate, cultural history and character. Death row has a number of unpleasant physical features. The cells are narrow, close, and without amenities. The toilets are small and cramped, little more than metal pipes wedged in each cell's floor. . . . The smells of death row are not offset by the aroma of prison food or by other qualities of the prison diet, though sometimes the scent of food is said to mask the odor of feces, urine, and sweat.

Source: Robert Johnson, *Condemned to Die: Life Under Sentence of Death* (Prospect Heights, IL: Waveland Press, 1981), pp. 43–45).

The Classical-Positivist Dilemma

Are humans free? Are criminals to blame for their acts? A great deal of scholarly inquiry and research has attempted to resolve these questions and to place punishment in its proper perspective. It is difficult to imagine a society entirely without punishment. Whether punishment prevents crime is one issue that has not been settled. Criminologists, politicians, philosophers, and just about everyone else has a view about why we should or should not punish criminals, how we should carry out punishment, and what results of punishment we should expect.

Dostoevski's Concept

Consider the case of the brilliant Russian writer Feodor Dostoevski. The czar had arrested and sentenced to death Dostoevski and the rest of the so-called Petroshevsky conspiracy, a group of liberal students. In an obviously cruel move, the czar allowed the "execution" ritual to proceed to the point of blindfolding and preparing the group for the shooting. At the last moment the czar stepped in and announced he would spare the lives of Dostoevski and his companions. The mock execution was designed to teach the conspirators a lesson. One of the reprieved went mad, but Dostoevski, after spending four years in Siberia, wrote the novel *Crime and Punishment* and became a writer of international reputation. The theme of *Crime and Punishment* is that *crime is its own punishment.* Did the threat of severe punishment cause insanity in one person and the birth of creative genius in the other? If so, what does this suggest about how well we can predict the results of punishments?

The Classical View of Crime

The **classical view** of crime believes that people are free to determine their own behavior and commit crime as a matter of choice. It logically follows, then, that because people have free will, punishment is proper. Because people choose to break the law, society has a moral responsibility to remind them that their actions are unacceptable. If people can freely choose whether to commit crime, then they can be freely condemned for wrong choices and be appropriately punished. The classical view strongly influences our criminal justice system. The use of determinate sentences implies that criminals are responsible for their actions and must suffer in amounts equal to or greater than the amount of suffering they have brought to others. When we believe that punishment is the goal of sentencing, we want potential criminals to know exactly what punishment they will suffer if they commit a particular crime.

However, freedom of choice is not necessarily absolute. People's selection of their behaviors is restricted by a variety of conditions, including immaturity, organic brain damage, epilepsy, alcoholism, drug addiction, compulsiveness, and strong social forces. The recognition in the seventeenth and eighteenth centuries that criminals often displayed these (and other) problems led to Cesare Lombroso's work. This was the beginning of positivism in criminology.

Classical view Perspective on crime that believes people freely choose their behaviors; criminal actions are seen as voluntarily chosen.

The Positivistic View of Crime

Positivistic view
Perspective that believes something causes or pushes people to commit crime; belief that something in biology, psychology, or social structures leads to criminal behavior.

Most social scientists take a **positivistic view** (sometimes referred to as a *utilitarian view*) of human behavior. Beginning with Lombroso's attempts to identify criminals by their less evolved physical, mental, and social characteristics, positivistic views of crime have always emphasized factors that cause or push people into crime. This view endorses a "value-free approach"[4] to uncover factors in the environment that explain why people engage in criminal behavior.

If their environments manipulate them, then people cannot be held completely responsible for their actions. If they are not morally responsible for criminal or delinquent behavior, then people should not be punished. This view is what philosophers would call *deterministic,* and it is contrary to the notion of free will in classical school explanations of crime. Rather, when individuals are "pushed" into crime, for whatever reason, they clearly need some type of help. With indeterminate sentences, where offenders can be sentenced to a range of time, individuals can get "help" and have an incentive (getting out earlier) to work through their problems.

Radical Views An interesting phenomenon occurred during the 1960s and continued to the early 1980s: the return of a Marxist point of view to explain criminal and delinquent behavior. Following a perspective the Dutch criminologist William A. Bonger made popular in the early part of the twentieth century,[5] some scholars reemphasized the economy when explaining crime. The distribution of wealth, coupled with significant corruption in the business world and in government, led to varying theories that saw the criminal justice system as the mechanism for maintaining power. In simple terms, the radical theorists blamed the capitalist system for the creation of crime and injustice.

It is almost impossible to find anyone, even a social scientist, who always makes completely value-free judgments. The highly respected American criminologist Edwin H. Sutherland, for example, who introduced the concept of white-collar crime, strongly advocated the belief that criminal behavior is just another form of social behavior. Yet Sutherland *condemned* white-collar crime as socially undesirable—a value judgment.

Post-modernism A perspective that criticizes the positivistic view and argues that social science should question the supposed causes of crime; also known as *post-structuralism.*

Post-structuralism
See *post-modernism.*

The predominant focus of the twentieth century has been toward positivism in the social and behavioral sciences. However, Western European influences, in the form of critiques of positivism known as **post-modernism** or **post-structuralism,** have become somewhat influential in the 1990s. This new critical perspective declared the positivistic school of thought as too narrow and guided by deterministic and unprovable assumptions. The post-modern critique has had little impact on corrections or correctional evaluations, but it has significantly influenced the way social and behavioral scientists approach the study of human behavior.

Natural Law   Legal scholars and philosophers, as well as behavioral scientists, have long attempted to determine whether patterns and trends of criminal behavior exist. The question is whether universal principles of law apply to aspects of criminal behavior that are independent of cultural influences. In recent times scholars of various philosophical persuasions have worked cooperatively in natural law institutes to find a common ground for communicating about the essentials of law.

Murder is an example of behavior deemed intrinsically wrong *(mala in se)*. Prostitution is an example of behavior deemed wrong because the law has prohibited it *(mala prohibitum)*.

Crimes were originally divided on the basis of ***mala in se*** (intrinsically wrong) and ***mala prohibitum*** (wrong merely because the law prohibited them). All common law offenses were considered *mala in se* because, in theory, common law did not punish offenses that were not wrong in and of themselves. Thus, breaches of the peace or public order, moral offenses, and injuries to people or property were considered *mala in se.*

Not appealing to positivists, the concept of **natural law** considers people to be free, moral agents who actively can and do choose to violate the laws of society. We are left, then, with the old dilemma between classical and positivistic thinking. The questions are whether humans have free will and how we identify and resolve conflicts between science and ethics.

Punishment in the Abstract

Long before punishment became an issue of concern for criminologists and correctional officials, philosophers debated the nature and intent of punishment. Because of its moral nature, punishment was originally and quite properly viewed as within the range of philosophic speculation; and it remains so.

Those disposed toward a treatment stance in corrections tend to believe punishment is unnecessary and inappropriate. In contrast, retributivists like Ernest van den Haag speak of the necessity of punishment and maintain that the state, if it threatens sanctions, must impose them: "Laws threaten, or promise, punishment for crime. Society has obligated itself by threatening. It owes the carrying out of its threats."[6]

The "left" or liberal writers attack punishment in the name of corrections as an instrument of political discrimination (like the Marxists). Jessica Mitford, for instance, puts it bluntly:

> Whereas formerly convicts tended to regard themselves as unfortunates whose accident of birth at the bottom of the heap was largely responsible for their plight, today many are questioning the validity of the heap. Increasing numbers of prisoners are beginning to look upon the whole criminal justice system, with the penitentiary at the end of it, as an instrument of class and race oppression.[7]

Those in the middle position appear to believe that offenders can be resocialized while also being punished. When put into practice, this approach would emphasize restrictions being placed on offenders rather than imposing pain on them. Punishment would be applied as a predetermined penalty, and it would need to be designed to assist in rehabilitative efforts.

Changing Ideologies of Corrections

If we examine the historical record, we see that different ideologies at different times have motivated punishments for criminals. Overall, we can identify six major theoretical positions: retribution, deterrence, rehabilitation, reintegration, incapacitation, and the just deserts

Table 3–1	Major Correctional Ideologies
Philosophy	**Major Tenets**
Retribution	■ Punishment is appropriate for wrongdoing. ■ Punishment serves a purpose for both society and the wrongdoer. ■ Wrongdoers should be punished.
Deterrence	■ Punishment will prevent future wrongdoing by the individual who is punished and by others. ■ To be effective, the punishment must outweigh the benefits gained by the wrongdoing.
Rehabilitation	■ It is possible to retrain wrongdoers to be law-abiding. ■ Society needs to assist wrongdoers to learn how to behave in socially appropriate manners. ■ Without learning acceptable behavior patterns, wrongdoers will not have the ability to behave in socially appropriate manners.
Reintegration	■ Wrongdoers need to be taught how to adapt to their environments in socially acceptable manners. ■ It is not the wrongdoers who need to be changed, but their ways of adjusting to the environment in which they live.
Incapacitation	■ Some wrongdoers cannot be changed and need to be segregated from society. ■ Society has the responsibility to protect law-abiding citizens from those whose behavior cannot be controlled.
Just Deserts	■ Society has a responsibility to both wrongdoers and others to reduce crime. ■ Punishments must be used, and potential wrongdoers must know that punishment is a certain outcome. ■ Punishments should be determined by one's offenses, not by characteristics of individuals or behavior displayed after punishment has begun.

model. Each position overlaps the others. However, we can also see an evolution in how and when each ideology has dominated in our thinking. The explanations presented in Table 3–1 of these six positions should be seen as broad generalizations and ideas that exist in the abstract. When an ideology is applied to real-life situations, the policies and programs it produces will vary somewhat from the ideal form presented here.

Retribution or Vengeance

Some people believe that lawbreakers simply *deserve* to be *punished.* This is known as **retribution.** This tells us that when punishment is justified on the basis of retribution or vengeance, two major concepts are involved:

1. Punishment is an end in itself.
2. The act committed *deserves* punishment.

Retribution The idea that a crime (or any wrongdoing) is reacted to with a punishment because the individual who commits a wrong deserves to be punished.

The first concept means that punishment is not designed to achieve any change in or to reform the criminal. If the primary justification for punishment is that the act deserves punishment (the second concept), then we restrict the results that we seek to achieve. Retribution does *not* include two important factors that other ideologies emphasize: any gain for society and any gain for the individual.

Retribution and vengeance have been practiced for many centuries. Not until the mid-eighteenth century did Immanuel Kant (1724–1804) and Georg Hegel (1770–1831) first spell out the underlying philosophy behind punishment for the sake of punishment. Kant held that punishment was a "categorical imperative" (an incontestable, self-evident truth), and Hegel insisted that punishment was the criminal's "right." Their ideas gave support to the classical school of criminology, and one of their major premises was that people's behaviors are a result of choice or of free will.

As a final, important aspect of retribution, it is always a reaction to an earlier event. Therefore, any attempt, whether punishment or treatment, to cope with a past criminal act is retributive. By definition, and as intended, any and all actions that arise from retribution are focused on the past. Thus, retribution as an ideology is not concerned with future events, but rather with past events.

Deterrence

Vengeance and retribution, the first ideologies guiding how societies responded to criminals, shifted to the belief in deterrence. The first major change in viewing how and why to punish criminals, **deterrence** suggests that punishing acts in the past will help prevent crime in the future. Until the mid-eighteenth century, European "correctional" efforts were primarily based on retribution. The state had succeeded the family or tribe in the role of taking vengeance against rule-breakers. However, as society became more sophisticated, complex, and forward-looking, so did responses to criminals.

There is a widespread public belief that punishment deters future crime. However, the majority of U.S. correctional officials would probably not agree. It is, in fact, impossible to determine whether severe punishment—particularly capital punishment—is a deterrent to crime. We can never know how many people have actually been guided away from becoming criminals. For that matter, it is also possible that law-abiding people are actually deterred by their own value systems rather than by their fear of punishment.

Deterrence Belief that punishing criminal actions will reduce crime in the future.

FYI

There is no definite answer to whether the death penalty deters people from violent crimes. Research results have been mixed. Some researchers find that publicized executions are associated with lower homicide rates in the days following those events. Other researchers have found the exact opposite: Publicized executions lead to increased homicide rates.

Contrasting Views An interesting minority viewpoint states that the primary purpose of punishment is not to change the criminal's behavior, but to reward law-abiding citizens. This "reward" comes in the form of visible evidence (the imprisonment of criminals) that those citizens' way of life is valued.[8]

What we have, then, are actually two different purposes or focuses for deterrence. **Specific deterrence** is the preventive effect that a punishment will have on a specific person. When Johnny is imprisoned for three years for assaulting Jimmy, we like to believe that the punishment of prison will "teach Johnny a lesson." That is, he will learn not to assault people again. **General deterrence** is the preventive effect that a punishment will have on all others who observe or have knowledge of the punishment given to a specific offender. So, in our example, general deterrence will be achieved if Johnny's

Specific deterrence Belief that punishing criminals will reduce the likelihood of their recommitting crimes.

General deterrence Belief that punishing criminals will prevent others who know of this punishment from committing crimes.

Strict sentencing of offenders often results in both specific and general deterrence.

friends and family members realize that they should not assault others if they wish to avoid the punishment that Johnny received.

Although the majority of people in the field of corrections and in related disciplines in the behavioral sciences do not agree with the theory, deterrence does have some current support. It also has some research failing to support it. Those who favor deterrence believe that people can learn from punishments both personally experienced and witnessed.

The incidence of serious crime rose rapidly and continually from the 1960s to the early 1980s and has been comparatively consistent since then. (See Table 3–2.)

This leveling off of the crime rate could suggest that deterrence is working. However, the number of violent crime attempts increased 11 percent from 1990 to 1991.[9] Furthermore, violent crime is primarily perpetrated against particular types of people: non-whites (especially African-Americans), persons under 25 years of age, and those with the lowest incomes. A hard-line deterrence approach, then, is an effort to protect the most victimized—the poor. The rationale is that deterrence may not be fully effective because of failures to arrest, convict, and imprison enough criminals. But as the poor are more likely than the middle and upper classes to be arrested, they would

Table 3–2	Uniform Crime Reports: Rate of All Index Crimes per 100,000 Population, 1960–1993		
Year	Rate	Year	Rate
1960	1,887.2	1977	5,055.1
1961	1,906.1	1978	5,109.3
1962	2,019.8	1979	5,521.5
1963	2,180.3	1980	5,950.0
1964	2,388.1	1981	5,858.2
1965	2,449.0	1982	5,603.6
1966	2,670.8	1983	5,175.0
1967	2,989.7	1984	5,031.3
1968	3,370.2	1985	5,207.1
1969	3,680.0	1986	5,480.4
1970	3,984.5	1987	5,550.0
1971	4,164.7	1988	5,664.2
1972	3,961.4	1989	5,741.0
1973	4,154.4	1990	5,820.3
1974	4,850.4	1991	5,897.8
1975	5,281.7	1992	5,660.2
1976	5,266.4	1993	5,482.9

Source: U.S. Department of Justice, Federal Bureau of Investigation, *Crime in the United States, 1975; 1980; 1988; 1992; 1993* (Washington, D.C.: Government Printing Office, 1976, 1981, 1989, 1993, 1994).

again be disproportionately victimized! This leads some critics to view the deterrence approach as simply a masked version of vengeance.

Though scientific evidence may never conclusively tell us whether punishment truly prevents crime, the studies and data that are available indicate that punishment is *not* an effective or efficient deterrent. As we saw earlier, over 200 offenses were punishable by death in England in the early nineteenth century. Yet the possibility of such severe punishment did not limit the frequency in which crimes were committed. More recently, however, the National Academy of Sciences concluded that jurisdictions with more severe penalties for crimes have generally lower rates of crime.[10] This correlation, however, does not say that the more severe penalties *caused* the lower crime rates. It simply says that both lower crime rates and more severe penalties were present in the same locations.

A major argument against the effectiveness of deterrence focuses on scientific evidence that most criminals simply do not consider the penalties for their crimes. Do robbers, traveling through several states, consult the laws of those states to determine the penalties that might be imposed for their robberies? Do burglars determine in advance the difference between first-degree and second-degree burglary (and their penalties), and do they plan burglaries on that basis? Do rapists choose one victim rather than another because they know the difference between statutory and forcible rape? And, in crimes of passion, which make up the vast majority of homicides, how often do murderers stop to think about whether their state enforces the death penalty?

Severity of Penalty Increasing crime rates give many people a natural reason to call for increasingly severe penalties. The loudest calls for increased penalties come in two forms: (1) calls for increasing imprisonment and longer prison sentences for drug offenders and (2) demands for increased and streamlined use of the death penalty.

Drug offenders, who receive comparatively lengthy sentences in the United States, make up the largest group of offenders contributing to the prison overcrowding. According to 1992 Justice Department figures, convictions for drug trafficking and possession accounted for 31 percent of all state court convictions. In the same year, violent offenders accounted for only 18 percent of all convictions; property offenders, for 33 percent. The likelihood of being incarcerated is very similar across all offense types: 70 percent of drug offenders and 70 percent of all convicted offenders being incarcerated.[11] However, because the population of drug offenders is large, the size of the prison population serving sentences for drug-related convictions is growing more rapidly than other offense populations. Add to this the fact that many drug offenses carry lengthy, mandatory sentences, and overcrowding is a problem we can expect to contend with for many years.

Common belief holds that the true deterrent effect of punishment can be most clearly seen in the case of capital punishment. This issue has raised serious scholarly debate, however. Until the mid-1970s social science had a general consensus that capital punishment did not deter people from homicide. This belief was seriously challenged, however, in 1975 when Isaac Ehrlich claimed that, based on a review of executions and homicide rates from the 1930s to the late 1960s, each execution carried out appeared to prevent 7 or 8 homicides. Also, in 1987 Steven Stack estimated that his review of the relationship between publicized executions and homicides revealed that highly publicized executions saved as many as 30 people from being homicide victims.[12] Despite the difficulties others have had in replicating Ehrlich's and Stack's results (coupled with criticisms of their research methods), their findings fueled the political and scientific debate about capital punishment. In the 1990s, based on results of several carefully controlled studies, social scientists are returning to general agreement that capital punishment has no deterrent effect.[13]

In addition to the practical question of whether punishment prevents crime, there may be a more important issue: the ethics of deterrence. This, though, is rarely discussed. If the sanctions (punishments) threatened for breaking laws are to be believed, they must be actually enforced. This issue is not new. Even the "father of deterrence," Jeremy Bentham, recognized the need to actually carry out threatened punishments. Because individuals weigh the costs and benefits of actions, Bentham believed that the severity of the punishment needed to just exceed the severity of the crime. To deter people from criminal acts, the costs of those acts must outweigh the benefits gained, but only somewhat.

It would be pointless to describe certain acts as criminal and yet provide no penalty for performing them. The concept of imposing

Prison sentences for drug offenders are on the rise, particularly for women.

sanctions to prevent future offenses, however, raises an entirely different issue—the issue of justice. This presents an ethical dilemma. Is it just to impose a penalty for a future behavior that may not be performed? The answer you offer to this question tells where you believe the focus of punishment should be: on what has happened in the past or on what may happen in the future.

JOB FOCUS: CORRECTIONAL CASEWORKER

Correctional caseworkers have the primary goals of assisting inmates both during their incarcerations and when they are preparing to return to the community and of using effectively the services provided within the institution as well as those of agencies and organizations in the community. These services assist inmates in any treatment programs and adjustments to living conditions.

Prison caseworkers are responsible for gathering and maintaining information about inmates' criminal and personal histories, assisting in resolution of personal and family problems, and guiding the process of planning for personal, social, occupational, and educational activities after release. Caseworkers are typically assigned a set of inmates for whom they take the responsibility for overseeing in what programs the inmates participate and sometimes mediating between the inmates and other institutional staff (job placement officers, disciplinary committees, and so on).

Caseworkers may or may not be required to have college degrees, although the trend is definitely toward hiring only people who have advanced educations. Caseworkers usually earn more than correctional officers, often earning $25,000–$30,000 per year to start. When caseworkers are expected to be responsible for a specialized set of inmates, such as those with severe substance abuse problems or mental retardation, advanced education in the specialized field may be either required or provided as part of the job.

Source: U.S. Department of Labor, Bureau of Labor Statistics, *Occupational Outlook Handbook,* 1994–95 ed., p. 137.

Rehabilitation or Reformation

The shift to a rehabilitative (or reformative) attitude toward criminals did not occur because of any one event or idea. Perhaps the most influential factor in this evolution was the emergence of scientific investigations of crime and punishments. The detachment and objectivity of the physical sciences were increasingly used to examine crime and criminal behavior. These same elements of investigation were successfully transferred to the developing behavioral sciences. Italian criminologists made an early contribution to the application of the scientific method to the social science of criminology. As an outgrowth of the Enlightenment, the rehabilitative ideal was attractive due in part to its supposed ability to recreate good citizens through the application of "humane" methods.[14]

Recognition that punishment was not accomplishing its stated objectives also increased. Specific reformative developments, such as probation and parole, helped change attitudes toward criminals and increased the possibilities of successfully changing behaviors. Another influence was an increased belief in the philosophy of humanism with its concern for human welfare. All these factors affected the development and growing implementation of the rehabilitative ideology.

The retributive philosophy dominated European correctional efforts until the mid-nineteenth century. In the society of titled landowners, who prevailed in the early Middle Ages, violation of property rights was not an important concept. The main concern was to prevent vengeance from developing into a blood feud. Crime was considered an act of war, and peace was maintained almost exclusively by the imposition of fines. The so-called criminal justice system was based on class distinctions, and the lower classes (as has seemingly always been the case), received harsher treatment than did the upper classes. The inability of the poorer classes to pay the fines gradually led to the introduction of corporal (physical) punishment. The economic inferiority of large numbers of people, the feudal lords' increasing domination of judicial rights, and the uncontrollable impulse to increase the revenue from fines were major factors that ultimately caused the end of the fines system.

After the fifteenth century, the number of poor people increased. This of course meant that the number of people who did not own property increased. In turn, the city populations increased, and jobs of skilled workers were threatened by the increase in population. The usual problems that accompany sudden population growth developed. When wandering bands of workers increased, landowners quickly hired this cheap labor. It could well be said that the exploitation of the masses caused the rise of capitalism.

The poorer the masses and the larger the visible mass of poor people became, the harsher were the punishments imposed for crimes. Physical punishments, originally substitutes for fines, became the rule. Once exceptions, execution and mutilation became common forms of punishment. During the entire reign of Henry VIII, an estimated average of five hangings occurred per day.[15] That is, approximately 72,000 major and minor thieves were hanged in 38 years.[16] Not only were many physical punishments imposed, but they also become increasingly brutal. With an overabundance of labor, the value of life decreased; and the whole system became increasingly harsh and physically extreme.

There were occasional, if somewhat isolated, reactions to the severities of punishment. Trial by ordeal, common in the thirteenth century, was outlawed. As early as the seventeenth century, the Quakers opposed inhumane treatment in the North American colonies. Their efforts, perhaps more than any other factor, caused Pennsylvania to become the cradle of prison reform in the United States. Houses of correction began operating in Britain, Europe, and North America. These institutions were, at least in part, concerned with the welfare of the young. The first European house of correction established in Amsterdam was one of the few that offered some hope of correction. Most, however, were miserable places.

In the eighteenth century, the thrust for reform was advanced by men like John Howard (1726–1790), perhaps the greatest of all prison reformers. Through his celebrated and widely read book, *The State of Prisons,* Howard brought to the world's attention the critical need for prison reform. Sir Samuel Romilly (1757–1818), a British lawyer, was an untiring opponent of the English criminal code with its excessive capital punishments. Through his efforts, England's first

FYI

During the Middle Ages simply putting an offender to death was not considered a severe enough punishment. Public humiliation and sometimes physical torture preceded the actual killing. Social values of the times, regarding both crime and persons of varying social statuses, are clearly evident in the following description of penalties from Italy in the Middle Ages:

> The execution ritual required that the condemned man or woman be marched from prison to the place where the offense had taken place. There, he or she would be mutilated by the removal of the offending member (usually a hand in the case of theft or murder). Then the convict was marched back to the place of execution, to be hung if a male or burned alive if a female. In Florence, the street crowds added to the ceremony by urging the official tormentors to keep torturing irons at high temperatures throughout these marches; executioners who failed to keep the convict howling by this method were occasionally killed on the spot by mob violence.

Source: Herbert A. Johnson, *History of Criminal Justice* (Cincinnati: Anderson Publishing Co., 1988), pp. 67–68.

modern prison, the Millbank Prison, was built. Four years after Romilly's death, as a result of the continuing reform of the criminal code, the death penalty was removed as the prescribed punishment for 100 petty offenses.

In the mid-nineteenth century, John Augustus in Boston and Alexander Maconochie in Australia reshaped correctional efforts by originating probation and parole as rehabilitative treatment devices. These moves, coupled with the initiation of religious and educational programs, truly pushed the rehabilitative ideology into practice.

The early pioneers in modern corrections believed that punishment alone was not effective. Further, their work and ideas were the basis for later efforts toward reformation and rehabilitation.

Today **rehabilitation** focuses on efforts to return individuals to their original (supposedly noncriminal) state. In recent American history the ideology of rehabilitation has relied heavily on the medical model. Rehabilitation rests on the positivistic explanations for crime; that is, the purpose of corrections is to identify and treat the causes of crime. People do not exercise free will in performing criminal acts.

Rehabilitation Belief that criminal offenders should receive treatment to change the aspect that led the individuals to commit crime.

Rehabilitation is focused on efforts to "correct" the problems that led to criminal behavior.

Rhodes v. Chapman, 452 U.S. 337 (1981).

In 1981 the United States Supreme Court rejected by an 8–1 margin an action filed on behalf of inmates of the maximum security prison in Ohio. The inmates claimed that their Eighth Amendment rights of protection from cruel and unusual punishment were being violated. The inmates argued that the prison policy of placing two men in a cell originally designed for only one inmate imposed such severe crowding on them that this constituted cruel and unusual punishment.

The Court ruled that double-celling is not in and of itself cruel and unusual punishment, so long as other conditions of the institution—heat, light, ventilation, quality and quantity of food, medical care, and program opportunities—were adequate. As stated by Justice Powell, "There is no evidence that double-celling under these circumstances either inflicts unnecessary or wanton pain or is grossly disproprotionate to the severity of crimes warranting imprisonment."

In simple terms, the Supreme Court held that punishment by incarceration need not provide inmates with the same standards of living as available in free society. In summary fashion, Justice Powell wrote: "The Constitution does not mandate comfortable prisons. . . . to the extent that conditions are restrictive and even harsh, they are part of the penalty that criminal offenders pay for their offenses against society."

Rather, something in their physical, psychological, or social environment draws or pushes them into criminal acts. The rehabilitation movement, then, focuses correctional efforts on medical and psychological treatments and on social skills training, all designed to "correct" the problems that led the individual to crime.

During the 1970s rehabilitation came under harsh criticism. As the widely known Martinson report[17] most clearly exemplified, nothing really seemed to achieve rehabilitative success. However, because the development and implementation of rehabilitation programs were expensive and because many still believed in rehabilitation, this guiding ideology remained important throughout the 1970s. Even today, neither correctional officials nor the general public[18] has completely discarded rehabilitation. In fact, governments and private oganizations are today returning to a belief in rehabilitation, emphasizing education. The belief today is that a "do nothing" attitude is highly inefficient and perhaps very dangerous (for inmates, correctional employees, and society as a whole). One of the motivations behind this change has included Robert Martinson's claims that his earlier work was flawed and seriously misinterpreted. His retraction and attempts to clarify his earlier work, however, have not been discussed as widely as his original claims.

As the late 1980s and early 1990s critiques proclaim, the "nothing works" claims are overstated and have neglected possible successes given improved inmate classification systems, better refined treatment programs, and more careful matching of offender needs/risks and programs. Today there are calls for a resurgence of rehabilitative efforts and claims that such a philosophy has not died, but has only been temporarily displaced. As David Shichor, a leading proponent of this view, explains:

> In spite of the fact that currently this orientation is on the decline, it has not vanished completely. This orientation has deep historical and traditional roots in Western, especially American, culture; and the fact that the alternative penal and social control approaches do not show much better results in social control contributes to the tenacity of this penal idea and policy, not only among social scientists, but in the public opinion as well.[19]

Reintegration

The ideology of reintegration is very similar in focus to and often confused with the ideals of rehabilitation. Whereas rehabilitation tries to "fix" individuals so they do not commit future crime, **reintegration** tries to "change" individuals so they can better fit into their communities. As a result, many correctional efforts geared toward reintegrating offenders to communities rely on community-based corrections, not incarceration. Included here are programs such as home incarceration, intensive supervision probation, and work-release programs. (These will be discussed in detail in Chapter 11.)

Reintegration programs attempt to provide offenders with social skills, to teach them positive behaviors, and to assist them in understanding and utilizing community resources. With their focus on preventing recidivism, these programs shape offenders in ways that do

Reintegration Belief that criminal offenders should receive treatment to assist them in returning to society in ways that will allow them to fit in better (and commit less crime) than they experienced previously.

Reintegration focuses on efforts to assist offenders to better fit into their communities.

not make it necessary (or even attractive) to commit additional crimes. Reintegration programs can also be found in prisons, most likely in the form of prerelease programs. Some prison systems provide soon-to-be-released inmates with special training at prerelease centers for up to 90 days preceding their release. The goal of these programs is to teach inmates the skills they need to successfully adjust to life outside of prison.

Incapacitation

Rehabilitation of criminals and protection of the public go hand in hand. If offenders can be successfully rehabilitated, then the public is that much safer. However, the philosophy has shifted from a focus on rehabilitating criminals to efforts designed to ensure the prevention of crime. This shift parallels the development of the social sciences and has been influenced mainly by sociology, psychology, and cultural anthropology (the study of differences between societies). Science showed an earlier tendency to seek a single explanation for crime, whether it be biological (caused by bodily deficiencies and differences), anthropological (caused by racial inferiorities), or psychological (caused by mental or emotional conflicts and instabilities). This single-cause focus has largely been abandoned, though, as a result of continuing discoveries in the physical and social sciences. Sociology has shown the influences that social institutions and social interactions have on behavioral patterns; cultural anthropology has shown the influence of culture and cultural conflicts on the development of behavior; and psychology has shown biases in how mental illnesses and traits are diagnosed and classified. All these disciplines have shown that many people become criminal or delinquent not simply because of free will and not because they were biologically inclined to act criminally. Rather, social injustices, deprivations, class inequities, cultural conflicts, and similar social and environmental factors led them to crime as a necessity or as the best of a very limited set of choices.

The dominant philosophy of the 1980s focused on **incapacitation,** or public protection and prevention. We incarcerate offenders for a period of time to protect society from this particular threat for that time period.[20] To incapacitate people is to remove their ability to commit further undesirable acts. This may mean sentencing criminals to prison to prevent their access to those in free society. There, criminals' only potential victims (theoretically) are other criminals. However, because of their status as criminals, these individuals are not defined as real (or, worthy of protection) potential victims. When our society shifted to a goal of separating criminals from free society, prison populations increased rapidly. This trend continues today as more and more offenders are segregated from society for longer and longer periods of time.

Incapacitation Belief that criminal offenders should be removed from opportunities to commit future crimes.

Just Deserts

Just deserts model
Belief that criminal offenders should receive punishments in amounts equal to the degree of harm they caused to other individuals and society.

As an outgrowth of the perceived failure of the rehabilitation models and coupled with increasing rates of crime and violence, a number of people subscribed to a punishment or equity model of criminal justice. This approach is known as the **just deserts model.** The belief here is that criminals should receive punishments equal to the negative experiences they caused society. Whereas earlier we saw that retribution promotes punishment solely for punishment's sake, just deserts adds an element of deterrence. That is, not only do criminals deserve to be punished, but also the punishments criminals receive should discourage others from committing similar crimes. Thus, just deserts is a combination of the retribution and deterrence ideologies.

The basic premises of just deserts may be summarized as follows:

1. The mission of the criminal justice system is to reduce crime and delinquency.

2. The best way to achieve this objective is to increase the risk for criminal behavior. This can be best accomplished by enhancing techniques for crime detection, certitude of apprehension, and sentencing.

3. Discretionary devices, such as good-time credits and parole, should be eliminated from the criminal justice system because they are inequitable.

4. Punishment is a valid objective of the criminal justice system; people should go to prison *as* punishment.

5. Certitude should prevail over severity, and confinement should be imposed only for offenses above a legislatively prescribed degree of serious behavior.

6. Sentences should be for specific and definite periods of time; recidivists should receive increased penalties; the employment of a weapon in an offense should result in an increased, mandatory penalty.

7. Plea bargaining should be eliminated.

Although just deserts may sound harsh, its principles reveal a strong belief in matching punishments to the size and severity of the crime to achieve justice. The movement toward acceptance of this view was spurred by the Martinson report, which pointed out the general failure of rehabilitation programs. However, a desire for justice, rather than simply a denial of the potential of "treatment," characterizes this new ideology.

Summary

Corrections today is not so much interested in "correcting" but rather in protecting society and dispensing punishment to known criminal offenders. Whereas we shifted from the rehabilitative ideal because of its perceived inadequacies, our goals today are also not being fully achieved. With consistently increasing prison populations, it is readily apparent that we are not producing a safer society. Due to the overcrowding of our prisons, we are also not able (in some people's minds) to adequately punish known offenders. So, the question is: What is our present correctional system accomplishing?

Today's correctional practices are a result of the general sense of failure attributed to earlier attempts at rehabilitation and the accompanying rapid growth in prison populations. Our focus is to integrate punishment (retribution and just deserts) and public protection (incapacitation) while also providing some preparatory skills to soon-to-be-released offenders (reintegration) in hopes of curbing our spiraling incarceration rates.

QUESTIONS FOR REVIEW

1. What are the similarities and differences between equity and equality?

2. How have the forms of punishment imposed by criminal justice systems changed over the course of history?

3. Why did the forms of punishment used to correct offenders change?

4. How do the classical and positivist views of crime differ in their approaches to explaining criminal behavior?

5. What are the recent variations in the classical-positivist debate about the origins of criminal behavior?

6. Identify and discuss the six major philosophies of punishment.

7. What are the conclusions of research testing whether deterrence is effective? Does deterrence work?

8. What is the difference between specific and general deterrence?

9. How effective are rehabilitation programs in corrections?

10. What is the just deserts model of corrections? How does this philosophy differ from the other major philosophies?

ACTIVITIES

1. Survey students and ask what they believe the purpose of corrections should be. Examine which of the six guiding ideologies they see as the appropriate purpose of corrections. Are there any patterns in the responses based on respondents' age, sex, race, or major?

2. Debate the possibility of a value-free approach to studying crime and working in corrections. Is it possible to work in a prison and maintain a value-free approach to one's work? Why or why not?

3. Research and discuss the specific ways that physical punishments were carried out.

4. Read Jack Abbott's *In the Belly of the Beast.* Identify the ways that Abbott sees prison inmates being "punished." Discuss what the positive and negative consequences of these punishments may be for both society and individual offenders.

ENDNOTES

1. Karl Menninger, *The Crime of Punishment* (New York: The Viking Press, Inc., 1968), p. 202.

2. Michel Foucault, *Discipline and Punish: The Birth of the Prison* (New York: Random House, 1977).

3. Robert Johnson, *Condemned to Die: Life Under Sentence of Death* (Prospect Heights, IL: Waveland Press, 1981); Robert Johnson, *Death Work: A Study of the Modern Execution Process* (Pacific Grove, CA: Brooks/Cole Publishing, 1990).

4. Max Weber, *Methodology of the Social Sciences* (Glencoe, IL: The Free Press, 1949), pp. 1–47.

5. W. A. Bonger, *Criminality and Economic Conditions,* translated by Henry P. Horton (Boston: Little, Brown and Company, 1916).

6. Ernest van den Haag, *Punishing Criminals* (New York: Basic Books, Inc., Publishers, 1975), pp. 14–15.

7. Jessica Mitford, *Kind and Usual Punishment* (New York: Alfred A. Knopf, 1973), p. 232.

8. Arnold W. Green, *Sociology,* 3d ed. (New York: McGraw-Hill Book Company, 1960), p. 554.

9. Lisa D. Bastion, *Criminal Victimization, 1991* (Washington, D.C.: Bureau of Justice Statistics, 1992).

10. Peter Greenwood, "Controlling the Crime Rate Through Imprisonment," *Crime and Public Policy,* James Q. Wilson, ed. (San Francisco: Institute for Contemporary Studies Press, 1983), p. 255.

11. *Felony Sentences in State Courts, 1992* (Washington, D.C.: National Judicial Reporting Program, 1995).

12. Steven Stack, "Publicized Executions and Homicide, 1950–1980," *American Sociological Review,* Vol. 52, No. 5, 1987, pp. 532–540.

13. William C. Bailey and Ruth D. Peterson, "Murder and Capital Punishment: A Monthly Time-Series Analysis of Execution Publicity," *American Sociological Review,* Vol. 54, No. 5, 1989, pp. 722–743; Franklin E. Zimring and Gordon Hawkins, *Capital Punishment and the American Agenda* (New York: Cambridge University Press, 1986).

14. David Shichor, "Following the Penological Pendulum: The Survival of Rehabilitation," *Federal Probation,* Vol. 56, No. 2, 1992, pp. 19–25.

15. Harry Elmer Barnes and Negley K. Teeters, *New Horizons in Criminology* (Englewood Cliffs, NJ: Prentice-Hall, 1950), p. 417.

16. George Rusche and Otto Kirchheimer, *Punishment and Social Structure* (New York: Columbia University Press, 1939), p. 19.

17. Robert Martinson, "What Works? Questions and Answers About Prison Reform," *The Public Interest,* Vol. 42, No. 22, 1974, pp. 22–54.

18. Frank Cullen and K. E. Gilbert, *Reaffirming Rehabilitation* (Cincinnati: Anderson Publishing Co., 1982).

19. Shichor, *loc. cit.,* p. 23.

20. G. Hawkins, *The Prison: Policy and Practice* (Chicago: University of Chicago Press, 1976).

CHAPTER 4

The Prison

CHAPTER OBJECTIVES

This chapter begins an examination of what most people believe is the centerpiece of the U.S. correctional system: the prison. Keeping the six major correctional ideologies in mind, after reading this chapter, you will be able to:

1. Understand the historical antecedents to the prison.

2. Identify the beginning of the penitentiary movement in the United States.

3. Compare and contrast the early competing systems of prisons in the United States.

4. Identify trends in the growth of the U.S. prison population.

5. Discuss the variations in incarceration rates across geographic regions and demographic characteristics.

6. Trace the development of the federal correctional system.

7. Identify the factors driving the expansion of the federal correctional system.

8. Discuss the federal correctional system, and identify similarities and differences with state correctional systems.

9. Identify areas in which the federal correctional system has been an innovator, a role model, and a leader for other correctional systems.

10. Identify common characteristics of offenders incarcerated in federal correctional facilities.

KEY TERMS

corporal punishment
penitentiary
Walnut Street Jail
Pennsylvania system
Auburn system
congregate work
lockstep

reformatory
incarceration rates
contraband
correctional
    institutions
community treatment
    centers

CHAPTER OUTLINE

The state prison at Osining, New York—otherwise known as Sing Sing.

History and Origin

I n 1928 Warden Lewis E. Lawes published a book about his well-known prison and called it *Life and Death in Sing Sing*. Despite its title, Lawes' book was mostly a story of death—the death of the human spirit, which had been present in that New York penitentiary and in many others across the nation for a very long time. One legend connected to Sing Sing is about the Sinck Sinck Indians, who roamed the land around the present site of the prison three centuries earlier. According to this legend, ghosts of the Sinck Sincks kept watch over the prison. The ghosts must have been amused, however, by the white man's lack of tracking skills. On one occasion the skeleton of a would-be escapee was accidentally discovered inside the prison compound—ten years after the deceased had attempted his escape![1]

The comments of an on-site observer, almost half a century later, indicated that the institution had made little progress:

> The conditions at Sing Sing are bad . . . the dirt in the mess halls and hospitals [is] repulsive. They still have the old style seating arrangements; metal benches and metal tables that extend across the hall; they really don't have much room to eat. And of course everything is old.[2]

After its inmates' infamous riot in 1971, Attica Prison in New York needed extensive repairs. A portion of the allocated repair funds was set aside for the installation of bathing facilities in the regular housing blocks. The inmates had not destroyed the bathrooms during the riot. However, before the riot inmates had to move in mass through "some of the longest corridors to be found in any American prison"[3] to get to the distant bathhouse. As you might expect, having to supervise inmates on this journey was dangerous and a highly inefficient use of staff time.

Dartmoor Prison, once known by the convicts housed there as "Halfway to Hell," still stands on the forbidding gray moors of Devonshire, England. Its old-fashioned architecture dates back to 1806 when it was built to house French prisoners. Almost 1,500 Americans and Frenchmen are among the dead buried in the cemetery.[4] An Old West analogy was once employed to describe the staff at Dartmoor. They were said to be like a small handful of whites on the American frontier battling many times their number of Apaches.[5] The motto chiseled in the institution's granite face is, ironically, *Parcere subjectis* ("Spare the humbled").[6] Dartmoor's infamy can be sensed

FYI

Another well-known prison has its essence summarized by an old quotation. The 1850s still echo in this quote about San Quentin of the 1970s:

> The rain will still flow up your pants leg on a windy day while standing under the shed on the upper yard. . . . or how about shower night with a whole tier under five or six showers, with ten or fifteen minutes to get down. Well, I could go on and on. . . . I don't feel very poetic today, which might be the result of seeing to [sic] much red [blood] over the past year.

Source: Personal letter (1971) from a convict who has been a frequent inmate of San Quentin since the early 1950s. The mention of "red" refers to prison killings of staff and inmates—excessive for the period cited.

in the still-sung lyrics of an old prison ballad that goes like this:

> The judge said stand by there
> And dry up your tears.
> You're sentenced to Dartmoor
> For twenty-one years.

It seems that we may recapture the historical past of prisons by simply examining the present. As we will see in this chapter, change comes slowly to the world of corrections. Progress in architecture, programming, administration, and official procedures comes very slowly—but it does come.

The Historical Perspective

Similar to every social activity, corrections has been influenced by customs, changes, and major social upheavals. We have already referred to the tight social system of feudal lords and serfs and to the changes that gradually destroyed this system. The dissolution of the feudal system determined not only the form that society took, but also society's attitude toward lawbreakers. Unfortunately for the poor, suppression of the monasteries accompanied the downfall of the feudal system. In the Christian tradition, monasteries had long opened their doors to those whom society rejected. However, when the monasteries closed their doors, the unfortunates were forced to join the hordes of unemployed, including the many soldiers whose military skills were no longer in demand. Beggars and paupers roamed the countryside in large numbers, and the situation reached a critical stage in the sixteenth century.

In 1563 the English Parliament passed a law requiring churches to collect alms. These were to be used for the relief of the poor, the diseased, and the helpless. The mayors of towns were also obliged to collect money for the poor. This legislative act is considered the beginning of the shift in responsibility for the indigent from church to state.[7] At the same time, however, the laws were very repressive. Beggars who were arrested once for loitering could have an ear cut off, and a second arrest for loitering subjected the beggar to hanging and a burial in a pauper's grave. In addition, the charitable person who dared to give alms directly to a beggar was subjected to a fine ten times the equivalent of the gift to the beggar.[8]

The widespread use of capital and **corporal punishment,** such as whipping, stoning, or burning, in the later Middle Ages discouraged the development of "holding facilities" (jails and prisons). The first generally used holding facility was a variation of what today we call a jail. At the Assize of Clarendon in 1166, Henry II ordered the construction of a "gaol" in each English county that did not already have one. However, several centuries would pass before anything like a modern prison arrived.

Corporal punishment Physical forms of punishment such as whipping, stoning, or burning.

The "First" Penitentiary

English criminal justice officials consider the English house of correction established at Bridewell in 1557 as the origin of the prison. American correctional officials, in contrast, give that credit to the Walnut Street Jail, which was built in Philadelphia in 1773 and remodeled as a state prison in 1790 by the Pennsylvania Assembly. The first prisons were referred to as **penitentiaries.** Which facility—Bridewell or Walnut Street Jail—was the first penitentiary is less important than the fact that both were developed. The Walnut Street Jail, in any event, was the birthplace of the penitentiary in the United States. Despite its name ("Jail"), Walnut Street operated as a prison.

Penitentiary First form of American prisons; institutions designed to encourage criminals to contemplate their actions and the consequences of them.

Antecedents of the Penitentiary

Many historical influences, including religion, architecture, philosophy, and social custom, combined to produce the penitentiary, but the penitentiary is basically an American contribution to corrections, not something we inherited from England or Europe.

Before the nineteenth century, a sentence to a penal institution as a punishment was not common. Political prisoners were imprisoned, of course, and people were put in jail for nonpayment of debts or for religious deviance to await trial or to be tortured. Some evidence suggests that jail sentences were imposed as punishments during the fourteenth century in Italy[9] and even earlier in England,[10] but not until the nineteenth century were the penitentiary system and conventional sentencing widely used.

JOB FOCUS: CORRECTIONAL OFFICER

The most basic, and usually first, job in corrections is that of a correctional officer. Most correctional systems require new employees to begin as correctional officers, unless they enter the system in one of a few special, professional jobs (doctor, nurse, psychologist, etc.).

Correctional officers focus on maintaining both perimeter and internal security for a correctional institution. They may be required to provide security for inmates who leave the institution to perform jobs in the community or on farms, ranches, or in forestry camps. Important skills include an ability to carefully watch large groups of inmates and not become easily distracted. They must also interact effectively with people from a wide range of social and cultural backgrounds. Also critical is an ability to respond to emergency situations, including medical and violent emergencies. Finally, correctional officers must prepare and maintain written records, forms, and reports.

The requirements for correctional officers include: at least 18 years of age (although in some systems, you must be 21), free of felony convictions, and, in most systems, no serious misdemeanor convictions on your record. Most government systems, but not private-contracted corrections, require applicants to pass a civil service test. Also, most systems have physical fitness requirements for new correctional officers. Finally, a high school diploma or GED is a basic requirement in almost all correctional systems. Some systems today require at least some college education. Whether required or not, a college education (especially in corrections, criminal justice, or some related field) is a strong positive mark for job applicants.

Correctional officers generally earn a beginning annual salary between $19,000 and $28,000. Most correctional officers have many opportunities for advancement and increases in pay. In government systems correctional officer positions also offer a full range of fringe benefits.

Source: U.S. Department of Labor, Bureau of Labor Statistics, *Occupational Outlook Handbook,* 1994–95 ed., p. 296.

The House of Correction   To deal with the increasing numbers of beggars and vagrant children, houses of correction were developed. The philosophy and purpose of these institutions were to force the inmates to perform hard, unpleasant labor, which was believed would deter crime and would convert idle drifters into disciplined, hard workers. Houses of correction spread throughout Europe; notable ones were established in Amsterdam in 1596 and at Ghent, Belgium, in 1773. Founded by Jean Jacques Philippe Vilain (1717–1777), the one at Ghent, known as a *maison de force,* is often considered, along with the Hospice of San Michel, as the beginning of the penitentiary idea.[11]

The Hospice of San Michel   Pope Clement XI established the Hospice of San Michel as the first home for delinquent boys in 1704. This institution was guided by the following motto inscribed over its door: "It is insufficient to restrain the wicked by punishment, unless you render them virtuous by corrective discipline." The value of work was central in the Hospice of San Michel and in other houses of correction. With an unquestionable Christian base and as the basis of the Protestant ethic, the value of work is still honored in the New World. At the Hospice of San Michel, reform was to be achieved via hard labor and silence. The Hospice's occupants were primarily orphan boys, boys sentenced by the court, and delinquent boys who were considered incorrigible. However, it is interesting to note that the Hospice also provided accommodations for over 500 infirm and aged men and women.

The Maison de Force   In 1773, 69 years after Pope Clement XI established the Hospice of San Michel, Vilain opened his house of correction in Ghent. The most significant differences that Vilain introduced were:

1. Felons and misdemeanants were separated.
2. Women and children had separate quarters.

A strict disciplinarian, Vilain was nonetheless a kind man. He believed all prisoners should serve at least a year to learn a trade and, thus, be reformed. Believing in individual cells, medical care, productive labor, and consistent discipline, Vilain was strongly opposed to life imprisonment.

Students of the late twentieth century may realize that many of the "new" ideas found in corrections today are not really new at all. Perhaps if we realize that solutions to "new" problems can be found in "old" ideas, we will be more able to cope with today's problems.

The Penitentiary Emerges: The Walnut Street Jail

With the houses of correction, Hospice of San Michel, and the Maison de Force as precedents, encouraged by the philosophy of John Howard, and spurred by notions of reform, the post-Revolutionary colonists attempted to improve the poor treatment of convicts. The **Walnut Street Jail** was turned into a penitentiary by legislative act, and John Howard's philosophy of separate and silent conditions was introduced into an American institution. Also introduced was a simple classification system that included segregation of the sexes and separation of debtors and witnesses from felons. In addition, there were a simplified form of inmate self-government, productive labor, and a provision for separate housing of hard-core offenders in a block of cells that became known as the "penitentiary house."

The Walnut Street Jail.

Despite the Walnut Street Jail's use of new ideas and techniques that attracted observers and scholars from abroad, the system soon realized some major problems. These problems included poor architecture, overcrowding, public apathy, and a lack of productive work opportunities for inmates. The Philadelphia reformers again petitioned the legislature to erect a penitentiary in which the correctional philosophy of solitary confinement and hard labor could be successfully effected.

The Pennsylvania System The Pennsylvania legislature authorized funding for the construction of two penitentiaries: one in Philadelphia for the eastern part of the state and the other in Pittsburgh for the western part. Together the two penitentiaries are referred to as the **Pennsylvania system.** The Eastern Penitentiary, opened in 1829, was called Cherry Hill because it was built on a site that was once a cherry orchard. It became more famous than the Western Penitentiary, which had opened three years earlier. In the Pennsylvania system, segregation of inmates was rigidly enforced, leading to its identification as the "separate" or "isolate" system. This is in contrast to the so-called **Auburn system,** which had developed in 1817 at Auburn, New York, and was known as the "congregate" system.

The Philadelphia prison consisted of seven blocks of outside cells, radiating from a central hub, and featured segregation and silence. Each cell had a private exercise yard in which the prisoner had two brief exercise periods daily. Prisoners worked, ate, and slept in their

Pennsylvania system Approach to correctional institutions that included silence and complete separation of inmates.

Auburn system Approach to corrections that emphasized silence but required collective work projects; developed to overcome problems associated with the Pennsylvania system.

The Eastern Penitentiary in Philadelphia opened in 1829.

cells; and their only visitors were prison personnel or officials from outside the prison, such as the members of the prison reform society of Philadelphia. Prisoners were blindfolded when first brought to the institution, and their blindfolds were not removed until they were placed in their cells. Inmates were thus prevented from observing other prisoners or the prison's basic architecture. Quickly recognized as a problem, complete isolation was believed to have caused many prisoners to become "incurably insane." As a result, officials soon realized that total isolation was impractical because of both overcrowding and the effects on the prisoners.

The Auburn System   In Auburn, New York, in 1817 a penitentiary was opened that differed in several important ways from the Pennsylvania system. By some architectural chance, the inside cells were too small for inmates to use spinning wheels and other vocational equipment. **Congregate work** (work performed by several prisoners in the same room) was therefore necessary. However, silence was to be maintained. Here the infamous **lockstep** was instituted to make supervision of inmates easier. By requiring inmates to walk—actually march—in unison, while holding the shoulder of the inmate in front of them, staff could easily detect troublemakers and those who might

Congregate work Practice of bringing inmates together to work in a common location on a common job.

Lockstep Practice of requiring inmates to walk/march in unison while holding the shoulder of the inmate in front of them.

require discipline. The modern U.S. prison was modeled on the Auburn system.

After Auburn and Pennsylvania In his pioneer, classic research on the prison social system, Donald Clemmer gave his opinion that 40 percent of America's prisons had not changed during the two decades in the mid-

twentieth century.[13] Clemmer attributed much of the failure to change to two major forces: (1) architecture that inhibited change and (2) political corruption. In spite of the fundamental truth of Clemmer's position, if it were possible to visit a U.S. prison in the second half of the nineteenth century and to compare it to one in the second half of the twentieth century, some dramatic changes would be noticed.

Most notably, one change has been the major trend toward specialized institutions.[14] Though this has defined prisons for several decades, other important developments include: more emphasis on treatment than on punishment; abandonment of silence and segregation; introduction of educational and recreational activities; community interaction on a much larger scale than the early Pennsylvania prison reformers could have imagined; and physically larger living spaces with more ventilation and light. Usually in gray or denim blue, uniforms are still common. The old-style stripes are gone, along with the lockstep. Some prisons no longer issue uniforms, unless inmates are unable to provide their own clothing. For the most part, changes have taken place in buildings of concrete and steel. However, major changes in the social aspects of institutions have been slower to develop and are oftentimes less significant.

The Elmira Reformatory

One of the most important changes in U.S. corrections occurred in the 1880s at Elmira, New York. The prison at Elmira was the first **reformatory** in U.S. corrections. Representing an ideological change about corrections, the reformatory was designed as a modification of the penitentiary. As such, the ideology shifted from believing that

Reformatory Correctional institution designed for younger, less-serious offenders; its purpose is to provide rehabilitative opportunities to offenders.

Example of a modern, institutional prison cell.

inmates should be passive and contemplate their wrongdoings to a belief that inmates should be active and be "reformed."

Opened in 1877, Elmira Reformatory was designed to house first offenders between the ages of 16 and 30. These were the criminals who could most likely be "changed." However, the plans for Elmira were never completely fulfilled. Because of overcrowding and the large numbers of sentenced offenders who were recidivists, about one-third of Elmira's inmates were repeat offenders.

To change inmates, they needed to be educated, to know the value of hard work, and to learn to work to achieve personal goals. In pursuit of these goals, the Elmira Reformatory operated on principles very different from those of the Pennsylvania or Auburn systems. First, inmates were grouped according to their progress in educational and work programs. This led to the second major difference at Elmira: the earning of "marks" (or points) for achievements. Inmates earned marks in order to gain more privileges and to eventually earn their releases from prison. However, earning their releases could be accomplished only through the use of indeterminate sentences. It was (and still is) believed that only with the incentive of earning release could inmates be motivated to truly improve themselves.

The reformatory idea was generally judged a success. By 1913, 37 years after Elmira opened, 18 other states had opened reformatories. These states copied the emphasis Elmira placed on education and work, rather than on industry. Whereas the Pennsylvania and Auburn systems focused on inmates' producing goods for sale (to offset expenses), Elmira's officials focused on activities that would improve the inmates, making them less likely to return to prison. In this way, the reformatory idea focuses on reducing expenses in the long term.

Prison Populations

The history of U.S. corrections is one of expanding populations. While dips and short leveling-off periods have occurred, the obvious and important trend has been one of rapid and continued population explosion.

The National Profile

Despite the population growth and the increase in serious crime, the total number of inmates in federal and state prisons has shown both dramatic upswings and periods of leveling off over the years. From the late 1960s until 1974, prison populations had been decreasing about 1 percent per year. This trend was dramatically and lastingly reversed in the mid-1970s. From January 1, 1974, to January 1, 1976, the national prison population increased by 22 percent. The increase in prison populations continued and expanded beyond most critics' imaginations during the 1980s. Prison populations increased annually during the 1980s at an average rate of 8.9 percent. From 1980 to 1994 the total population of U.S. prisons increased more than 150 percent! (See Figure 4–1.)

Some states and the federal system have prison populations larger than some mid-sized cities. In 1994 California incarcerated the most inmates, 125,605, roughly equivalent to the populations of Berkeley, California; Clearwater, Florida; or Waco, Texas.[15] On the opposite end of the range, some states have relatively small prison populations. In 1994 Vermont had a prison population of 1,301; Wyoming, 1,217; and North Dakota, only 536.

Figure 4–1 Prison populations, 1980–1995.

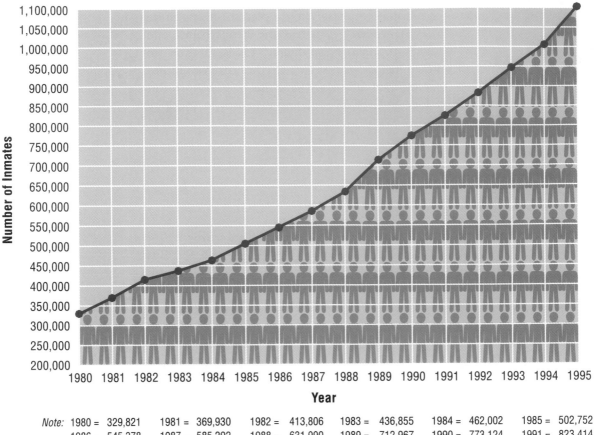

Note: 1980 = 329,821   1981 = 369,930   1982 = 413,806   1983 = 436,855   1984 = 462,002   1985 = 502,752
1986 = 545,378   1987 = 585,292   1988 = 631,990   1989 = 712,967   1990 = 773,124   1991 = 823,414
1992 = 882,500   1993 = 946,946   1994 = 1,012,851   1995 = 1,104,074

Source: Tracy L. Snell and Danielle C. Morton, *Prisoners in 1991* (Washington, D.C.: Bureau of Justice Statistics, 1992), Allen J. Beck and Darrell K. Gilliard, *Prisoners in 1994* (Washington, D.C.: U.S. Department of Justice, 1995), and Bureau of Justice Administration, Automated Telephone Information Source, 1995.

Incarceration rates
Number of people
in prison per
100,000 population.

However, more informative than the actual number of people in prison are the incarceration rates of various correctional jurisdictions. Nationally, 387 persons for every 100,000 Americans in 1994 were in a federal or state prison. This represents approximately a 150 percent increase since 1980 and an 11 percent increase from one year earlier. Only 10 percent of all prison inmates are held in the federal prison system. State prisons outnumber federal prisons, and state prisons hold the vast majority (90%) of all prison inmates. The jurisdictions with the highest **incarceration rates** (number of people in prison per 100,000) are: Louisiana (486), South Carolina (514),

Delaware (584), and the District of Columbia (1,859). In contrast, the jurisdictions with the lowest incarceration rates are: West Virginia (92), Minnesota (85), and North Dakota (75). On a more general level, the Southern states show the highest incarceration rate (365); and the Northeastern the lowest

(270). In the period from 1980 to 1994, the region with the most rapid growth in the incarceration rate has been the Northeast, followed by the Midwest, South, and West.

The number of female inmates in 1994 totaled 64,403. Eighty-nine percent of women prisoners are housed in state prisons while 87 percent of male prisoners are so housed. (See Figure 4–2.) Women accounted for about 6 percent of all inmates in state prisons and about

Figure 4–2 Distribution of inmates by gender housed in state and federal institutions.

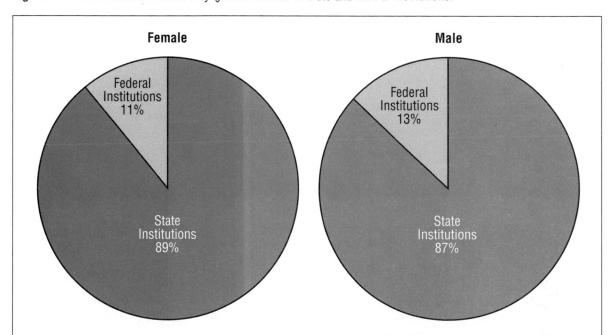

Source: U.S. Department of Justice, *Sourcebook of Criminal Justice Statistics* (Washington, D.C.: Bureau of Justice Statistics, 1994).

8 percent of federal inmates in 1994. The population of female inmates has been increasing more rapidly than the population for males. From 1993 to 1994 the total prison population increased 8.6 percent, but the population of female inmates increased 10.6 percent. Women have always been a small minority of prison inmates. As a result, many correctional systems have faced some unique housing problems. At the beginning of the 1990s, 19 of the 50 states had fewer than 300 female inmates (8 of these states had fewer than 100). Some states have very few women incarcerated; in 1994 Vermont held only 49 women, and North Dakota held only 16 women in prison at the beginning of 1995. While such low numbers may be reassuring, these "few" inmates need facilities, personnel, and programs. This means that although women make up a small fraction of all inmates, the cost of incarcerating them is not much less than that for males, in total.

Incarceration rates that differ by gender are well known. Also widely recognized (and often considered problematic) are differences in rates of incarceration based on race. Historically, African-Americans have represented larger percentages of prison populations than of the population in general. Contrary to many assumptions, however, since the end of the Civil War, the Northern, not Southern, states have had the largest overrepresentation of African-Americans incarcerated.[16] This continues today. At the end of 1994 African-Americans represented 44 percent of all prison inmates in the United States. In contrast, white Americans, who are socially and politically dominant in the United States, represent approximately one-third of all prison inmates in all U.S. regions except the West. (See Figure 4–3.)

Despite many dramatic and innovative developments in correctional treatment, U.S. prisons continue to show a commitment to the ideologies of retribution and incapacitation. Security and deprivations are the central aspects of our correctional institutions. Traditionally, the gaps between the staff and the inmates have been actively maintained. Staffs carefully observe prisoners and their housing facilities. Inmates' personal belongings are frequently searched and may be considered **contraband.** Contacts with members of the opposite sex are

Contraband Forms of personal property that are not allowed in correctional institutions.

Figure 4–3 Racial composition of prison population as of December 31, 1994.

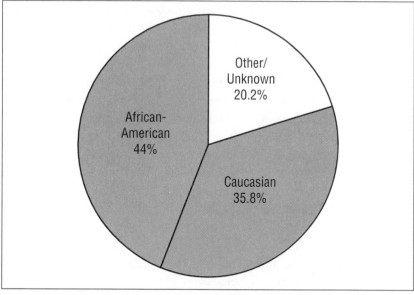

Source: Allen J. Beck and Darrell K. Gilliard, *Prisoners in 1994* (Washington, D.C.: U.S. Department of Justice, 1995).

rare and carefully monitored; religious activities may be restricted; and social pleasures and courtesies are rare.

Some Pragmatic Aspects

Criticism of prison systems grew very strong in the 1960s and 1970s. Many magazine articles contained harsh attacks by experts and quasi-experts. Also at this time, political upheaval was rampant throughout society. It was not just our prison systems that were so strongly criticized, but so were most aspects of life. The attacks on prisons continue today, although the criticisms seem to identify few, if any, new points of attack. This barrage of criticism is directed toward a multibillion-dollar industry in which only a small percentage of inmates are considered serious threats to public safety. A large percentage of inmates could do as well in community correctional programs. A group of wardens polled at an American Correctional Association Congress once estimated that the "dangerous" element in their prisons constituted no more than 10 to 15 percent of the inmate population.

The Federal System

The federal prison system, as we know it today, was a slowly emerging part of U.S. corrections. For over a century all persons convicted of violating federal statutes were held in facilities operated by either state or local governments. Not until 1870 did the federal government designate an official to oversee the placement of federal prisoners. Then, not for another 25 years was the first federal prison opened. When the old military stockade at Fort Leavenworth, Kansas, was converted to a federal penitentiary and opened in 1895, 2,241 prison inmates were under federal sentences and approximately 15,000 federal inmates were in local jails. This "used" military prison quickly proved inadequate, and Congress allocated money to construct a new prison at Leavenworth. Built largely with inmate labor, this "new" prison at Leavenworth opened in 1928.

However, before opening the new Leavenworth prison, the federal government authorized the construction or purchase of prisons in Atlanta and on McNeil Island in the state of Washington. However, even the addition of these two prisons did not house all federal inmates. To ease overcrowding, a fourth federal prison was authorized in 1925: a reformatory in Chillicothe, Ohio (based on the ideals of Elmira), for younger male offenders. Additionally, by 1924 Congress recognized the increasing number of female federal inmates and authorized construction of the 500-bed federal women's prison in Alderson, West Virginia, which opened in 1927.

Leavenworth Penitentiary, opened in 1895, was the first federal prison in the United States.

Even with the openings of Chillicothe and Alderson, problems remained. Because many new federal inmates were sentenced for violations of prohibition and immigration laws—which often brought sentences of less than one year—they could not legally be housed in the penitentiaries. This led to three federal jails opening during the early 1930s in New Orleans (where an old mint was renovated), La Luna, Texas (primarily for immigration violators), and Milan, Michigan.

The federal correctional system continued to grow during the 1930s. On May 14, 1930, Congress established the Federal Bureau of Prisons (FBP). Perhaps the most pressing problem facing the FBP was overcrowding, which led to the opening of more prisons. During the 1930s federal penitentiaries opened at Lewisburg, Pennsylvania, and Alcatraz Island in San Francisco, as did a second reformatory at El Reno, Oklahoma, and a mental hospital in Springfield, Missouri.

Even though the number of federal inmates leveled off between the 1930s to 1960, the federal prison system continued opening institutions to catch up with the bed space necessary to house federal inmates. Whereas in 1931 only 54 percent of federal prisoners were housed in federal institutions, by 1960 this number had increased to 88 percent. In 1960 federal prisoners accounted for 17 percent of all U.S. prisoners. There has been a steady decline in this rate ever since. By 1994 only about 10 percent of all inmates were federal prison inmates.

The Institutional System

In the coast-to-coast federal prison system, there are 79 **correctional institutions** and numerous **community treatment centers** (many privately contracted). Included are the large penitentiaries at Atlanta, Georgia; Leavenworth, Kansas; Terre Haute, Indiana; and Marion, Illinois; and modern correctional institutions with multiple programming at Butner, North Carolina, and Miami, Florida. There are, in addition, prerelease centers, in which inmates live while working in the community prior to actual release on parole, as well as a modern Staff Training Center at El Reno, Oklahoma. The Federal Bureau of Prisons also provides technical and training assistance to state and local correctional personnel through the National Institute of Corrections, which the Juvenile Justice and Delinquency Prevention Act of 1974 authorized and which is attached to the FBP.

The FBP is widely recognized as a leader in the development of sophisticated classification systems for inmates. Most notable is the six-level security classification system used to distinguish among the

Correctional institutions Facilities designed to hold and control convicted criminal offenders; include various types of prisons and jails.

Community treatment centers Lower level security institutions designed to house convicted offenders but to allow them interactions in free society.

Federal Correctional Institution at Estill, South Carolina.

federal correctional facilities. Most federal facilities are mid- to low-security level institutions. The "super-max" penitentiaries at Marion, Illinois, and Florence, Colorado, are the only Level 6 institutions in the federal system. The penitentiaries at Leavenworth, Kansas; Lewisburg, Pennsylvania; and Lompoc, California, are maximum-security institutions and classified as Level 5. The penitentiary at Terre Haute is the only Level 4 institution for general population male inmates; and the penitentiary at Atlanta is for a variety of special-needs inmates. All remaining federal correctional facilities, called federal correctional institutions or federal prison camps, are Level 3 or lower.

The Population Profile

At the end of 1994, inmates totaled 95,034 in the federal prisons.[17] This represents a 6.1 percent increase over the number of federal prisoners at the end of 1993. As is the case in almost all U.S. prison systems, population figures are rapidly increasing every year. Since the mid-1980s, the federal prison system has experienced a growth rate of 10–15 percent *every year*. Of the 95,034 inmates in 1994, 7,140 (or 7.5%) are females. The population of female federal inmates has been increasing even more rapidly than the overall federal inmate population.

The federal prisons are overcrowded, as are (at least officially) 45 of the 50 state systems. According to the Bureau of Justice Statistics, the federal prisons (not including private-contract facilities) were operating at 146 percent of their capacity population. This means that there are nearly three inmates for every two beds that federal prisons are designed to house.

One common misperception about federal corrections is that federal prison inmates are the most dangerous or "worst" criminals. While many federal inmates are very dangerous, the heinousness of inmates' offenses does not determine in which correctional system they are incarcerated. Inmates are in federal prisons because they were convicted in federal courts for violations of federal laws.

The offenses for which federal inmates are incarcerated actually show they may be less violent than state prison inmates. As shown in Table 4–1, the offenses that account for the greatest percent of federal inmates are (in decreasing order of frequency): drug offenses, immigration violations, property offenses, and crimes of violence.

Although some changes have occurred in the distribution of offenses over the last seven decades, the basic pattern remains: Federal prison inmates are not the "worst of the worst." This is not surprising, considering that most laws about personal and violent crimes are state, not federal, statutes. Without federal laws prohibiting particular acts, it is impossible to imprison someone in federal prison for those particular acts.

Table 4–1	Distribution of Offenses of Federal Inmates Sentenced, 1930–1993				
Offense	**1930**	**1950**	**1970**	**1983**	**1993**
Drug and liquor law violations	64%	30%	16%	27%	65%
Immigration violations	n/a	8%	9%	18%	2%
Property offenses	18%	48%	42%	24%	10%
Crimes of violence	1.4%	2%	10%	11%	13%
Other violations	16.6%	12%	23%	20%	10%

Sources: Margaret Werner Cahalan, *Historical Corrections Statistics in the United States, 1985–1986* (Washington, D.C.: Department of Justice, Bureau of Justice Statistics, 1987), Table 6-11, p. 156, and Allen J. Beck and Darrell K. Gilliard, *Prisoners in 1994* (Washington, D.C.: Department of Justice, Bureau of Justice Statistics, 1995).

Summary

The history of U.S. corrections is rooted in Western European correctional efforts. Criminal offenders were originally punished with little, if any, regard given to "correcting" behavior. Physical punishments, often grotesque and extreme, were the norm. The introduction of prisons as places to sequester and to reform offenders, instead of as places to hold offenders until physical punishments could be exacted, was heralded as a major humanitarian reform.

With the opening of the Walnut Street Jail in Philadelphia, the U.S. penitentiary movement began at the end of the eighteenth century. Walnut Street Jail and the subsequent Pennsylvania system focused efforts on reforming offenders to abandon crime. This was to be accomplished through complete isolation and silence. To overcome some of the Pennsylvania system defects, the Auburn system provided work opportunities in a congregate setting but enforced silence on inmates. Since the days of the Pennsylvania and Auburn systems, prisons both have and have not changed dramatically. While many of the structural components of prisons (including the actual physical prisons) have remained, the social and interactional natures of today's prisons are completely different. Today, many inmates are idle, spend almost all of their time in groups, and have an abundance of opportunities for activities.

The most notable characteristic of the U.S. prison population, both in the state and federal systems specifically, is overcrowding. A variety of factors—legal, social, and economic—has contributed to the rapidly escalating prison populations. Today, most prison systems are overcrowded, understaffed, and have too few resources. As an innovator, the federal prison system has developed better classification systems and treatment programs.

QUESTIONS FOR REVIEW

1. What are the historical forerunners of the modern prison?

2. When, where, and why did the United States begin using prisons?

3. How were the early European correctional institutions similar to and different from the first U.S. correctional institutions?

4. What have been the major contributing factors to the U.S. prison population growth?

5. What different information can be drawn from examining the numbers of offenders incarcerated and the incarceration rates of particular jurisdictions?

6. What patterns can we expect to find when examining incarceration rates by demographic categories?

7. Discuss the development of the federal correctional system. How was this similar to and different from the development of corrections in general in the United States?

8. Discuss the current status of the federal correctional system. How does the federal system differentiate inmates and provide for their needs?

9. In what ways has the federal correctional system distinguished itself as a leader and an innovator?

10. What are the common characteristics of inmates in federal correctional facilities? What are the similarities and differences between this group of inmates and inmates typically found in state correctional institutions?

ACTIVITIES

1. Visit a state or federal prison in your area. Interview the warden about changes in the prison. Why have these changes occurred? For both the prison staff and inmates, what have been the consequences of these changes?

2. Design a plan for a state correctional system to cope with the increasing numbers of inmates being sentenced from the courts. Include plans to effectively manage the changing demographics and offenses of inmates. Be sure to base your design on one of the guiding philosophies of corrections discussed in Chapter 3.

3. Research and debate the changes in U.S. drug laws in the last three decades. Support one of these arguments: (1) The changes in drug

laws have directly led to problems in U.S. corrections. (2) The changes in drug laws have *not* been the cause of emerging problems in U.S. corrections.

ENDNOTES

1. Lewis E. Lawes, *Life and Death in Sing Sing* (New York: Garden City Publishing Company, Inc., 1928), p. 76.

2. Personal correspondence from a New York corrections official, 1972.

3. Report of the Goldman Panel to Protect Prisoners' Constitutional Rights, Correctional Association of New York, November 15, 1971.

4. Justin Atholl, *Prison on the Moor* (London: John Long Limited, 1953), p. 11.

5. Thomas Mott Asborne, *Within Prison Walls* (New York: D. Appleton and Company, 1914), p. 137.

6. The complete motto, taken from Virgil, is: *Hae tibi erunt artes: pacisque imponere morem, Parcere subjectis et debellare superbos* ("Let those by your artes: to impose peace, to spare the humbled and abase the proud.")

7. See, for example, Res A. Skidmore and Milton G. Thackery, *Introduction to Social Work* (New York: Appleton-Century-Crofts, 1964), p. 41.

8. Arthur E. Fink, *The Field of Social Work,* 2d ed. (New York: Henry Holt and Company, Inc., 1947), p. 5.

9. Barnes and Teeters credit Professor Marvin Wolfgang with contributing the information that this occurred in the fourteenth century Florentine prison, Della Stinche. Harry Elmer Barnes and Negley K. Teeters, *New Horizons in Criminology,* 3d ed. (Englewood Cliffs, NJ: Prentice-Hall, Inc., 1963), p. 329, footnote 2.

10. Taft and England point out that sentences of imprisonment actually began in the reign of Edward I (1272–1307). Donald R. Taft and Ralph W. England, Jr., *Criminology* (New York: The Macmillan Company, 1964), p. 394.

11. Harry Elmer Barnes and Negley K. Teeters, *New Horizons in Criminology,* 1st ed. (Englewood Cliffs, NJ: Prentice-Hall, Inc., 1950), p. 475.

12. The definitive history of this institution is unquestionably Negley K. Teeters and John D. Shearer, *The Prison at Philadelphia: Cherry Hill* (New York: Columbia University Press, 1957).

13. Donald Clemmer, *The Prison Community,* 2d ed. (New York: Holt, Rinehart & Winston, 1966), p. xii.

14. Edwin H. Sutherland and Donald R. Cressey, *Criminology,* 8th ed. (Philadelphia: J. B. Lippincott Company, 1970), p. 491.

15. Allen J. Beck and Darrell K. Gilliard, *Prisoners in 1994*

(Washington, D.C.: U.S. Department of Justice, 1995).

16. William J. Sabol, "Racially Disproportionate Prison Populations in the United States: An Overview of Historical Patterns and Review of Contemporary Issues," *Contemporary Crises,* Vol. 13, 1989, pp. 405–432.

17. Beck and Gilliard, *op. cit.*

CHAPTER 5

Administration of the Prison

CHAPTER OBJECTIVES

In the previous chapter you read about the history and origin of prisons. In this chapter we examine more closely how prisons operate. After reading this chapter, you will be able to:

1. Understand the purpose and procedures of classification.

2. Identify types and distribution of inmates across security classification levels.

3. Identify the four primary administrative goals for prisons.

4. Describe barriers to achieving administrative goals.

5. Explain the organization of prison staff.

6. Contrast management styles of wardens.

7. Discuss principles of participatory management as it applies to prison.

8. Explain procedures for recruiting and training prison staff.

9. Discuss the move toward professionalization for correctional staff.

10. Discuss the emergence and effectiveness of correctional employee unions.

Administrative Goals
1) Security
2) Segregation
3) Discipline
4) Treatment

ate inmates are serving sentences

	of Inmates	Offense	% of Inmates
	24.8	Drug Offenses	21.4
	12.4	Trafficking	13.3
	4.9	Possession	7.6
	2.8	Other drug	0.5
	2.2		
	1.4		
	0.7		
	0.4		

KEY TERMS

classification

security

segregation

discipline

treatment

warden

deputies

captain of the guard

line officers

autocratic wardens

bureaucratic model

civil service

participatory
 management

Texas control model

consensus model

responsibility model

inmate council

iron law of oligarchy

professionalization

accreditation

collective bargaining

A prison disciplinary board meets with an inmate. Prison administrators are responsible for enforcing prison rules.

Inherent Defects in Prison Administration

In reviewing the origins and development of the prison, we have also examined the federal prison system and the variety of state penal systems. Many cogent reasons exist to characterize the prison as an archaic corrective instrument and to abolish it. However, this institution is unlikely to evaporate in the future. It is, therefore, appropriate at this point to examine prison management and staffing.

Since the 1960s several experts and critics of contemporary prison administration have drawn attention to the inherent defects in the methods employed to administer corrections. Among those experts and critics were the President's Crime Commission in 1967 and the National Advisory Commission on Criminal Justice Standards and Goals in 1973. The structure of correctional systems and the organizational bureaucracy of prisons have been described as "a basic barrier to the establishment of collaborate regimes focused on reintegration of offenders into the community."[1] These criticisms have highlighted the need to shift prisons from closed hierarchical systems, which focus on retribution and restraint, into open and flexible systems capable of rehabilitation and societal reintegration. These "new" goals were the hallmark of correctional developments from the 1970s through the late 1980s.

The prison, however, remains a generally closed hierarchical system that operates on a retributive philosophy. The prison community, a society similar to the outside world in some respects, is structurally quite different. Loss of liberty is the hallmark of prison society, and the citizens of prison communities are subject to special regulatory controls. Furthermore, within these communities stratification systems are based on an individual's violent prowess and reputation, not on the standard dimensions of stratification in the "free world" of wealth and prestige.

The Prison Classification System

Officials impose upon the prison a classification system. Every prisoner is given a custodial classification, which is essentially a control and management tool. Inmates considerably outnumber staff, and the rigid, numerous rules reflect the belief that control must be maintained strictly to prevent inmates from revolting. This philosophy of

Classification The practice of assessing inmates and assigning them to facilities and programs that suit their security and treatment needs.

fear is one of the major stumbling blocks to developing a more benevolent, rehabilitative, and humane atmosphere in many prisons.

Having gained widespread acceptance in the 1970s and using objective criteria and assessment methods, procedures known as **classification** are designed to determine how to best meet the needs of inmates and prison officials. Inmates are processed through classification procedures for four basic reasons.[2] First, classification determines what prison in the system is most suitable for the inmate. Second, classification determines what type of housing is appropriate for the inmate in the chosen institution. Third, the inmate is matched with treatment and work programs. Fourth, the inmate's necessary custody level is determined. Custody level determinations focus on predicting an inmate's potential for disruptive and violent behavior.

Most inmates are not classified in the upper, maximum security levels of custody. The majority of U.S. prisoners are classified at medium or lower security levels. Studying all adult men and women incarcerated in this country, we find that only 14 percent are held in maximum security institutions, 11 percent in high or close security, 33 percent in medium security, 22 percent in minimum security, and 20 percent in community or nonsecure facilities.[3] Most prisoners continue to be housed in lower-level security institutions, and this is expected to continue throughout the 1990s. The preference for lower-level security is reflected in the types of prisons being built

FYI

The Federal Bureau of Prisons in 1994 opened a new "ultra-maximum security" prison in Florence, Colorado, designed to house 484 inmates. Those sent to Florence are the most dangerous to staff and other inmates, are considered significant escape risks, and simply are not to be trusted to interact safely with other people.

The cells in which inmates live are specially designed to minimize maintenance, the need for contact with others, and are secure. Among the cells' features in the Florence Penitentiary are unmovable furniture made of cement, closed circuit television used for purposes such as educational programming and religious services, showers that are set on timers controlled by officers, sinks/drinking fountains operated by officers (to prevent inmates from flooding their cells), and only powdered soap (to prevent bar soap from being used as a weapon). Outside the cells more than 150 video cameras monitor all areas of the prison; more than 1,400 electronically operated gates and doors and all walls are made of cement, reinforced with steel bars; and corrections officers are heavily armed.

around the country. Between 1987 and 1990, 143 new prisons were constructed in the United States. Of these new institutions, only 29 percent were maximum or close security, 38 percent were medium security, and 33 percent were minimum or lesser security.[4]

Remember that the policies and recommendations for determining inmates' classifications are just that: recommendations. While national standards do exist to guide classification decisions, some correctional systems have adopted these standards completely, while others have adopted only portions of them. Some researchers have suggested that systems with smaller inmate populations are more likely to implement such policies and that adoption of ACA (American Correctional Association) standards is related to legal intervention.[5] (See Figure 5–1.)

Administrative Goals for Prisons

Prisons have four primary administrative goals. These goals may initially appear to be quite divergent, and at times their pursuit does cause conflict. But, in the daily world of prison administration, each goal must be weighed whenever any activity or policy is considered. The four primary administrative goals for prisons are: security, segregation, discipline, and treatment.

Security

Prison administrators' primary and most important goal is maintaining custody and **security** of all inmates. Above all else, prisons are expected to be secure facilities where the public can be assured that inmates will remain. Maintaining security means, among other things, preventing escapes of inmates and intrusions from outsiders and keeping order among inmates.

Segregation

Prison administrators are responsible not only for maintaining custody and ensuring the security of the *outside* community, but they are also responsible for maintaining security *inside* the prison. One primary way this is achieved is by **segregation;** that is, by classifying various types of offenders. Classification procedures protect inmates from other inmates and also reduce the potential for problems that could threaten the prison's internal and perhaps external security.

Security An administrative goal of maintaining order; the top priority in any correctional institution; includes preventing escapes, preventing intrusions from unwanted outsiders, and keeping order among inmates.

Segregation An administrative goal for prisons; involves classifying (segregating and separating) various types of prisoners to protect them from other inmates and to protect the prison's internal and external security.

Figure 5–1 American Correctional Association's national correctional policy on classification.

Introduction:

Classification is a continuing process basic to identifying and matching offender needs to correctional resources. This continuing process involves all phases of correctional management.

Statement:

Classification should balance the public's need for protection, the needs of offenders, and the efficient and effective operation of the correctional system. In developing and administering its classification system, a correctional agency should:

A. Develop written classification policies that establish criteria specifying different levels of security, supervision, and program involvement; establish procedures for documenting and reviewing all classification decisions and actions; describe the appeal process to be used by individuals subject to classification; and specify the time frames for monitoring and reclassifying cases;

B. Develop the appropriate range of resources and services to meet the identified control and program needs of the population served;

C. Base classification decisions on rational assessment of objective and valid information, including background material (criminal history, nature of offense, social history, educational needs, medical/mental health needs, etc.) as well as information regarding the individual's current situation, adjustment, and program achievement;

D. Train all personnel in the classification process and require specialized training for those directly involved in classification functions;

E. Use the classification process to assign individuals to different levels of control on the basis of valid criteria regarding risk (to self and others) and individual needs, matching these characteristics with appropriate security, level of supervision, and program services;

F. Involve the individual directly in the classification process;

G. Assign appropriately trained staff to monitor individual classification plans for progress made and reclassification needs;

H. Objectively validate the classification process and instruments, assess on a planned basis the degree to which results meet written goals, and, as needed, refine the process and instruments; and

I. Provide for regular dissemination of classification information to all levels of correctional staff and to involved decision-makers outside of corrections as an aid in the planning, management, and operation of the correctional agency.

Source: The National Conference on Correctional Policy (College Park, MD: ACA, 1987). Reprinted with permission.

Discipline

Prison administrators are also responsible for enforcing the prison's rules on both inmates and staff. To have a safe and secure prison, rules are needed, just as with any society. When inmates or staff break these rules, they need **discipline,** or punishment.

Treatment

As agents of "corrections," prison administrators have responsibility for providing treatment to inmates. One reason for guaranteeing a secure, safe, and orderly prison is to house inmates in an environment

Discipline An administrative goal for prisons; involves punishment for inmates or staff members who break a prison's rules.

LEGAL BRIEF:

Gittens v. Coughlin, 584 NYS 2d 670 (1989).

In this New York case, the state supreme court upheld a prison hearing panel's decision to take away an inmate's hand-drawn map showing major roads and landmarks around the prison.

The hearing panel found Gittens, an inmate at the Shawangunk Correctional Facility, guilty of violating the prison's disciplinary rule regarding contraband. The rule stated that "contraband is any article that is not authorized by the superintendent." At his hearing, Gittens claimed he was unaware that his hand-drawn map would be considered contraband. When found guilty of an institutional rule violation, Gittens then appealed to the state supreme court.

In making its ruling, the supreme court cited other case law establishing that corrections officials have both the right and responsibility to keep control over the property inmates have in the prison. Based on this reasoning, the supreme court ruled that the prison officials had not granted Gittens permission to possess his map. Therefore, Gittens had violated the rules about contraband. Adding to this, the supreme court cited the fact that in hiding the map under his bed, Gittens apparently knew that the map was contraband.

Treatment An administrative goal for prisons; involves psychological and substance-abuse counseling, basic and advanced education, and behavioral modification and job-training programs.

that is conducive to **treatment,** including psychological and substance-abuse counseling, basic and advanced education, and behavioral modification and job-training programs.

Working to Achieve Administrative Goals

While suggested as the ideals for all prisons, these administrative goals are met in varying degrees and by various methods. The key to individual prisons meeting these goals is both the financial and political support an institution receives.

With skyrocketing costs and shrinking budgets, many prisons and correctional systems have reduced their programs, services, staff, and physical maintenance and improvement projects. In doing so prison administrators have prioritized their goals and cut resources from lower priorities. When political decisions are made to reduce allocated funding to corrections, yet criminal statutes and public sentiments call for increasingly strict criminal sanctions, correctional administrators are caught in the middle. Such a situation usually means something must be cut.

In all circumstances custody/security goals are held as top priorities. Services to inmates that are not primarily focused on main-

A warden often meets informally with correctional staff.

taining custody and control are typically lower priorities. Therefore, these services are more likely to suffer in times of financial hardship. However, for those priorities that are not highly valued, middle range political decisions are also very important. Correctional administrators are more often than not politically appointed positions and, therefore, subject to rapid and sometimes unanticipated turnover. When top correctional administrators, who may hold their positions for relatively short time periods, decide to pursue particular forms of programs and organization, correctional personnel who are most directly affected by these changes may oppose them.

Correctional staff who have daily contact with inmates—in fact, all staff in prisons—may feel safely removed from the political workings of corrections and may believe that directives from top administrators are unrealistic and unworkable. Consequently, when staff believe administrators are not informed about daily life in prison and instead are concerned with politics, they may resist implementing changes. When combined with their belief that top-level administrators will rapidly turn over, middle management and other institutional workers commonly resist changes and maintain the status quo.

Consequently, prison administration is a field in which change happens very slowly. Due to the political nature of corrections management, the sheer size of the population with which most corrections systems work, and the restrictions of architectural designs, change is difficult to implement.

The Prison Staff

Every prison has a staff hierarchy. Figure 5–2 shows an example of a "typical" staff hierarchy. The director of the correctional system is supported by the **warden** or superintendent, who acts as the primary manager of an individual institution. Within each prison, the warden is assisted by one or two **deputies** or assistant wardens, who are commonly responsible for one of the two major sets of goals for the prison: security/custody (operations in Figure 5–2) and treatment/ programming (programs in Figure 5–2). Comparable in rank and authority to the counterpart in a military or police organization, the **captain of the guard** is the commanding officer of the custodial staff who directly supervises the inmates. The custodial staff consist of a number of watch lieutenants and sergeants and a larger number of correctional officers (sometimes called **line officers**).

Warden Top-level administrator who manages an individual correctional institution; also sometimes referred to as a *superintendent.*

Deputies Top-level assistants in an administrative structure; typically have daily responsibilities for particular areas of operation in a facility or program; also sometimes referred to as *assistant wardens.*

Captain of the guard Commanding officer of the custodial staff in a correctional institution.

Line officers Those who directly supervise the inmates of a correctional institution; also referred to as *correctional officers.*

Figure 5–2 Institutional table of organization.

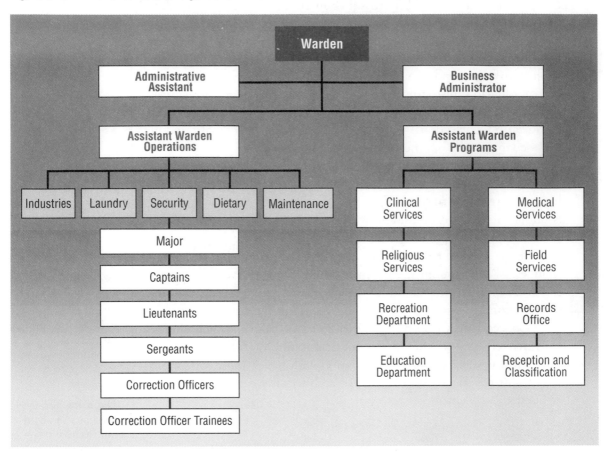

Source: Illinois' Menard Correctional Center. Reprinted with permission.

While the primary duties of a correctional officer are to maintain security and custody, this does not mean that an officer's main job is preventing escapes. The physical structure of the prison and perhaps a few armed officers in towers around the prison's periphery ordinarily ensure that inmates do not escape. Instead, the correctional officer is charged with maintaining control within the prison and seeing to it that both inmates and staff are kept safe. A correctional officer has the most frequent and intense forms of interaction with inmates. Therefore, the correctional officer also has the greatest impact on the behaviors of individual inmates. While primarily concerned with maintaining security (both internal and external) and discipline, the correctional officer is, perhaps, in a position where the most significant degree of treatment may occur.

Depending on the institution, the region of the country, the state, the budget for the particular department, and the prevailing philosophy and prioritized goals, the prison's treatment staff may be a variety of professionals. Prison treatment staffs may include psychiatrists, psychologists, sociologists, medical personnel, chaplains, substance abuse counselors, social workers, lawyers, academic teachers, and vocational teachers. Support staff in prisons include a variety of persons who oversee the business affairs, maintenance, public relations, and clerical functions as well as coordinate contacts between inmates and both institutional personnel and outside services and agencies.

Relations between correctional personnel and inmates are unpredictable and volatile yet usually impersonal and mild. A natural gap exists between staff and inmates, and the gap is aggravated by a range of sociocultural factors. Most prisoners come from urban areas, while most prisons are in rural settings. The inmate population is largely from lower socioeconomic classes, whereas most staff members' social classes are more economically and culturally privileged. Disproportionately large percentages of inmates are minorities; disproportionately small percentages of correctional personnel are minorities.

Since the late 1970s the number of women who work in corrections, both in treatment and custodial positions, has increased. This means that male inmates are under the direct supervision of women, a situation many lower class, urban, minority men find offensive and unacceptable. These facts obviously bring to the prison two different, often conflicting value systems and natural barriers to communication and the establishment of personal relationships.

Additionally, for many staff members in less progressive correctional systems, their positions and roles grant them status in their communities. This status differential is often used to emphasize the differences they perceive between themselves and the inmates they guard.

Prison Administrative Management Models

As the primary manager, the warden has responsibility for overseeing the prison's daily functions as well as imple-

Relations between correctional personnel and inmates are usually impersonal and mild.

menting programs and policies for pursuing the prison's administrative goals. In terms of demographic characteristics and work styles, wardens of the 1990s are very different from their predecessors. These changes are in large part a response to the evolving needs of inmates, staff, and the public.

JOB FOCUS: DIRECTOR, STATE DEPARTMENT OF CORRECTIONS

At the top of the corrections hierarchy is the person who is responsible for overseeing all aspects of the daily operations and for planning the system's future needs. As director of a state's corrections programs, this person is a political appointee who must work with both the practical needs of inmates, employees, and the public and the political agendas of a governor (who usually appoints the director), state legislators, and the public (who elect legislators and governors).

The director is a top-level administrator in most states. This means that most of the director's time and attention is consumed with large-scale issues. The daily issues, crises, and needs of correctional workers and clients are delegated to others who work under the director. Most states give the director the power to appoint/hire top assistants (although the governor or legislature must usually approve these appointments).

A director of corrections will almost always be college-educated, often with a graduate degree in criminal justice, law, psychology, or business administration. For many years the director of corrections job was considered a prime political job. However, as the needs of corrections have changed, the thinking today is that this person needs to have experience in corrections, as well as administrative experience. A director's salary is determined by statute and generally ranges from around $50,000 to well over $100,000, depending on level of experience.

Source: Harold E. Williamson, *The Corrections Profession* (Thousand Oaks, CA: Sage Publications, 1990).

Autocratic Wardens

Wardens of U.S. prisons originally had total control and discretion in how they ran their prisons. From the birth of the penitentiary movement until after World War II, politically appointed wardens were viewed as totalitarian leaders whose only concern was staying in the good graces of the governor. **Autocratic wardens** held responsibility for every aspect of the prison. However, because of the size of such a job, most autocratic wardens compelled compliance with their orders through a mix of terror, incentives, and favoritism. These management tools were used with both inmates and staff.

Bureaucratic Wardens

Following the end of World War II, most U.S. social institutions, especially those associated with government, moved toward an increasingly **bureaucratic model.** For corrections, this meant the development of statewide correctional systems. When individual prisons were tied more closely together in a state system, a new layer of supervision was created above the wardens. Whereas wardens had previously made and enforced policies as they pleased, these functions were now given to or supervised by a coordinating system office.

In the bureaucratic system, wardens' powers eroded, and relations between administrators and both staff and inmates changed significantly. Part of the bureaucratization of government included the implementation of a **civil service** system. Correctional staff had job security, and wardens could not dole out jobs as political favors quite so easily.

Because of the changes in the wardens' role, as well as other large-scale social changes, there have been major changes in the types of people who are wardens. Not until the 1960s did it become common for wardens to be college graduates, frequently with training in both corrections and management. Also, an influx of minorities and women has entered corrections, including top-level administration. Women serve as prison wardens for both women and men and as directors of systems in states as diverse as Maine, New Jersey, Louisiana, and California.

Participatory Management

One major change to occur after the implementation of a bureaucratic management model was the inclusion of correctional staff and inmates

Autocratic wardens Early form of prison administration; total power centered in the hands of the top-level administrator; individuals who held the authority to make any and all decisions about the operations, personnel, or inmates of a particular institution.

Bureaucratic model Form of correctional management that emerged following World War II; calls for specialization of tasks and dispersion of responsibility among numerous staff members and multiple levels of administration.

Civil service Part of the bureaucratic model of management where staff receive specialized forms of job protection as governmental workers.

Participatory management Management model where both correctional staff and inmates are included in decision-making processes.

Texas control model A form of participatory management where strong and powerful inmates were given authority to maintain order and security among segments of the inmate population; declared unconstitutional in 1982 by the Supreme Court in *Ruiz v. Estelle*.

Consensus model A form of participatory management in which administrators met with inmate groups to discuss changes to institutional policies and programs.

Responsibility model A form of participatory management that attempted to encourage a sense of community among inmates by imposing minimum restraints on daily life.

in management issues. **Participatory management** has been accompanied by a shift from considering wardens as specialists to viewing them as generalists in management. In a way this reflects the autocratic warden's role without the power. In a participatory management scheme, wardens see themselves as the individuals responsible for conceptualizing an overall plan for the prison and then developing a framework for implementing that scheme.

The participatory portion of the management approach enters when planning and implementing specific goals of the general plan. Groups of staff and inmates are involved, in one of several ways, to develop specific ways to implement the general ideas. There are two basic benefits to such an approach. First, the warden has the burden of developing and implementing all policies. Second, when people whom these policies and procedures will affect are involved in the planning process, they will less likely oppose them when implemented. In this way a participatory management approach helps to pursue all four primary administrative goals: security/custody, segregation, discipline, and treatment.

All has not gone smoothly for participatory management plans, however. In various states and individual prisons, problems have arisen when different groups, often correctional officers, have used their input to advance their own interests over those of the institution. In these instances, the participatory nature of the management plan has had to be reduced to avoid deep resentments and large-scale problems between inmates and correctional officers. This has, in part, led to the move toward unionization of correctional officers (discussed later in this chapter).

Various forms of participatory management have failed. The **Texas control model,** where strong and powerful inmates were recruited to maintain order in their units in exchange for special privileges, was ruled unconstitutional by the U.S. Supreme Court in the 1982 case of *Ruiz v. Estelle.* California's **consensus model** attempted to have administrators meet and discuss with inmate groups changes to institutional policies and programs. This model was designed to have inmate leaders endorse and convince other inmates to accept changes. However, when inmate gangs fought for dominance in the program, the model failed. Finally, Michigan's **responsibility model** attempted to encourage a sense of community among inmates by imposing minimum restraints on daily life. The intention was to build inmates' individual responsibility to ease reintegration to the community. The model failed when rather than building a commu-

One form of participatory management is having administrators and inmates discuss institutional policies and programs.

nity sense, inmates maneuvered and fought to gain power over other inmates. In essence, this model failed because inmates acted just like people in the free world.

One development that has survived in many prisons is the **inmate council.** These are groups of inmates, selected either by the administration or preferably by the inmate population, who are provided opportunities to lobby administrative representatives for the "inmate perspective." A similar development has been the inmate grievance council, an outlet for airing complaints about administrative and staff actions. With grievance procedures established, the buildup of tensions and the possibility of violence are less likely to occur.

Inmate council
Groups of inmates whom administrators select to inform or to make decisions about areas of institutional life.

The Prison's Influence on Staff

While the destructive effects of imprisonment on prisoners have been well documented, the prison's influence on the staff has received significantly less consideration. However, this has been changing in recent years.

"The Other Prisoners"

Prison staffs are commonly referred to as "the other prisoners" because of the pressures they experience being locked into institutions and having to live and work according to the strict rules, regulations, and restrictions. One observer, focusing on the impact of a correctional career on an individual's mental health, has concluded that:

> Prison conditions place a significant degree of strain on the workforce, strain which can actually be damaging to the personality of the employee, and thus . . . his effectiveness as a prison officer.[6]

This is what is sometimes called the "dehumanizing" effect of corrections. Not only are inmates reduced to numbers, but correctional officers may also find they are performing simply rote tasks, being something more similar to a robot than to a rational, responsive, and responsible person.

Many correctional officers initially enter their jobs with idealistic goals of helping rehabilitate inmates. However, they quickly realize these ideals are unrealistic and naive. Because of the high rates and frequency of contacts with abnormal behavior, brutality, racial conflicts, and general states of tension and anxiety, young correctional officers soon lose their enthusiasm.[7] Also, pressures to conform to peers' ideals and views lead many correctional officers to view inmates similarly to how their superior officers view them. Also leading to a loss of idealism is the high rate of recidivism. When officers (and other staff) see inmates whom they believed had in fact "rehabilitated" return to the prison, often in very short order, their hopes for rehabilitation are dampened. As a consequence, correctional staff's generally negative attitudes toward inmates and correctional efforts minimize the chances of such efforts being successful.

Selection and Training of Prison Staff

The success of prison programs depends not only on the prison's management style, but also on the staff's quality and attitudes. However, many prison staffs are relatively uneducated, unskilled, and insufficiently trained for their duties. While almost all prison employees are required to participate in specialized training, ranging from only a few days to several months, most of the "real" job training occurs on the job. This suggests that many of the correctional officer's early experiences are trial-and-error experiments. Some of these experiments lead to successes; others, to errors.

Inmates also provide much "training" for correctional officers. Novice officers and many experienced officers depend highly on securing the inmates' cooperation in carrying out their responsibilities. Inmate leaders frequently "help out" officers by enforcing rules within housing units and ensuring the cooperation of other inmates with administrative orders. While helpful in the short run, such "assistance" also guides officers to pursue particular methods of resolving conflicts and fulfilling their responsibilities. Inmates thereby have "trained" officers to function in particular manners. (This was one of many problems in the Texas model, which was ruled unconstitutional.)

Most correctional administrators would like to hire staff who have extensive training, both in corrections as well as in general educational fields. More exacting educational requirements have become commonplace for correctional officers through the past two decades. While administrators believe that educated officers mean a more emotionally mature, socially aware, and interpersonally skilled staff, education has not been shown to have a significant relationship to correctional officers' increased job satisfaction levels.[8]

Correctional officers need to develop inmates' voluntary cooperation in carrying out their custodial duties.

In 1947 the American Prison Association (now the American Correctional Association) firmly stated that personnel of uniformly high quality could best be recruited through a state system.[9] More recently the American Correctional Association has softened its stand on this issue, although the debate still stands regarding whether training and supervision should be controlled locally or through a centralized organization. Most recently the American Correctional Association has ratified as one of its recommended national policies on corrections a section on Staff Recruitment and Development. (See Figure 5–3.)

During the past several decades, public policy has moved in the direction of returning the control, management, and treatment of crime and offenders to local communities. A logical consequence of this move, it is argued, is for the recruitment and training of correctional personnel to be focused on the local level. This will not only place control over institutions and political decisions more firmly in local hands, but it will also involve local communities with corrections.

For top-level management positions, though, recruitment is generally believed necessary on a national scale. However, promotion of local personnel through the ranks is also considered a viable alternative. This brings to our attention the potential problems involved in mixing locally recruited and imported correctional personnel and administrators. Over forty years ago, the German sociologist Robert Michel pointed out that organizations and their leaders are necessarily practitioners of oligarchy.[10] A political fact of life, those in power tend to keep themselves in power mainly by giving leadership roles to their loyal followers, thus creating political machines. This is the essence of what Michel calls the **iron law of oligarchy.**

Iron law of oligarchy Idea that persons in positions of power strive to maintain their power through giving somewhat powerful subordinate positions to loyal followers.

Public relations problems have historically plagued recruitment to correctional positions. The general public has a very distorted and limited perception of the work involved in corrections. This has led many highly qualified and promising potential correctionalists to shy away from careers in the corrections field. They see the work as intellectually unchallenging, physically demanding, dirty, and undesirable. Additionally, the geographic location of prisons has meant that the local labor force from which institutions can draw is primarily rural and unfamiliar with the values, lifestyles, and cultures of the predominantly urban, minority inmate populations.

Many potential correctional workers believe that they need only "common sense" to fulfill the duties a job in corrections would require. With such an uninformed view, a correctional staff member

Figure 5–3 American Correctional Association's national correctional policy on staff recruitment and development.

Introduction:

Knowledgeable, highly skilled, motivated, and professional correctional personnel are essential to fulfill the purpose of corrections effectively. Professionalism is achieved through structured programs of recruitment and enhancement of the employee's skills, knowledge, insight, and understanding of the correctional process.

Statement:

Correctional staff are the primary agents for promoting health, welfare, security, and safety within correctional institutions and community supervision programs. They directly interact with accused and adjudicated offenders and are the essential catalysts of change in the correctional process. The education, recruitment, orientation, supervision, compensation, training, retention, and advancement of correctional staff must receive full support from the executive, judicial, and legislative branches of government. To achieve this, correctional agencies should:

A. Recruit personnel, including ex-offenders, in an open and accountable manner to assure equal employment opportunity for all qualified applicants regardless of sex, age, race, physical disability, religion, ethnic background, or political affiliation, and actively promote the employment of women and minorities;

B. Screen applicants for job-related aspects of physical suitability, personal adjustment, emotional stability, dependability, appropriate educational level, and experience. An additional requisite is the ability to relate to accused or adjudicated offenders in a manner that is fair, objective, and neither punitive nor vindictive;

C. Select, promote, and retain staff in accordance with valid job-related procedures that emphasize professional merit and technical competence. Voluntary transfers and promotions within and between correctional systems should be encouraged;

D. Comply with professional standards in staff development and offer a balance between operational requirements and the development of personal, social, and cultural understanding. Staff development programs should involve use of public and private resources, including colleges, universities, and professional associations;

E. Achieve parity between correctional staff and comparable criminal justice system staff in salaries and benefits, training, continuing education, performance evaluations, disciplinary procedures, career development opportunities, transfers, promotions, grievance procedures, and retirement; and

F. Encourage the participation of trained volunteers and students to enrich the correctional programs and to provide a potential source of recruitment.

Source: The National Conference on Correctional Policy (College Park, MD: ACA, 1987). Reprinted with permission.

could potentially have serious problems on the job. However, because of the traditionally poor working conditions, low pay, and geographic isolation associated with corrections work, a diverse pool from which correctional administrators can draw new personnel may not exist.

Since the late 1960s, correctional institutions and systems have made strong efforts to recruit diverse personnel. The move to increase minority group representation in the ranks of corrections personnel is designed to both counter the social and economic discrimination found in society in general and to work toward a more racially balanced institution.

As one moves up the hierarchy of correctional positions, discrimination has stronger influences and is more evident. Relatively few minority group members occupy top administrative positions. (See Figure 5–4.) Those who make it to the top ranks have greater demands and expectations imposed on them but receive less support.[11]

Recent Developments in Organization of Prison Staff

Two major changes in corrections during the past several decades have been the move toward a professional approach to correctional work and the emergence of unions. Both of these developments, which are related, have brought changes to how correctional institutions operate. However, neither change has been universal or complete.

Professionalization

Moving toward a professional approach to corrections work has accompanied a general trend in the United States toward professional-

Figure 5–4 Federal and state correctional personnel, by race.

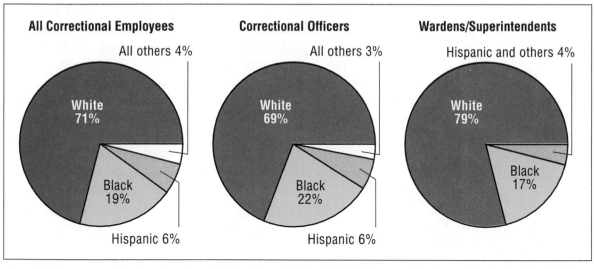

All Correctional Employees	Correctional Officers	Wardens/Superintendents
All others 4%	All others 3%	Hispanic and others 4%
White 71%	White 69%	White 79%
Black 19%	Black 22%	Black 17%
Hispanic 6%	Hispanic 6%	

Source: U.S. Department of Justice, *Sourcebook of Criminal Justice Statistics, 1994* (Washington, D.C.: Bureau of Justice Statistics, 1995).

ization of many occupations. Since the middle of the century, many services and technological occupations (law enforcement, social work, pharmacy, education, and so on) have attempted to alter their public perception by changing from an occupation to a profession. For most occupations, this change has occurred, but only in limited degrees. This is the case for corrections.

A simple definition of a profession contains four primary elements:

1. A profession is grounded on acquisition of a theoretical body of systematic knowledge through a prolonged period of academic study. This knowledge is unique to the members of the professional group.

2. Members of the profession are motivated by social or community concerns, not self-interest.

3. The individuals and organizations of the profession are largely self-regulating.

4. The members of the profession establish and distribute rewards based on values unique to the profession.[12]

Perhaps the greatest degree of progress toward **professionalization** of corrections has occurred in developing a theoretical body of

Professionalization
The process through which an occupation changes status to a profession.

Recent Developments in Organization of Prison Staff   **125**

systematic knowledge. However, corrections differs from many other emerging professions in this regard. That is, corrections has no unique body of knowledge but draws heavily from the theoretical bodies of a number of social sciences and academic disciplines. Thus, the systematic "knowledge about corrections" is not a body of knowledge unique to those in the corrections field.

Evidence both supports and refutes correctional workers' community-interest motivation. While the relatively low pay that many corrections staff receive suggests these people are not motivated by self-interest, ample evidence also suggests that people choose corrections because the jobs are convenient and offer stable employment. This directly relates to a system of rewards for correctional workers. Because they are usually government positions, the jobs themselves do not create the monetary and status rewards. However, people who enter corrections to pursue community interests may find personal satisfaction in social interaction opportunities and stable jobs. Of course, this largely depends on the individuals and their goals and desires.

> **FYI**
>
> Although their general education level has increased in the past several decades, correctional officers overall still have low levels of education. In 1992 only 18.5 percent of the more than 9,200 correctional officers in the Federal Bureau of Prisons had a college degree. At the other end of the scale, fully 46.5 percent of the correctional officers in federal prisons had no college education at all. Minority correctional officers are slightly more likely than white correctional officers to have advanced educations. Among white correctional officers, 17.7 percent hold college degrees, while 24.2 percent of African-American correctional officers in the Federal Bureau of Prisons have degrees.

The increasing level of education of corrections staff has contributed to the movement toward professionalization. See an insider's view on professionalization in Figure 5–5. The percent of college-educated correctional officers continues to increase. This is not to say that correctional officers necessarily have a degree when they start their jobs. Rather, many officers are encouraged to return to college and may be seen in college classrooms (even in corrections classes!).

Self-regulation, similar to the theoretical body of systematic knowledge, is an emerging characteristic of corrections. Again, because of the hierarchical structures that provide the framework for correctional systems and institutions, the degree to which correctionalists can be self-regulating is limited. Professional associations (such as the American Correctional Association) do not determine work tasks and are able to render only recommendations and

Figure 5–5 An insider's view on professionalism.

The following Letter to the Editor was printed in a small-town newspaper in Indiana on December 23, 1994. The writer is responding to the way the media reported on the murder of a correctional officer at an Indiana prison.

To the Editor:

With the recent stabbing of "prison guard" Phillip Curry at the Indiana State Prison in Michigan City, I feel that a few points should be made. First, the idea of "prison guard" has been around for quite some time; however, I think it should be brought to the public's attention that in this professional field, we are classified as "correctional officers" and not as "prison guards."

Also, we have been trained to deal with rehabilitation of offenders on all levels, from the ones for the pettiest crimes to those incarcerated for the more violent crimes. This is a rather extensive training course for all new correctional officers and lasts for several weeks. When you have finished the course, hopefully you will know how to handle yourself in a professional manner. I realize that this training did not stop what happened to Phillip Curry, but I do feel he deserved the recognition of being known as "Correctional Officer Phillip Curry of the Indiana State Prison" and not as a "prison guard."

Furthermore, it seems to be that when a police officer or other public official is killed in the line of duty, it is well publicized. And on most news stations it is the top story and on the front pages of most newspapers. Even when Indiana had an execution earlier this month, most news stories gave it top priority. However, after the killing of Correctional Officer Phillip Curry, it seems to have been downplayed by most of the media. In some manner, correctional officers are public officials for we spend our 40 hours-plus work week with those offenders, doing our best to keep them as secure and safe as possible, thereby performing our service to the public. The answer is not, "If you don't like it, quit." Someone has to do the job and handle this responsibility.

The flags were flown at half-staff until after Correctional Officer Phillip Curry was buried; and I wonder how many residents of the State of Indiana didn't know why, or even cared.

So maybe for future reference, when the unfortunate happens to a correctional officer, that individual will receive the recognition they so deserve.

Correctional Officer Michael Litz
Indiana State Farm

Source: Michael Litz, Letter to the Editor (Greencastle, IN: *Banner-Graphic*, December 23, 1994).

accreditation standards. That is, they do not enforce standards. Also important: The majority of individuals involved in correctional work are not members of professional organizations. Having no membership in professional associations means having no assistance from them.

Accreditation Process by which correctional institutions and programs are declared to meet a minimum set of professional standards; professional organizations create and enforce this process.

Finally, individuals involved in correctional work do not determine their own schedules, tasks, or responsibilities. Correctional work is largely reactive, not proactive. This means that work in corrections involves responding to situations as they arise, not predicting possible problems and working to avoid them.

Where does this leave the issue of professionalization, then? It appears that corrections is moving toward but has not yet fully achieved a professional status. Rather, it may be more accurate to view corrections as an "emerging profession."[13] As such, corrections appears to have achieved the structural elements of a profession. However, it has yet to fully achieve the attitudinal elements necessary to be considered a full-fledged profession.

This is not a negative view of corrections' potential as a profession in the future. Numerous researchers have suggested that professionalism is most significantly influenced by prisons' structural elements (organization of staff, lack of interaction among staff, and a sharp distinction between staff and inmates). Once a professional perspective is adopted, it tends to remain stable.[14] Therefore, the move toward professionalization can be expected to continue. As people with a professional perspective continue to be recruited and to retain their view as structural elements of prisons are modified, professionalization can be expected to continue.

Unionization

As guaranteed by the freedom of association clause of the First Amendment to the U.S. Constitution, public- and private-sector employees have the right to join unions. This is a right to choose to join; it is not a mandate to join. (However, employees who do not join but stand to benefit from a union's efforts may be required to pay what amounts to a "user's fee.")

As in many occupations, correctional employees' unions arose as a response to what workers perceived as a general lack of official concern with their safety, security, and working conditions. Some early union organizers may have achieved some personal gains (increased pay, promotions, new assignments, and so on) in the unionization process. However, the unionization process in corrections has been a late developer when compared to most other state employee occupations. In many states, correctional employees were the last group of state employees to form a union (if they have unionized at this time).[15]

The unionization movement grew out of correctional officers' frustrations of feeling powerless to influence their working conditions. Although the era of the autocratic warden disappeared by the 1940s, little change had been made by the 1970s or 1980s for lower-level employees. Correctional employees' frustration level differs across systems. This is obvious when some states permit administrators and supervisors to join unions, and other states prohibit their joining. As most aspects of U.S. society moved toward bureaucratization, the unionization movement also prospered, except for correctional workers.

Attempts to unionize correctional workers have met strong community resistance, largely due to the public's fear of what might occur if unionized correctional officers were to go on strike. The public fears that a strike would mean mass inmate escapes and general chaos in society. Correctional officers have gone on strike in many states, although strikes by public employees are generally illegal. The results of strikes have varied, but very rarely have the consequences even come close to the public's fears. When a strike occurs, prisons will be staffed in one of two ways: The National Guard will be called in to run the prisons or both correctional administrators and the state police will be used as staff persons, as happened in Wisconsin and in Ohio and Washington, respectively.

Because strikes are illegal, correctional officers' unions have as their main tool the powers of **collective bargaining.** Through their collective bargaining, unions have introduced improvements in physical conditions and pay/benefits and have served as advocates for securing due process rights for correctional workers.

Many observers, however, believe that unions have not succeeded in providing sufficiently for correctional officers. Hawkins and Alpert[16] identify three main reasons for the general failure of unions. First, when a correctional system makes its initial move to unionize, the competition intensifies among groups to represent workers. This competition, rather than allowing correctional workers to negotiate beneficial relationships, actually serves to raise employees' expectations unrealistically high and to distract workers from their tasks at hand. Second, correctional unions have historically failed to represent the increasing diversity of correctionalists. Whereas one function of unions should be to eliminate discriminatory treatment, unions have served primarily to re-create and, thereby, magnify status hierarchies.

Collective bargaining Process whereby a labor union (or other group representing a collection of individuals) negotiates a contract of wages, benefits, and working conditions for staff with an employer's administrative agents.

Third, the fact that unions cannot legally strike hurts their effectiveness in two ways. First, if the union remains within the boundaries of legal action, the strike (as a very effective union tactic) is unavailable. Second, if it does strike, which is illegal, the union loses some (if not all) of its credibility in the eyes of the public. This, in turn, makes any other action of the union less effective.

Summary

Prisons are institutions that can be very difficult to manage. Management of a prison requires administrators to identify and overcome numerous obstacles. In pursuit of the basic goals of security, segregation, discipline, and treatment, the administrator must ensure that inmates are properly classified (to best meet the needs of both inmates and the prison). Administrators also need to recognize that their staff predominantly comes from backgrounds different from those of inmates. The experience of working in a prison has profound effects on staff, as does the management style that administrators adopt. The role and style of wardens have changed dramatically during the twentieth century, from autocratic rulers to directors of a bureaucracy to participatory managers who attempt to involve inmates and staff in daily decision-making processes. In response to both these internal developments and external social changes, correctional workers have become increasingly professional and have unionized in many states to protect their interests.

QUESTIONS FOR REVIEW

1. What are the four primary administrative goals for prisons?

2. What are the various types of treatment programs that are commonly available in prison?

3. What are some reasons why changes in prison administration occur very slowly?

4. What is the tone of typical inmate-staff interactions?

5. What are the differences between an autocratic and a bureaucratic warden? Why did these differences come about?

6. What are the duties of a prison warden? What types of people are wardens?

7. How does participatory management work in prison? What are the advantages and disadvantages of such an administrative strategy?

8. What are some problems associated with recruiting a high-quality, stable staff?

9. Is correctional work a profession? Why or why not?

10. What is the role of unions in corrections? How effective are unions?

ACTIVITIES

1. Interview people in your community and ask their impressions about prisons, prison inmates, and correctional officers. Compare responses and consider from where these impressions come.

2. Develop a model program for recruiting and training staff for a new prison to be built in your community.

3. Discuss how correctional officers who are unhappy with their jobs can work with prison administrators to try to correct problems in the institutional administration and hierarchy. Try role-playing a discussion, taking the role of warden, correctional officers, union representative, and concerned community member.

ENDNOTES

1. President's Commission on Law Enforcement and Administration of Justice, *Task Force Report: Corrections* (Washington, D.C.: U.S. Government Printing Office, 1967), p. 59.

2. Robert B. Levinson, "A Clarification of Classification," *Criminal Justice and Behavior,* Vol. 9, No. 2, 1982, pp. 133–142.

3. *ACA Directory, 1990* (Laurel, MD: American Correctional Association, 1990), pp. xxvi–xxvii.

4. *Ibid.*

5. Patrick M. Clark, Jo E. Weth, and David Canales-Portalatin, "Inmate Classification in the United States: Advancements in Policy and Procedure," paper presented at the annual meeting of the American Society of Criminology, New Orleans, 1992.

6. Paul Schlacter, "Concept of Self and Perceived Stress: A Study of Correctional Officers," unpublished doctoral dissertation, The Ohio State University, Columbus, OH, 1980, p. 81.

7. A. Guenther and M. Guenther, "Screws and Thugs," *Society,* Vol. 11, July–August 1974, pp. 42–50.

8. Nancy C. Jurik, Gregory J. Halemba, Michael C. Musheno, and Bernard V. Boyle, "Educational Attainment, Job Satisfaction and the Professionalization of Correctional Officers," *Work and Occupations,* Vol. 14, No. 1, 1987, pp. 106–125.

9. *Handbook on Classification in Correctional Institutions* (New York: American Prison Association, 1947), p. 15.

10. Robert Michel, *Political Parties: A Sociological Study of the Oligarchi-*

cal Tendencies of Modern Democracy (Glencoe, IL: The Free Press, 1949).

11. James A. Bush, "The Minority Administrator: Implications for Social Work Education," *Journal of Education in Social Work,* Vol. 13, No. 1, 1977, pp. 15–22.

12. E. C. Hughes, "Professions," in K. S. Lynn (ed.), *The Professions in America* (Boston: Houghton-Mifflin, 1965).

13. R. C. Kearney and C. Sinha, "Professionalism and Bureaucratic Responsiveness," *Public Administration Review,* Vol. 48, 1988, pp. 571–579.

14. Robert Blair and Peter C. Kratcoski, "Professionalism Among Correctional Officers: A Longitudinal Analysis of Individ- ual and Structural Determinants," in Peter J. Benekos and Alida V. Merlo (eds.), *Corrections: Dilemmas and Directions* (Cincinnati: Anderson Publishing, 1992); F. T. Cullen, F. E. Lutze, B. G. Link, and N. T. Wolfe, "The Correctional Orientation of Prison Guards: Do Officers Support Rehabilitation?" *Federal Probation,* Vol. 53, 1989, pp. 33–41; J. T. Whitehead and C. A. Lindquist, "Determinants of Correctional Officers' Professional Orientation," *Justice Quarterly,* Vol. 6, 1989, pp. 69–87.

15. Richard Hawkins and Geoffrey P. Alpert, *American Prison Systems: Punishment and Justice* (Englewood Cliffs, NJ: Prentice Hall, 1989).

16. *Ibid.*

CHAPTER 6

The Prisoner

CHAPTER OBJECTIVES

In the previous two chapters you learned about the history, origin, and administration of the prison. This chapter begins an examination of the prisoner and how the culture of and programs offered in the prison affect an inmate. After reading this chapter, you will be able to:

1. Understand the size and characteristics of the U.S. prison population.

2. Identify the effects of long-term imprisonment.

3. Relate the effects of aging among prison inmates to the challenges this population presents to correctional administrators.

4. Identify the ways that the prison experience impacts inmates' sense of self and social status.

5. Examine the means by which inmates construct a social structure, including an economy, social norms, and social control efforts.

6. Explore the range of commonly offered programming options for adult inmates.

7. Understand the impacts of prison industries on both treatment of inmates and economic benefits for correctional systems.

8. Identify the forms of programming available to inmates.

9. Examine the effectiveness of prison programs.

10. Understand the effects of incarceration on the ex-prisoner.

The institution of prison creates its unique culture and code of conduct.

Prisons and Prisoners

We have already examined the reasons prisons were established, the methods prisons have historically used to dole out punishments or to achieve other goals with inmates, the historical evolution of prisons, and the major issues in prison administration. This chapter focuses on those people who are the real reason for prisons' existence: prisoners.

In this chapter we will study prison inmates: who they are and how their lives are structured within the **total institution** of the prison. We will also examine how prison programs attempt to change prison inmates. Finally, we will discuss how prison impacts the lives of former inmates.

Total institution An approach where others regulate and control all aspects of an individual's life and activities.

Prison Populations

With more than 1.1 million adults incarcerated in state and federal prisons at the end of 1995,[1] the United States has one of the largest prison populations in the world today. This total population is more than 200 percent larger than it was in 1980. During the 1990s alone, the total number of imprisoned adults has been increasing by nearly 7.5 percent every year.[2] Increases in population have been greater in the federal system than in the state systems. Only five states—Maine, New Jersey, North Dakota, Oregon, and Wyoming—had a decrease in their prison populations during the early 1990s.[3]

It is interesting to note, however, that the size of a state's inmate population is not necessarily correlated with that state's total population or violent crime rate. Table 6–1 presents the 50 states' rankings of total population and violent crime and incarceration rates (number of inmates per 100,000 residents).

While some states, such as Alabama, Louisiana, South Carolina, and Maryland, have high violent crime rates *and* high incarceration rates, several states have significant disparities between their rankings for violent crime and incarceration rates. Among the states with the greatest disparities between high incarceration rates and relatively low violent crime rates are Arizona, Oklahoma, Virginia, and Mississippi. In contrast, some states are ranked significantly lower in incarceration rates than in violent crime rates (Texas, Florida, New York, California, Tennessee, Illinois, New Mexico, and Massachusetts). What quickly becomes obvious is that the states with the comparatively lower incarceration rates are the generally more populous states. Since

Table 6–1

State	Population Rank	Violent Crime Rank	Incarceration Rate Rank
Alabama	22	12	7
Alaska	48	15	27
Arizona	23	18	6
Arkansas	33	23	18
California	1	2	14
Colorado	26	24	26
Connecticut	27	31	19
Delaware	46	19	12
Florida	4	1	10
Georgia	11	17	9
Hawaii	40	43	40
Idaho	42	41	29
Illinois	6	7	23
Indiana	14	29	28
Iowa	30	38	38
Kansas	32	28	31
Kentucky	24	30	24
Louisiana	21	4	2
Maine	39	48	47
Maryland	19	6	11
Massachusetts	13	10	43
Michigan	8	11	8
Minnesota	20	37	49
Mississippi	31	32	13
Missouri	16	16	20

States' Rankings of Total Population, Violent Crime, and Incarceration Rates

Source: Biennial Report (St. Paul: Minnesota Department of Corrections, 1995).

incarcerating a higher percentage of their larger populations would only aggravate overcrowding, populous states apparently must be more selective about which offenders to imprison.

Such analysis is only part of the picture, however. We gain additional understanding of inmates and population-status impacts on correctional systems by reviewing the inmate distribution based on

Table 6–1   *Continued*

State	Population Rank	Violent Crime Rank	Incarceration Rate Rank
Montana	44	46	36
Nebraska	37	36	45
Nevada	38	9	5
New Hampshire	41	47	42
New Jersey	9	22	22
New Mexico	36	8	34
New York	2	3	17
North Carolina	10	20	21
North Dakota	47	50	50
Ohio	7	26	16
Oklahoma	28	21	4
Oregon	29	27	41
Pennsylvania	5	33	33
Rhode Island	43	34	37
South Carolina	25	5	3
South Dakota	45	45	32
Tennessee	17	13	25
Texas	3	14	1
Utah	34	39	44
Vermont	49	49	46
Virginia	12	35	15
Washington	15	25	35
West Virginia	35	44	48
Wisconsin	18	42	39
Wyoming	50	40	30

offenses and demographics across prison populations in individual states. As shown in Tables 6–2 and 6–3, variations exist from overall national figures in the individual state systems, but the general trends hold steady. Most notable about U.S. prison inmates is the sex distribution—only 6 percent of all U.S. inmates are female. In 1991, 30 percent of prison admissions were for drug offenses; 31 percent

Table 6–2	Comparison of State Correctional System Inmates: Offenses				
State	Total Population	Total Prison Population	Percent Violent Offense	Percent Property Offense	Percent Drug Offense
National totals[1]	255,078,000	745,000	29.0	31.0	30.0
California[2]	30,407,000	101,808	42.3	26.4	24.5
Texas[3]	17,683,000	51,592	51.0	27.0	17.0
Florida[4]	13,483,000	47,012	52.5	23.0	20.3
Kentucky[5]	3,715,000	9,638	53.0	30.0	14.0
Colorado[6]	3,370,000	6,720	43.7	35.2	10.7
Minnesota[7]	4,468,000	3,627	—	—	—
Vermont[8]	571,000	1,351	50.3[9]	49.7	

1. Statistics as of 6/30/92.
2. Statistics as of 12/31/91.
3. Statistics as of 8/31/92.
4. Statistics as of 6/30/92.
5. Statistics as of 1/27/92.
6. Figures represent averages for the year 1991.
7. Statistics as of 7/1/92.
8. Statistics as of 2/93.
9. Statistics as of 8/92; Vermont does not report drug offenses separately but distinguishes only among crimes of violence (against person), property, and other.

Source: Biennial Report (St. Paul: Minnesota Department of Corrections, 1995).

for property offenses; and 29 percent for violent offenses. National figures on inmates' race show that 46.3 percent of inmates are white or Hispanic, 47.9 percent are African-American, and 5.3 percent are other races.[4]

Experiences of Long-Term Imprisonment

Long-term incarceration Serving more than 7 or 8 years in a correctional institution.

What qualifies as **long-term incarceration** varies. Most researchers determine the cutoff to be serving either 7 or 8 years, although others apply such terminology only to those inmates serving a minimum of 20 years.[5] Most long-term inmates are unmarried white men who are in their late 20s or early 30s when first imprisoned and who remain incarcerated until they are elderly. In fact, the population of elderly inmates is rapidly growing. (See the discussion of "Elderly Inmates.")

State	Percent Male	Percent White	Percent African-American	Percent Hispanic	Percent Previously Incarcerated
*National totals[1]	94	33	48	13	N/A
California[2]	94	29	35	31	38
Texas[3]	96	28	48	24	52
Florida[4]	95	39	58	—	52
Kentucky[5]	95	68	32	—	34
Colorado[6]	95	46	23	25	34
Minnesota[7]	—	57	30	4	—

*Note: These figures have been rounded to the nearest whole number.

1. Statistics as of year-end 1990.
2. Statistics as of 12/31/91.
3. Statistics as of 8/31/92.
4. Statistics as of 6/30/92.
5. Statistics as of 1/27/92.
6. Figures as of 6/30/91.
7. Statistics as of 7/1/92.

Source: Biennial Report (St. Paul: Minnesota Department of Corrections, 1995).

All prison inmates experience a number of problems beyond the simple disruption of their lives. However, long-term inmates face difficulties that may be more intense and have a greater impact than what short-term inmates face. Most notable, the problems that impact inmates most severely are social: disruption of relationships with outsiders and problematic relationships with fellow inmates.[6] Many long-term prisoners have an almost obsessive fear that they will deteriorate (physically and mentally) before their release. However, psychological studies have systematically failed to demonstrate significant deteriorations.[7]

What most characterizes long-term inmates is their common development of alternative modes of adjustment, which are often exaggerated. Some of these adjustments may have negative consequences for both

FYI

The majority of prison inmates are not serving sentences for violent crimes against people. Among prison inmates, drug offenses and property crimes are most common.

individuals and the institution. Those who serve lengthy sentences have more cases of prison suicides,[8] psychological disorders,[9] and detachment from significant others outside correctional institutions.[10] Long-term inmates also suffer a lowered sense of self-efficacy (individuals' assessment of their effectiveness, competence, and ability to influence events).[11] These issues pose additional programming, classification, and supervision difficulties for correctional officials. Consequently, it becomes obvious that not only do inmates experience long-term imprisonment differently, but correctional personnel as well have different experiences with long-term inmates.[12]

Elderly Inmates

Similar to the general U.S. population, the population of prison inmates is growing older. By the year 2000 more than 34 million Americans will be over 65; by 2010 one-third of all Americans will be older than 50.[13] These increases have had and will continue to have two impacts on prisons: increasing incarceration rates for older people and increasing numbers of offenders serving longer sentences. During the 1980s the number of inmates over age 55 increased by more than 50 percent. More recently, from 1990–1993, inmates aged 55 or older increased 30 percent. In 1993 more than 25,000 inmates were 55 or older.[14] As Edith Flynn argues in her article "The Graying of America's Prison Population," "the issue of the graying of this country's corrections population has not yet reached a crisis stage. If left unattended, however, it surely will."[15]

Most important in this area is the need to modify facilities and services to accommodate the needs of **geriatric inmates.** Inmates who present a set of health concerns and problems unique to older persons are one example of **special needs inmates.** Since most prison inmates come from economically disadvantaged backgrounds, they are more likely to have health problems. This is especially true for incarcerated elderly inmates, who have higher rates of health problems than do nonincarcerated elderly people.[16]

However, elderly inmates are not a homogeneous lot. More accurately, the population of elderly inmates is comprised of three types of individuals. First, and numerically the smallest of the three groups, are those offenders of advanced age who are arrested for the first time and subsequently sentenced to prison. Oftentimes these individuals are incarcerated for killings. Second are those offenders who have been in and out of the criminal justice system for many years and who are

Geriatric inmates Elderly inmates who present unique health and social needs.

Special needs inmates Inmates who require special programming, housing, or health services.

returned to prison at an advanced age. In popular discourse, these are referred to as **career criminals.** Third, and the group with the most significant impact on contemporary corrections, are individuals who have aged in prison. Convicted and sentenced for especially severe offenses or for a large number of serious offenses, these offenders have lengthy sentences and spend many years in prison.

Elderly inmates, similar to long-term inmates (as there is considerable overlap between these categories), experience some special

Career criminals
Offenders who are in and out of corrections and who spend the majority of their lives involved in some type of criminal activity.

LEGAL BRIEF:

Statutory Laws Regulating Prison Recreation

*I*n *1994 a number of states made significant changes to their state statutes and administrative laws that severely restricted inmates' access to common recreational programs. Most of these changes focused on inmates' access to television, weight-lifting equipment, and other forms of recreation. Some of the legal changes that have recently been made include:*

- California: *Senate Bill 1260 narrows the "inmate bill of rights" to allow prison authorities to bar "obscene publications" and materials that may incite violence. Senate Bill 22 follows up on a Los Angeles County sheriff's order that will do away with weight-lifting equipment. This law requires that as equipment is broken or wears out, it will not be replaced.*
- Wisconsin: *Governor Tommy Thompson issued orders ending inmates' access to free weights and tennis courts.*
- Louisiana: *House Bill 226 forbids inmates' training in martial arts (judo, karate, etc.).*
- Mississippi: *Various pieces of legislation were passed that take away private televisions, radios, tape/compact disc players, and all weight-lifting equipment from inmates. Also, a return to inmate uniforms with stripes (different color stripes for different classifications) was passed into law.*

Also in 1994 similar laws were considered (but failed to pass) in Florida, New York, North Carolina, Ohio, and South Carolina.

Elderly inmates present special problems to correctional officials.

problems and present some special needs to correctional officials. Vito and Wilson have identified the following major categories of problems and special needs of offenders:[17]

1. *Adjustment to imprisonment.* Elderly first-time offenders may have greater difficulties adjusting to the conditions of imprisonment. These adjustments are primarily concerned with social environments (being supervised by younger, culturally diverse people and coping with loss of one's well-established daily routines) and loss of one's culture and material possessions.

2. *Vulnerability to victimization.* Elderly inmates are often viewed by predatory inmates as easy targets for exploitation, especially economic and sexual exploitation.

3. *Adaptation to physical conditions.* Elderly inmates must live in physical facilities that may aggravate or cause physical problems. Things such as concrete floors and walls, stairs, long corridors separating housing, food services, and program offices make incarceration more difficult for many elderly inmates.

4. *Lack of suitable programs.* Most prison recreational programs (primarily sports-related) are geared to younger inmates, as are most educational, vocational, and counseling programs. Because of the cultural isolation most elderly inmates perceive in prisons, they often feel unwelcome, uncomfortable, or vulnerable if they attempt to participate in available programs.

5. *Diversity of the elderly inmate population.* When institutions attempt to serve the needs of the elderly, they must realize that such efforts need to be culturally diverse. Elderly inmates are not a homogeneous group; the only thing they share universally is age. They have cultural, educational, economic, and social/political differences. This diversity must be addressed in any programming efforts; failure to acknowledge such differences will most likely mean the failure of such efforts.

Contemporary correctional systems have not accommodated many of these problems and needs. As late as 1992, only 20 state systems had some kind of specialized or housing facilities for elderly inmates. Assignments to these units were most commonly determined by inmates' levels of disability, not their age. Consequently, present programming does not focus on the cultural and generational distinctiveness of elderly inmates.

FYI

Contrary to some assumptions, even the oldest Americans can violate laws and be imprisoned. In 1994 a 94-year-old Jacksonville, Florida, man was sentenced to seven years in prison for assault and gun possession. Wesley (Pop) Honeywood was arrested for assault charges while on probation for attempted sexual battery of a 7-year-old girl.

When sentenced, Mr. Honeywood was given the option of being sent to a nursing home or to prison. He quickly chose prison, saying, "If I go to jail, I may be out in a couple of years. If I go to a nursing home, I may be there the rest of my life."

The Culture of Prison

In 1940 Donald Clemmer, a sociologist at the Menard Prison in Chester, Illinois, began his classic study of the prison as a separate culture or community. His perceptive observations and description of the formal organizational structure of the prison counterculture were the first of numerous systematic efforts.[18] Since the publication of Clemmer's work, many other studies have been made. Nearly all of these studies have agreed on the power, influence, organization, and pathology of the prison culture. It has a code, a normative order, a status hierarchy, and a language of its own, typically referred to as **prison argot.**

Prison argot A language that is unique to a prison.

Similar to someone moving to a different country and needing to speak and understand that culture's language to survive, the correctional professional must know the language spoken in prison. However, prison language can differ among institutions. For this reason, staff must carefully listen to the words used (and their specific meanings) when entering a new prison or jail. The influence of language on behavior is clearly evident in the work of those who adhere to **labeling theory.** This school of thought believes that the labels, or names, we attach to people and actions significantly influence our self-concept and subsequent behavior. For example, people who are repeatedly told that they are stupid or worthless will eventually believe these statements. As a result, they will have very low self-esteem and expectations for themselves.

Labeling theory Belief that the names and terms used to identify people shape the identities and behaviors of such people.

While incarcerated, inmates are effectively removed from free society and are subjected to life within a controlled, restrictive, and punitive structure. As a consequence, inmates experience suffering or, as Sykes says, "pains of imprisonment."[19] First is the deprivation of liberty. As its most basic function, prison serves to segregate offenders from society, thereby depriving inmates of their freedom. Second, inmates are deprived of or have limited access to material goods (food, clothing, entertainment devices, personal care products, etc.) and to professional and care services. Third, inmates suffer deprivation of heterosexual relationships. Although opposite-sex staff are fairly common in prisons, strict rules govern sexual relationships between staff and inmates. Only a few states (most notably California and Mississippi) allow inmates **conjugal visits,** where spouses can spend time together in private (and have sex), but these are relatively rare. Fourth, and perhaps surprising to some, inmates suffer a deprivation of security. Prison is filled with people who are often violent, predatory, and threatening. As we will discuss in more depth in Chapter 8, prison can be a very violent place, and many inmates sense vulnerability. Finally, inmates suffer a loss of autonomy. The highly structured nature of many prisons means that inmates do not make many decisions about their daily or long-term activities. In many ways inmates are treated as if they were children, unable or too irresponsible to

Conjugal visits Time that inmates are allowed to spend with family and spouses in private; usually thought of as opportunities for spouses to visit inmates and to engage in sexual activity.

make intelligent decisions. As a result, inmates are taught not to make intelligent decisions.

However, the experience of incarceration not only creates "pains" for individuals, but, because it is stressful, imprisonment also magnifies problems people bring to jail and prison. Many people who are incarcerated are dependent on alcohol or other drugs. They may be mentally ill, may have chronic medical conditions, and may be responsible for the welfare (or survival) of significant others and children. Many find that the support networks on which they have long relied are stretched beyond their useful points. Thus, when initially incarcerated, many people have a myriad of problems with which to cope. As a result, they may not be able to handle any specific problem particularly well.

Depersonalization in Prison

One of the most distressing by-products of prison life is **depersonalization.** The processes and structures of corrections remove inmates' individualities and reclassify them as simply "other inmates," indistinguishable from each other. In effect this "dehumanizes" or converts "individuals" to simply members of the mass of nonindividuals.

Depersonalization
Result of living in a total institution where individuals lose their sense of individuality and identify themselves as simply members of a set of similar individuals.

An inmate surrenders his or her personal identity upon entering prison.

Status degradation ceremony Procedures where individuals are officially declared no longer to occupy particular social roles and statuses and are symbolically and officially placed into a less valued social position.

Depersonalization first occurs when new prisoners enter an institution used as a reception and classification center. Here, as new inmates are given orientation to life in prison, the process of removing individual identities begins.[20] It happens when their names, their marks of individuality, are taken away and are substituted with numbers. It continues when drab prison uniforms are issued—after degrading searches of their naked bodies and every opening in them, often by a disrespectful examiner. It is emphasized when the cell door first slams shut and when they are left either in complete isolation or with other officially depersonalized inmates. These processes serve official functions; they symbolically proclaim inmates as disgraced people. This is the foundation of reference to such processes as a **status degradation ceremony.**[21]

Here, such processes function to place inmates within the prison's social structure, not necessarily to erode individuals' self-esteem. Although many academics debate the conclusions, a few studies show that long-term incarceration leads to a decline in self-esteem. Overall, however, there is no support for significant self-esteem differences between inmates and noninmates.[22]

We live in a materialistic society, and employment is a major way we identify ourselves and develop our self-esteem. Working at a low-level prison job (or left to sit idle) is, therefore, a major blow to inmates' identities. No longer can or do they achieve some goals; now

Maintaining family ties while in prison facilitates post-release success for the inmate.

they are simply inmates. Entry into the prison community also means that individuals lose most of the personal belongings that give them feelings of worth and identity. This stripping of personal possessions further lessens individuals' concepts of self-worth and identity.

Losing personal relationships and interactions with significant others may be the most difficult experience for inmates. When their social networks are removed, inmates can anticipate numerous difficulties. Maintaining family ties while in prison is important to inmates and to society in pursuit of three goals: maintenance of the family unit, enhancement of individual family members' well-being, and facilitation of post-release success for inmates.

Inmates who are parents feel more acutely the loss of social/family contacts. Recognized as central to inmates' adjustment, visitation privileges and opportunities are allowed. **Contact visits** are the norm for female inmates. Here, inmates and visitors can visit in a setting where they can actually touch one another and not be separated by a glass, mesh, or metal partition. Further, some institutions for women have made visiting areas more attractive and comfortable, and have extended visiting hours. A few institutions allow young children to stay overnight with their incarcerated mothers.[23] Incarcerated fathers' inability to fulfill their paternal roles may directly lead to their loss of self-esteem.[24] Frequently at their own wishes, imprisoned fathers do not have visits with their children.[25]

Contact visits Visiting in a setting where inmates and visitors are not separated by a partition.

Separating the Inmate From the Subculture

Can treatment efforts effectively prevent prisoners from identifying with the prison subculture? Much evidence relates that treatment is ineffective in this way, but some evidence suggests that it is effective. Daniel Glaser, in studying how the prison experience affects various types of offenders, found that a majority of ex-prisoners, when asked if they had identified with the convict population while in prison, had tried actively to remain apart from the other prisoners. Three-quarters of the 250 "successful" releasees (those not rearrested) studied replied as such. Glaser discovered that their identification with other prisoners and the prison culture was higher during the middle period of imprisonment than it was at the beginning or just before release.[26]

Clemmer's original work focused on the process of **prisonization,** whereby inmates internalize the institution's norms, values, and activity patterns. This is the process of learning, internalizing, and adhering to the cultural milieu of the correctional institution. How-

Prisonization Process where inmates internalize the institution's norms, values, and activity patterns.

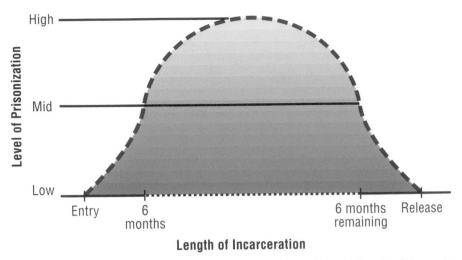

Figure 6–1 Levels of prisonization by length of incarceration.

Source: Adapted from Stanton Wheeler, *Social Organization and Inmate Values in Correctional Communities,* proceedings of the eighty-ninth annual American Correctional Association, Miami Beach, FL, 1959.

ever, for decades correctionalists debated the presence and form of the prisonization process. This debate culminated in the 1960s, when Stanton Wheeler found that the prisonization process does not simply result in greater degrees with increasing length of incarceration. Rather, during both the first and last six months of incarceration, inmates have low levels of adherence to prison culture. During the remaining, middle period, prisonization increases to a peak and then decreases as inmates approach release.[27] (See Figure 6–1.)

More recently other researchers have argued that new inmates, especially those with relatively short sentences, may pursue adaptation strategies whereby they "suspend" their pre-prison identities and adopt a new, temporary identity that serves their needs as inmates.[28] However, such strategies are not completely successful. Unable to totally leave behind their pre-prison selves, inmates are unable to completely recapture their original senses of identity after leaving prison. In contrast, Sykes claimed that some inmates do not conform to the convict culture. Rather, these inmates seek to maintain a sense of personal dignity, to keep strong ties to the outside, and to display an ability to tolerate imprisonment.[29] Generally defined as "easy to manage," these inmates have an easier time readjusting to life on the outside.

Wheeler had earlier pointed out that inmates differ in their responses to the prison community. His general conclusion was that the degree of identification depended on how much contact inmates had with other prisoners and how long they had been in prison.[30] Thus, thrown into contact with each other in the reception centers, new inmates share the cultural values formed before entering prison. However, before integrating to institutional culture, new inmates must work through a grief process similar to what terminally ill patients experience.[31] Beginning with a stage of denial and working through the stages of anger, bargaining, depression, and finally acceptance,[32] new inmates experience a range of stresses and emotions. The stresses can cause emotional and psychological damage and can potentially place inmates in positions of physical vulnerability.

As new inmates involve themselves in the prison's daily activities and structure, they are increasingly exposed to the prison culture and its code of conduct. Eventually they give their loyalty to the prison society, rather than to the administration. Then, as release approaches, many inmates shift their identification to those reference groups with whom they identified before prison. Mabli and his colleagues found that as inmates of one federal correctional institution approached their release dates, they experienced increased levels of stress, exhibited in both their mood and behaviors.[33] Taking this a step further, inmates who adopted behaviors conforming to the institutional culture were more likely to experience difficulties readjusting to free society upon release than were those inmates who actively resisted conformity pressures while incarcerated.[34]

These generalizations, however, are not true of all prisoners. Thoroughly institutionalized criminals, for example, do not identify with the free culture *regardless of whether in or out of prison.* In addition, most institutions by their very nature are not treatment-oriented. Treatment, therefore, cannot overcome the negative influences of the prison subculture. Some observers have identified one major dilemma that subcultural participation helps inmates overcome: the lack of personal control. When people are restricted in controlling the outcomes of their actions, have no choices of actions, and cannot predict their future actions, they will cease taking responsibility for their actions. They will also seek ways to regain these forms of personal control.[35] This is one contribution that the inmate subculture can make to participating individuals. Similarly, participation in prison programs has helped inmates adjust to life while in prison, but not to life after release.[36] This suggests that programs provide inmates with opportunities to control some aspects of their lives while in prison.

Nor can one assume that prisoners are part of a unified, loyalty-based subsystem. Inmates' greatest enemies are often other prisoners, who may be psychotic, exploitative, or simply violent.

Penetrating the Subculture

To prevent becoming hard-core "convicts," inmates must overcome the negative aspects of the prison culture. Some inmates have been successful in their efforts. The closer an institution is to minimum security, the more progress inmates can make. In minimum-security institutions, inmates have fewer negative psychological and social impacts of tight custody and fear. In contrast, if placed in institutions where custody is the main goal, prisoners will be segregated in a convict-ruled subculture and controlled by fear. Under such circumstances, treatments or rehabilitational efforts will be less successful. Security, of course, cannot be abandoned, but it can be kept at a reasonable level. This is where classification schemes become clear.

Using minimum-security prisons and correctional institution camps are ways that correctional professionals attempt to overcome the high social costs of incarceration. Although many Americans express great disappointment and outrage when white-collar offenders (and others considered little or no immediate danger to society) are incarcerated at fenceless camps, the reason for such actions should now be quite clear. Incarcerated in highly restrictive, inmate-dominated prisons, these offenders could easily become "worse"

An aerial view of a minimum-security prison, the Vienna Correctional Center, in Illinois.

rather than "better." In minimum-security facilities, the effects of prisonization can be held in check.

The **inmate code** has been clearly understood. Considering the evolving nature of prison norms, correctional officials can now make serious attempts to control or neutralize its impacts. Sykes has made the clearest statements regarding the inmate code's components. According to Sykes, the basic tenets of this normative system are to "do your own time" and "don't inform on another convict." More specifically, the universal aspects of the inmate code include:

1. *Don't interfere with inmate interests.* This is the idea that one should mind his or her own business and not become involved in other prisoners' activities, whether legal or not.

2. *Don't fight with other inmates.* Devote your attention to your own affairs, and do not make things more difficult on yourself or on others by fighting.

3. *Don't exploit other inmates.* If you do become involved in dealings with others, be true to your word and do not try to manipulate others.

4. *Be strong.* Accept the conditions of your imprisonment. Excessive complaining or showing signs of physical, psychological, or emotional weaknesses are dangerous to one's status in the prison community.

5. *Don't trust the staff.* This also includes not adhering to staff's or officials' values and desires. At the base this norm says that an inmate is to value other inmates, and what they believe and stand for, over staff at all times and in all situations.[37]

Obviously, these norms are not always maintained in the prison community. However, similar to the basic norms and laws of society in general, they provide the foundation upon which the prison community's normative structure is based. When inmates violate norms of the inmate code, other inmates may sanction them. Or, just as in society in general, if those violating the norms hold enough social power, they may escape social sanctioning.[38]

Prison Economic Systems

Two economic systems exist inside prison: legitimate and illegitimate systems of exchange. The legitimate system centers on the wages inmates earn at prison jobs and on other monies that people outside

> **Inmate code** Set of norms and values that structure the informal patterns of life among inmates; these are the "rules" that inmates impose on their community.

Inmates may make purchases at the prison store, sometimes called the "canteen."

Contraband Forms of personal property that are not allowed in correctional institutions.

the prison place in institutional accounts. Inmates are permitted to draw a set amount from their accounts to make purchases at the prison store (sometimes called the "canteen"). This allows inmates to obtain name-brand toiletries, rather than prison-issued generic brands, snack foods, and small amenities for their cells and personal activities (stationery, pens, stamps, etc.). In some states inmates are allowed to carry a small amount of cash as well.

The prison's illegitimate economy centers on the distribution of **contraband,** or any unauthorized substance or material possessed by residents. Contraband goods and services can be summarized in nine general categories: drugs, alcoholic beverages (usually homemade), gambling, appliances, clothing, institutional privileges, weapons (both homemade and smuggled), food, and prostitution. Inmates may obtain contraband goods and services by

FYI

In 1847 the following items were contraband in New York's Sing Sing Prison: "newspapers, storybooks, *History of Buccaneers, Comic Almanac, Family Almanac* . . . pictures, chalk, writing desk . . . writing paper . . . lice and bedbugs . . . pocketbooks . . . slate and pencil . . . paintings . . . *French Grammar, Chronological Dictionary . . . Lives of Females* . . . letters and songs."

Source: *Journal of Correctional Education,* Vol. 34, No. 3, 1983, p. 79.

either barter or purchase. Purchases can be made with cash (which may be contraband itself), vouchers used to draw on one's institutional account, or most common, packs and cartons of cigarettes. Barter systems work most effectively for those inmates who have special skills that others desire (legal skills, tattoo paraphernalia, or handicraft work) or who are willing to trade sex for goods.

The two economic systems overlap and influence each other. Goods and services obtained on the legitimate market may be introduced to the illegitimate market in exchange for contraband. Also, the legitimate system, by its very structure and operation, makes possible the existence and profitability of the illegitimate market. As Kalinich concluded from his study of the institutional economy at the State Prison of Southern Michigan:

> The legitimate economic system supports and facilitates the sub-rosa system in two ways. Many of the institutional assignments place residents in positions of trust and allow them freedom of movement, which permits them to deal rather freely in the sub-rosa system. Residents may buy and sell contraband by having funds placed in the supplier's personal bank account or resident fund from the buyer's bank account or outside contacts. This system can be and often is used to transfer money from one resident's fund to another.[39]

Prisons do have active economies, and inmates expend much time and energy to maintain the system. Inmates benefit from their underground economy by easing the pains of imprisonment. However, institutional authorities also benefit. Maintaining their economic system occupies many inmates' time and minds. Also, the system serves many inmates' needs, which would be too costly for the institution to meet. Finally, the introduction of some contraband items, specifically alcohol, drugs, and prostitution, may actively work to prevent stress, frustrations, and potential violence.

Prisoners' Views on Homosexuality

Most prison inmates express strong negative feelings about homosexuality,[40] but sex does occur between inmates, especially male inmates.[41] (For a discussion of homosexuality among female inmates, see Chapter 9.) Sexual relations in prison take one of three forms: consensual sex, prostitution, or sexual assaults/rapes. (Sexual assaults will be dealt with in depth in Chapter 8.) Inmates who engage in sexual relations with other inmates may be labeled as "fags" or "punks" and may be relegated to the lowest rungs of the inmate social structure.

However, not all inmates who engage in sex with other men are so labeled. Inmates who fulfill the "passive" or "feminine" role are stigmatized. So, it is not simply participation in homosexual acts, but inmates' roles in such acts, that determines how they are viewed in the prison subculture. Men who are sexually aggressive or dominant are viewed as "normal," while men who are sexually passive are despised.

Prison regulations prohibit sexual contacts between inmates (as well as between inmates and staff). When "caught" having sex, inmates are disciplined. Attempts are made to separate sexual predators from highly vulnerable inmates. However, keeping such inmates apart is nearly impossible. As a result, correctional officers may expect inmates to devise ways to protect themselves. This is a common cause of violence, as will be discussed in Chapter 8.

Prison Treatment Programming

As a student in the classroom setting, you are exposed to ideal concepts. However, you must understand that the ideal is not always practiced in the real world. Innovative treatment programs implemented in prisons deserve attentive discussion, but the treatment-oriented prison does not now, nor has it ever, dominated U.S. corrections. Instead, custodial functions dominate the staffing of correctional facilities.

Over the last several decades, correctional managers have been severely criticized as ineffective and inefficient. These criticisms claim current management styles are highly restrictive toward not only inmates, but also staff. Only in limited cases have institutional management teams been innovative and worked to prevent problems. After all, corrections is largely reactive, not proactive. The idea of a team approach to inmates' treatment needs, which was one innovation of the federal corrections system, has become the dominant approach to prison treatment programming. Not only are treatment professionals (psychologists, psychiatrists, counselors, teachers, and social workers) involved in such teams, but so are correctional officers. These team members work together in the classification and decision-making processes affecting inmates. In this way, the individual having the most frequent contact with inmates—the correctional officer—is an integral part of the treatment process, instead of being an uninvolved, perhaps detrimental, force in inmates' lives.

Punishment Versus Treatment

With little commitment to the treatment approach in the U.S. correctional system, proving that treatment is more effective than punishment is difficult. Only a small number of people, both staff and inmates, are actually involved in treatment programs. Also, the treatment philosophy in corrections has substantial opposition. These two factors prevent careful scientific analysis of the treatment approach. Furthermore, a relatively new development in the penal field, treatment has never been given sufficient opportunity to demonstrate its utility.

Prisoners are not voluntary "patients," and the prison setting is minimally conducive to therapeutics. Neither the setting, nor the treatment applicators, nor those receiving treatment are primarily devoted to treatment. After all, custody and security are the primary goals of correctional staff. Therefore, it is no surprise that treatment programs have commonly been viewed as "ineffective." This is especially true for higher-level security prisons. Here, the inmates are supposedly more serious offenders, and the restrictions that institutional authorities impose are more stringent. Treatment and custody tend to have an inverse ratio.

Recreational activities, such as sports, play an important role in effectively managing the prison population.

The job of planning and supervising inmates' recreational activities is often viewed as being like a party director or an elementary school gym teacher. However, we must remember that prison inmates have large amounts of time on their hands. By keeping inmates busy in activities they enjoy (or, at least, do not dislike), we can manage an institution more efficiently and effectively. These facts mean that staff who design and oversee organized recreational activities can be a very important part of a treatment approach.

Recreational leaders are responsible for organizing activities that will occupy inmates' vast array of interests. Common activities that are organized include sports leagues, individual sports equipment (such as free weights), crafts classes and workshops, and individual or small group activities (cards, board games, movies, etc.). Recreational leaders need to interact well with inmates and to be sensitive to the needs of all inmates, not simply those involved in sports.

Most correctional systems prefer recreational leaders to have college degrees in a related field (corrections, criminal justice, recreation management, education) and to have experience organizing recreational activities in other settings. Most prisons have a very small recreation staff, usually between one and five people. Because people in these jobs have some specialized knowledge and skills, their pay is often slightly above that of correctional officers. Most recreational leaders will begin making between $15,000 and $20,000. These jobs are often good ways to explore other options available in prisons, and many people move from recreational specialist jobs to other treatment-type positions in the prisons.

Source: U.S. Department of Labor, Bureau of Labor Statistics, *Occupational Outlook Handbook,* 1994–95 ed., p. 135.

The split between those who do and do not believe in the potential for rehabilitation can be quite wide. However, many who work in corrections do believe that at least some inmates can be successfully rehabilitated. Cullen et al. conducted a national survey of prison wardens. This study found that "while placing a prime emphasis on maintaining custody and institutional order, wardens remain supportive of rehabilitation."[42] Wardens did not, however, naively believe that their institutions could rehabilitate all offenders. They instead suggested that approximately one in four of their inmates was a good candidate for rehabilitation. Not only do the top administrators hold hopes for rehabilitation. Somewhat surprisingly, despite their often negatively charged interactions with inmates, correctional officers are often supportive of rehabilitative efforts.[43] However, the degree of their support usually weakens with lengthier experience.[44]

Academic Education in Prison

Many developments in prison programming and treatment have been encouraging. Among the most notable are those in educational policy and activity. Some observers see this as a reaction to the harsh and restrictive measures originally implemented by the Pennsylvania and Auburn systems, while others suggest that this is simply a delayed imitation of the move toward better education in all segments of our society. Regardless of why educational programs initially began, they are today recognized as the most promising major **treatment modalities** used in corrections.[45] Additionally, change will be most successful when education is combined with the establishment of an alternative community that incorporates normative and value systems different from those of the general prison population.[46]

Treatment modalities General approaches to providing rehabilitation and/or reintegration programming for inmates.

Numerous researchers have demonstrated that inmates do not lack intelligence, but are merely undereducated. Deficits in education and skills have long been theorized as contributors to crime.[47] If they are unable to support themselves, people may believe they have no alternatives except to turn to crime for survival.[48] Economic, and perhaps physical, survival in our society depends largely on literacy. As early as the mid-1970s policy makers addressed concern that many correctional institution inmates possessed inadequate academic skills. According to one report, approximately one-half of U.S. imprisoned adults were functionally illiterate.[49] Many correctional experts believe this is a very low estimate. The costs to society of such academic deficits are staggering. According to one researcher, functional illiteracy costs the United States $237 billion in unrealized lifetime earnings and another $224 billion in indirect costs (welfare, unemployment, crime, etc.).[50] Hence, basic academic programming is very important in preparing offenders for return to society.

Today, prison inmates are able to participate in educational programs ranging from mastering basic reading, writing, and math skills through earning college degrees. In some select institutions, inmates may complete graduate degrees, including most requirements for a doctorate. Many states today require inmates to attend school if they do not possess basic skills, and some correctional systems require inmates who do not have a high school diploma to work toward their General Equivalency Degree (GED).

Educational programs help prepare inmates to return to society.

Over 80 percent of U.S. prisons have offered college degree-granting programs in one form or another.[51] Typically rather small, however, the majority of prison-based college programs have fewer than 100 students.[52] Such programs are offered and administered by many different types of colleges and universities, but are most commonly affiliated with community colleges or small, four-year liberal arts institutions. Most prison-based college programs offer inmates opportunities to earn degrees. A national survey conducted in the early 1980s reported that one-half of all programs offer opportunities to earn at least an associate degree or program certificate, slightly more than one-quarter of programs offer bachelor's degrees, and master's degrees are available in 3.4 percent of prison-based college programs.[53]

The obvious and often asked question here is: "Who pays for inmates to earn college degrees?" The answer is that inmates pay for their educations the same way we all do, either by absorbing the cost themselves or by receiving assistance from financial aid programs. However, inmates receiving financial aid and competing for it with traditional students is a hotly debated issue in the 1990s.

Attempts to prohibit inmates from receiving federal financial aid have been made. In 1991–1992 Congress debated and ultimately defeated legislation that would have restricted inmates from receiving Pell grants. However, this restriction did become law in the 1994 Crime Bill. As Senator Jesse Helms of North Carolina remarked upon introducing the legislation:

> American taxpayers are being forced to pay taxes to provide free college tuitions for prisoners at a time when so many law-abiding, taxpaying citizens are struggling to find enough money to send their children to college.[54]

Such a position obviously relies on assumptions that (1) inmates receive a significant portion of such funds and (2) inmates are not needy or deserving. The lobbying against this legislation pointed out that the first assumption is false. Only 1.2 percent of all Pell grants are issued to inmates. However, the emotional element of inmates receiving educations ultimately won.

Vocational Training

Improved academic education for inmates who have the need and ability should be part of the prison resocialization program. Vocational training is an equally critical and valuable need. This is especially true when a correctional system emphasizes the goal of reintegration. As just discussed, most prisoners are undereducated. They also lack job skills. In short, prisoners do not lack ability or

LEGAL BRIEF:

Smith v. Van Boening, 29F 3d 634 (9th Cir 1994).

This case concerns an inmate, Smith, in the Washington correctional system, who tried to apply for a college correspondence course but was denied access to the enrollment papers.

According to the prison officials, they did not allow Smith to receive the application because they believed their responsibility was to keep inmates from contracting with people outside the prison to protect the public. If inmates entered into contracts, there would be a good chance they would be unable to fulfill their obligations (such as pay for services). In July 1994, the Ninth Circuit Court of Appeals ruled in favor of the prison officials, saying that this was a legitimate government interest.

Smith argued that in denying him access to a college correspondence course, the institution was denying him access to educational opportunities. However, the prison officials and the courts denied this claim, citing Smith's access to the degree program offered in the institution through the Walla Walla Community College.

trainability, but they have interrupted the process of acquiring education and vocational skills to become criminals. Since most inmates have inadequate education and few job skills, the prison should be equipped to fill their vocational needs.

Prison Industries

Traditionally, most vocational training has occurred through employing inmates in **prison industries.** However, the vast majority of prison inmates, perhaps as many as 90 percent, are not employed while in prison.[55] Inmates have historically worked under one of four different models of prison industries.

First, under the **leasing system** contractors provide the materials, equipment, training, and supervision of inmates who labor to make products while inside prison facilities. This system served as the model for creating factories inside prisons and using inmates as laborers. Originally the leasing system operated on a basis of renting inmates for a period of time to outside entrepreneurs who took them out of prison and assumed responsibility for housing, feeding, and supervising them. This was a popular practice in the Southern states during the years following the Civil War when prison space was limited and Reconstruction projects were common. Critics, however, decried this system and compared it to a new form of slavery.

Second, the **price-piece system** uses inmates to produce products from materials that outside businesses supply to the prison. Under this system, outside entrepreneurs have fewer contacts with inmates than they do under a leasing system. The business usually provides the materials, equipment, and supervision and pays the prison a set per-unit price for the product being manufactured. This industrial model, similar to the leasing system, calls for a minimum investment of prison resources.

Third, the **state use system** eliminates the involvement of outside businesses and operates prison industries for the state's benefit. Here, prisons establish and operate their own manufacturing of products, which the state government exclusively uses. Products may include furniture, printed materials, clothing, or the well-known license plates. Contained within the government are all benefits of the industrial setup. Inmates are put to work and are taught vocational skills. Also, the savings that are realized by not purchasing products elsewhere benefit the prison or the government.

Prison industries
Vocational training offered to inmates through employment in manufacturing jobs provided in the prison.

Leasing system
Early form of prison industries where inmates were rented to individuals who put them to work and who assumed responsibility for providing necessities and security to inmates.

Price-piece system
Form of prison industry where private contractors supply prison officials with raw materials and tools that inmates use to produce finished goods; contractors pay a specific per-unit price to the institution for goods produced.

State use system
Form of prison industry where inmates produce goods that, rather than being sold on the open market, are used by state agencies.

The state use model of prison industries includes inmate manufacturing.

Fourth, and primarily a Southern system, is the **plantation system.** Many states, especially Southern states, operate prison farms and plantations that produce food and other agricultural products for inmates' and others' use (similar to the state use system).

Finally, vocational training, such as the federal system's Unicor prison industries program, may take the form of a government-operated, for-profit corporation. This model assumes vocational training will be sophisticated, will keep up with changing technology, and will allow the business to remain competitive.

Religious Programming

The oldest and most consistently present form of prison programming is religious worship. From the earliest days of the Walnut Street Jail, religious materials and worship services have served as cornerstones of the correctionalist's attempt to alter offenders' behavior. The founding of the penitentiary was based on separating individuals from society and encouraging their self-reflection and search for spiritual guidance.

Today, all prisons are legally required to provide for inmates' religious needs. (See Chapter 7.) Inside the prison are essentially all forms of religious services available in free society, including worship

Plantation system
Form of prison industry based on agriculture; inmates are housed and work on large farms where they produce food and other agricultural products for consumption in the correctional system.

services, Bible study, and individual counseling. Traditionally, both Protestant and Catholic clergy have been regularly available for conducting worship services and for counseling inmates. In some institutions Jewish clergy have also been made available, and since the 1960s many prisons have also provided Muslim clergy.

In meeting inmates' religious needs, correctional officials have difficulty identifying clergy who are interested, willing, or able to work in the prison. The low pay offered by and the often remote locations of correctional institutions make it very difficult for clergy to survive financially and to combine prison chaplaincy with other work. Consequently, volunteer groups offer many of the religious programming options available to prison inmates and hold weekly meetings or conduct study groups. Such outreach efforts are frequently considered

LEGAL BRIEF:

Boone v. Commissioner of Prisons, 1994 WL 383590 (Ed PA).

Boone, an inmate at the Frackville State Correctional Institute, claimed that his constitutional rights to freedom of religious expression were violated when prison officials refused to allow him to attend what he argued were religious activities.

One founder of the United Christian Community Church, Boone held group meetings on the prison yard. Prison officials believed these meetings posed a security risk and informed Boone that they would no longer be permitted. However, when Boone continued to organize the meetings, the officials searched his cell and confiscated items related to the United Christian Community Church. When Boone complained about these actions, disciplinary action was taken against him.

When Boone challenged the actions in court in July 1994, the U.S. District Court in the Eastern District of Pennsylvania found no violations of constitutional rights. The court ruled that the officials' actions were justified in the pursuit of institutional security. Being the least restrictive means available, the officials' actions were in pursuit of institutional security and overrode Boone's right to the free exercise of religion.

important components of congregations' ministries and are valued outside contacts for inmates.

The Ex-Prisoner

No matter what constructive activities occur in the prison, when all is said and done, it will be an unproductive investment if the community will not reaccept the former inmate. How many men and women discharged from our "correctional" systems find themselves in a hostile and rejecting community? When this occurs—and it commonly does—how can we expect them not to readopt criminal ways because their community exercised discrimination and rejection and proved inflexible?

Returning ex-inmates have many built-in psychological barriers between themselves and their communities. Former inmates have lived in an artificial community for some time. They have had little contact with the opposite sex. Although they are rational people with decision-making abilities, almost all their decisions have been made for them. Things have changed on the outside; and the longer they have been away, the more difficult it is for them to readapt. In addition, they must relearn relations with loved ones and friends.

Another type of barrier is related to ex-inmates' vocational plans. Having higher vocational goals, they expect more specialized occupations and more rapid salary increases than they receive.[56] Also, the stigma of being "ex-cons" can have serious negative effects on their employability. Combined with the usually low-level skills and education that most inmates (and, therefore, ex-inmates) possess and their interrupted or absent employment record, it is no surprise that the vast majority of released offenders are confined to the secondary labor market. This is the world of unskilled, poor-paying, and nonsecure work, temporary employment, jobs without benefits, and part-time or seasonal work. Essentially, as undesirable employees, ex-inmates are relegated to jobs that most people take only when they have no other options.

FYI

When released from prison, inmates are not, contrary to popular belief, provided with new clothing, job referrals, and general assistance in returning to the community as law-abiding citizens. In most states, inmates receive only the clothes they wore when they were imprisoned and a small amount of money ($50–$100). They are expected to find their own support systems.

Many believe that to maximize the likelihood of ex-inmates succeeding (not recidivating) after their releases, intensive services should be provided to them. However, recent research has reported that intensive supervision, when focused on surveillance rather than on service provision, leads to increased, not lower, recidivism rates.[57]

When released from prison, inmates are typically provided very little material or treatment/vocational assistance. (See Chapter 12.) This means that inmates must plan for their releases and gather their own resources. Many inmates save portions of their institutional incomes, but these rarely amount to significant totals. Therefore, released inmates rely very heavily on their families and friends for support.

However, many released inmates find this support to be either partially or completely absent. A criminal conviction, especially when accompanied by a prison sentence, is highly stigmatizing. The public's misunderstandings of and the myths about life in prison make most people fear being with "ex-cons." Many people also fear that their own characters may be tarnished if others know they associate with ex-inmates. Such negative repercussions not only affect ex-inmates, but they also directly impact offender's families and close friends. **Courtesy stigmas** are those negative labels others apply to people whom they perceive as associated with known or suspected offenders. Because of others' negative perceptions, as well as the shame, embarrassment, and anger they feel, many family members and friends do not continue relationships with released offenders. This means that ex-prisoners have yet more obstacles to overcome in their quest to remain free in the community.

Courtesy stigmas
Negative labels others apply to individuals whom they perceive as associated with known or suspected criminals.

Summary

The U.S. prison population has increased during the last decades to the point where correctional authorities have exceptional difficulty meeting inmates' basic needs of security, housing, feeding, and perhaps treatment. Our prison population is changing, most notably in terms of inmates serving longer sentences and growing older. This presents a range of special needs and demands on correctional systems and staff.

The growing number and changing characteristics of prison inmates mean that the creation and existence of a distinctive inmate subculture become ever stronger. While prisons exert control over both the major and minor aspects of inmates' lives, inmates covertly develop their own systems of status. Within a prison population exist complex and carefully defined roles, systems of exchange, and social relationships.

Encouraged by the political rhetoric of the 1960s and 1970s when correctional systems emphasized attempts to "rehabilitate" inmates, prison programming opportunities significantly expanded in the 1970s and 1980s. Although some programming (religious, academic, and work programs) has been present in some form and frequency since the earliest days of U.S. penology, these and other programs are now more common. This is beginning to change in the mid-1990s, though. Many systems are reducing their programs and provisions for inmates. In relation to programming, the process of providing programs for inmates will often conflict with the institution's primary goal of security. Although prison wardens and other staff may be strong supporters of programs, the inevitable conflicts will necessarily impose limitations on programming options.

The effects of prison sentences do not end with inmates' releases, however. Social stigmas follow ex-inmates, who consequently experience numerous difficulties in readjusting to life in free society. These difficulties mean that some ex-inmates may find it beneficial, or necessary, to return to crime. With their return to prison likely or, at least, possible, the cycle of increased prison population begins once again.

QUESTIONS FOR REVIEW

1. What is the size of the U.S. prison population? What has been the growth trend of the prison population over the past few decades?

2. How does the experience of long-term imprisonment negatively impact inmates?

3. Why are elderly inmates considered special needs inmates? What are the unique challenges posed by an aging prison population?

4. What are the long- and short-term psychological consequences of incarceration? What are the social consequences?

5. What does the term *inmate culture* mean? What are the economic structures and processes in prison?

6. How do prison programs coordinate with the prison's goal of punishment?

7. What are the academic programming options available in U.S. prisons? How common are these programs?

8. What are the reasons for vocational training programs in prisons?

9. Who benefits and how do they benefit from the variety of prison industry programs commonly found in U.S. prisons?

10. How does the experience of imprisonment impact individuals after release?

ACTIVITIES

1. Contact your local parole office and interview a parole officer about how ex-inmates adjust to their return to the community.

2. Construct an economic structure based on consumable goods with your classmates, roommates, or family and friends. Spend a day or two living without money, checks, and credit cards, and trade your newfound form of currency with each other for all goods and services that you need/want. Consider how your transactions are similar to and different from those in your usual daily life.

3. Put yourself in a prison inmate's place, and assume that you will be allowed to communicate with your significant other for only one 1-hour visitation period per week. Compose a list of things you will want to discuss, and plan how you can cover all your topics in a one-hour period. What are the difficulties in maintaining a relationship this way?

4. Contact a staff person at several local prisons or jails and ask him or her to provide you with a list of common argot language. Compare the meanings of these terms to determine if speaking the language of one institution would cause problems if it were spoken in another institution.

ENDNOTES

1. U.S. Department of Justice, *Mid-Year Report.* (Washington, D.C.: Bureau of Justice Statistics, December 3, 1995).

2. U.S. Department of Justice. *Prisoners in 1994.* (Washington, D.C.: Bureau of Justice Statistics, 1995).

3. U.S. Department of Justice, *Prisoners in 1992* (Washington, D.C., Bureau of Justice Statistics, 1993).

4. U.S. Department of Justice, *Sourcebook of Criminal Justice Statistics, 1993* (Washington, D.C.: Bureau of Justice Statistics, 1994).

5. Barry Richards, "The Experience of Long-Term Imprisonment: An Exploratory Investigation," *British Journal of Criminology,* Vol. 18, No. 2, 1978, pp. 162–169; Cindie A. Unger and Robert A. Buchanon, *Managing Long-Term Inmates* (Washington, D.C.: National Institute of Corrections, 1985); Deborah G. Wilson and Gennaro F. Vito, "Long-Term Inmates: Special Needs and Management Considerations," *Federal Probation,* Vol. 52, 1988, pp. 21–26; Edith Flynn, "The Graying of America's Prison Population," *The Prison Journal,* Vol. 72, No. 1–2, 1992, pp. 77–98.

6. Richards, *op. cit.*

7. R. J. Sapsford, "Life-Sentence Prisoners: Psychological Changes During Sentence," *British Journal of Criminology,* Vol. 18, No. 2, 1978, pp. 128–145.

8. Deborah G. Wilson, *Inmates' Suicides in the Kentucky Corrections System: 1973–April, 1986* (Frankfort, KY: Kentucky Corrections Cabinet, 1986).

9. Hans Toch, *Men in Crisis, Breakdowns in Prisons* (Chicago: Aldine, 1975).

10. Wilson and Vito, *op. cit.*

11. Edward A. Parker, "The Social–Psychological Impact of a College Education on the Prison Inmate," *Journal of Correctional Education,* Vol. 41, 1990, pp. 140–146.

12. However, other researchers dispute these findings and, in fact, claim that most inmate suicides are in the earliest days of a sentence (if not prior to sentencing) and that long-term inmates actually display more positive functioning on psychological tests than do shorter-term inmates. J. Stephen Wormith, "The Controversy Over the Effects of Long-Term Incarceration," *Canadian Journal of Criminology,* Vol. 26, No. 4, 1984, pp. 423–437.

13. K. Moritsugu, "Inmate Chronological Age Versus Physical Age," *Long-Term Confinement and the Aging Inmate Population: A Record*

and *Proceeding* (Washington, D.C.: Federal Bureau of Prisons, 1990).

14. U.S. Department of Justice, *Sourcebook of Criminal Justice Statistics, 1993* (Washington, D.C.: Bureau of Justice Statistics, 1994); *Directory: Juvenile and Adult Correctional Departments, Agencies and Paroling Authorities* (Laurel, MD: American Correctional Association, 1992).

15. Flynn, *op. cit.,* p. 79.

16. E. O. Moore, "Prison Environments and Their Impact on Older Citizens," *Journal of Offender Counseling, Services and Rehabilitation,* Vol. 13, No. 2, 1989, pp. 175–191.

17. Gennaro F. Vito and Deborah G. Wilson, "Forgotten People: Elderly Inmates," *Federal Probation,* Vol. 49, 1985, pp. 18–24.

18. Donald Clemmer, *The Prison Community* (New York: Holt, Rinehart & Winston, 1966).

19. Gresham Sykes, *The Society of Captives* (Princeton, NJ: Princeton University Press, 1956).

20. Erving Goffman, *Asylums* (Garden City, NY: Anchor Books, 1961).

21. Harold Garfinkel, "Conditions of Successful Degradation Ceremonies," *American Journal of Sociology,* Vol. 61, February 1956, pp. 420–424.

22. Lynne Goodstein and Kevin Wright, "Inmate Adjustment to Prison," in Lynne Goodstein and Doris Layton (eds.), *The American Prison: Issues in Research and Policy* (New York: Plenum, 1989); R. J. Homant and D. G. Dean, "The Effect of Prisonization and Self-Esteem on Inmate Career Maturity," *Journal of Offender Counseling, Services and Rehabilitation,* Vol. 12, No. 2, 1988, pp. 19–40.

23. Virginia V. Neto and LaNelle Marie Bainer, "Mother and Wife Locked Up: A Day With the Family," *Prison Journal,* Vol. 63, No. 2, 1983, pp. 124–141.

24. A. D'Andrea, "Joint Custody as Related to Paternal Involvement and Paternal Self-Esteem," *Conciliation Courts Review,* Vol. 22, No. 2, 1983, pp. 81–87.

25. C. S. Lanier, "Fathers in Prison: A Psychosocial Exploration," paper presented at the annual meeting of the American Society of Criminology, Montreal, Canada, 1987.

26. Daniel Glaser, *The Effectiveness of a Prison and Parole System* (New York: The Bobbs-Merrill Company, Inc., 1964), pp. 89–117.

27. Stanton Wheeler, "Social Organization and Inmate Values in Correctional Communities," proceedings of the eighty-ninth annual American Correctional Association, Miami Beach, Florida, 1959.

28. Thomas Schmid and Richard Jones, "Suspended Identity: Identity Transformation in a Maximum Security Prison," *Symbolic Interaction,* Vol. 14, No. 4, 1991, pp. 415–432.

29. Sykes, *op. cit.*

30. Wheeler, *op. cit.*

31. Carolyn Brastow Pledger, "Do Incarcerated Offenders Experience the Five Stages of Grief as Do Terminally Ill Patients?" *Journal of Offender Counseling* Vol. 6, No. 1, 1985, pp. 9–17.

Chapter 6   *The Prisoner*

32. This stage model of grief for the terminally ill was originally proposed by Elisabeth Kubler-Ross in *On Death and Dying* (New York: Macmillan Publishing, Inc., 1969).

33. Jerome Mabli, Steven M. Glick, Marilyn Hilborn, Jerry Kastler, David Pillow, Kevin Karlson, and Scott Barber, "Prerelease Stress in Prison Inmates," *Journal of Offender Counseling, Services and Rehabilitation,* Vol. 9, No. 3, 1985, pp. 43–56.

34. Lynne Goodstein, "Inmate Adjustment to Prison and Transition to Community Life," *Journal of Research in Crime and Delinquency,* Vol. 16, No. 2, 1979, pp. 246–272.

35. Lynne Goodstein, Doris Layton MacKenzie, and R. Lance Shotland, "Personal Control and Inmate Adjustment to Prison," *Criminology,* Vol. 22, No. 3, 1984, pp. 343–369.

36. Harjit S. Sandhu, "Recidivist and Non-Recidivist Perceptions of Prison Experience and Post-Prison Problems," *Free Inquiry in Creative Sociology,* Vol. 14, No. 2, 1986, pp. 193–196.

37. Sykes, *op. cit.,* pp. 63–108.

38. James W. Marquart and Julian B. Roebuck, "Prison Guards and 'Snitches': Deviance Within a Total Institution," *British Journal of Criminology,* Vol. 25, No. 3, 1985, pp. 217–233.

39. David Kalinich, *Power, Stability & Contraband: The Inmate Economy* (Prospect Heights, IL: Waveland Press, 1980).

40. Mark Fleisher, *Warehousing Violence* (Newbury Park, CA: Sage Publications, 1989); Katy Richmond, "Fear of Homosexuality and Modes of Rationalization in Male Prisons," *Australian and New Zealand Journal of Sociology,* Vol. 14, No. 1, 1978, pp. 51–57; Norman E. Smith and Mary Ellen Batiuk, "Sexual Victimization and Inmate Social Interaction," *Prison Journal,* Vol. 69, No. 2, 1989, pp. 29–38.

41. Richard Tewksbury, "Measures of Sexual Behavior in an Ohio Prison," *Sociology and Social Research,* Vol. 74, No. 1, 1989, pp. 34–39; Wayne S. Wooden and Jay Parker, *Men Behind Bars* (New York: Plenum Publishing, 1982).

42. Francis T. Cullen, Edward J. Latessa, Velmer S. Burton, Jr., and Lucien X. Lombardo, "The Correctional Orientation of Prison Wardens: Is the Rehabilitative Ideal Supported?" *Criminology,* Vol. 31, No. 1, 1993, p. 69.

43. Francis T. Cullen, Faith Lutze, Bruce G. Link, and Nancy Travis Wolfe, "The Correctional Orientation of Prison Guards: Do Officers Support Rehabilitation?" *Federal Probation,* Vol. 53, 1989, pp. 33–42.

44. *Ibid.;* Nancy C. Jurik, "Individual and Organizational Determinants of Correctional Officer Attitudes Toward Inmates," *Criminology,* Vol. 23, 1985, pp. 523–539.

45. Douglas Lipton, Robert Martinson, and Judith Wilks, *The Effectiveness of Correctional Treatment* (New York: Praeger Publishers, 1975).

46. Rick Linden and Linda Perry, "The Effectiveness of Prison Edu-

cation Programs," *Journal of Offender Counseling, Services and Rehabilitation,* Vol. 6, No. 4, 1982, pp. 43–57.

47. H. H. Goddard, *Feeblemindedness: Its Causes and Consequences* (New York: Macmillan, 1914); W. Shockley, "A 'Try Simplest Cases' Approach to the Heredity-Poverty-Crime Problem," *Proceedings of the National Academy of Sciences,* Vol. 57, No. 6, 1967, pp. 1767–1774; Travis Hirschi and Michael J. Hindelang, "Intelligence and Delinquency: A Revisionist Review," *American Sociological Review,* Vol. 42, 1977, pp. 572–587.

48. Albert K. Cohen, *Delinquent Boys: The Culture of the Gang* (New York: The Free Press, 1955); Richard A. Cloward and Lloyd E. Ohlin, *Delinquency and Opportunity: A Theory of Delinquent Gangs* (New York: The Free Press, 1960).

49. Janet Carsetti, *Literacy Problems and Solutions: A Resource Handbook for Correctional Educators* (Washington, D.C.: American Bar Association, Clearinghouse for Offender Literacy Programs, 1975).

50. O. D. Coffey, "Book 'em: No Read, No Release," *Corrections Today,* Vol. 49, June 1987, pp. 116–118.

51. John F. Littlefield and Bruce I. Wolford, "A Survey of Higher Education in U.S. Correctional

Institutions," *Journal of Correctional Education,* Vol. 33, No. 1, 1982, pp. 14–19.

52. Ken Peak, "Postsecondary Correctional Education: Contemporary Program Nature and Delivery Systems in the U.S.," *Journal of Correctional Education,* Vol. 35, No. 2, 1984, pp. 58–62.

53. Ken Peak, "Directors of Correctional Education Programs: A Demographic and Attitudinal Profile," *Journal of Correctional Education,* Vol. 34, No. 3, 1983, pp. 79–83.

54. Quoted in Jon Marc Taylor, "Pell Grants for Prisoners," *The Nation,* January 25, 1993, p. 90.

55. Timothy J. Flanagan and Kathleen Maguire, "A Full Employment Policy for Prisons in the United States: Some Arguments, Estimates, and Implications," *Journal of Criminal Justice,* Vol. 21, No. 2, 1993, pp. 117–130.

56. Glaser, *op. cit.,* pp. 311–316.

57. Susan Turner and Joan Petersilia, "Focusing on High-Risk Parolees: An Experiment to Reduce Commitments to the Texas Department of Corrections," *Journal of Research in Crime and Delinquency,* Vol. 29, No. 1, 1992, pp. 34–61.

CHAPTER 7

Prisoners' Rights

CHAPTER OBJECTIVES

In this chapter we will examine how the legal system continues to influence the daily lives of prison inmates and prison administration. After reading this chapter, you will be able to:

1. Understand the historical evolution of judicial intervention in corrections.

2. Understand the historical developments in prisoners' having no legal rights to being considered citizens with legal disabilities.

3. Identify political and social factors that initiated current approaches to legal issues in corrections.

4. Contrast the positive and negative consequences of courts' involvement in correctional matters.

5. Explain how society decides whether correctional practice are cruel and unusual punishments.

6. Discuss the legal restrictions placed on inmates' visits with family and friends, sending and receiving mail, and religious practices.

7. Explain the legal requirements necessary for providing medical services to inmates.

8. Discuss the importance of inmates' legal right to access the courts.

9. Understand the development and evolution of inmates' rights.

Prior to judicial intervention, a prisoner had no legal rights.

Prisoners' Rights in a Historical Context

I n simple terms, the history of prisoners' rights has evolved from considering inmates as people who had absolutely no legal rights to considering inmates as citizens who have legal disabilities. The changes that have occurred in the last four decades have been immense, and prisoners' rights have been an outgrowth of larger, societal-wide legal developments. In fact, prisoners' rights evolved when large-scale (some might say "radical") changes in citizens' rights—especially in minority citizens' rights—occurred.

Judicial Intervention

The history of **judicial intervention** in corrections, or courts deciding whether certain practices violate the Constitution, is a relatively short story. Throughout history, including most of U.S. history, judges have approached corrections with a **hands-off policy.** Not really a specific policy, hands-off is an approach judges use to explicitly avoid involvement in correctional issues. Instead of ruling on cases that contest the policies, procedures, and conditions of correctional institutions, judges have stated that their limited expertise leaves them incapable of deciding how prisons should operate. Rather, judges have (both explicitly and implicitly) deferred to correctional "experts" and have relied on their decisions. These experts, of course, have been the administrators of correctional systems and institutions. So, in terms of judicial intervention in corrections, the courts have avoided issues and have placed trust in the judgment of officials. Therefore, for most of our nation's history, the courts have rendered few decisions about changes in prison operations.

Under English common law, the forerunner to our U.S. system, conviction for certain felonies such as treason or outlawry carried with it **civil death,** which was the legal equivalent of physical death. Convicted felons were deprived of all their normal legal capacities such as inheriting property. Before the various U.S. states modified the principle by statutes and constitutions, civil death was commonly applied to all people who received life sentences. The idea still persists that all convicted felons (whether imprisoned or not) are civilly dead. In fact, in almost all cases, the rights that offenders lose at the time of conviction can be restored.

Some states do permanently remove convicted felons' rights. However, which rights and in what states vary considerably. For

Judicial intervention Actions of the courts to determine whether the actions of correctional officials are legal and within constitutional boundaries.

Hands-off policy Practice of the courts throughout U.S. history to avoid involvement in correctional matters.

Civil death Practice of legally transforming a convicted criminal to a non-being; the civilly dead individual was stripped of all legal rights, private property, and claims to inheritance and relationships.

instance, 11 states permanently deny convicted felons the right to vote.[1] Imprisoned felons may have their parental rights terminated in 16 states.[2] While 6 states prohibit previously incarcerated felons from holding public office or government jobs,[3] 4 other states[4] explicitly forbid convicted felons from holding jobs that could have direct connections to the offenses for which they were convicted. Several other states also have specific criteria that limit the types of public employment convicted offenders can hold.

Instead of the formalized, total, and permanent loss of rights in our culture, we commonly encounter a varying set of **collateral consequences.**[5] Many legal restrictions imposed on convicted offenders are very similar to those imposed on the mentally ill and incompetent.[6] In the area of forfeited civil rights, the most common collateral consequences are losing the right to sit on juries and filing for divorce on the grounds of a spouse's incarceration. In some states, people may also lose their parental rights, may permanently lose their rights to public sector employment, and may be required to register their names, addresses, and other vital information with local, regional, or statewide criminal authorities.[7]

Convicted criminals have been historically considered as individuals undeserving of legal rights. Having shown their inability or unwillingness to live within the law, criminals were considered as undeserving of any protections of the law. In other words, convicted criminals have commonly been viewed as deserving civil deaths. Thus, for most of our nation's history, convicted felons were stripped of essentially all legal rights, except those guaranteed by the Constitution. The primary basis of these rights, of course, is the Eighth Amendment to the Constitution, which contains the well-known protection from "cruel and unusual punishment," as well as restrictions against *excessive* bail and fines. (See Figure 7–1.) This one sentence, however apparently clear-cut, has been the focus of some very long, complex legal battles. As we will see in the following section, nothing in the law is really "clear-cut."

Collateral consequences Loss of privileges and rights that accompany a criminal conviction.

Figure 7–1 Text of the Eighth Amendment.

> **EIGHTH AMENDMENT TO THE UNITED STATES CONSTITUTION**
> Excessive bail shall not be required, nor excessive fines imposed, nor cruel and unusual punishments inflicted.

Source: The United States Constitution.

Today, we consider inmates as legally disadvantaged citizens. This is in sharp contrast to the situation that existed for many decades in the United States. The government's relationship with convicted criminals is similar to an authority figure's relationship with a younger, perhaps disabled, immature individual. Put more simply, our government's relationship with convicted criminals is essentially a relationship between parents and their children. In fact, this legal principle, **parens patriae,** has guided many U.S. correctional experts for decades. That is, the government (correctional officials) should take responsibility for supervising children (inmates) and all others who cannot properly care for themselves. *Parens patriae* is also the basis of the judicial hands-off policy regarding involvement in the actions of the "parental" correctional system.

Lack of judicial intervention and change in U.S. corrections can also be attributed to the explicit legal devaluing of convicts. For most of our nation's history, convicts and inmates were considered as having less legal value than "good" citizens. This status was explicit and guided both our popular and legal beliefs about criminal convicts. Although best known for abolishing slavery, the Thirteenth Amendment to the Constitution, ratified in 1865, made criminal convicts forfeit all their legal rights. While it eliminated slavery, the Thirteenth Amendment left open the door for slavery-like treatment of convicts. As this Amendment reads:

> Neither slavery nor involuntary servitude, except as punishment for crime whereof the party shall have been duly convicted, shall exist within the United States.

This position held sway in the United States for the better part of a century. Following on the heels of the Thirteenth Amendment, a Virginia court clearly stated in the 1871 case *Ruffin v. Commonwealth* that:

> As a consequence of his crime [he] not only forfeited his liberty, but all his personal rights except those which the law in its humanity accords to him. He is for the time being the slave of the state.[8]

Although convicts held no rights, the Supreme Court charged the federal government with the responsibility of protecting from "lawless violence all persons in their service or custody in the course of administering justice."[9] This would later give inmates a foundation upon which to build their cases for freedom from cruel and unusual punishment, for access to the courts, and for medical care. However,

Parens patriae Legal doctrine that says the state must provide parental-like protections to those who are unable to care for themselves; applied to convicts when popular ideology holds that criminals have shown themselves unable to act like adults.

during the nineteenth century, convicts' status as slaves permitted the perpetuation of the courts' hands-off policy.

The "finding" or emergence of prisoners' rights has primarily been a product of judicial decisions regarding the First and Fourteenth Amendments. These emerging legal rights have been recognized only during the last 40 years, the period during which the prisoners' rights movement has been active. This is also the period during which social scientific research on prison culture and evaluations of correctional programs, administrative styles, and correctional practices have received greater recognition and acceptance.

The Prisoners' Rights Movement

Only in the past four decades have the courts increasingly moved toward guaranteeing prisoners' rights. As Burton, Cullen, and Travis

The social changes inside U.S. prisons coincided with the civil rights movement in U.S. society.

conclude, "with few exceptions . . . and despite a broader swing recently toward 'get tough' criminal justice policies, states generally are becoming less restrictive in depriving the civil rights of offenders."[10]

The 1961 Supreme Court ruling in *Monroe v. Pape*,[11] which made the Civil Rights Act of 1871 applicable to prison inmates, triggered the modern prisoners' rights movement. The Civil Rights Act provided newly freed slaves the opportunity to sue state officials in federal court, and the 1961 decision extended this opportunity to state prison inmates. Under Section 1983 of the 1871 Civil Rights Act, prison inmates could sue public officials for monetary damages in response to violations of clearly established constitutional rights. That is, inmates could argue that they had "clearly established constitutional rights" and the courts could then validate those rights.

Accompanying these legal changes, some important social changes within prisons facilitated the development of the prisoners' rights movement. First, during the 1960s and 1970s, the prison population increased dramatically. Second, the longer sentences given to convicted felons added to the problem of overcrowding in our prisons. Third, the inmate population became increasingly diverse, less educated, more likely to be substance abusers, and increasingly violent. All these factors added to the stressful nature of most prisons and created a context in which the need for change was obvious.

The social changes inside U.S. prisons and in U.S. society created a tense situation that demanded legal changes. The societal changes that spurred the prisoners' rights movement were the growing diversity of our nation's population and the advances of the civil rights movement. Not only were prisons becoming more diverse racially, economically, and culturally, but so was society. Additionally, minority groups became increasingly politically active in the 1960s and 1970s. This resulted in changing legal statuses for minorities in society and for those inside our prisons.

The flood of court cases did, in fact, validate many inmate claims. Following on the heels of the civil rights movement, the prisoners' rights movement established an ever-widening range of constitutional rights for prison inmates. Although we have never seen a direct overturning of the statements in *Ruffin* and the Thirteenth Amendment, the words of the landmark 1974 case *Wolff v. McDonnel* clearly show the new view of prison inmates: "Though his rights may be diminished . . . a prisoner is not wholly stripped of constitutional protections."[12]

This leads us, then, to the question: Which rights are stripped from prisoners? The primary achievement of the prisoners' rights movement has been establishing legal and procedural precedents for the judicial system to abandon its hands-off policy and to become actively involved in the structured, daily operations of correctional facilities. Important outgrowths of these precedents have been the substantive rulings of appeals courts that have required changes to prison operations. In these changes of prison operations, the courts have established and specified prisoners' legal rights.

JOB FOCUS: PRISON PARALEGAL

Because the Constitution requires prisons to provide inmates with access to the courts, prison paralegals assist inmates in preparing legal documents and processing their legal challenges against the prison and its staff. While such jobs do not require a law degree or specialized legal competence, paralegal work does require discretion and independent judgment in applying specialized knowledge of particular laws. In simple terms, prison paralegals become intimately familiar with a very narrow segment of the law and how to both apply the law to real-life situations and how to coordinate agency and institution operations to remain within the parameters of the law.

To be qualified for a job as a prison paralegal, one must have either a certificate or associate's degree in paralegal studies. Most correctional systems prefer people who have had experience in criminal law work and, ideally, some familiarity with corrections. Either hourly or salaried, paralegals have a wide range of pay scales. An important factor in the pay is whether the position is full-time or part-time. The national average annual compensation for a paralegal with six years on the job is $32,000.

Source: Marge Dover, "1995 National Utilization and Compensation Survey Report," *Facts & Findings: The Journal for Legal Assistants,* Vol. 22, No. 4, 1995, pp. 18–20.

The Rights of Inmates

Inmates—in fact, all convicted criminals—do not have all their legal rights removed. Instead, inmates of the 1990s take many of their basic citizenship rights with them to prison. However, they do not retain some rights. As we shall see shortly, individuals forfeit some not-so-obvious rights when they are convicted of felonies.

Two rights that individuals forfeit when convicted of felonies are holding public office and voting in elections. **Disenfranchisement** is the loss of the right to vote, which is commonly paired with a loss of the right to hold public office. The legal basis for placing these restrictions on convicted felons is found either in statutory law or in a state's constitution. Although laws vary somewhat from state to state, they are ordinarily stated in precise language. Even so, some confusion exists in interpreting them. Individuals can regain the rights lost, including disenfranchisement, in one of four ways: (1) by executive clemency, (2) by discharge, (3) by pardon, or (4) by special legislative act.

Executive clemency is a special power granted to certain elected officials that permits them to overrule particular types of court decisions. The constitutions of most states (and the Constitution) allow governors to dismiss criminal courts' convictions and sentences of offenders. Granted very rarely, clemencies are used only in cases where the public considers a conviction inappropriate or a sentence much too extreme. Since clemencies can also be politically dangerous, governors usually grant them at the end of their terms of office.[13]

However, when discussing prisoners' rights, it is not so much a matter of examining what rights they forfeit, but what legal rights they retain. In keeping with our historical foundations, we assume that people convicted of felonies give up all their rights, *except those specifically enumerated by law.* Case law, or occasionally statutory law, covers the area of prisoners' rights. This tells us that the majority of legal rights inmates retain is a result of changes in the judicial system's hands-off policy.

Today, inmates have a number of specific rights guaranteed to them by the Constitution. Included are the rights to be free from cruel and unusual punishment (the Eighth Amendment), to receive visitors, to send and receive mail, to practice their chosen religion, to receive necessary medical care, and to have access to the courts.

Disenfranchisement
Loss of the right to vote.

Executive clemency
Special power granted to elected office holders that permits them to overrule some court decisions.

Freedom From Cruel and Unusual Punishment

The Eighth Amendment to the U.S. Constitution expressly forbids "cruel and unusual punishments." The courts have interpreted this prohibition to apply to the sentences imposed, to the conditions in which convicts are imprisoned, and to an institution's internal disciplinary procedures.

Our founding fathers may have known exactly what they considered cruel and unusual punishment. For us, however, this concept is neither a clear nor a precise legal principle. The U.S. Supreme Court has repeatedly offered differing interpretations of that concept. Furthermore, the Supreme Court has argued that "cruel and unusual," being linked to contemporary cultural standards, can be interpreted differently at different points in history. Specifically, in 1910 the Supreme Court stated that the Eighth Amendment "is not fastened to the absolute but may acquire meaning as public opinion becomes enlightened by humane justice."[14]

However, the question still remains: What is cruel and unusual punishment? Perhaps the best answer to this question is: There is no one answer but several related answers. A 1991 decision by the U.S. Supreme Court[15] established that the Eighth Amendment contains both an objective and a subjective component. For any particular correctional action or sentence to be declared in violation of the Eighth Amendment, it must violate both components of the Amendment's prohibitions. To be in violation of the objective component of the Eighth Amendment, the practice in question must be shown to violate "contemporary standards of decency."[16] Usually a correctional practice will be declared to violate this standard if it results in a serious physical or psychological injury. However, a practice may also violate this standard if it has an imminent threat of actual injury, and this threat could be (but is not) prevented.[17] Whether a practice or action violates the subjective component depends on whether it was performed *as a punishment.* If something is done that harms or injures an inmate, but it is not done to punish, then it cannot be in violation of the Eighth Amendment.[18] Remember: The Constitution provides protection only from cruel and unusual *punishment.*

Capital punishment is the most notable application of the Eighth Amendment to specific sentences. The death penalty has historically been the most common form of criminal punishment in the world. In contemporary U.S. society, our judicial system has usually interpreted the penalty of death for crimes other than intentional homicide with aggravating circumstances (or treason at the federal level) to be "too severe."

Conditions of confinement are the prisons' actual physical conditions and the positive/negative impacts they have on inmates. The Constitution guarantees that inmates will be held in physical facilities that do not impose undue hardships or dangers to their safety and health. *Holt v. Sarver,* a 1969 federal district court ruling, is one significant court case in this area of law. In this case the inmates of two prison farms in Arkansas claimed that the combined, overall conditions in these institutions were cruel and unusual punishment. The court agreed with the inmates, declaring the Arkansas correctional system to be in violation of the Eighth Amendment because of its **totality of conditions.** As the court stated:

> Confinement itself within a given institution may amount to cruel and unusual punishment prohibited by the Constitution where confinement is characterized by conditions and practices so bad as to be shocking to the conscience of a reasonably civilized people . . . .[19]

Holt v. Sarver opened the doors, and courts found entire institutions or even correctional systems to be in violation of the Eighth Amendment. When this is done, courts typically specify either detailed and specific changes or establish broad guidelines for changes that prisons must make to improve conditions that are *not* cruel and unusual punishment. (See Table 7–1.)

The Eighth Amendment also impacts the specific treatment and disciplinary procedures that prisons use with inmates who violate institutional rules and regulations. Most significant here is that correctional personnel no longer have complete and open access to use corporal punishment or physical force on inmates. In only five situations may correctional personnel use physical force with an inmate:

1. As an act of self-defense against inmate aggression.
2. As an act of defense to protect a third party under attack by an inmate.
3. As an act to enforce prison rules and regulations (but only when all other, less severe methods to bring about compliance have been exhausted).
4. As a means to prevent an escape.
5. As a means to prevent the commission of a crime.

Conditions of confinement The prisons' actual physical conditions and the positive or negative impacts they have on inmates.

Totality of conditions An institution's complete set of physical and social circumstances; during the prisoners' rights movement, this was the focus of lawsuits claiming that prisons/jails were in violation of minimum constitutional standards.

Table 7–1	Reasons for Prisons to Be Under Court Orders to Limit Population	
Reason		**Total No. of Prisons**
Total		1,207
Not under court order or consent decree for specific conditions of confinement		965
Under court order or consent decree for specific conditions of confinement		242
Crowding		186
Medical facilities		172
Administrative segregation		121
Staffing		155
Food services/nutrition		136
Education		139
Disciplinary policies		114
Recreation		127
Visiting/mail policies		130
Fire hazards		114
Counseling programs		106
Inmate classification		121
Library services		122
Grievance policies		113
Other		41

Source: U.S. Department of Justice, *Sourcebook of Criminal Justice Statistics, 1993* (Washington, D.C.: Bureau of Justice Statistics, 1994). Statistics as of June 29, 1990.

Until the late 1960s, corporal punishment was the norm for reacting to inmates who violated prison rules and regulations. In the 1968 case of *Jackson v. Bishop,* the U.S. Court of Appeals for the Eighth Circuit ruled that whipping inmates who violated institutional rules violated their Eighth Amendment protection from cruel and unusual punishment.[20] This case was a major precedent for later cases, and today any form of corporal punishment a correctional institution uses is interpreted as illegal behavior.

Visitation

Receiving visitors while incarcerated is not a fundamental right. Rather, it is a right that must be balanced against the needs of insti-

Two types of acceptable visiting conditions: (1) clear partition and (2) open visitation room.

tutional security.[21] The restrictions on visitation procedures and permissible visitors must be precise.[22] Examples of policies that have been deemed unconstitutional include: an Ohio restriction on visits from individuals whose conduct is "objectionable"[23] and a California ban on visitation between persons of different races.[24] Finally, the prison must provide some degree of privacy for visits, and visitors and inmates must be able to simultaneously see each other and converse. Consequently, visits must be conducted in either an open, unrestricted area or in visitation booths. If the latter, then only clear partitions can separate inmates and their visitors, and communication must be facilitated through open screens or over effective, modern voice communication apparatus.[25] However, contact visits, while allowed in many prisons, have not been declared a right of inmates.

Use of the Mails

Inmates' right to send and receive mail is the result of judicial interpretations of the First Amendment to the Constitution. Specifically, the right to use the mail is guaranteed by: "Congress shall make no law . . . abridging the freedom of speech, or of the press." This is considered one of the most fundamental rights of inmates. Most correctional officials would not want to restrict or eliminate inmates' use of the mail, as this is perhaps the most common form of contact inmates have with the outside world. Without outside contacts,

The Rights of Inmates   **187**

inmates display weakened morale, increased tensions (and, consequently, more rule violations and violence), and difficulties readjusting to society upon release.

To ensure that communications are maintained with people outside the prison, inmates are guaranteed the right to be provided with stationery and stamps if they cannot afford these themselves.[26] Prison officials restrict inmates from receiving stamps from outsiders. However, prison officials are not required to provide inmates with typewriters/computers or funds for certified mail.

The restrictions placed on mail focus on maintaining institutional security. Specifically, officials are concerned with controlling

LEGAL BRIEF:

Hershberger v. Scaletta, 861 F. Supp. 1470 (N.D. Iowa 1993).

On August 26, 1994, the Eighth Circuit U.S. Court of Appeals upheld an Iowa local court ruling concerning provision of postage to inmates. The specifics in this case involved Hershberger, an inmate at the Iowa State Reformatory, who did not have money to pay for postage.

Housed in an administrative segregation unit, Hershberger had only limited privileges. While in the unit, Hershberger argued that he should be provided free postage since he had no access to money to purchase it. The regulations of the Iowa State Reformatory allowed no free postage for personal mail, but inmates were advanced a maximum of $7.50 for postage on legal mail. Additionally, the prison assessed a service fee of $.50 per month to inmates with an outstanding balance on this advance.

When challenged in court, these regulations were upheld as legal. The local court ruled that the prison did not have to provide free postage for personal mail but did have an obligation to provide a minimum of one free stamp and envelope per week for legal mail (to ensure the right to access to the courts). On appeal, the Eighth Circuit upheld the lower court's ruling.

Inmates have limited rights to send and receive mail.

contraband. Prior to 1974 prison officials routinely censored inmates' mail to monitor contraband and escape plans. However, in 1974 the U.S. Supreme Court ruled in *Procunier v. Martinez* that officials' censoring of mail could be done within the confines of known standards.[27] Included in the category of mail subject to special conditions are correspondences with inmates in other institutions (these may be prohibited), with former inmates now outside of the prison,[28] with one's attorney and the courts (these may not be restricted or read), and with outgoing mail to news media (officials may not simply prohibit contact with the media).

To balance inmates' First Amendment rights and prison officials' security concerns, a "correspondence list" (individuals approved for mail exchanges) may be required for all inmates. Prison officials may open incoming mail but only to determine whether it is actually from an approved person. Censorship of mail, unless containing contraband or information dangerous to institutional functioning (such as escape plans), is prohibited. Incoming mail from attorneys may be opened and shaken out in the inmate's presence (to check for contraband), but prison personnel cannot read it.

Religious Rights

Other First Amendment rights prohibit government establishment of religion and guarantee protection of religious freedom. Religious teachings and worship have been core components of U.S. corrections. They also were one instigating factor behind the American colonists' first correctional efforts. However, not until the Black Muslims brought legal challenges in the 1960s were inmates' constitutionally guaranteed religious rights recognized.

The prohibition of government establishment of religion centers on the separation of church and state. This clause of the First Amendment has consistently been interpreted to mean that states cannot use public resources to create and to impose on people religious organizations and practices. Consequently, correctional officials cannot force inmates to attend any form of religious activity. Since inmates would not have access to religious services and counseling if these were not provided, the courts have broadened the range of permissible (and, in fact, required) governmental actions to require equal provision of services across religious faiths. The Supreme Court uses the guiding principle that state governments neither favor nor hinder religion.

This right becomes problematic for correctional authorities when inmates demand clergy. Prisons are required to provide clergy to tend to the spiritual needs of inmates.[29] However, this does not mean that prisons must provide staff clergy for any and all religious groups. Clergy are to serve the needs of all inmates, not only those of particular faiths.[30] Similarly, institutions need not provide special, individual facilities for worship. One facility that faiths share meets the constitutional requirement.[31]

While the state cannot establish religion, it must provide opportunities for inmates to freely practice their religions. However, there are permissible restrictions here. One restriction focuses on whether a particular form of religious practice would potentially threaten institutional security and order. Another restriction questions whether the religion to be practiced is in fact a religion. Several widely known federal court decisions have examined what practices qualify as a "real religion."[32] Inmates must show the presence of a set of comprehensive beliefs that address fundamental and ultimate questions concerning imponderable matters. Also, formal and externally recognizable symbols must identify the religion. Most important, the "practicing" followers must show sincerity.

Religious services can be restricted when necessary to ensure institutional order and security. To legally prevent a religious group gathering, correctional officials must show that the teachings and/or practices present a "clear and present danger" to the prison's functions. Also, correctional officials can prohibit attendance of individual inmates who can reasonably be expected to cause disruptions or other security problems. This is a valid security measure, especially when alternative forms of religious services are provided.[33] Clearly, the courts have placed issues of institutional security (which affect all institutional people) above issues of individual rights.

Medical Care

The governmental body responsible for incarcerating inmates is also responsible for their safety and health. Inmates have a constitutionally guaranteed right to receive necessary medical care while incarcerated, and denial of such care has been deemed cruel and unusual punishment. This right to care extends to both physical and psychological ills.[34] However, this has not always been the situation.

The major turning point in establishing inmates' rights to medical care came in the 1976 Supreme Court ruling in the landmark case of *Estelle v. Gamble*.[35] Here, the Supreme Court introduced the new standard for determining whether and when provided medical care fulfilled the constitutional requirements for adequacy. From this point forward, inmates who claimed they did not receive proper medical care would need to show "deliberate indifference to serious medical needs" on the part of corrections officials. This does not mean that inmates must be cured of any and all medical problems (whether real or imagined).[36] Neither does "deliberate indifference" mean that all medical care must be effective. Simply put, inmates must be provided with "necessary" medical care to maintain them at "reasonable" levels of health. However, the draw on the correctional system's resources need not be so severe as to seriously detract from other, necessary services.

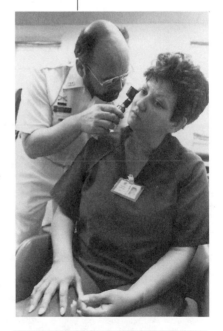

Inmates have the right to proper medical care.

The Cost of Medical Care The simple fact is, however, that providing "necessary" medical care for inmates is very expensive. A 1989 survey of 47 of the 51 U.S. correctional systems (50 states plus the Federal Bureau of Prisons), as well as a 1993 federal review of state prison budgets, show that approximately 9.5 percent of correctional systems' annual expenditures go for health care.[37] This translates to an average of $1,906 per inmate, or a total average expenditure of $24,569,436.[38] Both small and large expenses contribute to this total cost. Common diseases and injuries are one source of expenses. So are the more major costs: heart attacks, cancer, organ transplants, and HIV/AIDS. Table 7–2 shows the distribution of funds for a sampling of state correctional system budgets.

To control these costs and to limit "abuses" of the free medical care provided, many states are now investigating the possibility of charging inmates a nominal fee ($2 to $5) for visits to the infirmary and for prescriptions. While this makes life in prison more similar to life on the outside (most health insurance requires some type of co-payment), such a plan poses problems. For example, most inmates have few, if any, financial resources. What if they cannot pay? How should a prison administrator determine whether an inmate can or cannot pay? Might their inability to pay keep inmates from seeing a doctor or nurse and then having a major (that is, more expensive) problem later? These are just some issues that will need to be resolved before charging inmates for medical care can be fully instituted.

HIV/AIDS in Prison   One new—and more financially draining—medical issue facing correctional administrators today is how to care for and manage inmates with HIV. Specifically, this issue poses three complex sets of problems for correctional administrators:

1. How should issues of testing inmates for HIV antibodies be handled?

Table 7–2	Distribution of Funds for Selected State Correctional System Budgets (by percent)				
State	**Custody/ Security**	**Treatment Programs**	**Inmate Health Care**	**Maintenance**	**All Other Expenses**
California	38	2	10	N/A	50
Florida	45	4	13	4	34
Illinois	55	5	16	10	16
Nevada	65	N/A	18	1	16
Massachusetts	82	2	13	0	3
South Carolina	44	3	12	4	37
Texas	36	3	8	3	50

Source: U.S. Department of Justice, *Sourcebook of Criminal Justice Statistics, 1994* (Washington, D.C.: Bureau of Justice Statistics, 1995).

2. How should the somewhat unique needs of HIV-positive inmates be addressed?

3. How should the medical care of inmates with HIV (including AIDS) be met?

HIV testing is one issue that has the clearest answer at this time. Correctional systems may subject all inmates to mandatory testing.[39] However, many states have recently abandoned this practice in favor of testing only certain categories of "high risk" offenders (sex offenders, injection drug users, etc.) due to the high cost of testing such large numbers of people. All states provide some form of voluntary HIV testing. Critics of the mandatory testing policies argue that such actions constitute a violation of privacy and/or a violation of Fourth Amendment rights protecting inmates from unreasonable searches and seizures. The courts have not upheld either argument.

In managing HIV-positive inmates, some states have chosen to segregate them from the general prison population. This has been upheld as legal.[40] It is also legally permissible to restrict HIV-positive inmates from particular work assignments, but only when the goal is to maintain institutional order and security, not due to any suspected risk of infection to other inmates. (There is no infection risk, so long as other institutional rules are abided.)[41] The trend in the 1990s, however, is to integrate HIV-positive inmates with the general population. Only when their medical condition necessitates segregation are most inmates removed from the general population.

Prison officials are also responsible for tending to HIV-positive inmates' medical needs. However, officials have not demonstrated "deliberate indifference" when they withhold treatments whose effectiveness has not yet been fully established.[42] The issue of providing medical treatments to HIV-positive inmates is especially serious because of the dire consequences for both parties. Without proper care, HIV-positive inmates will cer-

FYI

The impact of HIV and AIDS on correctional populations is a growing problem in the United States. More than 11,500 cases of AIDS are reported among the nation's prison inmates, but the distribution of these cases is not evenly spread across the country. Nationwide, almost 2.5 percent of prison inmates have tested HIV-positive, but the rates of infection vary significantly by region. The lowest rates of infection are in the West and Midwest (0.7%) with higher rates in the South (1.5%) and the Northeast (8.1%).

Source: T. M. Hammett, L. Harrold, M. Gross, and J. Epstein, *1992 Update: HIV/AIDS in Correctional Facilities* (Washington, D.C.: National Institute of Justice, 1994).

tainly die, most probably relatively quickly. By providing proper care, prison officials encounter huge financial costs. One year's worth of AZT, a drug used in the treatment of HIV infection, can easily cost $8,000 to $10,000. Other medications and treatments quickly add to this cost.

Access to the Courts

The foundation right for inmates is their ability to air grievances and to seek judicial solutions to what they perceive as violations of their legal rights. Originally stated in the 1961 Supreme Court case of *Ex parte Hull,* prison officials may not impair an inmate's right to apply to a (federal) court for redress of grievances.[43] Inmates' mail to and from courts and legal officials generally may not be censored or read by correctional officials.[44]

In addition, not only must inmates be allowed access to courts, but they must also be allowed assistance in preparing their cases for court submission. This can take the form of permitting self-taught **jailhouse lawyers** to assist inmates.[45] Or, if a correctional system

Inmates have the right to access the courts.

chooses to prohibit such assistance, then it must make available attorneys or other forms of "professional legal assistance." However, the courts have not been very consistent in ruling on what constitutes acceptable forms and amounts of provided professional legal assistance. Some states allow law school students to come to the institution; some provide paralegals; and some provide attorneys for a varying number of hours per week.

Providing legal assistance alone does not satisfy the requirement of providing access to the courts. Also required is access to legal materials, including law books and materials for the actual petitions to the courts. Prison officials must provide access to a law library, whether on-site or by providing services to gather and deliver requested materials to inmates. Because of the costs (financial and personnel) of gathering such materials, most states stock law libraries in each institution.

LEGAL BRIEF:

Beeks v. Hundley, 34 F2d 658 (8th Cir. 1994).

One recent development in inmates' rights focuses on keeping monetary damages they are awarded as a result of suits brought against correctional officials.

In a 1994 Iowa case, Beeks v. Hundley, *four inmates at the Iowa State Penitentiary received monetary awards for violations of their Fourteenth Amendment rights. Two of the inmates deposited the money into their prison accounts, and correctional officials promptly seized all but $50 of each inmate's account. This was done to pay the costs each inmate was expected to cover in the state's victim restitution program.*

The Eighth Circuit Court of Appeals upheld this seizure, saying that paying restitution to victims is not in conflict with inmates being compensated for violation of rights. However, in a somewhat similar Missouri case, the Eighth Circuit Court of Appeals barred correctional officials from seizing an inmate's judicial award under Section 1983 to pay the cost of the inmate's incarceration (as is called for under Missouri's Incarceration Reimbursement Act).

Evolution of Inmates' Rights

Prison inmates are recognized as people with legal rights. The flood of litigation began in the 1960s and continues today, although it appears that the courts have slowed the momentum of change. Between 1980 and 1986, an average of 261,997 civil and criminal cases were filed in U.S. district courts each year. These cases contended that inmates' civil, due process, and treatment rights or protection from cruel and unusual punishment had been violated.[46] While the great majority of these cases will eventually be dismissed, a significant minority will find that inmates' rights have been violated. Changes (and perhaps monetary damages) will be ordered. Also, in a few cases new inmates' rights will be "discovered." However, a review of Supreme Court prisoners' rights cases decided in the late-1980s and early-1990s suggests that "without a doubt . . . the U.S. Supreme Court has made it exceedingly difficult for inmates to prevail in lawsuits against prison officials."[47] Specifically, the Court has raised the standards that inmates must meet to show they have suffered cruel and unusual punishment, have experienced inhumane living conditions, or have reason to challenge the basic legality of their detention. Perhaps this is indicative of future judicial trends. It appears the tide is turning, and the progression of inmates' rights will begin to erode.

Much of this erosion can be credited to both public and legal community sentiments that inmates are abusing their rights to access the courts. It is commonplace to hear and read media reports about supposedly "ridiculous" lawsuits that inmates brought, challenging what appear to be trivial rules and practices in prisons. The backlog of cases in our court system can be upwards of several years in many parts of the country. This means that not only are civil suits out of prison waiting this long to be heard, but so are other cases involving supposedly more important issues. Reducing court backlogs is important if we hope to achieve the goal—as set forth in the Sixth Amendment—of providing all with a "speedy" trial.

The difficulty is in balancing these concerns. Yes, it is important to have a judicial system that operates quickly. It is also important to have a judicial system that actively works to protect the rights of all citizens, including incarcerated citizens. How is this balance to be achieved, though? Several potential solutions have been proposed. First, we could return to a judicial system that recognized the expertise of correctional officials and administrators, thereby essentially removing prison cases from the courts. Second, we could enlarge the judicial system to increase the number of courts, judges, and opportunities for cases to be heard. If we make the system larger—and the number of incoming cases does not increase—we could (theoretically) resolve cases more quickly. Or, third, as some federal district courts propose, we could designate specific individuals or offices attached to the courts to deal exclusively with prison cases. This would allow us to rely on specialists (similar to the experts on whom judges of the hands-off era relied) to handle prison cases and to remove such cases from court dockets where other types of cases are handled. Which solution is best? The answer probably will depend on the specifics of a jurisdiction's size and current practices. As the saying goes, only time will tell.

Summary

Once considered "slaves of the state," inmates are today viewed as citizens with legal disabilities. Based on English common law traditions, U.S. society deemed criminals as civilly dead. While changed in form and practice slightly, these basic ideas held prominence until the 1960s and 1970s. Following on the heels of the civil rights movement, the prisoners' rights movement pushed U.S. courts out of their hands-off policy and into an active role in reviewing and demanding changes in correctional practices and policies.

With the prisoners' rights movement, inmates made significant gains in retaining major portions of the Bill of Rights when they went to prison. This led to today's view that inmates do have rights. However, for reasons of necessity, usually to maintain institutional security, these rights may have to be altered or, in extreme cases, removed. At the most basic level, inmates are guaranteed protection from cruel and unusual punishments and the right to gain access to the courts. These two basic rights form the foundation upon which the more specific rights that influence daily life in prison are based.

The 1990s is witnessing a change in how the courts, as well as many people, view the inmates' legal challenges. Today, many recognize that it is an abuse of inmates' rights to limit access to the courts, and the number of inmates' lawsuits adds to the huge backlog of cases. In light of this, a movement grows to limit inmates' access to the courts and to limit the range of rights the courts may "find" for them.

QUESTIONS FOR REVIEW

1. In what ways are prisoners' legal rights different today than they were four decades ago?

2. What social factors accompanied the changes in philosophy about prisoners' rights?

3. What are the positive aspects of judicial intervention in corrections?

4. What are the negative aspects of judicial intervention in corrections?

5. What are the criteria for determining whether something is "cruel and unusual punishment"?

6. What are the legal requirements for inmate visitation, mail privileges, and religious practices?

7. What inmate health conditions must be provided medical attention?

8. Why is access to the courts considered a basic legal right?

9. What are the expected future trends in inmates' rights?

ACTIVITIES

1. Contact a local attorney who specializes in civil rights. Ask him or her to discuss the similarities and differences in legal rights of prison inmates, persons on probation, and yourself.

2. Visit a local law library and find two prisoners' rights cases. Make sure one case is from before the prisoners' rights movement (it would be best to get one from the 1800s) and one from the last several years. Read each case to see how the language has changed in referring to both prison inmates and their rights.

3. Contact or visit a local community organization that works to provide education about HIV/AIDS. Ask what it does with prison and jail inmates. How are their efforts in a correctional facility different from their other work?

ENDNOTES

1. These states are: Alabama, Arkansas, Florida, Iowa, Kentucky, Mississippi, Nevada, New Mexico, Rhode Island, Tennessee, and Virginia.

2. These states are: Alabama, Arizona, California, Colorado, Indiana, Kansas, Massachusetts, Michigan, Mississippi, Nevada, Oregon, Rhode Island, South Dakota, Tennessee, Wisconsin, and Wyoming.

3. These states are: Alabama, Delaware, Iowa, Mississippi, Rhode Island, and South Carolina.

4. These states are: Arizona, Florida, Pennsylvania, and Wisconsin.

5. Velmer S. Burton, Jr., Francis T. Cullen, and Lawrence F. Travis, III, "The Collateral Consequences of a Felony Conviction: A National Study of State Statutes," *Federal Probation,* Vol. 51, 1987, pp. 52–60.

6. Velmer S. Burton, Jr. "The Consequences of Official Labels: A Research Note on Rights Lost by the Mentally Ill, Mentally Incompetent, and Convicted Felons," *Community Mental Health Journal,* Vol. 26, No. 3, 1990, pp. 267–276.

7. *Ibid.*

8. *Ruffin v. Commonwealth,* 62 Va. (21 Gratt.) 790 (1871).

9. *Logan v. U.S.,* 144 US 263 (1892).

10. Burton, Cullen, and Travis, *op. cit.,* p. 60.

11. *Monroe v. Pape,* 365 US 167 (1961).

12. *Wolff v. McDonnel,* 418 US 539, 71 Ohio Op. 2d 336 (1974).

13. Patricia Gagné, "The Battered Women's Movement in the 'Post-Feminist' Era: New Social Movement Strategies and the Celeste Clemencies," unpublished doctoral dissertation, The Ohio State University, Columbus, Ohio, 1993.

14. *Weems v. United States,* 217 US 349 (1910).

15. *Wilson v. Seiter,* 111 S Ct 2321, 2323 (1991).

16. *Hudson v. McMillian,* 112 S Ct 995, 1000 (1992).

17. *Helling v. McKinney,* 113 S Ct 2475, 2482 (1993).

18. *Hudson v. McMillian,* 112 S Ct 995, 998 (1992); *Whitley v. Albers,* 475 US 312, 320 (1986).

19. *Holt v. Sarver,* 309 FSupp 362 (EDArk 1970), at pp. 372–373.

20. *Jackson v. Bishop,* 404 F2d 571 (8th Circuit 1968).

21. *McMurray v. Phelps,* 533 FSupp 742 (WDLa 1982).

22. *Feazell v. Augusta County Jail,* 401 FSupp 405 (WDVa 1975).

23. *Taylor v. Perini,* 413 FSupp 194 (NDOhio 1976).

24. *Martin v. Wainwright,* 525 F2d 983 (CA5 1976).

25. *McMurray v. Phelps.*

26. *Morgan v. LaVallee,* 526 F2d 221 (CA2 1975).

27. *Procunier v. Martinez,* 416 US 396 (1974).

28. *Farmer v. Loving,* 392 FSupp 27 (WDVa 1975).

29. *Thericault v. Carlson,* 339 FSupp 375 (NDGa 1972).

30. *Gittlemacker v. Prasse,* 428 F2d 1 (CA3 1970).

31. *Cruz v. Beto,* 405 US 319 (1972).

32. *Africa v. Pennsylvania,* 662 F2d 1025 (CA3, 1981); *Fulwood v. Clemmer,* 206 FSupp 370 (DDC 1962); *Thericault v. Carlson, Remmers v. Brewer,* 361 FSupp 537 (SDIowa 1973).

33. *Belk v. Mitchell,* 294 FSupp 800 (WDNC 1968); *Cooper v. Pate,* 382 F2d 518 (7th Circuit 1967).

34. *Bowring v. Godwin,* 551 FSupp 44 (CA2 1977).

35. *Estelle v. Gamble,* 429 US 97 (1976).

36. *Priest v. Cupp,* 545 P2d 917 (Or.Ct. App. 1976).

37. B. Jaye Anno, "The Cost of Correctional Health Care: Results of a National Survey," *Journal of Prison & Jail Health,* Vol. 9, No. 2, 1990, pp. 105–133. No data were available for the state correctional systems in Hawaii, Indiana, Mississippi, and North Dakota; U.S. Department of Justice, *Sourcebook of Criminal Justice Statistics, 1993* (Washington, D.C.: Bureau of Justice Statistics, 1994).

38. *Ibid.* B. Jaye Anno.

39. *Harris v. Thigpen* (USDC, MDAlabama) CA87, 1109 (1990).

40. *Ramos v. Lamm,* 639 F 2d 559 (10th Cir. 1980).

41. *Farmer v. Moritsugu,* 742 F Supp 525 (WD Wis 1990).

42. *Wilson v. Franceschi,* 735 F Supp 395 (USDC MO Florida, 1990).

43. *Ex parte Hull,* 316 US 546 (1961).

44. However, there are a few states which have had regulations upheld for restricting the mailing of legal papers for inmates. See for instances *Kirby v. Thomas,* 336 F2d 462 (6th Circuit 1964) and *In re Green,* 669 F2d 779 (CA8 1981).

45. *Johnson v. Avery,* 393 US 483 (1969).

46. Administrative Office of the U.S. Courts, *Annual Report of the Director* (Washington, D.C.: U.S. Government Printing Office, 1970–1986), Tables C-1, D-1.

47. Rudolph Alexander, Jr. "Slamming the Federal Courthouse Door on Inmates," *Journal of Criminal Justice,* Vol. 21, 1993, p. 114.

CHAPTER 8

Prison Unrest

CHAPTER OBJECTIVES

In the last two chapters you learned about prisoners and their rights. In this chapter we look closely at some prisoners' activities, specifically forms of violence. After reading this chapter, you will be able to:

1. Identify the forms of violence in prisons.

2. Understand the factors that contribute to the likelihood of victimization for inmates.

3. Examine the functions of violence in maintaining social control and order in prisons.

4. Identify the similarities and differences in prison disturbances and riots.

5. Explain the various theories of violence in prisons.

6. Explore the effects of material losses and overcrowding on inmate behavior.

7. Discuss the consequences of a high frequency of mental illness among inmates.

8. Trace the development of organized violent episodes in U.S. correctional history.

9. Illustrate the process and development of riots through extended examples.

10. Explain the reasons for collective violence in prisons.

KEY TERMS

routine activities
  theory

protective custody

physical coercion

sexual violence

riot

organized disturbances

prison gangs

absolute deprivation

relative deprivation

neurotics

psychotics

amnesty

snitches

predisposing factors

precipitating factors

CHAPTER OUTLINE

Weapons confiscated from inmates.

Forms of Prison Violence

Violence is a common way of dealing with group conflict or individual dissatisfaction, and prisons are not immune to the increased disposition toward violence. In the past, prisoners were expected to accept their "just rewards" without complaining. This is epitomized in the well-known inscription on the wall of the federal penitentiary at Terre Haute, Indiana:

> Whatever is brought upon thee, take cheerfully,
> And be patient when thou are changed to a low estate,
> For gold is tried in fire
> And acceptable men in the furnace of adversity.

Prison revolts, it can be said, not only represent protests against specific conditions, but they also constitute rejection of the ancient dogma that convicts are obliged to be resigned to their lot. Seen in this light, violence in prison provides positive consequences for inmates seeking both to express their dissatisfaction with their environments and to materially improve their condition.

Violence in prisons is of various forms and degrees of severity. Eight main forms of violence occur in prisons:

1. Physical violence by inmates on inmates
2. Physical violence by inmates on staff
3. Physical violence by staff on inmates
4. Sexual violence (usually confined to inmate on inmate)
5. Self-inflicted physical violence
6. Psychological violence (among both staff and inmates)
7. Economic violence
8. Organized disturbances and riots

We will now examine each form of violence in detail, by focusing on the prevalence and specific forms of each type.

Physical Violence by Inmates on Inmates

Violence among inmates is perhaps the most common form of violence in correctional facilities. However, accurate statistics on inter-inmate violence are difficult to find. Inmates simply do not report many incidents, and institutional personnel do not enter some incidents into any official reporting mechanism. However, both those who work and those who live in prisons (as well as in jails) know that violence among inmates commonly occurs.

Due to institutions' cultural and population differences, profiles of inmate perpetrators and victims of physical violence are difficult to generalize. However, based on his study of two close-security institutions, Wooldredge suggests:

> The likelihood of being victimized by personal crime during incarceration is greater among inmates who are physically disabled, those without children, those with fewer prior felony convictions, those who are closer to the ends of their sentences, those who spend fewer hours each day in vocational training, and those who spent more days in segregation.[1]

Additionally, "common knowledge" has long told us that inmates convicted of certain types of crimes (those even prison inmates see as "wrong") are more likely than others to be victimized. These include sex offenders and those who victimize children. These characteristics support a **routine activities theory** of crime, suggesting that inmates' usual, daily activities place them in contact with others who have opportunities to victimize them.

Who commits acts of physical violence in prison? The single most effective predictor is the one who commits violent acts in the community.[2] These are the inmates most likely to be violent, and they are most likely to commit violent acts during the early stages of their sentences. In the words of Adams:

> Recent violent offenders are likely to show greater disruptiveness and greater violence in prison settings and that these propensities are not limited to particular [periods] of a prison career.[3]

Violence presents the greatest concern in the murder of inmates. In 1992 and 1993, 32 and 47 inmates respectively in U.S. prisons were killed by other inmates. Only 11 (or 14%) of those murdered were federal inmates.[4] An additional 327 inmates' deaths were classified as being of "unspecified cause"; but one may suspect that at least some of these deaths were homicides. However, these numbers are not unexpectedly high. Rather, the 47 inmates murdered in 1993 represent only about 0.2 percent (or 1 per every 5,000 U.S. inmates) of individuals in prison on any given day. Furthermore, some patterns exist in the characteristics of inmates killed by other inmates. One study of homicide victims in Canadian federal correctional institutions suggests that, compared with the late-1960s and 1970s, incidents of inmates killing other inmates during the early-1980s are more likely to include multiple assailants (perhaps gangs) and to be motivated by

Routine activities theory People's usual, daily activities that place them in contact with others who have opportunities to victimize them.

revenge concerning drug or gambling debts.[5] Perhaps inmates could avoid victimization by changing their behavior patterns.

However, physical violence among inmates impacts all inmates. While not all inmates are physically victimized, the realization that they might be is ever-present. When they fear being victimized, inmates commonly exhibit high levels of tension, anxiety, or depression, have little energy, and cannot concentrate on tasks.[6] Also, when fearful some inmates may interpret innocuous actions of others as threatening and may strike out in self-defense.

However, not all inmates respond in this manner. Rather, inmates adopt two other patterns of behavior as personal precautions against victimization.[7] Older inmates and inmates who are not as tightly integrated to the institutional culture tend to use passive, avoidance techniques. However, other inmates could interpret this approach as signs of weakness and vulnerability. Younger offenders more commonly adopt a more aggressive, proactive technique of self-protection.

Protective custody
Highly restrictive, special housing units where inmates who require extra protection are placed.

All three approaches—striking out in fear, avoidance, and aggressive displays of strength—highlight the potential for increasingly self-destructive cycles of violence. Therefore, the answer to the question many new correctional staff ask, "How do I protect myself?" may be that there is no completely effective method of ensuring one's self-protection. However, one of the oldest laws regarding prisons establishes prison staffs' responsibility to minimize violence and to protect both staff and inmates from "lawless violence."[8]

FYI

Most prisons have **protective custody,** a special housing unit where those inmates who require extra protection are placed. The inmates in protective custody are usually those who have been sexually assaulted, who are known to be targeted for murder, or whom officials have special reason to believe may be in danger.

Life in protective custody includes few of the "privileges" that "regular" inmates receive. Most protective custody inmates are not eligible for most programs and are locked in their housing units most of the day (if not the entire day). Because the protective custody unit (usually referred to as "PC") is highly restrictive, many inmates who have been assaulted or threatened choose *not* to live there.

Physical Violence by Inmates on Staff

Of greater personal concern to most correctional personnel are acts of violence that inmates direct toward staff. Again, while reliable and valid statistics are very difficult to find, anecdotal evidence consistently warns correctional staff of the dangers of working in prison. Violent acts that inmates commit against staff run the range from simple blows to throwing objects (chairs, cans of food, feces, etc.) to beatings by individual or groups of inmates to stabbings, biting, and occasionally homicide. For this reason, most correctional systems require all personnel who work inside prisons to complete extensive personal defense training.

Protective gear for correctional personnel is available when it is needed.

However, while danger is inherent in correctional officers' work, the frequency of injuries among correctional staff is relatively low. Also, correctional officers are not the only targets for inmates' violence. Treatment staff, office workers, maintenance workers, and management personnel have all been recipients of inmates' violence. One study of inmate violence directed against prison staff in California reported that from 1977 to 1987 the annual number of assaults system-wide increased from 110 to 914.[9] Of course, this increase coincides with the 257 percent increase in institutional population during the same period. Furthermore, the increase is in assaults without weapons; the victimization rate for assaults with weapons has remained low at 0.2 per 100 inmates.

Physical Violence by Staff on Inmates

Prison observers often overlook (or support) acts of violence that prison staff direct toward inmates. As discussed in Chapter 7, physical assaults by staff on inmates are generally considered violations of the Eighth Amendment, unless such actions qualify as self-defense, defense of a third person, a last resort to enforce institutional rules, prevention of escape, or prevention of criminal acts.

Physical coercion
The use of force to make someone follow orders.

However, security staff often use **physical coercion**—the use of force to make someone follow directions—as an easily accessible and immediately effective manner to secure compliance with orders. In analyzing the methods of Massachusetts' correctional officers for controlling inmates, Kelsey Kauffman reports that officers use six primary approaches to secure power: authority, persuasion, inducement, manipulation, force, and coercion.[10] Inexperienced correctional officers may frequently use force, an act to remove an inmate's element of choice to follow an order. However, force has serious, negative consequences in the long term. As Kauffman says:

> Force is a form of power within a prison. Legal limits exist on the length of time an inmate can be forced to spend in lockup. . . . More fundamental, force is not effective in compelling performance of complex tasks. Nor can it be realistically relied upon for the *routine* accomplishment of even very simple tasks.[11]

LEGAL BRIEF:

Rutledge v. Springborn, 836 F. Supp. 531 (N.D.I. 11.1993).

In 1993 the U.S. District Court heard the case of Steve Rutledge, a convicted murderer serving a 70-year sentence in Illinois' Joliet Correctional Center. In June of 1990 Rutledge found out that several of his fellow inmates were planning an escape. Rutledge informed the prison's officials about the plan and even gave them names of inmates who would be participating.

Knowing that snitches are not respected among inmates, Rutledge was concerned for his own safety. Officials promised him they would keep the fact that he provided this information confidential. However, Rutledge was repeatedly threatened by other inmates, burned by having hot liquids thrown on him, and generally harassed by other inmates. According to Rutledge, the prison's officials did nothing to protect him. He believed this was in retaliation for being a jailhouse lawyer who had helped other inmates sue the prison and its officials in the past.

Because he was not adequately protected, Rutledge sued the prison and officials, claiming that his Eighth Amendment rights had been violated. In ruling on his claims, the U.S. District Court said that officials had violated his rights. In returning Rutledge to the same housing unit, the prison officials had been deliberately indifferent to his welfare. In other words, the prison officials had intentionally failed to protect Rutledge from the other inmates.

Staff may then become frustrated with their ineffective use of force and may escalate the violence, thereby pushing inmates to respond violently themselves. The real danger in staff's use of violence, whether for legitimate goals or not, is that inmates' violent responses may be triggered.

Rather than using violence, staff will have more effective results if they respond to threats and attacks by using well-developed communications skills. Being able to rationally and calmly talk *with* (as opposed to *to*) inmates is a widely recognized way to achieve smooth prison operations. Also, many correctional systems today train their staffs in conflict management skills.

Sexual Violence

Sexual violence Using sexual activity to bring harm to another person; in prison this comes in forcible rape, coerced sex, and coerced prostitution.

Sexual violence and assaults in men's prisons are of three basic forms: forcible rape, coerced sex, and coerced prostitution. (For a discussion of sexual violence in women's prisons, see Chapter 9.) Sex in prison is more about power than sex. Being able to control another man and "make him into a woman" is the most common goal of sexual assaults. Most media and academic attention is devoted to forcible rape, although this is probably the least common form of sexual violence. Coerced sex refers to inmates who are pressured or persuaded to perform sexual acts to avoid physical attacks or who are "trapped" into sexual acts when they cannot repay accumulated debts. Inmates who prostitute themselves usually do so because of pressure from physically intimidating inmates.

The incidence of rape in prison is difficult to assess accurately. Alan Davis, in his research on the Philadelphia prison (jail) system in the late-1960s, first addressed the issue.[12] Based on interviews with more than 3,300 inmates, Davis concluded that

FYI

For gay inmates there can be much pressure to have sex with large numbers of other inmates. This means that gay inmates are especially vulnerable to sexual victimization. As shown in the following quotation of one gay inmate, who wishes to remain anonymous, an ability to establish one's strength as a person can be a key to avoiding sexual victimization:

They're not after the ones who are out, because there's nothing you can do to them. I'd say, 'Hey, you want to f*** me? Fine, I can lay here. You're not going to have much fun, I'm not going to help you one little bit, but I'm not going to fight you either.' But the kid who just came in and is good looking, maybe he's straight, maybe he's not, but he's not going to say one way or the other, he's the one. He's going to fight back, he's going to make it interesting. That's the one they want. . . . That's the whole thing in there, intimidation. If they can intimidate you and scare you, then they got you.

more than 1 in 25 inmates had been sexually assaulted. Other researchers have placed the victimization rate higher, sometimes suggesting that nearly 3 in 10 inmates have been victims of attempted or completed sexual assaults.[13]

While many researchers have attributed prison rapes to racially motivated hostilities,[14] others have argued that the significant difference between victims and perpetrators is gender presentations and displays of physical strength. Basically, the strong dominate and victimize the weak. Inmates who are targeted for sexual assault are commonly young, nonviolent, first-time offenders who have slim builds, are white, and may have a history of mental illness.

However, the potential of prison rape impacts inmates' fears of victimization and guides their interactions. Inmates who report the greatest levels of fear of sexual assault are those who are shorter of stature and are heavier.[15] These characteristics are associated with their perceived inability to physically defend themselves.

Inmates coerced into sex or prostitution also react to feelings of vulnerability for physical violence. Some men may be forced to prostitute themselves to benefit a gang, or some men may be intimidated into a one-on-one relationship with another who promises to protect him from rape and physical violence. Even so, however, he is victim-

Inmate in a protective custody cell.

ized by the "protector" and sometimes by the protector's friends and associates.

Self-Inflicted Physical Violence

Inmates sometimes perpetrate violence against themselves. This includes suicide and self-mutilation. While suicides may be more publicly known, self-destructive behaviors may be more common and perhaps more difficult for correctional officials to manage.

Suicide among prison inmates is relatively rare; it is more common among jail inmates than among those in prisons. However, in 1990 a total of 134 prison inmates committed suicide, and 88 inmates did so in 1991.[16] When viewed in context of the total prison population this means that less than 0.01 percent of inmates successfully committed suicide. Figure 8–1 shows the geographic distribution of inmate suicides by region in 1991. The most common method of

Figure 8–1 Geographic distribution of inmate suicides, 1991.

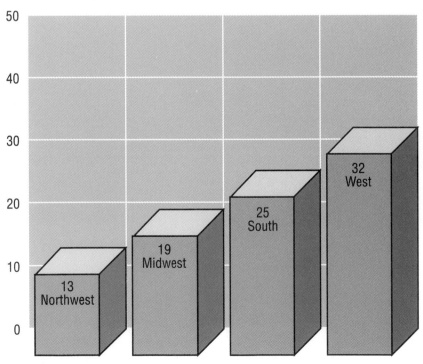

suicide among prison inmates is cutting, followed by hanging. However, inmates may commit suicide in many ways that are not always officially counted as such, including overdosing on drugs, jumping from upper tiers, or deliberately instigating situations where other inmates will kill them.

In addition, 35 inmates died in prisons during 1991 due to "accidental self-injuries." Whereas accidental deaths are one leading cause of deaths for young adult Americans, they account for only 1.9 percent of the 1,802 total deaths among 1991 prison inmates.[17] Ironically, then, it could be said that life in prison is "safer" than life on the outside (at least in terms of accidents).

Self-mutilating behavior, often considered a sign of mental illness, most often involves such acts as inmates cutting themselves, starving themselves, or injuring themselves by beating their heads on walls, floors, and furnishings. Attempting to control such acts can be extremely difficult. However, correctional staff have the responsibilities (1) to protect both other inmates and staff from injuries that result from such behavior and (2) to protect inmates' right to be held in a safe place while under the government's care. Also, numerous problems, including lowered morale, interpersonal physical violence, and other health concerns, may arise when inmates injure themselves and bleed in the presence of others. However, inmates determined to pursue self-mutilating behaviors may be nearly impossible to stop. Numerous creative ways exist to inflict self-injury, even without any potential "weapons" available.

Psychological Violence

Psychological violence, or continued threats of physical or sexual attacks, is most difficult to identify. The most common form of psychological violence is intimidation. Such acts are usually for the perpetrator's material benefit.

The impact of psychological violence is commonly believed more damaging and more constant in prison inmates' lives than any other form of violent victimization. Because psychological intimidation and fear last long after perpetrators leave the targeted inmates' immediate presence, psychological violence impacts more than just the victims' immediate activities. Psychological victimization may extend into the period following release from prison.

Psychological violence may then appear to have no obvious benefits for anyone. However, perpetrators gain social status and a sense of power. These gains can then, in turn, be materially beneficial to perpetrators. So, in the end, psychological violence *is* a self-benefiting behavior, although the benefits might be realized only indirectly.

Economic Violence

Economic violence involves both property and personal crimes against inmates and provides direct material benefits to perpetrators. Common forms of economic violence are extortion, blackmail, robbery, burglary, and larceny. As discussed in Chapter 6, prison inmates are deprived of most material goods. However, all inmates do have valuables, whether these be the basic grooming and hygiene goods supplied by the institution or accumulated personal property (both legitimate and illegitimate).

Some inmates, especially those who are physically and socially stronger than others, may coerce others into forfeiting their goods or may simply steal from other inmates. After all, as most corrections personnel will remind you, they all have committed crimes on the outside, and now that they are in prison, why not continue such behaviors?

Inmates who are the likely victims of economic violence are largely those who are targets for physical, sexual, and psychological violence as well. One study of inmates in Ohio prisons reports that the inmate most likely to be a victim of property crimes is: "Anglo-American with at least a high school degree who has served over three-fourths of his sentence, (and) spends most of his day engaged in education, vocational training, and recreation."[18]

Again, the routine activities theory explains economic violence victimization. When compared with the characteristics of inmates most likely to be victims of physical violence, inmates' daily activities put them at risk for physical and economic violence. Theft is most likely for those inmates who have collected and are away from their possessions. So, inmates with material possessions who have work assignments, school, or other regular activities away from their cells or dorm areas are most likely to have things stolen.

Of course, economic violence is directly tied to other forms of violence. As discussed earlier, some inmates may be coerced into prostitution because they have no possessions or they desire additional possessions. Or, some inmates may be coerced (or physically forced) into sexual relations as a result of their indebtedness to others. Or, in retaliation for economic victimization, some inmates may use physical violence. Or, some inmates may display physical violence to protect themselves from economic victimization.

Organized Disturbances and Riots

Organized disturbances and riots have been part of U.S. correctional institutions since their earliest days. **Organized disturbances,** or planned and coordinated uprisings that are minimally disruptive and damaging, are more common than full-blown riots. For an uprising to be considered a **riot,** it must be an incident "when authorities lose control of a significant number of prisoners, in a significant area of the prison, for a significant amount of time."[19]

The Walnut Street Jail experienced organized uprisings, as did the first American attempt at incarceration in an abandoned mineshaft in Simsbury, Connecticut. In today's world, prison riots are not rare and unique events, although they also are not everyday occurrences. Between 1970 and 1990, over 300, or an average of slightly more than 1 riot per month, occurred nationwide.[20]

Prison riots tend to occur in waves. The twentieth century has had four distinct periods during which prison riots reached epidemic proportions. The first wave coincided with the outbreak of World War I and led to alterations in strict internal security measures and increases in "moral regeneration" activities.[21] The second wave occurred during 1929–1930, the start of the Great Depression. The next wave of prison riots came during the Korean War. This period saw an unprecedented number of riots. For instance, between April 1952 and September 1953, 40 riots occurred in the United States, exceeding the total number recorded in the preceding 25 years.[22] Finally, accompanying the civil rights movement, the birth of the prisoners' rights movement, and the general sense of social upheaval of the 1960s and early-1970s, prison riots reached record numbers.

Our systems of immediate and mass communication lend a new, interesting facet to the pattern of prison disturbances and riots in today's society. One prison uprising can commonly trigger other prison disturbances and riots. This is clearly seen in the repercussions of uprisings at the State Prison of Southern Michigan in 1981 and in 1993 at Lucasville, Ohio. These uprisings were quickly followed in

Organized disturbances Planned and coordinated uprisings that have only minimal disruptive and damaging effects.

Riot An incident when authorities lose control of a significant number of prisoners in a significant area of the prison for a significant amount of time.

prisons elsewhere. The implication for correctional staff is clear: Whenever a prison, anywhere, experiences a riot, security demands a tightening of control.

What appears is a sad truth: While not rare events, disturbances and riots cannot be fully anticipated. This means that correctional staff may not be able to avert impending uprisings. Consequently, correctional staff must recognize as a reality the possibility of uprisings, at any time and place. In the words of Dinitz: "Like seismologists, we are aware of the internal rumbling and the occasional belching of fumes, but powerless to prevent the periodic 'blowouts' and violent eruptions."[23]

Disturbances and riots are uniquely individual events. The causes, courses, and consequences of riots vary widely. The following discussion elaborates on these differences, as well as on the similarities across disturbances and riots.

Explanations for Violence in Prison

Explanations for why violence occurs in prison are often complex and frequently contradictory. However, many of them are worthy of our consideration. We will examine these explanations: Prison inmates are simply violent by nature; violence is a necessary adaptation to conditions of deprivation; gangs are a major cause of violence; overcrowding leads to violence; and the high incidence of mental illness among inmates explains the high incidence of violence.

Violent Inmates

One common, apparently logical explanation for violence in prisons focuses on the violent natures of the inmates themselves. According to this view, because many prison inmates have histories of violent behavior, this behavior is expected to continue when individuals are confined with other, also violent people.

This explanation is apparently logical when these facts are considered: Over the last four decades the frequency and severity of violent acts in prisons have increased, and this has accompanied increases in the number of violent inmates incarcerated. Violence is not, of course, characteristic of all prison inmates. Those with histories of violence on the streets and who possess certain social statuses are the most likely to be violent. Examinations of which prison inmates are good candidates for violence show that common characteristics include: younger, nonwhite, having parents who divorced before the inmate reached 16, no father figure, low educational achievement, prior incarceration (either adult or juvenile), first arrest by age 12, and a history of disciplinary problems while incarcerated. In other words, the violent inmate usually has an unstable background and a long history of violence.

So, this explanation suggests that inmates do not normally *become* violent while incarcerated. Instead, violence in prison is simply a relocated version of violence from the outside.

Prison Gangs

A variation on the "violence is due to violent people" explanation focuses more specifically on the presence of particular types of violent inmates: gang members. Many people believe that **prison gangs** are based on racial and ethnic divisions. While this is frequently the case, it is not always true. Prison gangs are often extensions of gangs in the free community. When incarcerated in the same prison, several members of a street gang reinitiate gang activities and recruit new members.

Prison gangs exist in almost all U.S. correctional systems. The exceptions are the least populated and least urban states (Montana, North and South Dakota, Vermont, and Wyoming). Gangs are also in federal prisons. According to some estimates, as many as 6 percent of federal prison inmates may be members of prison gangs. A survey by the American Correctional Association in 1992 identified 1,153 gangs with more than 46,000 members.[24]

Prison gangs
Groups of inmates, usually organized along racial or ethnic lines, who victimize other inmates to improve the gang members' quality of life.

Prison gangs exist in nearly all U.S. correctional systems.

The most notable fact about members of prison gangs is that they are largely the same as non-gang members, at least in terms of personal and social characteristics. In comparison to nonmembers, members are slightly more likely to abuse drugs and alcohol, are slightly more likely (40% to 58%) not to have held a legitimate job, and have, on average, a greater number of juvenile court referrals. In addition, gang members have significantly more arrests as adults and are more likely to have used weapons during the crimes for which they are incarcerated.[25] Gang members also have more disciplinary infractions, especially for fighting or abusing drugs (but not other forms of contraband) and are less likely than nonmembers to participate in prison programs.

Prison gangs present management difficulties for prison administrators. A 1992 nationwide survey of 316 prisons concluded that more than 1 in 4 institutions "expressed the belief that prison gangs had significantly affected their correctional environment."[26]

Institutions with higher security levels are more likely to house gang members and to have associated problems. A full one-quarter of prisons indicate that gang members present problems by threatening staff. However, only one-tenth of prisons report any assaults by gang members on staff.

Gangs in prisons clearly present numerous difficulties, both in their propensity for violence and in their often uncooperative approach to the incarceration experience. This problem is not fading, though. Throughout the coming decades correctionalists will have to cope with the presence and presented difficulties of gangs.

LEGAL BRIEF:

Knight v. Gill, 999 F.2d 1020 (6th 1993).

On December 9, 1989, Wilford Knight, an inmate at the Luther Luckett Correctional Complex in Kentucky was attacked by his cell mate, John Loran. In attacking Knight, Loran poured boiling water on him.

Knight brought suit against several prison officials, claiming that they violated his Eighth Amendment rights when they denied his repeated requests to be permanently moved to a new cell. Instead of a permanent move, Knight was offered a temporary transfer to a protective custody unit where his privileges and movements would be severely cut back. Knight refused this move. He argued that since Loran had previously been under psychiatric care for violent behavior in the institution, his requests for a permanent transfer being denied constituted cruel and unusual punishment. His argument was based on the idea that the responsible officials showed deliberate indifference to his welfare.

The Sixth Circuit U.S. Court of Appeals ruled in 1993 that the prison's offer of a temporary move, to prevent Knight from being victimized, meant that it did show a good-faith effort to protect him. Therefore, Knight's claim that prison officials had acted "wantonly" in disregarding his safety and welfare was unfounded.

Adaptations to Deprivation

Some inmates' violent actions are simply attempts to cope with the new, stressful environment of prison. Many inmates, especially those who once had luxurious possessions and significant power, endure great hardships when imprisoned. When incarcerated, these inmates may find deprivation of so many important aspects of their lives too difficult. They may reestablish some semblance of their pre-prison lifestyles by exerting power over others. Having power allows them to regain some of their social clout. Also, with power inmates can accumulate personal possessions that, while not nearly what they possessed on the outside, are more and better than those of other inmates.

Inmates may turn to violence to resolve feelings of both absolute and relative deprivation. **Absolute deprivation** is that state when people simply do not have adequate resources for survival. More commonly, inmates use violence to avoid feelings of **relative deprivation.** This is the condition of having less than others in the same environment, regardless of the actual amount of possessions and resources owned. Remember: Survival in prison depends on one's image of power and strength. To have less than others may be interpreted as a sign of weakness. More accurately, having more "stuff" than others is likely to be interpreted as a sign of strength. Violence is both easily accessible and important in constructing an image of strength. Therefore, many inmates will turn to violence to overcome their sense of deprivation.

Absolute deprivation The state of not having sufficient resources to survive.

Relative deprivation The state of having less than others in the same environment with whom individuals compare themselves.

Overcrowding

One controversial explanation for prison violence centers on the issue of overcrowding. When the number of inmates in a correctional institution significantly exceeds the facility's housing capacity, many observers believe that violence is an expected consequence. Overcrowding may lead to violence as inmates have even less privacy and

Tents are often used in warm climates to relieve overcrowding.

opportunity to escape interactions with large numbers of other inmates. Considering the fact that those with whom one is forced to interact are probably violent people, who seek to overcome experienced deprivations and who may be mentally ill, the increased potential for violence in an overcrowded institution becomes clear.

That most U.S. prisons are overcrowded is simply a fact of life in contemporary corrections. However, our courts have also found some prisons to be so overcrowded that their conditions violate the Eighth Amendment protection against cruel and unusual punishment.[27] Our courts have interpreted the Eighth Amendment to include a guarantee of a "healthy habilitative environment."[28] One central component of such an environment is adequate living space. In early court cases about overcrowding, the courts adopted the standards of the American Public Health Association. These standards require a minimum of 60 square feet per inmate in cells and a minimum of 75 square feet per inmate in a dormitory arrangement.[29] However, in later challenges to prison conditions, these standards were abandoned in favor of those requiring less space.

When overcrowding is so severe as to make violence likely, correctional officials are in violation of constitutional standards. The courts have ruled them as exhibiting deliberate indifference to their obligation to protect inmates from attacks.[30] These legal rulings rely on both social science data and common sense. When inmates are crammed into increasingly crowded facilities, they are likely to resort to violence both to protect themselves and to establish their individuality (and to overcome increasingly severe deprivations).

High Incidence of Mental Illness

Most correctional workers staunchly believe that many inmates have mental illnesses. However, accurate estimates of the prevalence of mental illness among inmates are difficult to make. Research literature

JOB FOCUS: CORRECTIONAL COUNSELOR

Because a large number of prison inmates have mental illnesses or problems in dealing with others, people trained as counselors are greatly needed in our prisons. A correctional counselor works with inmates both individually and in groups to guide them in making decisions about their lives and to work through problems.

Qualifications for a correctional counselor include a bachelor's degree. In most jurisdictions a master's degree is either required or preferred. The degrees usually need to be in some human services field such as social work, counseling, psychology, or education. More important than the academic degrees are personal abilities and skills. Correctional counselors must work effectively with a wide array of persons and be able to handle large amounts of stress.

Correctional counselors are paid on a very broad scale. Depending on the actual qualifications possessed and the institution's specific needs and resources, correctional counselors' pay can range from $17,000 to start to perhaps $40,000. If individuals have professional credentials (such as a licensed psychologist), their pay can be as high as $90,000.

Source: U.S. Department of Labor, Bureau of Labor Statistics, *Occupational Outlook Handbook*, 1994–95 ed., p. 126.

has reported anywhere from 1 percent to 77 percent of prison inmates have a "mental illness."[31] Such discrepancies, of course, result from varying definitions of mental illness and when these criteria can be diagnosed in individuals. Most common among mentally ill inmates are **neurotics,** those with milder forms of illness, or people who are "in contact with the real world but extreme anxiety usually interferes with an ability to deal effectively with it."[32] From 0.3 percent to 40 percent of prison inmates have neuroses, while **psychotics,** the more seriously disturbed inmates, account for between 1 percent and 7 percent of prison populations.[33]

Violence is common not only among inmates with mental illnesses, but also among those who are mentally retarded (developmentally disabled). Some estimates suggest that as many as 10 percent of prison inmates have some degree of mental retardation.[34] In comparison to the mentally ill, the mentally retarded have more difficulties understanding complex (and sometimes simple) tasks and may not possess the capabilities to understand and abide by social norms. This also means they can be easily manipulated and easily convinced to do things that are prohibited or dangerous. Also, other inmates target the mentally retarded for sexual, economic, and psychological victimization.

Neurotics Individuals with milder forms of mental illness and whose extreme forms of anxiety interfere with their abilities to effectively cope with daily life.

Psychotics Seriously disturbed, mentally ill people who experience reality differently than do individuals who are not mentally ill.

Prison Riots

One form of prison violence easily captures the public's attention: the prison riot. Rioting prisoners are often perceived as the greatest threat to public safety. However, the likelihood of a mass escape, or even individual escapes, during a riot is minute. When a riot breaks out, correctional and law enforcement officials respond immediately and en masse, and armed personnel—including the National Guard—will often surround the facility. Escapes simply do not happen during riots; the general public is not in danger. Those in danger are the inmates and any staff taken hostage or trapped inside the prison.

Not all prison riots are similar in form or process. Some riots may be designed to call attention to conditions within the institution; some may be symbolic retaliations toward correctional and political officials; or, as sadly appears to be the recent trend, some may simply be opportunities for inmates to seek revenge on other inmates. Regardless of their targets, the inmates themselves suffer longest and perhaps most dramatically during and after a riot. The physical destruction from a riot is often very great and costly. Also, the facilities destroyed or damaged during a riot are often those that allow inmates opportunities for self-improvement and recreation. As summarized by Dinitz:

> By the perverse logic of prison rioters, the targets of destruction have been the school, shops, and infirmaries inside the walls. Counseling centers, chapels, and recreational facilities have been torched with regularity.[35]

Such acts naturally mean that inmates will be without many services and opportunities for prolonged periods of time.

We will now take an in-depth look at three prison riots. First, we will focus on the 1971 riot at Attica, where inmates were highly organized and sought political changes both within and outside the prison. Next, the extreme violence and destruction of the Santa Fe, New Mexico, riot of 1980 will be examined. Santa Fe signaled a sharp change in U.S. prison riots. Here, inmates never issued demands but focused their efforts on exacting revenge on other inmates. Finally, the related incidents at the U.S. Penitentiary at Atlanta and at the Alien Detention Center in Oakdale, Louisiana, in 1987 will be discussed. These riots were not only politically motivated, but they are also important for showing us the interrelatedness of prisons and the importance of both inmate culture and modern communications on prison violence. Each discussion focuses on a different geographical region, during different historical periods, and with quite different motivations, progressions, and results. However, the similarities in these events should be clear, despite the obvious contrasts.

Attica

Opened in 1931, the Attica Correctional Facility in upstate New York was the most expensive prison built to that date. Its 6,700-foot-long outside wall alone cost over $1.2 million in Great Depression dollar values! The prison's total cost was about $9 million, averaging approximately $4,500 per inmate. The prison had a maximum capacity of 2,370; at the time of the riot, it housed 2,254.

Attica's design is an interesting but—as was to be seen—poor one. Laid out in a square, the prison's four sides are known as Cellblocks A through D. Other buildings, including the administration building, stand outside the main square. A separate building, E block, houses infirm and elderly inmates. Inside the four cellblocks is a huge

The riot at Attica Prison in upstate New York occurred in 1971.

yard cut across by two enclosed and intersecting corridors, thereby cutting this huge yard into four smaller squares. The intersection of the corridors, known as "Times Square," provides access to the four yards and is a critical point in controlling the prison. At the time of the riot, only a single guard worked this crucial post.

After gaining control of A block, the rioting inmates captured B, C, D, and E blocks. The prison staff regained control of A, C, and E blocks. Therefore, the center of the riot activities was B and D blocks, and D block yard became the headquarters of the rebellion as well as the location of later negotiations.

The atmosphere at Attica before the riot was rather tense; and inmates, about 54 percent of whom were African-American, were demanding changes. At approximately 3:45 P.M. on September 9, 1971, as the inmates were flowing into the yards after work assignments, a minor misunderstanding broke out. This disturbance would later serve to ignite the four-day riot. When correctional officers tried to break up what they believed was a fight and to take the inmates to the segregation unit, the inmates escaped into the crowd. Later that night, the inmates believed to be involved in the fight were taken from their cells to segregation. However, rumors quickly spread that at least one of the inmates was beaten on his way to segregation.

The next morning, when returning from breakfast, inmates erupted into collective violence. The responsibility for overseeing the official reaction to the riot fell to Russell G. Oswald, commissioner of corrections, recognized as one of the most progressive correctionalists in the nation. Relatively quickly the negotiations became centered on a list of demands that the prisoners issued. (See Figure 8–2.) Commissioner Oswald met with the inmates and eventually agreed to 26 of the inmates' demands, but he refused to promise full **amnesty** (protection against prosecution). Oswald also requested that the hostages be released as a condition for further negotiations. The prisoners refused. Meanwhile, the army of state troopers, sheriff's deputies, and prison guards assembled outside the prison walls had grown to more than 1,000. On September 13, Commissioner Oswald made one last effort to negotiate an end to the riot, but the inmates refused to release their hostages by the Commissioner's 9 A.M. deadline.

At 9:46 A.M. a waiting helicopter was ordered to drop tear gas on the inmates. The police stormed into the area, firing at least 400 rounds. When the firing ended, 43 were dead—32 prisoners and 11 hostages (4 of whom were civilian employees). However, several after-the-fact investigations have supported the fact that the inmates had killed none of the hostages when the officials retook the prison.

Amnesty Protection against prosecution.

FYI

In July 1994, an inmate of the Southern Ohio Correctional Facility in Lucasville, Ohio, was sentenced to an additional 10–25 years after pleading guilty to participating in the beating death of another inmate during the 1993 riot at the facility.

Santa Fe

After Attica the public feared that prison riots would become highly politicized, extremely violent, and relatively frequent events.[36] Those fears were largely not met. After Santa Fe, Americans had their fears of rioting inmates rekindled. This time, however, the fears focused on the unthinkable—inmates imposed random, extreme degrees of abuse and suffering. Luckily, Santa Fe has not become the "model" for modern prison riots.

The Penitentiary of New Mexico was long known as one of the least desirable places to be incarcerated in the United States. Plagued

Figure 8–2 List of inmates' demands at the Attica riot.

1. Adequate food, water, and shelter.
2. Permission for prisoners to return to their cells voluntarily.
3. Application of the New York State Minimum Wage Law to inmate labor.
4. Appointment of an ombudsman (an impartial official who investigates complaints).
5. Freedom of political activity.
6. Religious freedom.
7. End of censorship of reading material.
8. Unrestricted communication with anyone outside the prison, at the inmate's expense.
9. Realistic rehabilitation programs.
10. A modernized educational facility.
11. An effective narcotics treatment program.
12. Adequate legal assistance.
13. Reduction of cell time; that is, more recreation.
14. A healthy diet; fewer pork dishes.
15. Adequate medical treatment; addition of Spanish-speaking doctors and other personnel to the staff.
16. Recruitment of black and Spanish-speaking officers.
17. A grievance commission with inmate representation and inmate power in decision-making.
18. Investigation of the charge that inmate funds had been taken over by the state.
19. Penal-law change to end the practice of administrative resentencing of parole violators.
20. Prompt parole violation hearings with legal counsel present.
21. Expansion of work-release programs.
22. Removal of screens between inmates and their visitors.
23. A maximum of 30 days in segregation.
24. An end to the practice of charging violation of parole for minor traffic offenses.
25. Access to outside doctors and dentists at the inmate's expense.
26. Supervision by the "observer committee" to make sure that the above demands were carried out.

by overcrowding, corrupt and frequently changing administrations, and powerful cliques of officers and administrators who intimidated inmates into informing on one another, Santa Fe was a place many inmates dreaded. All these factors, combined with a few others, culminated in the most violent prison riot in U.S. history on February 2 and 3, 1980.

The bloody riot at Sante Fe's Penitentiary of New Mexico occurred in 1980.

The riot actually began late on the evening of February 1. In one of the overcrowded open dorms (E2), a group of inmates were partying and getting drunk on homemade liquor. This group overtook four guards on their routine checks of the institution, thereby initiating the riot. These officers, as the first hostages, were stripped, bound, blindfolded, and beaten. More important, the inmates took the guards' keys to several other units in the prison. This allowed the E2 inmates to spread out and methodically take over the institution. Correctional officers were either taken hostage or forced to flee.

The critical point in the institution's capture, though, occurred when a mass of inmates descended on the control center, dragging a half-naked guard by a belt around his neck and demanding access to the control center. When the two officers inside refused, the inmates brutally beat the hostage. When the control center officers still refused them access, the inmates attacked the control center's bulletproof (but not shatterproof) window and easily broke it with pipes and fire extinguishers. As the officers inside fled, the inmates took control of all keys and lock controls.

Taking advantage of their access, the inmates found riot control gear (including tear gas grenades and launchers, batons, and helmets) and tools and torches being used to renovate one cellblock. The inmates subsequently used these tools to abuse the officer-hostages and, more important, to get revenge on personal enemies.

The inmates housed in the special protection unit of the institution, Cellblock 4, bore the brunt of the violence. Here were housed inmates known or believed to be **snitches,** the lowest of the low in the inmate social hierarchy. Inmates took special attention to torture and mercilessly kill many Cellblock 4 inmates. Although they treated hostages abusively, the inmates did not kill them during the riot. The system of social control that the penitentiary administrators regularly used focused on inmate informers. Therefore, rather than directing their rage against official captors, the inmates most hated the "traitors" among them and, consequently, chose them as the primary targets of their violence.

Negotiations were attempted throughout the riot. However, the inmates who formed the negotiation team had no authority in the prison. After the riot ended, many inmates claimed to have not known that negotiations had been taking place. Since hostages were not under any central group's control, they could not easily be used for bargaining. While some hostages were traded for concessions or released after especially brutal beatings,[37] others were assisted in escaping through torch-cut holes in cellblock walls.

Throughout the riot, a steady stream of inmates defected from the prison into secured areas. Many of them recognized the violence as too extreme and too dangerous. By the time authorities retook the prison, only about 100 of the total 1,136 inmates were still inside. After taking large quantities of pills found in the infirmary, many inmates were so drugged that they either slept through significant portions of the riot or were unable to actively participate. Also, those inmates in the honor dormitory declined to join the riot and jammed their entrance door to barricade themselves from those on the outside.

Inmates left a majority of the prison in total ruin. However, the targets for their destructive impulses appeared selective, as evidenced by the areas not significantly defaced. The inmates' library, the Catholic chapel, and the hobby shop were largely left intact. However, the administrative offices, the psychological clinic, and the cellblocks and dormitories were completely destroyed.

The riot has been attributed as being a direct cause of some significant improvements in the penitentiary's living conditions. In the years following the riot, overcrowding was reduced, correctional officer brutality was reported to have decreased, more programming options were offered, and the reliance on a "snitch" system was significantly reduced. In the end, 33 were dead; dozens of inmates and

Snitches Inmates who inform on other inmates to institutional officials; lowest of the low in the inmate social hierarchy.

staff suffered serious injuries; hundreds of inmates were beaten, raped, and abused; a prison was in ruins; more than $30 million in repairs had to be done; and New Mexico had to address a major political dilemma.

Oakdale, Louisiana/Atlanta, Georgia

Between November 21 and December 4, 1987, both the U.S. Penitentiary at Atlanta and the U.S. Detention Center at Oakdale, Louisiana, experienced lasting and related disturbances that at times resembled riots.[38] At both prisons, rioting Cuban inmates' actions were highly instrumental and goal-directed. At Oakdale, the primary reason behind the disturbance was a mass escape attempt. At Atlanta, the inmates' intentions were to take hostages and to demand access to mass media to air their grievances.

The Oakdale and Atlanta riots were the culmination of nearly 8 years of frustrations on the part of Cuban detainees (who were largely members of the 1980 Mariel boatlift out of Cuba) and repeated disturbances and violence at the 11 sites used across the country for housing the detainees while administrators made decisions and plans regarding the Cubans' possible release. Due to repeated small riots and destruction of property, the identified criminals among the Cuban detainees were consolidated at the U.S. Penitentiary at Atlanta.

The Cubans at Atlanta were housed in the penitentiary, originally constructed in 1902 and scheduled to be closed in 1981. However, because of the overcrowding attributed largely to the Cubans' influx, the prison was being renovated. While whole cellblocks were being renovated, inmates were either crowded into dormitories or moved to a converted Alien Detention Center in Oakdale, Louisiana. Oakdale was a "looser" institution; Atlanta was on lockdown status from November 1984 until 1986.

The announcement on Friday morning, November 20, 1987, that about 2,500 Cubans would be deported triggered the riots. The first real sign of trouble occurred on Friday evening at Oakdale. About 100 Cubans disrupted dinner by overturning food service trays and throwing food and other objects. This disturbance was quickly brought under control. However, later that evening when prison officials tried to remove the drunken instigator of the disturbance from his unit, other inmates turned the staff back to protect him from expected abuse. Throughout Saturday, inmate informants repeatedly told staff that problems would break out that night. However, because

The Atlanta riot occurred in 1987.

the Cubans were notorious but unreliable snitches, the staff disregarded these warnings.

When the 4 P.M. shift came on duty on Saturday, they were warned of the rumors and issued mace and handcuffs. The rumors proved to be true. At 6:45 P.M. in response to a preplanned signal, between 200 and 300 Cubans, many armed with small weapons, rushed the front entrance to the building. A riot squad on standby repelled the growing mass of inmates for two charges, but the squad was forced to retreat by a third charge. By their third charge, the detainees had picks, axes, pipes, and other "weapons" taken from buildings housing the prison industries. The Cubans had also set numerous fires throughout the detention center.

When things settled and officials acknowledged that the detainees had control, 10 of 14 buildings were destroyed, 28 people were presumed to be hostages, and the prison administration recognized that their attempt to control rising tensions via "talking" and "calming" had been a mistake.

The following day, Sunday, the Cubans struggled to find leadership to negotiate with officials. Essentially no movement occurred. On Monday, negotiations took place, and the Cubans were assured that a storming of the prison would not occur. The inmates frequently moved hostages about, welded closed several doors (this would also happen at Atlanta), and made knives, swords, and machetes as weapons. The Oakdale riot ended by negotiation with no major violent incidents occurring after the initial takeover.

In the wake of the Oakdale difficulties, officials at Atlanta called in extra staff during the first weekend of the riots. This was necessary as the Cuban detainees heard of the Oakdale riots essentially at the same time the officials did via the mass media.

On Sunday, correctional officers and other staff heard rumors of impending violence. Again, due to the Cuban snitches' reputation for unreliability, administrators gave little weight to this information. However, as rumored, while at work assignments on Monday morning at approximately 10:30, the Cubans methodically took over the institution. The Atlanta warden took one significant step to quietly evacuate the women from the general units of the penitentiary. As the Cubans took over, they rounded up staff as hostages, produced weapons, and quickly had control of the entire prison with the exceptions of the administration building and two large cellblocks at the front of the facility. The Cubans took and protected 102 hostages, who represented their means to demand access to the media.

Over the siege's course, the Cubans released several small groups of hostages but held the remaining hostages in several groups located throughout the detainee-controlled prison. Finally, on December 4, 1987, the Cubans released the remaining hostages, and the Federal Bureau of Prisons regained control of the U.S. penitentiary.

Explanations for Prison Riots

There are a number of explanations for why prison riots occur. However, scholars of corrections have never reached consensus regarding an explanation for prison riots. As the preceding discussions make clear, prison riots break out for a number of reasons.

As early as 1953, the American Prison Association (now the American Correctional Association) established a committee to study the causes of prison disturbances. After consultations with correctional administrators across the United States, the committee listed seven basic causes of prison riots:

1. Inadequate financial support
2. Substandard personnel

3. Enforced idleness

4. Lack of professional leadership and programs

5. Institutions that are too large and overcrowded

6. Political domination and motivation of management

7. Bad sentencing practices

Most striking about this list: Most of these conditions have changed very little in the past five decades. Therefore, it should be no surprise that these same conditions are central in most current theoretical explanations for prison riots. The following discussion focuses on five frequently advanced explanations for prison riots.

Environmental Conditions The most commonly cited reason for the outbreak of prison riots centers on poor physical and social conditions. This explanation, relied on in whole or in part by most after-the-fact investigations, argues that inmates riot to force officials to improve the deprivations and unsatisfactory conditions of prison life.

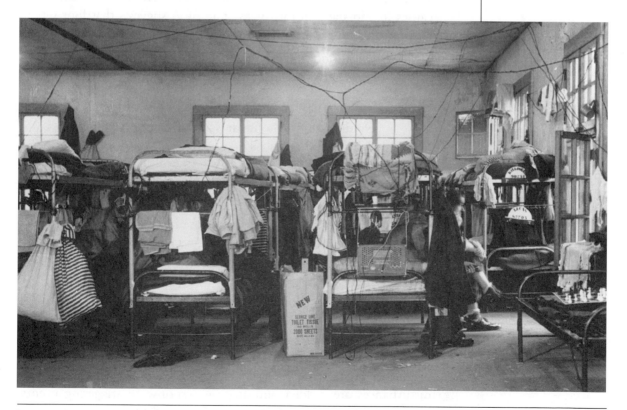

Many riots are a result—in part—of poor physical conditions within the prison.

Investigations of riots try to identify the "causes" that can either be eliminated or "fixed" to avoid future riots. By pointing to aspects of the physical facility or personnel, officials can easily devise plans of action to prevent future acts of collective violence. Among the most commonly cited environmental factors that instigate riots are:

- Poor, insufficient, and/or contaminated food
- Overcrowding
- Lack of professional leadership in the institution
- Substandard training of staff (especially in communication skills)
- Inadequate or absent treatment programs
- Lack of recreational, vocational, educational, and work opportunities/programs
- Presence of gangs
- Public indifference to conditions

Regardless of how observers explain riots, prisons' environmental conditions must bear at least some of the blame. This is clear in the 1981 American Correctional Association's (ACA) classification of causes for riots and disturbances. The ACA suggests that four sets of factors contribute to riots:

1. Institutional environment
2. Characteristics of the inmate population
3. Administrative practices
4. Noninstitutional (outside societal) factors shaping prison policies and activities

Obviously, the first three sets are conditions of the prison environment, and the fourth influences the shaping of the other three.

However, environmental conditions typically cited as causes of prison riots do not usually apply to those institutions that have riots. The question, then, must be: In addition to such environmental conditions, what special combination of factors or what other factors lead to a riot?

Spontaneity Model   One explanation, which is really no explanation, says that prison disturbances are essentially unplanned, spontaneously occurring events. Rather than conscious reactions to inhumane conditions or attempts to force change in institutional policies, inmate disturbances are sudden outbursts in response to triggering events. The spontaneity model suggests that while disturbances may occur with some frequency, only a select few disturbances will progress into full riots.

When we view riots as out-of-control disturbances, we must study the immediate set of circumstances that facilitate riot development. This means we must consider both **predisposing factors** and **precipitating factors**.[39] The constantly present environmental conditions that impose stresses and deprivations predispose inmates to riots. While routines and relatively uneventful days are present in predisposing factors, the impact of a precipitating factor triggers rioting. Precipitating factors may range from an attempt to lock down an institution to a minor scuffle between inmates or between inmates and staff. Once a precipitating event begins, the energy may quickly spread, incorporating more inmates and quickly growing out of control.

When it erupts, a riot has a natural life cycle. Fox has proposed a five-stage model for prison riots:[40]

1. Explosion (the precipitating factor).

2. Organization (as inmates communicate and draw more people and territory into the riot).

3. Confrontation (the period of facing off with officials, whether through demands, negotiation, or defiance).

4. Termination (the retaking of the institution either by force or negotiated agreement).

5. Reaction and explanation (the post-event investigations, political fallout, and steps toward implementing any changes in the facility).

Even though this model establishes the basic, expected progression of events, a vast amount of latitude is still available for individual riots to develop differently. This is the core of the spontaneity model: We must examine the immediate, uniquely individual sets of circumstances involved in a riot to explain why it occurred. Disturbances are largely sudden and unplanned, and may or may not grow into full-fledged riots.

Conflict Model The conflict model is based on the assumption that the official forms of control and repression typical in prisons have two consequences that may contribute to a riot. First, official use of social control creates value conflicts between the institution officials and the inmate population. Neither side understands nor fully accepts the other's actions and apparent values. Second, the structural nature

Predisposing factors
Circumstances in an institution that make people willing to take action to change conditions.

Precipitating factors
Circumstances that trigger actions.

whereby one group holds total (or near total) control over another group imposes on the controlled group a severely limited range of available means to express dissatisfaction.

This theory says we should not be surprised when inmates turn to collective action in such an environment. Violence should not be viewed as abnormal, perverse, or pathological. Instead, we need to review the options inmates have for expressing their value differences and the means they have for better understanding and changing those conditions with which they are dissatisfied. Inmates have very limited options. Collective violence is one of the few potentially effective means of expression.

Also, the prison culture emphasizes strength, power, and control. This is evident both within the inmate society and in how institutional officials maintain security and order. Therefore, inmates are cut off from "normal" avenues of expression and on a daily basis are shown models that use repressive powers and force to achieve goals. Therefore, violence is construed as a "normal" response to frustrations and difficulties. When a riot erupts, then, we should not be surprised. Instead, we should have expected it.

Collective Behavior/Social Control Model   This explanation focuses on riots erupting when the institution's daily social control processes are disrupted. The breakdown in social control means that inmates have no structure to guide their basic interactions. To fill this absence, some inmates may take control and impose their wills on officials and other inmates.

This argument hinges on the idea that a correctional institution's primary control mechanism is not force but, instead, a web of informal and reciprocal social relationships. In other words, inmates and staff maintain control in prison by silently agreeing to cooperate with one another and to trade favors. When something—a policy change, a staffing change, a crackdown on contraband—disrupts the relationships inmates and staff have negotiated, the delicate balance of power in place is threatened.

Whenever change occurs, stress follows. In prison this stress may be magnified because of the restricted range of options and experiences available to inmates. So, when inmates perceive a threat to the balance of power, they may logically respond in one of two general ways. Inmates may either work to restore the balance, or they may see an opportunity to improve (if only temporarily) their condition and therefore act (riot) to achieve such goals.

Riots, then, result from a correctional institution's breakdown in either its formal or informal control mechanisms. When no stable, recognized power structure exists, we should expect some or all of a prison's inmates to act to fill the resulting void.

Rising Expectations/Relative Deprivation Model   Similar to the collective behavior/social control model is the rising expectations/relative deprivation model for explaining prison riots. Whereas our previous theory says that change induces stress, this explanation focuses more specifically on how change causes the stresses that may culminate in riots.

Rising expectations/relative deprivation explanations suggest that when people believe a sizable gap exists between what they believe they deserve or should have and what they actually receive, they will experience high levels of frustration and perceive themselves as significantly deprived. The rising expectations portion of the explanation enters when a group of people who are slowly realizing improvements in their social conditions, have their progress suddenly and unreasonably stopped.

Applying these ideas to prison, inmates see the conditions of their lives improving, have reason to believe that these improvements will continue to develop, but suddenly have these improvements stopped or removed. The inmates feel highly deprived. The most obvious example of curtailing inmates' rising expectations is when officials tighten security and reduce their tolerance of contraband, sex, and activities for inmates. In response to these experienced frustrations, inmates may take collective action to convince officials to reinstate the improved (at least from the inmates' perceptions) conditions.

Summary

Commonly occurring in U.S. prisons, violence is performed by both inmates and correctional staff. However, most violence is contained within the inmate population. The goal of inmate violence—whether physical, sexual, psychological, economic, individual or collective—is to gain/maintain power and self-determination. Correctional staff use violence as one of several available means to maintain order, while inmates rely on actual or threatened violence as their primary available tool to maintain their culture.

The reasons for violence in prisons include factors unique to both the individuals' and to the institutions' physical conditions. Theoretical explanations also focus on factors both imported to the prison and created within the boundaries of the sociocultural system. Inmates are often violent individuals to begin with, so their violence inside is expected. Similarly, when gang members are moved to prison, they often continue their gang activities. A high percentage of inmates have diagnosable mental illnesses, which may lead to violent episodes. Generated within the prison, some factors such as overcrowded conditions and deprivation of material goods and services contribute to violence.

Prison riots, the most feared forms of prison violence, are situations in which inmates collectively take control of institutions. Riots and their less serious counterpart, organized disturbances, may be inmates' attempts to force changes in physical, cultural, and psychological conditions. However, as evidenced at Santa Fe, riots may arise spontaneously or result from inmates' attempt to address conditions by which their captors interact with them and maintain control.

Violence is a common feature of prison life. Attempts to control or at least limit violence within a correctional institution is one of the major challenges facing the modern correctionalist. If any of corrections' explicit goals are to be achieved and if the state's responsibilities are to be fulfilled, violence must be kept in check.

QUESTIONS FOR REVIEW

1. What are the most common forms of prison violence?
2. What factors contribute to the likelihood of victimization for inmates?
3. How does violence function to maintain order in prison?
4. What are the differences between prison disturbances and riots?
5. Why does violence occur in prison?
6. In what ways do overcrowding and limiting personal property contribute to inmate violence?
7. How common is mental illness, and what are its effects in the prison inmate population?
8. How have the frequency and form of collective violence in prisons evolved?
9. How are the riots at Attica, Santa Fe, and Oakdale, Louisiana/ Atlanta, Georgia similar and different?
10. Why do prison riots occur?

ACTIVITIES

1. Role-play ways for correctional officers to calm potentially violent inmates.
2. Write a plan for activities and policies to minimize the amount of violence in a prison.
3. Obtain a copy of a local prison's riot control plan. Review the plan and suggest how it could be improved.

ENDNOTES

1. John Wooldredge, "Correlates of Inmate Victimization in Ohio Correctional Facilities," paper presented at the annual meeting of the American Society of Criminology, San Francisco, November 1991.

2. Kenneth Adams, "Prison Violence: A Longitudinal Study of Inmate Behavior," paper presented at the annual meeting of the American Society of Criminology, Baltimore, Maryland, November 7, 1990.

3. *Ibid.,* p. 2.

4. U.S. Department of Justice, *Sourcebook of Criminal Justice Statistics, 1993* (Washington, D.C.: Bureau of Justice Statistics, 1994).

5. Frank J. Porporino, Phyllis D. Doherty, and Terrence Sawatsky, "Characteristics of Homicide Victims and Victimizations in Prisons: A Canadian Historical Perspective," *International Journal of Offender Therapy and Comparative Criminology,* Vol. 31, No. 2, 1987, pp. 125–135.

6. Richard C. McCorkle, "Fear of Victimization and Symptoms of Psychopathology Among Prison Inmates," *Journal of Offender Rehabilitation,* Vol. 19, No. 1–2, 1993, pp. 27–41.

7. Richard C. McCorkle, "Personal Precautions to Violence in Prison," *Criminal Justice and Behavior,* Vol. 19, No. 2, 1992, pp. 160–173.

8. *Logan v. United States,* 144 US 263 (1892).

9. Michael Agopian, "Inmate Violence Against Employees in the California Department of Corrections," paper presented at the annual meeting of the American Society of Criminology, Baltimore, Maryland, November 7, 1990.

10. Kelsey Kauffman, *Prison Officers and Their World* (Cambridge, MA: Harvard University Press, 1988).

11. *Ibid.,* p. 61.

12. Alan J. Davis, "Sexual Assaults in the Philadelphia Prison System," in J. H. Gagnon and W. Simon (eds.), *The Sexual Scene* (New York: Aldine, 1970).

13. Daniel Lockwood, *Prison Sexual Violence* (New York: Elsevier, 1980); Wayne S. Wooden and Jay Parker, *Men Behind Bars: Sexual Exploitation in Prison* (New York: Plenum Press, 1982).

14. Leo Carroll, "Humanitarian Reform and Biracial Sexual Assault in a Maximum Security Prison," *Urban Life,* Vol. 5, No. 4, 1977, pp. 417–437; Anthony Scacco, *Rape in Prison* (Springfield, IL: Charles C. Thomas, 1975).

15. Richard Tewksbury, "Fear of Sexual Assault in Prison Inmates," *Prison Journal,* Vol. 69, No. 1, 1989, pp. 62–71.

16. U.S. Department of Justice, *Correctional Populations in the United States, 1990* (Washington, D.C.: Bureau of Justice Statistics, 1991); *Correctional Populations in the United States, 1991* (Washington, D.C.: Bureau of Justice Statistics, 1992).

17. *Correctional Populations in the United States, 1991. op. cit.*

18. Wooldredge, *op. cit.*

19. Bert Useem and Peter Kimball, *States of Siege: U.S. Prison Riots 1971–1986* (Oxford: Oxford University Press, 1991), p. 4.

20. *Ibid.*

21. Simon Dinitz, "In Fear of Each Other," *Sociological Focus,* Vol. 16, No. 3, 1983, p. 158.

22. *Collective Violence in Correctional Institutions: A Search for Causes,* (Columbia, SC: South Carolina Department of Corrections, 1973), Appendix B.

23. Dinitz, *op. cit.,* p. 155.

24. G. Camp and C. Camp, *Prison Gangs: Their Extent, Nature and Impact on Prisons* (Washington, D.C.: U.S. Department of Justice, 1985). American Correctional Association, *Gangs in Correctional Facilities: A National Assessment* (Washington, D.C.: The National Institute of Justice. n.d.).

25. Randall G. Shelden, "A Comparison of Gang Members and Non-Gang Members in a Prison Setting," *The Prison Journal,* Vol. 71, No. 2, pp. 50–60.

26. George W. Knox and Edward D. Tromanhauser, "Gangs and Their Control in Adult Correctional Institutions," *The Prison Journal,* Vol. 71, No. 2, p. 15.

27. Kim Ellis, "Prison Overcrowding, Inmate Violence and Cruel and Unusual Punishment," *Criminal Justice Journal,* Vol. 13, Winter 1991, pp. 81–99.

28. *Battle v. Anderson.* 564 F2d 388, 395 (10 Cir. 1977).

29. *Ibid.*

30. *Riley v. Jeffes,* 777 F2d 143, 146 (3rd Cir. 1985).

31. Anthony Swetz, Marcel E. Salive, Thomas Stough, and T. Fordham Brewer, "The Prevalence of Mental Illness in a State Correctional Institution for Men," *Journal of Prison and Jail Health,* Vol. 8, No. 1, 1989, pp. 3–13.

32. *Correctional Officer Resource Guide* (College Park, MD: American Correctional Association, 1983).

33. Ken Adams, "Addressing Inmates' Mental Health Problems: A New Direction for Prison Therapeutic Services," *Federal Probation,* Vol. 49, December 1985, pp. 27–33; J. Monahan and H. Steadman, "Crime and Mental Disorder: An Epidemiological Approach," in M. Tonry and N. Morris (eds.), *Crime and Criminal Justice: An Annual Review of Research, Vol. 4* (Chicago: University of Chicago Press, 1983).

34. B. Brown and T. Courtless, *The Mentally Retarded Offender* (Washington, D.C.: National Institute of Mental Health, 1971).

35. Dinitz, *op. cit.,* p. 158.

36. This discussion of the Santa Fe riot is drawn primarily from the following accounts: Useem and Kimball, *op. cit.,* pp. 85–113; Dinitz, *op. cit.,* pp. 155–167.

37. Some hostages were released when inmates feared they might die. If a hostage dies, all inmates involved in the riot might be charged with murder, thereby significantly lengthening their prison stays. Therefore, hostages in very poor physical condition are commonly released by rioting inmates.

38. This discussion is drawn directly from Peter L. Nacci, "The Oakdale-Atlanta Prison Disturbances: The Events, the Results," *Federal Probation,* Vol. 52, No. 4, 1988, pp. 3–12.

39. Vernon Fox, "Why Prisoners Riot," *Federal Probation,* Vol. 35, No. 1, March 1971, pp. 9–14.

40. *Ibid.*

CHAPTER 9

Corrections for Women

CHAPTER OBJECTIVES

In the previous chapters you have studied the general structure, purposes, and culture of corrections. This chapter addresses corrections for women. After reading this chapter, you will be able to:

1. Compare the amount and typical forms of crime committed by women with that of men.

2. Contrast and explain the reasons for the different rates of imprisonment for women and men, and explain reasons for these differences.

3. Trace the historical development of corrections for women in the United States.

4. Understand the goals and procedures of women's corrections.

5. Compare state-level correctional programming efforts for female offenders.

6. Explain the federal correctional system's programs for women offenders.

7. Discuss the unique experiences of incarcerated women who are mothers.

8. Understand the variety of rehabilitative programming options available to incarcerated women.

9. Identify the legal rights of women in prison.

10. Discuss the obstacles that women face after release from prison.

KEY TERMS

gender

status offenses

two-track system

cottage system

pseudofamilies

cocorrectional
institution

equal protection

life skills

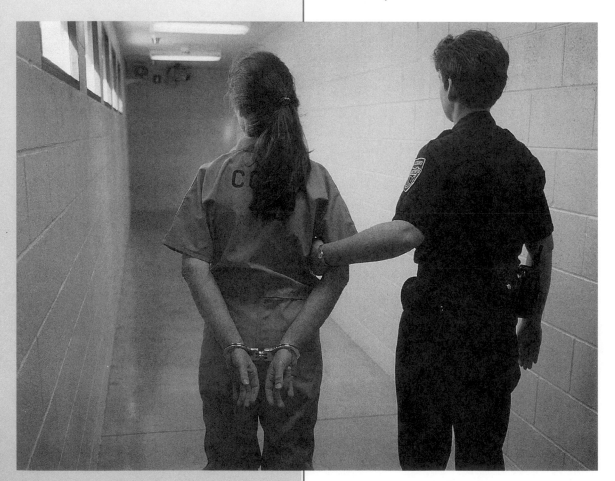

Crime rates among women have slowly risen over the past two decades.

The Extent of Female Criminality

Women's criminality has long been assumed a minor problem in our society. Traditional cultural beliefs and attitudes have held that women are too nurturing, soft, and sheltered to commit crimes in similar fashions and at similar rates as men do. Consequently, correctional efforts for women have largely been ignored. In fact, the ten-volume report produced by the 1967 President's Commission on Law Enforcement and Administration of Justice made no mention of female offenders.[1] Today, correctionalists recognize that women can and, in fact, do commit serious crimes, sometimes with great frequency.

Women's criminality has been historically viewed as largely biologically determined. While biological explanations for men's criminality have been harshly criticized, such explanations for women's crime have met little resistance. However, such theories and the research they produced fail to consider social influences. What we have are examinations exclusively of sex, not of gender. Sex, the biological component, may very well influence our behavior, but social scientists today strongly believe that our **gender**—our socially created roles, attitudes, and perceived "appropriate" activities—plays a greater role than biological sex in determining behavior.

Women today account for between 51 percent and 52 percent of our nation's population. However, women commit only 13 percent of all violent crime,[2] account for only 14 percent of all people under correctional supervision, and comprise only about 6 percent of all U.S. prison inmates.[3] These rates, however, have been slowly rising over the past two decades in response to women's changing social roles and to women's increasing participation in crime. According to some observers, women, especially younger, urban women, are not only becoming more involved in crime, but they are also becoming involved in forms and manners of committing crime more traditionally associated with men.[4] As we will see, this often means women are becoming heavily involved in drug-related crimes.

FYI

Although women commit only a minority of all violent crimes, violence by women has become a problem in our society. In 1993, arrests of women accounted for 9.4 percent of all murders, 15 percent of assaults, 8.5 percent of robberies, and 1.3 percent of rapes.

Source: Federal Bureau of Investigation, *Crime in the United States, 1993* (Washington, D.C.: Department of Justice, 1994).

Gender Social roles based on presumed qualities associated with a person's sex.

Women are becoming involved in forms of crime more traditionally associated with men, such as gang-related offenses.

There are those who hold that the resurgence of the women's rights movement in the 1960s, coupled with an increasing level of poverty among female-headed households, has led to women being more frequent participants in criminal activity. According to some theorists, this increase in criminality accompanies women's general movement into traditionally male roles. According to others, this is largely due to cultural conditions forcing women to turn to crime as a means of survival. Rita Simon[5] has argued that women's increased involvement in the workforce, as well as changes in attitudes toward women (as a result of workforce involvement), has led them into more frequent participation in crime.

Women's Offenses

Statistics on women offenders and women's offenses must be viewed skeptically. Many people believe that significant degrees of under-reporting and unofficial filtering mar any statistics on women's criminality. This is largely due to discretionary practices of law enforcement officials who elect not to arrest women in situations where they would most likely arrest men.[6] However, the most recent research suggests that it is not simply the offender's sex that influences such decisions, but instead it is women's display of "appropriately feminine" behaviors.[7] Or, as noted earlier, women's gender role performance, not biological sex, has more significant impact on our behavior. As one observer notes, "Police officers respond to female suspects on the basis of the image that they project, rather than the type of offense that they may have committed."[8]

Such attitudes and actions may very well prejudice the characteristics of women who are drawn into the criminal justice system. Overall, the characteristics of female offenders are not very different from those of male offenders. Female offenders tend to be poor, nonwhite, and undereducated. They also have children and histories of alcohol and drug abuse.

In 1993 a total of 2,290,420 women were arrested in the United States, accounting for 19.5 percent of all arrests.[9] (See Figure 9–1.) While the personal characteristics of male and female offenders are very similar, the offenses for which women and men are arrested tend to be very different. For instance, fewer women than men are arrested for all FBI index offenses. In 1993 men accounted for at least 84 percent of seven of the eight index offenses. The exception is the crime of larceny, for which men account for "only" 67 percent of the arrests.[10] The offenses for which women are most commonly arrested are larceny-thefts, prostitution, fraud, and embezzlement. However, since the early-1980s women's participation in violent crime has increased more rapidly than men's. During the 1980s men's violent

Figure 9-1 Distribution of all arrests, by gender.

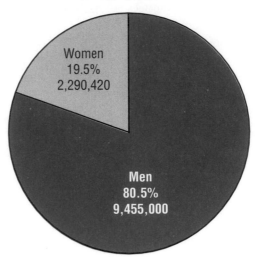

Women
19.5%
2,290,420

Men
80.5%
9,455,000

Source: Federal Bureau of Investigation, *Crime in the United States, 1993* (Washington, D.C.: U.S. Department of Justice, 1994).

crime rate increased 28 percent; women's, 33.6 percent. This means the rate of violent crimes by women increased at a rate 18.5 percent faster than that for men. Figure 9–2 shows the 1993 percent of index offense arrests for males and females.

As cited above, one study argues that women's increased presence in the workforce affords them greater opportunities to commit crime. However, data from the FBI indicate that there is *no* link between women's changing occupational roles and criminal behavior. Women's offenses (bad checks, credit card or welfare fraud, and larceny-theft) are not usually tied to work roles. Even in those occupations where women are the majority and opportunities to steal are common—such as retail sales—men are more likely to steal than women.[11]

The differences between women's and men's experiences with crime and criminal justice do not end at this point, however. Instead, the different experiences just begin. Discretion and, according to some observers, discrimination continue to occur after criminal cases reach the courts. Differences are most obvious at the stage of sentencing convicted offenders.

Research from the 1960s and 1970s on sentencing and gender revealed a general trend that women are treated more leniently than men. Most often this difference is explained as "chivalry-based" behavior. Women, as a group, are viewed as needing men's protection

Figure 9–2 Arrest rates for each index offense, by gender.

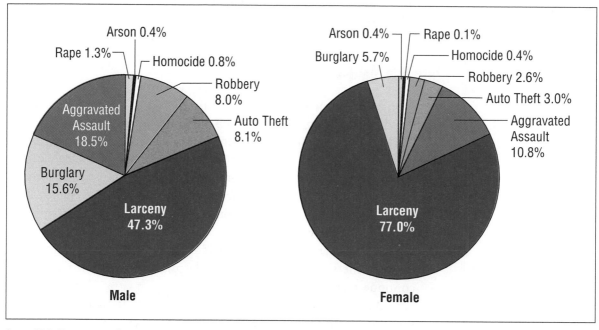

Male

Arson 0.4%
Rape 1.3%
Homocide 0.8%
Robbery 8.0%
Aggravated Assault 18.5%
Auto Theft 8.1%
Burglary 15.6%
Larceny 47.3%

Female

Arson 0.4%
Burglary 5.7%
Rape 0.1%
Homocide 0.4%
Robbery 2.6%
Auto Theft 3.0%
Aggravated Assault 10.8%
Larceny 77.0%

Source: U.S. Department of Justice, *Sourcebook of Criminal Justice Statistics, 1993* (Washington, D.C.: Bureau of Justice Statistics, 1994).

and special caretaking. However, leniency is not applied across the board to all women offenders. For instance, female defendants who are married and/or have children are treated more leniently than both their male counterparts and women who are not married and are childless.[12] In addition, one recent investigation using data from the mid-1980s suggests that an offender's gender does not necessarily influence sentencing. Instead, "judges are driven by two focal concerns, *blameworthiness* and *practicality*."[13] Also, juvenile girls are more likely to be referred to court for **status offenses**[14] and to receive harsher treatment than juvenile boys for lesser crimes, but the difference disappears for more serious offenses.[15]

Whether sentencing differences are based on assumptions about women's respectability or on beliefs about women's roles is a debate within corrections. This leads many, especially feminist, observers to argue that women do not receive leniency, but simply discrimination. Women are punished not only for violations of the law, but also for violations of "appropriate feminine behavior." Again, the importance of gender, not simply sex, is clear. The important points, regardless

Status offenses Acts of conduct that are illegal for juveniles but not for adults; activities that are illegal only because the individuals involved have the status of juveniles.

The Extent of Female Criminality

249

of how approached, are: Women are treated differently than men when sentenced, and women of different social statuses are treated differently.

Statistics on Female Incarceration

Women are a small but growing minority of U.S. prison inmates. At the close of 1994 a total of 64,403 women were inmates in the United States.[16] This number represents 6.1 percent of all inmates in our nation's prisons and a 16 percent increase over the 1993 female inmate population. As with the male inmate population, a large majority of female inmates (87%) are incarcerated in state prison systems. Most states have only a small number of women inmates; 23 states have fewer than 500 women inmates.[17] This means that while the percentage of inmates who are female is slightly increasing, the differences between the sizes of male and female prison population remain and continue to grow. (See Figure 9–3.)

As to race U.S. female inmates, like male inmates, show a disproportionately large population of minorities. As seen in Figure 9–4, white female inmates account for less than one-half of all female inmates. Furthermore, regions differ in racial compositions of female inmate populations, with the largest minority populations being in the South.

As women's incarceration rates increase and the proportion of female inmates slowly climbs, women inmates' criminal histories and sentences resemble those of male inmates. For instance, today more than two-thirds of women in prison are repeat offenders, with nearly one-third having three or more prior periods in prison or on probation.[18] One in ten female inmates is serving time on a sentence of more than ten years.[19] Thus, long-term incarceration issues will become more common and relevant to women's institutions.

Also reflective of women's increasing similarity to men's criminality, the number of women under the influence of drugs at the time of their offenses is increasing. In fact, among state prison inmates, women are actually *more* likely than men both to have used drugs during the month preceding the offense for which they are in prison and to have been under the influence of drugs at the time of their offense.[20] For instance, one-third of women inmates report drug use at the time of the offenses for which they are incarcerated.[21] Also, women are more likely to report using both powder and crack cocaine in the month leading up to their offenses.[22]

Figure 9–3 Growth in male and female inmate populations, 1980–1994.

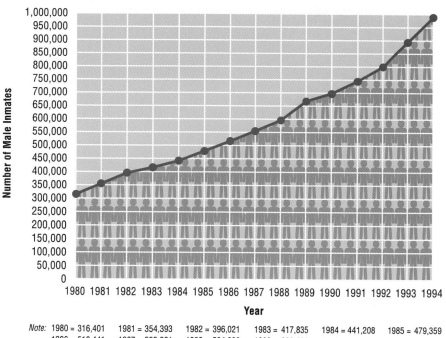

Note:
1980 = 316,401	1981 = 354,393	1982 = 396,021	1983 = 417,835	1984 = 441,208	1985 = 479,359
1986 = 518,441	1987 = 555,961	1988 = 594,996	1989 = 669,498	1990 = 699,416	1991 = 745,808
1992 = 800,676	1993 = 893,516	1994 = 989,335			

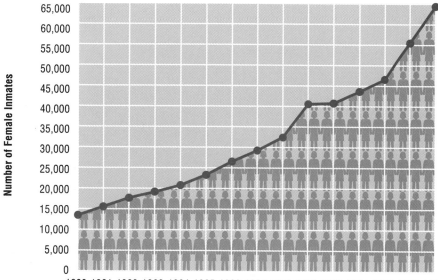

Note:
1980 = 13,420	1981 = 15,537	1982 = 17,785	1983 = 19,020	1984 = 20,798	1985 = 23,148
1986 = 26,531	1987 = 29,123	1988 = 32,592	1989 = 40,556	1990 = 40,564	1991 = 43,802
1992 = 46,595	1993 = 55,365	1994 = 64,403			

Sources: Lawrence A. Greenfeld and Stephanie Minor-Harper, *Women in Prison,* Special Report (Washington, D.C.: Bureau of Justice Statistics, 1991); U.S. Department of Justice, *Prisoners in 1993* (Washington, D.C.: Bureau of Justice Statistics, 1994); U.S. Department of Justice, *Prisoners in 1994* (Washington, D.C.: Bureau of Justice Statistics, 1995).

Figure 9–4 Race of female inmates by region, 1990.

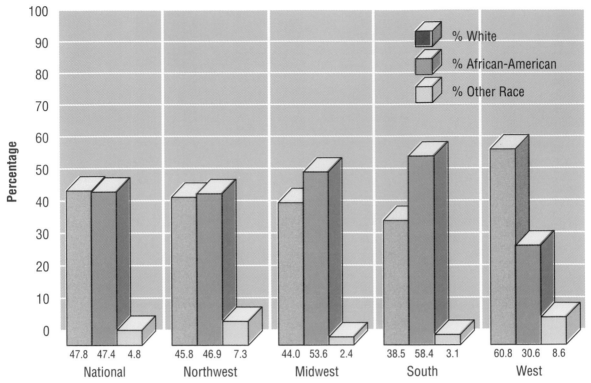

	White	African-American	Other Race
National	47.8	47.4	4.8
Northwest	45.8	46.9	7.3
Midwest	44.0	53.6	2.4
South	38.5	58.4	3.1
West	60.8	30.6	8.6

Source: U.S. Department of Justice, *Correctional Populations in the United States* (Washington, D.C.: Bureau of Justice Statistics, 1991), Table 5.8.

However, women inmates continue to differ from male inmates in terms of previous experiences as victims of sexual and physical abuse. Forty-one percent of all women inmates, most of whom are violent offenders, report having been sexually or physically abused.[23] Obviously, women in prison present a range of significant needs for a variety of counseling programs, as well as educational and vocational training programs.

The History of Women's Corrections

The history of women's corrections in the United States can best be summarized as an achievement of "partial justice."[24] That is, justice is only partial because two factors that differentiated women's corrections historically, as seen, continue to influence women in today's criminal justice system. First, prison administrators often reacted to women's rule infractions with greater leniency. However, while some situations were treated with more leniency, women were presented with a range of additional, often unmet needs and dilemmas. Second, women were numerically a small minority of all prisoners. Historically, this has meant that few, if any, institutions, personnel, and programs were devoted to the imprisonment of women. The options and opportunities for "correcting" women inmates frequently did not exist. Because there were so few women, institutions viewed it as a luxury to hire female staff or to devote a cellblock or building to female inmates.

This means that for a significant portion of U.S. and especially British history, from which our system evolved, women were confined either with men or simply in separate quarters within institutions for men. Therefore, women were either directly vulnerable to male aggression or completely isolated for their own protection. Consequently, women have historically been cut off from opportunities for visitation, exercise, social interactions, and sometimes even supervision.

Many early conceptions about female offenders rested on the idea that women were morally weak and needed a greater degree of supervision.[25] Male administrators used harsh discipline and greater degrees of control, because they believed women could not be trusted to control their behaviors. Women were oftentimes subjected to cruel and humiliating public punishments that intended to make them more obedient and subservient to their husbands.[26] In essence, adult women were considered less to blame for their actions than adult men for the same reasons children are not held fully responsible for their actions: they were considered incapable of such self-control.

British reformer Elizabeth Fry was the first person to address the unique problems of women in prisons. After visiting the Newgate Prison in 1813, Fry realized that the conditions in which women (as well as men and children) were housed were deplorable. As one historian says, women inmates in the early-1800s "were totally at the mercy of their male keepers and the male prisoners who contrived means to enter the women's ward."[27] For these reasons early feminists called for female administrators and staff during the development of institutions specifically for women in the United States. However, this was never fully realized, and even today, instances of sexual, psychological, and emotional abuse of women inmates by male staff occur.

In 1817 Elizabeth Fry returned to Newgate Prison and convinced the administrators and, more important, the imprisoned women to work with her to establish a school for the children within the women's ward. Later, Fry took her cause to the outside and organized the Ladies' Newgate Committee to gather clothing for the prisoners and later to obtain materials for teaching the imprisoned women to sew. Elizabeth Fry, then, is the mother of vocational training and prison industries for incarcerated women.

By the late nineteenth century, nearly all of the states had opened separate prison units for women. Many of these units were simply separate wings of men's institutions or free-standing buildings in or near the grounds of the men's prisons. These were attempts to free women from the problems associated with their being imprisoned with men. However, from the beginning these women-only facilities

> developed their characteristic tradition of inmate neglect. In them, prisoners received care inferior to that given their male counterparts. The further they were removed, the more were women cut off from personnel, who left the main prison to visit the female department only in emergencies.[28]

Two-track system
In women's corrections, the historical development of prisons and reformatories; both types of institutions were used for several decades, had different goals, and were designed to serve different types of inmates.

Women's corrections developed into a **two-track system** starting in the 1860s. The first of these two tracks, custodial prisons, were for women considered "lost" to habitual crime. As the second track, reformatories were for those women deemed salvageable. The reformatories viewed their women as needing guidance and treated them like children. The goals of reformatories were to instill "feminine values" in women convicted of petty offenses.

The two-track system of women's corrections lasted into the 1930s. By this time a number of states had established both a custodial prison and a reformatory for women. However, custodial institutions tended to have small populations, while reformatories for misdemeanants the correctional system wished to "save" were filled. Economic hardships during the Great Depression forced most states to combine their two institutions, generally moving custodial inmates to reformatories and converting the women's custodial institution into a prison for men. Also, by merging the women's institutions, most misdemeanant women were forced out of the correctional system,

LEGAL BRIEF:

Canterino v. Wilson, 546 F. Supp. 174 (1982).

In 1982 a major class-action lawsuit by Kentucky Correctional Institution for Women (KCIW) inmates was concluded. The ruling ended the use of management and treatment procedures in the Kentucky correctional system deemed to result "in massive disparities within Kentucky's penal system between male and female prisoners in the availability of privileges and opportunity to fulfill basic human needs."

The lawsuit challenged three major issues at KCIW: the use of the Levels System, availability of vocational education and training, and general conditions of confinement. The U.S. District Court found all three areas to be discriminatory against women in Kentucky and took greatest issue with the use of the Levels System. As a five-tier system in which inmates earned privileges based on nondisruptive behavior and staff evaluations, the system appears logical. However, none of the Kentucky men's institutions had a similar system. Even more important, many of the "privileges" women had to "earn" were taken for granted at the men's institutions. For example, because they were still classified as Level 1 or 2, over 50 percent of KCIW inmates were not allowed to display pictures of their families, were required to be in bed by 9:30 P.M., had to wear a "state dress" that was shapeless and admitted by prison administrators to be "demeaning," and were permitted only one 5-minute telephone call per month. However, male inmates in Kentucky had virtually unrestricted access to telephones, and inmates in disciplinary segregation at the maximum-security men's institution were allowed more visitation than most of the women at KCIW.

The court found that even Kentucky corrections administrators could not provide justification for the policies, observing "the Levels System is harmful to the [women inmates]. It is punitive and unsupported by any valid correctional goal." It then stated as its guiding principle that "male and female prisoners must be treated equally unless there is a substantial reason which requires a distinction to be made," the court struck down the KCIW policies. In concluding the case, the court remarked that "inferiority of programs and discrimination . . . are not always the result of conscious sex discrimination. They are often attributable to oversight, omission, and traditional views of female offenders, which have not kept pace with the changing inmate population."

thereby bringing the correctional systems for men and women onto more similar tracks.

However, not until the 1960s were women inmates able to successfully challenge sentencing laws in many states that provided both minimum and maximum times on men's sentences but specified no minimum and extended the maximum periods for women on similar offenses.[29] Similarly, not until 1982 did women successfully challenge sex discrimination such as rehabilitative schemes where "programming" was directly responsible for more punitive treatment of women. Numerous states, in their effort to train women offenders to be "proper ladies," had established systems that many considered discriminatory.

Women in Prison

As discussed earlier, until the nineteenth century all prisoners, regardless of offense, conviction status, age, or sex, were housed together. This began to change when prisons specifically for women opened. In 1873 the Indiana Reform Institute for Women opened, the first correctional institution specifically for females.

A 1916 view of the poultry yard at the Indiana Reform Institute for Women, which was opened in 1873.

In almost all instances, women inmates today are segregated from male inmates. However, a large number of male staff members work in women's prisons. When originally conceived, women's separate institutions were to be staffed and administered exclusively by *women.* However, because society lacked confidence in women's abilities to run a correctional institution, plans and laws were quickly altered to allow men to work in women's prisons.

Through the 1970s male staff were largely found in positions with minimal or no direct contact with inmates. However, by the 1980s men constituted 31 percent of correctional officers in women-only prisons, although this varied widely from no male correctional officers in Delaware and Arkansas to 81 percent male officers in Colorado.[30]

Women inmates generally do not oppose the presence of male staff members, even as correctional officers. Generally, female inmates are more receptive to supervision by men than are male inmates to supervision by women.[31] The few areas where women inmates express a preference for female correctional officers are those areas involving privacy: discussing personal problems, doing strip searches, and supervising shower and toilet areas.[32]

The Form and Structure of Institutions for Women

Women's correctional institutions are usually different in design, structure, and culture from men's institutions. Most notably, facilities for women tend to be rather small. No mega-prisons (population over 1,000) exist for women. Instead, women are typically incarcerated in institutions with fewer than several hundred inmates and live in settings that appear more similar to a college campus than a stereotypical "prison." Women's prisons are usually designed on a **cottage system** model and have historically emphasized small group (family-like) living arrangements. Rather than being in one large building, women are housed in separate buildings, each containing a dormitory or rooms for inmates, recreational facilities, and perhaps dining facilities. Women's institutions also expect inmates to be more responsible for maintaining the housing facility than men's institutions expect of their inmates.

Although changing somewhat in the 1990s, the emphasis on security and discipline in women's institutions is less than that in men's institutions. This is based on the belief that women are neither a significant escape threat nor likely initiators of violence. However,

Cottage system A housing pattern most common for women and juveniles; inmates are housed in house-like buildings, in small groups, and with staff who stay in the building, acting as "parents" overseeing the inmates' activities.

women inmates of the 1980s and 1990s have displayed aggressive and violent behavior more frequently than they did in decades past.[33] However, the proportion of aggressive or violent women inmates remains rather low. Also, the factors that generally predict which male inmates will be violent—age and drug use—are not significant predictors with women inmates. Instead, what appears most important is women's childhood family structures. Specifically, women inmates who were raised in homes with both parents present display greater likelihoods of violence while incarcerated, perhaps suggesting that more conflict was present in these homes than in homes where parents were separated.[34]

Daily life in a women's institution allows inmates more freedom of movement, encourages more interactions between staff and inmates, and devotes more time, energy, and resources to counseling and attempts to "help" women. The reformatory movement of the nineteenth century stressed these factors. This is not to say that more programs are available to women, but that there is more hope of rehabilitating women, primarily via personal interactions and informal socialization.

The culture of most women's prisons is more peaceful than that in men's. Contrary to many media portrayals, women's prisons have

An aerial view of a women's prison in South Carolina.

little violence, and inmates will frequently develop close friendships. One major difference between men's and women's prison cultures is the phenomenon of **pseudofamilies** within the women's prison. While not as common as in previous years,[35] the pseudofamily provides emotional, social, and material supports to women in prison. Groups of women develop social structures and roles based on the traditional roles in extended families, including "marriages" and male roles. Those women most in need of support and assistance in adjusting to incarceration—new arrivals—are most likely to become involved in such relationships.[36] In men's prisons, while some men may—either voluntarily or due to force and coercion—form one-on-one relationships, they do so for primarily sexual purposes, not to provide mutual support.

The issues surrounding same-sex sexual activity in women's prisons are very different from those in men's prisons. In institutions for men, homosexuals are severely stigmatized, and a small but significant number of men may be subjected to sexual assaults. In women's institutions, same-sex relationships are seen as a more normative adaptation to the conditions of incarceration, and sexual assaults are rare.[37] Lesbians and lesbian sexual activity are not necessarily stigmatized and devalued. Male prisoners despise homosexuality because such actions suggest one is "taking the role of a woman" and lowering himself in the gender hierarchy. These are not relevant issues in a world of women.

While women inmates may not have some of the typical problems found in men's prisons, they do face several situations and problems that male inmates do not commonly encounter. Specifically, all women within a jurisdiction are usually housed in one institution; so, classification schemes are difficult to maintain. Also, incarcerated women must usually cope with separation from their children, a situation that, while relevant to male inmates, impacts women more. Finally, women inmates have generally fewer programming opportunities, and often those offered are based on stereotypes of what a "lady" should know and be.

Next, we will examine several specific state correctional systems and the Federal Bureau of Prisons' corrections for women. After these overviews, we will review more specifically some of the unique factors involved in the incarceration of women.

State Systems

A great deal of disparity exists in the size and structure of state systems' correctional efforts regarding women. As mentioned earlier, most states have a relatively small number of women inmates and have only one prison for women. This means that clas-

Pseudofamilies A social phenomenon in women's prisons where inmates assume statuses and roles that create family-like situations; developed to offset the emotional and psychological differences between life in prison and on the outside.

sification, programming, and discipline must be handled differently than they are typically dealt with in regard to male inmates. In the following overviews of selected state correctional systems' efforts with women, these differences will become clearer.

Florida.[38] One of the nation's most populous female correctional systems, the state Department of Corrections in Florida houses approximately 3,100 female inmates in 4 major institutions. These 4 institutions range in size from just over 1,000 inmates to a small facility for only about 150 women. The cost of incarcerating a woman in Florida averages 142 percent the cost of incarcerating a man ($54.57 versus $38.29 per day, respectively).

The population of Florida's women's institutions is 36 percent white and 57 percent African-American.[39] Comprising just under 10 percent of all admissions to the Florida system, women tend to be under 30 and are most likely sentenced for possession, sale, or manufacture of drugs or for grand theft. However, nearly two-thirds of Florida's female inmates have sentences of 3 years or less. However, 5 women (3 white, 2 African-American) are on death row in Florida.

Texas. The state Department of Corrections in Texas is another of the nation's larger prison systems. Just over 7 percent of Texas' approximately 120,000 inmates are women (8,839).[40] Nearly all of Texas' women inmates (with the exception of those in hospitals, etc.) are housed in 1 of 2 facilities, both located north of Gatesville, Texas, just southwest of Waco. Both are fairly large institutions, with the Mountain View facility having a capacity of 653 and the Gatesville facility (including reception center) having a capacity of 1,781. Distinguishing itself as somewhat unusual, Texas operates a Special Alternative Incarceration Program (boot camp) program for women, a program usually reserved for young men.

Minnesota.[41] The state Department of Corrections in Minnesota, a much smaller department, houses approximately 250 women inmates in 2 different institutions. One facility is a minimum-security institution exclusively for women, and one is a **cocorrectional institution.**[42] While the female inmate population is comparatively small and accounts for only 5 percent of all Minnesota inmates, it has grown over 300 percent in the last 15 years. Because of this rapid growth, Minnesota was forced to open a unit for women at the Willow River/Moose Lake Correctional Facility, effectively making this a cocorrectional facility in 1990.

Kentucky.[43] The state Department of Corrections in Kentucky operates 1 facility for women, a medium-security institution exclusively for women. A total of approximately 650 inmates are in the

Cocorrectional institution An institution that houses both male and female inmates in different units of the institution.

Kentucky Correctional Institution for Women, of which 60 percent are white.[44] Women incarcerated in Kentucky are equally likely to be incarcerated for violent and property crimes (36 percent and 37 percent, respectively) and tend to have sentences of 5 years or less (41 percent of the population). However, 14 percent of inmates are serving sentences of life or longer than 20 years. In addition, just over one-half of Kentucky's incarcerated women come from the state's two largest counties (out of 120 total counties).

Federal Institutions   The Federal Bureau of Prisons houses women inmates in 14 different facilities. (See Figure 9–5.) Six of these are institutions exclusively for women, and 7 are cocorrectional institutions that house both men and women (in different units of the institution).

Of the total 7,410 females in the Federal Bureau of Prisons' custody on December 31, 1994, about one-third of the women were

Figure 9–5 Location of federal women's prisons.

at the Federal Medical Center in Lexington, Kentucky. The Federal Prison Camp at Alderson, West Virginia, the first and best known of the federal institutions for women, held 15 percent of the women under federal correctional supervision.[45]

The Federal Bureau of Prisons' flagship institution for women is the Federal Prison Camp at Alderson. Opened in 1928, Alderson was devoted to housing and attempting to rehabilitate the few women under federal correctional authority. Since its opening, Alderson has housed women with high rates of sexually transmitted diseases who are undereducated and who most likely have substance abuse problems. However, despite difficulties convincing the powers that be in the Federal Bureau of Prisons to accept them, Alderson initiated a range of innovations in classification procedures, treatment programs, and supervision of individual inmates' progress. Ironically, the federal system eventually adopted many of these programs as policy.[46]

An overwhelmingly large portion of the women inmates in federal prisons are sentenced for drug offenses. Women inmates have always presented higher rates of substance use than the general population. However, the nearly two-thirds (63.9%) of today's female federal prison population on sentences for drug charges is largely a development of the 1980s. As a point of comparison, only 56 percent of male federal inmates are incarcerated for drug violations. This is also a major difference when compared to women in state prisons. Most frequently, women in state prisons are serving time for property or violent offenses, with only 12 percent of women in state prisons serving sentences for drug-related offenses.[47] In 1981 only 26 percent of both women and men in federal prisons were serving time for drug offenses. This means the percent of federal inmates on drug-related charges more than doubled during the 1980s. These numbers tell us that when women commit serious criminal activity, they are more likely than men to involve drug offenses.

A majority, approximately 60 percent, of women in federal prisons are white, and nearly one-third are age 30 or younger. The average age of women in the federal prisons is 36, and only 4 percent of these women are elderly (over age 55). Perhaps the most significant difference between federal female and male inmates is the fact that 75 percent of the women are classified as minimum or low security, compared with only 49 percent of the men. Whether this indicates a real difference in the degree of danger that female versus male inmates pose, or this is yet another indication of a chivalrous approach to women in corrections, is open to debate.

Women Inmates as Mothers   Female inmate populations, both across jurisdictions and across history, have consistently been comprised of a majority of mothers. Today, more than three-quarters of women in prison are mothers, two-thirds of whom have children under the age of 18.[48] Women inmates are slightly more likely than male inmates to report having children. This means that women are more likely than men to have an additional, serious dilemma to cope with while incarcerated. Of necessity, someone else must care for the offenders' children, and women commonly report anxiety regarding whether their children will develop stronger bonds with their new caretakers and how their eventual reunions with their children will proceed.[49]

When a parent—especially of a minor child—is sent to prison, the family system, not simply the individual offender, feels the impact. Families of incarcerated offenders experience a range of social and personal problems and may explicitly blame the offender for their hardships. As summarized by one observer, "The major problems encountered by inmates' families are related to stigmatization, finances and housing, loneliness, management of the children, and visits with the inmate."[50] To combat the negative impacts of separating mothers and children when the mother is incarcerated, some states are experimenting with programs where children can stay overnight (or the weekend) with their mothers. This, of course, requires special facilities where the inmates can be kept in a secure setting but where the children can feel comfortable with their mothers.

Female inmates visiting with their children.

In addition, issues of who will care for the offenders' children must be addressed. Generally, when family members are available and willing, they will assume responsibility for an incarcerated woman's children. Incarcerated men's children almost always are cared for by the children's mother. However, incarcerated women rely more heavily on the children's grandparents or other caretakers. (See Figure 9–6.) This is not just a matter of concern for women inmates, though. As researchers focus attention on the experiences of incarcerated men who have children, evidence emerges that fathers in prison may very well experience depression and stress related to their parenting role.[51]

Figure 9–6 Where children are placed when a custodial parent is incarcerated.

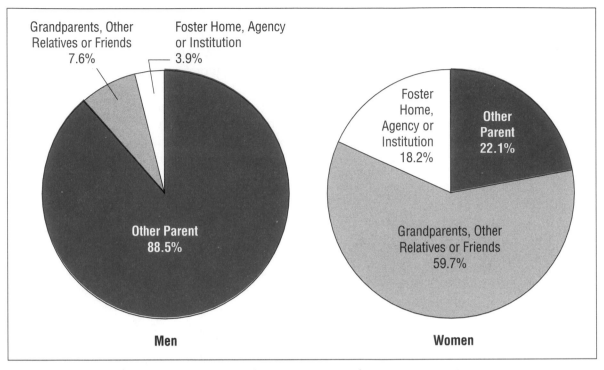

Source: U.S. Department of Justice, *Women in Prison* (Washington, D.C.: Bureau of Justice Statistics, 1991).

Programming for Women Inmates

Generally, women in prison have been discriminated against and offered fewer, often lower-quality programming options. It is clear from the preceding discussions that this results from a historical neglect of women's corrections, as well as from institutionalized sexism. The small number of incarcerated women leads correctional systems to neglect programming for them. Also, the programming opportunities typically offered have focused on stereotypically feminine social roles and occupations. Even mental health counselors have frequently operated on this basic assumption: To be mentally healthy, women need to adopt "traditional" women's roles, not to prepare themselves for independent economic survival after returning to the community. Such approaches, however, do not serve imprisoned women's real needs. According to the *Corrections Compendium,* the most needed programs for women inmates are in vocational training, parenting skills, and independent living.[52]

Programming for incarcerated women began to change in the 1980s. Researchers had consistently found fewer occupational, educational, and social programs, as well as inadequate health and mental health services, in women's institutions.[53] However, as the prisoners' rights movement took hold in women's corrections in the early 1980s, women filed class-action lawsuits claiming violations of their Fourteenth Amendment rights to **equal protection** of the law. The courts have tended to agree with women inmates and have ordered correctional systems to minimize or eliminate the inequalities in their institutions.

As a result of court orders, many women's prisons exhibited significant changes in their operations by the mid-1980s. Ralph Weisheit, in a review of programming options available to incarcerated women, reported in 1985 that alcohol and drug programs were near universal. Also, many women's institutions had programs for **life skills** and parenting training. These programs provide inmates with the basic tools (using transportation, finding housing, budgeting, improving communication skills, etc.) necessary to care for themselves and their children.

One recent review of women's prison programming reports that 84 percent of prison systems offer incarcerated women some form of parenting programs.[54] These programs not only offer incarcerated mothers opportunities to visit with their children, but they also emphasize instruction in communication skills, self-esteem, and parenting skills. In addition, volunteers such as Parents Anonymous come to a number of institutions to conduct classes and meetings with mothers.

Also, the vocational training opportunities, while still heavily weighted toward "women's work," have been showing a wider range of options. The most common job training programs were in the fields of secretarial work (86% of prisons), sewing (83% of prisons), food service (78% of prisons), and domestic work (56% of prisons). Nontraditional training programs, which

Equal protection Legal requirement from the Fourteenth Amendment that, regardless of sex or race, inmates of various groups must be treated similarly.

Life skills Basic tools for adequate social functioning in society; includes such things as household management, simple financial management, communication skills, and parenting skills.

FYI

The Fourteenth Amendment, together with the Thirteenth (abolishing slavery) and Fifteenth (granting the right to vote regardless of race, color, or previous condition of servitude), was a measure the victorious Union used to maintain control of the defeated, rebellious Confederacy. However, the scope and importance of the Fourteenth Amendment have been much greater than anyone could have imagined. Today, this legal principle forms the backbone of many lawsuits against all branches of government (including correctional systems) when individuals believe they have been discriminated against.

Figure 9–7 The Fourteenth Amendment to the United States Constitution.

FOURTEENTH AMENDMENT:
All persons born and naturalized in the United States, and subject to the jurisdiction thereof, are citizens of the United States and of the State wherein they reside. No State shall make or enforce any law which shall abridge the privileges or immunities of citizens of the United States; nor shall any State deprive any person of life, liberty, or property, without due process of law; nor deny any person within its jurisdiction the equal protection of the laws.

lead to much higher-paying jobs after release, were less frequently available and open to a smaller number of women. Among such programs the most common were carpentry (42% of prisons), plumbing (33% of prisons), welding (25% of prisons), and auto repair (22% of prisons).

Educational programs, of many varieties and at all academic levels, are just as important for imprisoned women as they are for men. Without opportunities to complete a basic education, women may be doomed to recidivate. Women and men are equally likely to participate in academic and vocational training, with approximately one in three state prison inmates of both sexes receiving some such training

Female inmate in a nontraditional job training program.

while in prison.[55] Because of the additional social obstacles women face in our society, it is even more important for women to have opportunities for advanced educational pursuits than for men.

Two areas of programming where women's unique needs are most apparent are counseling and medical care. During the last several decades, people have recognized that women in general have much higher rates of sexual abuse, especially as children, than do men. Nearly all women's prisons today offer several counseling programs, most often group therapy, to address women's experiences with abuse. Also, groups in most women's prisons address domestic violence and physical abuse issues.

Many Americans experience difficulties accessing and affording medical care. Knowing that people (both men and women) who are imprisoned are usually poor and have histories of alcohol and drug use and abuse, we should expect inmates to have a variety of health problems. Among women inmates the most common, persistent health problems are severe psychological disturbances, substance abuse, obesity, and gynecological disorders, along with many stress-related problems.[56]

One very important area where women inmates' health care needs are more acute than men's and which correctional administra-tors may find surprising is in HIV infection. HIV and AIDS have historically been viewed as primarily men's health concerns. However, a study of prisons conducted in 1994 reported that among female inmates HIV infection rates were as high as 20 percent of institutional populations. In 90 percent of the facilities or jurisdictions, women had higher

> **FYI**
>
> Although a major concern about HIV/AIDS in corrections centers on male homosexual activity, HIV infection is more common among women inmates. HIV may have more long-term, broader-reaching impact among women inmates because of their greater likelihood of being parents.

rates of infection than men, especially for those under 25 and non-white inmates.[57] HIV has introduced to women's health care in prisons both obvious and legal issues. Among the obvious issues are managing a highly stigmatized and serious physical impairment and bearing significant increases in costs of providing health care. Legal issues concern what treatments can and should be provided and how such inmates are to be managed within the institution.

Women Inmates' Legal Rights

In the broadest sense, women inmates' legal rights are the exact same as those of imprisoned men. The Fourteenth Amendment guarantees "equal protection of the laws" to all U.S. citizens. However, though the Fourteenth Amendment was ratified in 1868, not all citizens have been granted true "equal protection of the laws" since that time. Rather, judicial discretion determines what counts as "equal," under what circumstances, and for whom.

Women inmates face some unique legal challenges. The major differences in female inmates' legal status arise from women's unique social statuses and the historical pattern of differential treatment of women in corrections. Compared with their male counterparts, women inmates have had distinct experiences with legal rights in three main areas:

1. Segregation and differential treatment issues
2. Health care issues
3. Parental rights

This does not imply that all aspects of housing, treating, and maintaining security over female and male inmates must be the exact same. In fact, in a limited range of cases, the courts have deemed differential treatment of the sexes acceptable. However, this is acceptable only if the correctional system can show that a "substantial" relationship exists between the differential treatment and an "important statutory purpose."[58] This means that it is legal (and obviously logical) to house males and females separately. Separate, in this situation, does not equate to different and illegal.

For those states that have few women inmates, the practical aspects of having women's correctional facilities present a range of problems. At the conclusion of 1994, 6 states (Maine, Montana, North Dakota, Vermont, West Virginia, and Wyoming) had fewer than 100 women inmates. To alleviate huge financial burdens, some of these states entered into contractual agreements with other states to house their female inmates. Generally speaking, courts have frowned on this practice, deeming such actions as infringements of female prisoners' equal protection of the law.[59] States may incarcerate women out of state, but only if they make efforts to minimize the use of such actions and if they grant individuals sent out of state a due process hearing first.

In terms of health care, women inmates are entitled to "adequate" health care, just like men, as established in *Estelle v. Gamble*.[60]

However, legal issues have arisen regarding "women's health." Notable among these issues are feminine hygiene supplies and medications for menstruation, pregnancy, abortion, and childbirth. Most controversial is whether a woman in prison has a right to an abortion. At this time, if a woman is imprisoned in a state that permits abortions, she carries that right with her into prison.[61] However, states may not be required to provide free abortions. So, while women inmates may be permitted access to abortions, their access may be curtailed if they do not have sufficient money to pay for the service.

LEGAL BRIEF:

Dodson v. Indiana, 377 N.E. 2d 1365 (1978).

Convicted of first-degree murder for killing James Young, who was on a fishing trip with a friend on June 8, 1976, Ralph Dodson was sentenced to life imprisonment at the Indiana State Prison. Dodson's motion to be sentenced to the Women's Prison was dismissed without a hearing.

The dismissal of his petition was one of the grounds on which Dodson filed appeals. Dodson claimed that it was unconstitutional sex discrimination to house him in a sex-segregated facility, whereby he was arbitrarily denied his right to engage in sexual intercourse with consenting members of the opposite sex. This, according to Dodson, amounted to a violation of the Eighth Amendment prohibition of cruel and unusual punishment. According to Dodson, homosexual inmates did not face such situations. Dodson argued that a forced lifetime of celibacy was contrary to an inmate's natural biological drives.

When the Supreme Court of Indiana heard Dodson's case, it ruled, not surprisingly, that there was no violation of constitutional rights. According to the court ruling, the state had a compelling reason to impose separation of the sexes, which did not constitute cruel and unusual punishment. As the court stated, if it found that an inmate had a right to be sentenced to a prison designed for the opposite sex, there would have been an overflow at the Women's Prison. This, in turn, would have caused numerous administrative and security problems. Therefore, prison inmates do not have a right to be housed in an institution for the opposite sex.

Pregnant inmates may pose some unique security issues for institutions. For instance, pregnant inmates may not be compelled to submit to vaginal searches, as this has consistently been upheld as a

JOB FOCUS: ACADEMIC TEACHER

In all prisons, education is one primary form of programming. This means that teachers are needed. Most prisons offer a wide range of educational opportunities, from the most basic literacy training to college or graduate level education.

Academic teachers in prisons are required to have the same credentials as needed in any comparable-level school in free society. Some variation exists across the states, but teachers for all levels through high school or GED classes are usually either employees of a local school district that contracts with the prison to offer classes, or employees of a centralized school district that the state department of corrections operates. Instructors of college-level courses are faculty members of the college or university that administers the prison program.

The job tasks of prison academic teachers are very similar to those of public school teachers. However, there are some important differences. Most prison inmate students have had negative experiences with formal education and, therefore, are not overly enthusiastic about "school." Also, many of these students have very poor basic skills, meaning that teachers must have a great deal of patience, creativity, and a commitment to work with individual students.

To be academic teachers in prison, candidates must have teaching certificates (which, of course, require a four-year college degree) and clean criminal background checks. Salaries for prison academic teachers vary widely and are set by the school district that administers the prison programs. Usually prison teachers earn the same salaries as teachers outside of prison with the same experience and credentials, averaging about $36,000 a year.

Source: U.S. Department of Labor, Bureau of Labor Statistics, *Occupational Outlook Handbook,* 1994–95 ed., p. 156.

threat to a fetus. Also, prenatal care is guaranteed to women, both as adults and as juveniles.[62]

When women who have children are imprisoned in states with civil death statutes, they may lose their parental rights. By being imprisoned, parents can be deemed "unfit" and thereby lose their legal parental rights. Their children can then become wards of the state or be placed for adoption.

These legal situations signal a sharp change from the past. For many years in U.S. correctional history, mothers were allowed to keep their young children with them inside the prison. While some jurisdictions may still permit this on a limited basis, keeping children with their mothers has never been established as a constitutionally guaranteed right. Interestingly, in no state is a child permitted to remain in prison with a father, even when the father is the child's sole caretaker.

Because there is no legal right to have their children with them in prison, either a statute or administrative order must permit this practice. In most states, when an incarcerated woman gives birth, she and her newborn will spend a maximum of 48 hours together before the child is taken to either a foster home or a state institution or is turned over to relatives outside the prison.

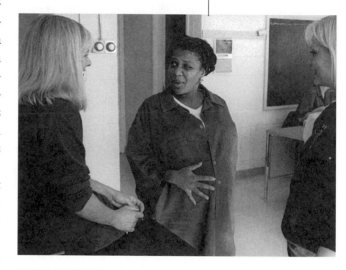

A concern unique to female institutions is inmate pregnancy.

After Prison

In some ways the conditions of women's incarceration may be "less" or "easier" than those for men. However, because of the social stigmas associated with criminal records and institutionalized sexism, women leaving prison face a number of additional, perhaps more imposing, obstacles than do their male counterparts. The words of Camilla Zimbal, a federal probation officer, need to be considered:

> Every female ex-offender automatically has two strikes against her: She is female and she is an ex-offender. The odds of her rehabilitation are formidable. Because she is female she suffers from a number of well-documented

discriminatory practices which affect all women who want to work. . . . Because she is an ex-offender, she suffers from the prejudice of prospective employers.[63]

The relationship between successful readjustment to the community and employment is well documented. For women leaving prison, employment is not only critical, but the jobs must allow women time to care for their children and pay enough to allow women to provide for themselves and their dependents. With women earning approximately two-thirds of what men in comparable jobs earn, this means that female ex-offenders must do more and better than their male counterparts to have similar chances at "success."

Summary

Although all U.S. citizens are presumed to be treated equally, "equality" is not necessarily an appropriate term to describe U.S. corrections for men and women. While women account for only a small portion of the official crime statistics in our country, the number and level of severity of women's criminal offenses have been increasing significantly.

Women have always been a small portion of correctional populations and, consequently, have almost always been subjected to lower-quality housing and programming efforts. Women's prisons did not become separate from men's prisons until the mid-nineteenth century. However, because of the small numbers of women in corrections, facilities were very poor and conditions were generally worse than those provided for men. Developing into a series of efforts to "save" those women deemed as salvageable, women's corrections expanded into a two-track system of institutions: custodial prisons for hardened criminals and reformatories designed to convert misdemeanant women into proper ladies. This attitude has remained in U.S. corrections, to some extent, until the present day.

Women's institutions today are structured very differently from men's prisons. Women are most frequently provided with few vocational training opportunities, and those that are available fall in stereotypically feminine fields. Women's institutions are less likely to see violence and thus place less emphasis on security and discipline. Instead, women offenders are treated as errant children who need guidance and ways to pursue a moral and legal lifestyle.

Following in the footsteps of the prisoners' rights movement, women inmates have used the judicial system to secure relatively equal access to programming and services. However, some programs and opportunities, which are considered uniquely or largely women's issues, have simultaneously become more restrictive. Women who are incarcerated and have children must concern themselves with finding someone to care for their children. Also, when women give birth while in prison, today they must pass their children to other caretakers in a matter of hours. Children were historically allowed to remain with their mothers; today, this is possible in only a few jurisdictions and for only a limited amount of time.

Women share all the legal rights of male inmates and also have a few additional legal rights. Women have had to secure their Fourteenth Amendment rights to equal protection of the law in issues of segregation and service provision, reproductive health, and parental rights. In addition, women who leave prison also face additional challenges when compared with their male counterparts. Women ex-prisoners must return to the community and face both the stigmas associated with being ex-convicts and the obstacles of institutionalized forms of sexism.

QUESTIONS FOR REVIEW

1. How does women's and men's criminal behavior differ?
2. Why are women such a small percent of all U.S. prison inmates?
3. What factors have influenced the historical development of women's corrections?
4. What are the goals of women's corrections?
5. How do women's prisons differ in structure, architecture, and daily procedures from men's prisons?
6. How do the federal and state correctional systems differ in their handling of women inmates?
7. In comparison with incarcerated men, what unique challenges do incarcerated women face?
8. What are the typical programming opportunities available to women inmates? How do these compare with those available to male inmates in terms of quality, size, and frequency?
9. How do women inmates' legal rights differ from those of male inmates?
10. What problems do women commonly encounter after they are released from prison?

ACTIVITIES

1. Visit your local jail and compare the facilities for male and female inmates. What are the differences? Are there differences in the activities available to male and female inmates?
2. Ask 10 male and 10 female acquaintances what they believe causes men to commit crime. Then ask them what they believe causes women to commit crime. Compare their answers to see whether differences exist between men and women concerning their beliefs about male and female criminality.
3. Develop a plan for a program to assist women inmates and their children to maintain a relationship. Make sure your plan ad-

dresses issues such as security, costs, transportation, and the safety of the children.

ENDNOTES

1. Thomas O. Murton and Phyllis Jo Baunach, "Shared Decision-Making in Prison Management: A Survey of Demonstrations Involving the Inmate in Participatory Management," in M. G. Herman and M. G. Haft (eds.), *Prisoners' Rights Sourcebook* (New York: Clark Boardman Company, 1973), p. 573.

2. Federal Bureau of Investigation, *Crime in the United States, 1993* (Washington, D.C.: U.S. Department of Justice, 1995).

3. U.S. Department of Justice, *Prisoners in 1994* (Washington, D.C.: Bureau of Justice Statistics, 1995).

4. Anne Campbell, *The Girls in the Gang: A Report from New York City* (New York: Basil Blackwell, 1984).

5. Rita Simon, *The Contemporary Woman and Crime* (Rockville, MD: National Institute of Mental Health, 1975).

6. Martin R. Haskell and Lewis Yablonsky, *Crime and Delinquency* (Chicago: Rand McNally, 1973); Ray R. Price, "The Forgotten Female Offender," *Crime & Delinquency,* Vol. 23, 1977, pp. 101–108.

7. Imogene L. Moyer, "Police Responses to Women Offenders in a Southeastern City, *Journal of Police Science and Administration,* Vol. 10, No. 4, 1982, pp. 376–383; Christy A. Visher, "Gender, Police Arrest Decisions, and Notions of Chivalry," *Criminology,* Vol. 21, No. 1, 1983, pp. 5–28.

8. Visher, *op. cit.,* p. 23.

9. *Crime in the United States, 1993,* p. 430.

10. *Ibid.*

11. Alice Franklin, "Criminality in the Work Place: A Comparison of Male and Female Offenders," in Freda Adler and Rita Simon (eds.), *The Criminology of Deviant Women* (Boston: Houghton Mifflin, 1979), pp. 167–170.

12. Kathleen Daly, "Structure and Practice of Familial-Based Justice in a Criminal Court," *Law and Society Review,* Vol. 21, 1987, pp. 267–290; David P. Farrington and Allison M. Morris, "Sex, Sentencing and Reconviction," *Journal of British Criminology,* Vol. 21, 1983, pp. 229–249; Candace Kruttschnitt and Daniel McCarthy, "Familial Social Control and Pretrial Sanctions: Does Sex Really Matter?" *Criminal Law and Criminology,* Vol. 76, 1985, pp. 151–176; Rita Simon, *Women and Crime* (Lexington, MA: D. C. Heath, 1975).

13. Darrell Steffensmeier, John Kramer, and Cathy Steifel, "Gender and Imprisonment Decisions," *Criminology,* Vol. 31, No. 3, 1993, p. 439.

14. Howard N. Snyder and Terrence A. Finnegan, *Delinquency in the United States, 1983* (Washington, D.C.: U.S. Department of Justice, 1987).

15. Hugh D. Barlow and Theodore N. Ferdinand, *Understanding Delinquency* (New York: Harper Collins, 1992).

16. *Prisoners in 1994, loc. cit.*.

17. Darrell K. Gilliard and Allen J. Beck, *Prisoners in 1993* (Washington, D.C.: U.S. Department of Justice, Bureau of Justice Statistics, 1994).

18. Lawrence A. Greenfeld and Stephanie Minor-Harper, *Women in Prison* (Washington, D.C.: Bureau of Justice Statistics, 1991).

19. *Ibid.*

20. U.S. Department of Justice, *Survey of State Prison Inmates, 1991* (Washington, D.C.: Bureau of Justice Statistics, 1993), p. 22.

21. Greenfeld and Minor-Harper.

22. *Survey of State Prison Inmates, 1991,* p. 23.

23. Greenfeld and Minor-Harper.

24. Nicole Hahn Rafter, *Partial Justice: Women in State Prisons, 1800–1935* (Boston: Northeastern University Press, 1985).

25. R. Dobash, R. Dobash, and S. Gutteridge, *The Imprisonment of Women* (New York: Basil Blackwell, 1986).

26. *Ibid.*, p. 23.

27. Herbert A. Johnson, *History of Criminal Justice* (Cincinnati: Anderson Publishing, 1988), p. 153.

28. Rafter, *op. cit.*, p. xxi.

29. *Ibid.*, p. 184.

30. Linda Zupan, "Men Guarding Women: An Analysis of the Employment of Male Correction Officers in Prisons for Women," *Journal of Criminal Justice,* Vol. 20, 1992, pp. 297–309.

31. T. Holland, M. Levi, G. Beckett, and N. Holt, "Preferences of Prison Inmates for Male Versus Female Institutional Personnel," *Journal of Applied Psychology,* Vol. 64, 1979, pp. 564–568; Zupan, *op. cit.*

32. Zupan, *op. cit.*

33. Lee Bowker, "Gender Differences in Prisoner Subculture," in Lee Bowker, *Women and Crime in America* (New York: Macmillan, 1981), pp. 409–419; Candace Kruttschnitt and Sharon Krmpotich, "Aggressive Behavior Among Female Inmates: An Exploratory Study," *Justice Quarterly,* Vol. 7, No. 2, 1990; Coramae Mann, *Female Crime and Delinquency* (Tuscaloosa: University of Alabama Press, 1984).

34. Kruttschnitt and Krmpotich.

35. J. Fox, "Women's Prison Policy, Prisoner Activism, and the Impact of the Contemporary Feminist Movement: A Case Study," *The Prison Journal,* Vol. 64, No. 1, 1984, pp. 15–36.

36. Doris Layton MacKenzie, James Robinson, and Carol Campbell, "Long-Term Incarceration of Female Offenders: Prison Adjustment and Coping," *Criminal Justice and Behavior,* Vol. 16, No. 2, 1989, pp. 223–238.

37. Rose Giallombardo, *The Social World of Imprisoned Girls* (New York: Wiley, 1974); Esther Heffernan, *Making It in Prison: The Square, the Cool, and the Life* (New York: Wiley, 1972).

38. All information in this subsection is drawn from the 1993/1994 Annual Report of the Florida Department of Corrections. Beck and Gillard, *Prisoners in 1994, op. cit.*

39. Statistics as of December 1993.

40. Statistics as of December 31, 1994.

41. All information in this subsection is drawn from Beck and Gilliard, *Pris-*

oners in 1994, op. cit.; the 1993–1994 Minnesota Department of Corrections Biennial Report.

42. Statistics as of June 30, 1992.

43. All information in this subsection is drawn from Gilliard and Beck and the 1994 Profile of Institutional Population, Kentucky Department of Corrections.

44. Statistics as of January 27, 1994.

45. Sue Kline, "A Profile of Female Offenders in the Federal Bureau of Prisons," *Federal Prisons Journal,* Vol. 3, No. 1, 1992, pp. 33–36.

46. Esther Heffernan, "The Alderson Years," *Federal Prisons Journal,* Vol. 3, No. 1, 1992, pp. 21–26.

47. Kline, p. 34.

48. Greenfeld and Minor-Harper.

49. Linda Abram Koban, "Parents in Prison: A Comparative Analysis of the Effects of Incarceration on the Families of Men and Women," *Research in Law, Deviance and Social Control,* Vol. 5, 1983, pp. 171–183; D. DuBose, "Problems of Children Whose Mothers Are Imprisoned," in Phyllis Jo Baunach, "Critical Problems of Women in Prison," in Imogene L. Moyer (ed.), *The Changing Roles of Women in the Criminal Justice System,* (Prospect Heights, IL: Waveland Press, 1992.)

50. Donna Hale, "The Impact of Mothers' Incarceration on the Family System: Research and Recommendations," *Marriage and Family Review,* Vol. 12, No. 1–2, 1987, p. 148.

51. C. S. Lanier, "Affective States of Fathers in Prison," *Justice Quarterly,* Vol. 10, No. 1, 1993, pp. 49–65.

52. Todd Clear and George F. Cole, "Female Offenders," *Corrections Compendium,* Vol. 5, No. 10, 1984, pp. 1–10.

53. Suzanne Sobel, "Difficulties Experienced by Women in Prison," *Psychology of Women Quarterly,* Vol. 7, No. 2, 1982, pp. 107–118.

54. Mary J. Clement, "Parenting in Prison: A National Survey of Programs for Incarcerated Women," *Journal of Offender Rehabilitation,* Vol. 19, No. 1/2, 1993, pp. 89–100.

55. U.S. Department of Justice, *Survey of State Prison Inmates, 1991* (Washington, D.C.: Bureau of Justice Statistics, 1993), p. 26.

56. Catherine Ingram-Fogel, "Health Problems and Needs of Incarcerated Women," *Journal of Prison and Jail Health,* Vol. 10, No. 1, 1991, pp. 43–57.

57. This study, conducted by Johns Hopkins School of Public Health and the Centers for Disease Control, is reported in W. Travis Lawson, Jr., and Lena Sue Fawkes, "HIV, AIDS, and the Female Offender," *Federal Prisons Journal,* Vol. 3, No. 1, 1992, p. 29. Ted Hammett "AIDS in Correctional Facilities, 1994" (Washington, D.C.: U.S. Department of Justice, 1995).

58. *Reed v. Reed,* 404 US 71 (1971).

59. *Park v. Thompson,* 356 F.Supp. 783 (DHaw 1972).

60. *Estelle v. Gamble,* 429 US 97 (1976).

61. *Doe v. Jennings,* Civil Act No. 79-681 (WDPa 1979); *Commonwealth v. Aldridge,* (Cir. Ct, Arl Co, Va 2/27/79).

62. *Morales v. Turman,* 383 F.Supp. 53 (ED Tex 1974).

63. Camilla K. Zimbal, "Hiring Women Ex-Offenders: What We Can Do," *Federal Probation,* Vol. 47, No. 3, 1983, p. 42.

CHAPTER 10

Local Corrections

CHAPTER OBJECTIVES

In the last chapter we focused our discussion on women inmates. In this chapter we direct our attention to a frequently overlooked portion of the U.S. correctional system: local corrections. After reading this chapter, you will be able to:

1. Understand the evolution of local U.S. correctional ideologies, goals, and organizations.

2. Explain the scope of local correctional populations and why many facilities are overcrowded.

3. Distinguish population variations of local correctional facilities based on demographics and geographic locations of jurisdictions.

4. Understand typical models of jail administration.

5. Identify alternative models of jail administration and explain their advantages and disadvantages.

6. Identify the major problems of contemporary jails.

7. Describe the conditions of local correctional facilities and the problems encountered in correcting problems.

8. Discuss programming opportunities for inmates of local correctional facilities.

9. Explain the reasons for and consequences of poor staff recruitment and training in local correctional facilities.

10. Understand the range of, reasons for, and dilemmas posed by health problems among jail inmates.

KEY TERMS

jails

lockup

gaols

first generation jails

second generation
 jails

intermittent
 supervision

new generation jails

direct supervision

cooperative jail
 administration

privatization

social density

spatial density

work-release

accredited

CHAPTER OUTLINE

I. Evolution of Local Correctional Efforts

II. Local Correctional Populations

   A. Demographic Variations

   B. Geographic Variations

III. Administration and Management of Local
Correctional Facilities

   A. City/County Government Administration

   B. State Government Administration

   C. Cooperative Administration

   D. Private Corrections

IV. Problematic Aspects of Jails

   A. Substandard Physical Facilities

   B. Minimal Programming Opportunities

   C. Staffing Deficiencies

   D. Health Status of Inmates

V. Summary

Local correctional facilities, typically referred to as "jails,"
are administered by local communities.

Evolution of Local Correctional Efforts

Local correctional facilities include all existing institutions that local communities administer to hold people who violate local laws, who are convicted of violating misdemeanor statutes, who await processing (arraignment, trial, or sentencing) within a local court, or who await transfer to a prison. Typically referred to as **jails,** local correctional facilities also include institutions known as lockups, workhouses, local houses of corrections, and county prisons.

This chapter provides an in-depth look at the historical development and the population characteristics of local correctional facilities and examines the administrative structure and common problems of U.S. jails. Jails are more numerous than prisons and process more people. In the study of U.S. corrections, jails have largely been unexplored. Not only do the U.S. public and media devote more of their time to understanding prisons, but so do students and professors of corrections.[1] This chapter seeks to correct this traditional oversight. Essentially all offenders pass through jails, and as crime rates continue to escalate, jails offer many career opportunities for those interested in corrections.

Jails exist today to detain both convicted and accused offenders. Jails typically hold people for between 48 hours and 365 days. Shorter stays usually mean that people are confined to a **lockup** at a law enforcement agency. That is, they have not been detained long enough to be fully processed into a jail. The law in most jurisdictions limits jail sentences to not more than 365 days for misdemeanors. Longer sentences, more than one year, accompany felony convictions, and felons are incarcerated in prisons. However, some people may spend longer than one year in jail as they await arraignment, trial, and sentencing (if convicted).

Our nation's jail population is about evenly distributed between those who have been convicted of crimes and those who have not. Presently, those who are unconvicted are the slight majority, 51 percent.[2] This means that the structure and operations of local correctional facilities, by law, must be different from those of prisons. Since many people in jail have not been convicted of any crimes, they need to be afforded different degrees of legal rights. Also, many Americans believe those who have not been convicted of any crimes warrant a qualitatively different form of treatment and custody.

This has not always been the case with the situation and functions and, consequently, the structure of jails in the United States.

Jails Local correctional institutions designed to hold both convicted misdemeanants and people charged with crimes and awaiting judicial processing.

Lockup A holding center for people who have not been detained long enough to be fully processed into jail.

Gaols Early forerunners of modern jails; first established in 1166 in England.

The colonists originally imported from England the idea of a place to detain people in the community. The British first established **gaols** in 1166. King Henry II decreed that all county sheriffs would create facilities to hold people charged with crimes until they could be tried. This often meant that alleged offenders had to spend months or years in confinement awaiting a judge's arrival. British judges were responsible for a number of court circuits that they traveled. In some communities, judges were present two or three times a year; in more remote locations, judges might be available only every five to seven years. This meant that alleged offenders spent long periods of time in facilities that offered little or no standard comforts of life.

When the North American colonies were being settled, the British legal system had undergone a number of changes. Gaols were no longer simply places to hold persons until trial or after conviction until punishment. Instead, gaols became places to confine petty criminals as a form of punishment. The colonists brought this idea with them to North America.

The first jail in the colonies was established at the Jamestown, Virginia, settlement in 1606. Early colonial jails included a fee system, meaning that those confined had to pay a fee for admission or release. The fee in the Virginia colony jails was two pounds of tobacco.[3] The purpose of the jail was to hold people until the time of trial or after trial until the time they were physically punished. The jail, then, was not initiated as a form of corrections. Rather, jails began as a complement to correctional efforts. Not established for punishment or treatment, jails instead ensured that offenders were available for legal processing and punishment.

Perhaps the most notable and most important change in U.S. jails has been in their actual physical structures. An evolution has occurred—and, in fact, is still occurring—in the architectural design of local correctional facilities. These changes in jails' physical layout and design have been accompanied by changes in their function and administration. The evolution of U.S. jails has occurred in three phases or generations.

First generation jails were essentially holding pens for all varieties of people. These were usually large rooms inside a building, or a building itself, into which most or all people awaiting trial or punishment were placed. Of course, wealthy, powerful community members who were able to bribe officials remained free.[4] Inmates were provided very little, if anything, inside first generation jails. In fact, inmates were responsible for their own food, clothing, safety, and welfare. However, many jailers provided food, clothing, and firewood

First generation jails Early correctional facilities in which all prisoners were held in one communal room or building.

to inmates, but only for a fee. This meant that a class system was established inside jails. Those with the resources—financial or otherwise—to buy or trade for goods and services could obtain them, while others were left to the mercy and charity of their fellow inmates. Thus, the poor, unpopular individuals in our early jails commonly died of starvation or disease.[5]

First generation jails, despite their numerous problems—disease, exploitation, lack of classification—had their advantages for a limited population: those who administered the jails. Making a great deal of money from their inmates, jailers also had opportunity to sexually exploit their inmates (especially females). Also, jailers had relatively easy jobs. They had very little responsibility except securing inmates and perhaps minimizing the disruptions, exploitations, and violence among them. From an administrative standpoint, the first generation jails made sense.

However, a major change occurred in viewing the rights of those in jails. To provide for those removed from their families and livelihoods, second generation jails developed during the early-1800s. **Second generation jails** were seen as a progressive step forward. They segregated types of inmates, and they were also more secure than earlier facilities. This is the "typical" jail design that most Americans recognize. Second generation jails consist of rows of side-by-side cells with jail staff having an office or station at the end of the row(s). This design, referred to as *linear,* allows **intermittent supervision.** This means that staff do not observe inmates constantly, but periodically. Observation occurs only when a staff person walks in front of the cell or when a camera that can view the cell is activated. Since second generation jails separate inmates, they permit increased safety for inmates, give staff better opportunities to control problematic inmates, and allow inmates greater opportunities for self-reflection and penitence (as advocated by the early prison designers and administrators).

First generation jails were essentially holding pens.

Second generation jails Correctional facilities operated by local governments and designed with rows of side-by-side cells, with offices located at one end of the building.

Intermittent supervision Periodic, not constant, supervision of inmates.

The daily routines in second generation jails have varied over time, across locations, and by local administrations. However, in this jail design inmates commonly spend most or virtually all of their

Second generation jails were developed during the early-1800s and remained relatively unchanged until the mid-twentieth century.

New generation jails Modern design of local correctional facilities; individual cells/rooms are placed around the outside of a large room with officers' stations in the middle of the facility, allowing constant observation of all cells/rooms; includes common areas in the building's open spaces where inmates spend most of their time.

Direct supervision Opportunities for jail or prison staff to continuously and directly monitor inmates' activities; made possible by technologies or new generation architecture.

time in cells and have few, if any, opportunities to participate in recreation, counseling, or other programs. However, the conditions of such facilities, sometimes having cells with dozens of inmates, remained largely unknown in our society until the 1960s. With the social upheavals of the 1960s and the increasing numbers of arrests of "respectable," middle-class people (especially the young adult and adolescent children of the middle class), greater attention was focused on the conditions of jails. Consequently, calls for jail reform were common during the 1960s and early-1970s.

Some reform measures were implemented during the 1960s, but these were almost exclusively attempts to clean up or correct conditions within existing jails. In the 1970s and 1980s many jurisdictions found it necessary (or perhaps easier) simply to build new facilities. With new building projects underway, many administrators, architects, and politicians devoted their energies to design facilities that promoted more positive living atmospheres, less stress on staff and inmates, and more cost-efficient management. These goals culminated in the development of the **new generation jails.** Borrowed from juvenile corrections and drug treatment programs in federal prisons, the design of such jails is not an entirely new concept. However, the new generation design was first used in the Federal Metropolitan Correctional Centers in New York, Chicago, and San Diego in 1975.

During the decade of 1973 to 1983, the height of the modern jail reform movement, more than 1,000 new jails were built in the United States.[6] While the majority of these new facilities were constructed on the second generation design, some were instead based on an architectural design that promotes staffs' direct and constant supervision. This model has a central area similar to a dayroom, where inmates congregate and engage in group activities and interactions. Around the central area is one or two tiers of cells. The absence of bars and stationary, spartan furnishings strike most observers as the immediate difference in this design. Instead, each individual "room" or cell has a door with a window, and all furnishings simulate the appearance of those in outside life. In addition, staff are present in the living areas 24 hours a day to both supervise and ensure security and to serve as resources for inmates.

More advantageous than those of the second generation design, new generation jails rely on the management method known as **direct supervision.** Here, staff are given opportunities to continuously monitor inmates' activities. New generation jail proponents believe that

The new generation jail was designed to promote a more positive atmosphere for both inmates and staff, as well as to be more cost-efficient.

inmates in linear model jails engage in violent, destructive behavior to demonstrate dominance over their environment and to demand provision of materials and attention. In contrast, the design of new generation jails allows staff to continuously and directly supervise inmates to prevent their illegal and deviant behavior. In this way, because inmates are constantly under surveillance, the emphasis is on *institutional* control, not *inmate* control.

A direct supervision method of jail management not only offers advantages in effectively overseeing and controlling inmate behavior, but it also offers financial advantages. Approximately 70 percent of a jail's annual operating costs are expenditures on personnel.[7] Compared with intermittent supervision jail designs, direct supervision jail designs allow fewer officers to supervise growing numbers of inmates. By being physically present in the housing unit, and not having to circulate among the facility's cells, dayrooms, and programming areas, one officer can fill the functions that previously required several officers. Also, by having constant observation, inmates are less likely to hurt themselves or others. This limits the liability that the jail, jail staff, and responsible government entity may encounter as a result of injuries.

In addition, financial savings can be realized in new generation jails. Staff in such facilities report higher levels of morale, decreased tension, reduced use of sick leave, decreased frequency of conflicts between staff and inmates, and decreased destruction to facility property.[8] These savings measures are offset slightly by additional training of staff. However, this increase can be balanced over time as the positive results eventually reduce rates of staff turnover.

Of course, one important factor to consider when designing a jail is its anticipated population. U.S. jails vary widely in size, from those facilities in small towns and rural areas that can hold only handfuls of people to large, urban jails that hold several thousand people. The "typical" U.S. jail is very small, and 44 percent of our nation's jails have fewer than 25 cells. These facilities hold only 4 percent of our nation's jail inmates. Fully 45 percent of our nation's jail inmates are incarcerated in the 4 percent of jails that are the largest (and in our largest metropolitan areas).

Most U.S. jails are too small to hold the number of people arrested in their jurisdictions. Nationwide, our jails are overcrowded, although many of our smaller jails have empty cells every single day. Most likely to be overcrowded are jails serving jurisdictions with populations of more than 250,000.[9] Jurisdictions have addressed the overcrowding problem by renovating existing facilities and constructing new ones that have higher capacities. From 1993 to 1994 alone, the total population capacity of our nation's jails increased 6.6 percent. However, even this growth has not kept pace with the rapidly rising number of people arrested and incarcerated. As seen in Figure 10–1, over the past 15 years the rapid growth of jail populations has reached—and today continues to exceed—the capacity of our jails.

Numerous reasons contribute to the overcrowding situation in jails. Jail personnel and administrators could change and control some of these factors, but others are not under their control. From the jail administrators' perspective, one frustrating cause of overcrowding is court orders to limit their populations. Consequently, when at their legal maximum capacity, some prisons will refuse to accept new inmates whom the courts have sentenced. This means that inmates must remain in local jails until beds open up in the prisons. This inmate backlog

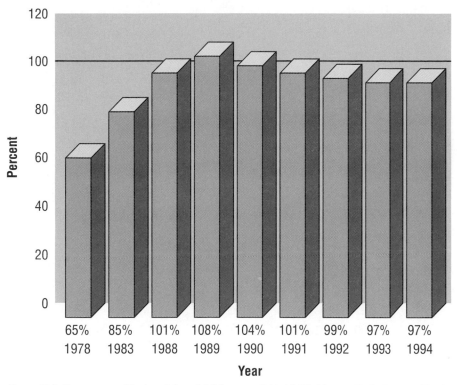

Figure 10–1 Percent of jail space occupied.

65%	85%	101%	108%	104%	101%	99%	97%	97%
1978	1983	1988	1989	1990	1991	1992	1993	1994

Year

Source: U.S. Department of Justice, *Jails and Jail Inmates, 1993–94* (Washington, D.C.: Bureau of Justice Statistics, 1995).

causes overcrowding in our jails, which is not jail administrators' fault. However, just as our judicial system has been unwilling to accept extreme overcrowding in prisons, so too have they refused to allow jails to operate at highly overcrowded levels. This means that jail administrators are left to develop plans to resolve their overcrowding problems, which are not necessarily of their making.

Local Correctional Populations

As mentioned previously, the population of our nation's jails is rapidly increasing. At midyear-1994, local jails held a total of 490,442 people. This represents an increase of 6.6 percent over the total population figure at midyear-1993.[10] As shown in Figure 10–2, the total number of people in our jails on a daily basis has consistently increased over the past two decades.

Figure 10–2 Rate of increase in jail populations, 1972–1993.

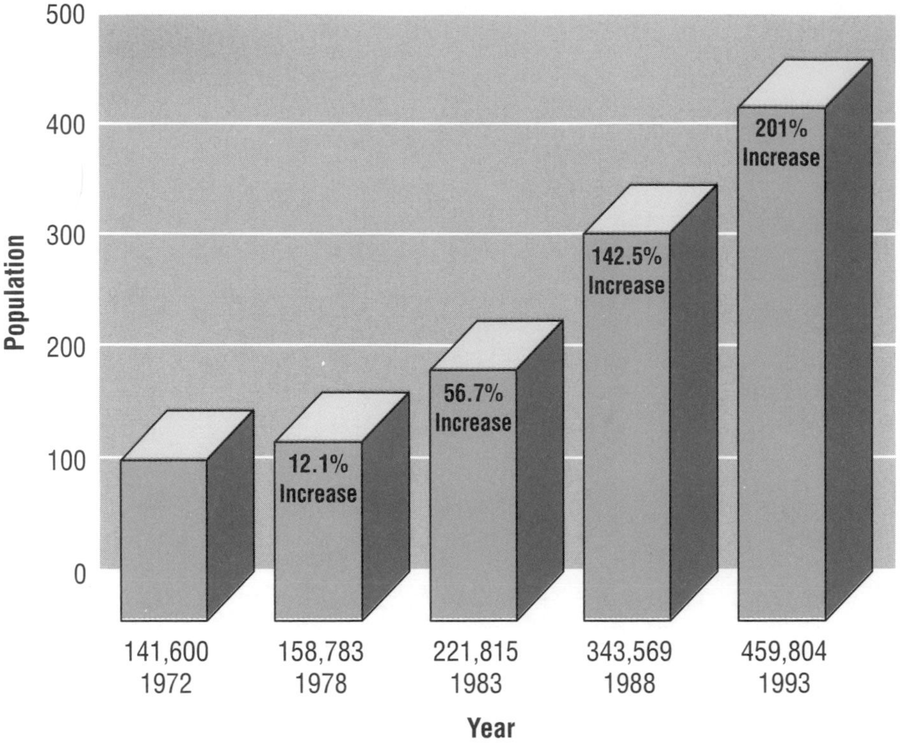

Source: U.S. Department of Justice, *Jails and Jail Inmates, 1993–94* (Washington, D.C.: Bureau of Justice Statistics, 1995).

Even more striking are the statistics regarding the total number of admissions and releases in our jails. In the year from midyear-1990 to midyear-1991, more than 20 million individuals were admitted or released from jail. We need to exercise care when interpreting these statistics, however. This is not to say that more than 20 million *different* people were processed through our local correctional systems. That is, many individuals were arrested and processed through jail more than once. This is especially true for alcoholics, who may be arrested a dozen or more times a year on charges of public intoxication.

Demographic Variations

Just as there are definite demographic patterns for our prison population, so are there similar trends in our jail population. Most striking is the overrepresentation of racial minorities and men. This is not surprising, however, as these statistics reflect those for known criminal perpetrators, convicted offenders, and prison populations. As shown in Figure 10–3, African-Americans slightly outnumber white Americans in our jails (43.9 percent and 39.1 percent, respectively). Furthermore, Hispanics (15.4 percent) are also overrepresented compared with their proportion (10.3 percent) of today's population.

Although they still account for fewer than 1 in 10 jail inmates, women have been increasingly incarcerated in jails during the past two decades. In 1978 only 5.9 percent of jail inmates were women. This figure nearly doubled by 1993, when fully 10 percent of jail inmates were women.[11] Women in jail differ from their male counterparts, however. They are somewhat more likely than men to serve sentences following convictions.[12] Women are also more likely to be in jail for drug-related offenses but less likely than men to be in jail for violent crimes. In addition, female jail inmates are more likely than male jail inmates to be first-time offenders. In 1989 nearly 1 in 3 women in jail, but only about 1 in 5 men, were first-time offenders.[13]

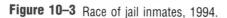

Figure 10–3 Race of jail inmates, 1994.

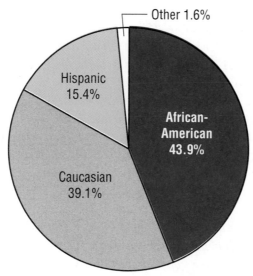

Source: U.S. Department of Justice, *Jails and Jail Inmates, 1993–94* (Washington, D.C.: Bureau of Justice Statistics, 1995).

Geographic Variations

Jails may vary widely according to their geographic locations. For instance, we might expect the racial demographics to vary between populations of jails in cities versus those in rural areas or between cities in different regions of the country. We would expect to find a larger proportion of Hispanic inmates in Texas, New Mexico, and Arizona jails than in Vermont, North Dakota, or Arkansas jails.

However, the most notable difference is that metropolitan area jails have much larger populations than county jails outside cities. This means that these facilities also are more likely to encounter overcrowding and problems among both staff and inmates. Jails that hold

LEGAL BRIEF:

Alford v. Osei-Kwasi, 48 S.E. 2d 79 (1992).

In this 1992 case the Court of Appeals of Georgia upheld a lower court ruling in favor of a jail lieutenant whom a female jail inmate sued. The inmate, Yolanda Alford, claimed that when she was 7 1/2 months pregnant, Lt. Osei-Kwasi used unnecessary force to transfer her out of her cell. According to Ms. Alford, the lieutenant shot her with a Taser gun. (A Taser gun fires darts attached to a 9-volt battery.) Lt. Osei-Kwasi did not dispute using the Taser gun but instead argued that his use of the Taser was justified due to Alford's belligerent and defiant response to his attempt to move her.

The Court of Appeals based its ruling on the legal precedent of Whitley v. Albers (475 US 312, 1986), saying that a determination of whether force was necessary must look at whether the force used was a good faith effort or a malicious and sadistic intent to cause harm to the inmate.

Based on this guidance, the Georgia court ruled that the situation did not establish the use of the Taser gun as wanton, malicious, or sadistic. In fact, the court argued this was obvious because inmate Alford, despite being pregnant, did not suffer any serious injury.

20 or 30 people are obviously very different in structure and function from those that hold 200, 300, or even 3,000 people. In these instances the differences doubtlessly outnumber the similarities between these jails.

As we would expect, jails with the largest capacities are in our largest cities. Most of our major cities operate more than one facility to allow some degree of classification and to ensure order and security. The 10 largest jail systems in the United States, as shown in Table 10–1, account for 20 percent of the nation's total number of jail inmates.

Because of their size, problems, and location in areas with large populations, these facilities receive the most public attention. However, they are, in fact, the minority among all jails. Fully two-thirds of all U.S. jails have an average daily population under 50. This means that in our less populated counties and towns, the local correctional facilities serve fewer people, while they draw basic funding from a smaller base. Consequently, they have less money for improvements as well as basic maintenance and staffing. Thus, many of the nation's smaller (and older) jails are some of the most oppressive and in the poorest condition.

Table 10–1	Locations of the Ten Largest Jail Systems (Number of Facilities and Average Daily Populations, 1994)	
Jurisdiction	**Number of Facilities**	**Average Daily Population**
Los Angeles County, CA	9	19,725
New York City, NY	15	18,091
Harris County, TX	4	10,282
Dallas County, TX	6	9,321
Cook County, IL	1	8,950
Dade County, FL	7	6,656
San Diego County, CA	11	5,651
Orleans Parish, LA	11	5,231
Tarrant County, TX	4	5,167
Shelby County, TN	2	4,891

Source: U.S. Department of Justice, *Jails and Jail Inmates, 1993–94* (Washington, D.C.: Bureau of Justice Statistics, 1995).

Administration and Management of Local Correctional Facilities

The number of U.S. jails has been decreasing throughout the past two decades. For instance, between 1972 and 1988 the number declined by over 15 percent. Although many new jails were constructed during this time period, many of these facilities replaced two or more existing facilities. At the same time, though, as previously discussed, the number of jail inmates in 1988 was 142.5 percent higher than it was in 1972. As we might expect, this has meant that our jails are overcrowded. To control the overcrowding problem, jurisdictions have built larger jails or have adopted alternative methods of jail administration. With more large jails being built (those with capacities for more than 500 inmates), how jails are administered and managed has also changed.

This section discusses the four main forms of jail administration and management: 1) city/county government, 2) state government, 3) cooperative administration, and 4) private corrections. While city or county government is still the most common form of administration, the move toward alternative models of administration and management, especially privatization, has rapidly increased.

City/County Government Administration

Municipal or county governmental bodies administer approximately 82 percent of jails. Most often, state constitutions grant the office of sheriff the authority and responsibility for jail administration.[14]

Sheriffs do not, however, have complete authority and control over their jails. While they may have authority to make decisions about jail operations, sheriffs almost always are held politically and financially accountable to both the voters who elect them and to county commissions (or similar bodies controlling the funding of county agencies). This means that other political actors often check and limit sheriffs' authority.

State Government Administration

Only in 6 of the 50 states—Connecticut, Hawaii, Rhode Island, Delaware, Alaska, and Vermont—does the state government administer adult jails. In part this is done to centralize the function of local corrections. These 6 states have generally small populations (ranking 27th, 40th, 43rd, 46th, 48th, and 49th, respectively, in population)[15] and relatively small numbers of jails and jail inmates. Therefore, for these states, centralizing all local correctional authority, responsibility, and services is advantageous.

Ideally, jails administered by a centralized body of state government offer four advantages over those administered by local governments.[16] First, this setup would allow for more equal distribution of resources and, therefore, more stable delivery of services and maintenance of facilities across the state. Second, administration of jails could be streamlined as the state government could more easily develop and implement statewide standards for local correctional facilities. Third, costs could be controlled by sharing resources and ensuring that space, personnel, and other expensive resources are not underutilized. Finally, state-run jails could be advantageous by removing jails from the local political arena, thereby allowing greater focus on the daily operations of jails rather than on public (that is, voter) reaction.

Most states grant authority for jail administration to the office of sheriff.

These identified advantages might lead some to expect a number of states to take over local corrections. However, this has not been the case and can be attributed to political fighting between state and county/local governments. Despite the difficulties encountered in running jails, many local governments want to maintain the authority they hold in this area. Some state governments, also, have not pursued centralizing jail operations because they are overwhelmed and overburdened with the responsibilities they currently hold. This means that we should not expect much, if any, movement toward centralizing jail operations within state government.

Cooperative Administration

Centralized jail operations offer several significant advantages to local correctional facilities. However, balancing the disadvantages of centralization located in state government has discouraged most jurisdictions from pursuing such a setup. Rather, some jurisdictions have sought other ways to combine their operations to achieve more

JOB FOCUS: EXECUTIVE DIRECTOR, AMERICAN JAIL ASSOCIATION

The executive director of the American Jail Association is responsible for managing the daily operations of the Association's central office. The executive director has ultimate responsibility for supervising the personnel, financial matters, and editorial policies of the Association, which represents the interests of the member local correctional facilities and their employees.

The American Jail Association has among its chief objectives facilitating the organization of all professionals concerned with the custody and care of inmates in local facilities and those professionals concerned with overseeing the conditions and systems used for detaining people locally. The Association, under the leadership of the executive director and a 12-member board of directors, operates on an annual budget of $1.25 million to advance the interests, needs, concerns, and proficiencies of the profession. Specifically, the American Jail Association strives to achieve professionalism through training, exchanging information, and providing technical assistance, publications, and conferences. The Association also provides leadership in developing and implementing standards, legislation, management models, and programs and services.

The executive director serves as the symbolic leader of all jail personnel and, therefore, is expected to have a history of lengthy and illustrious experience in jail administration, as well as a minimum of a bachelor's degree. To successfully fulfill the job, this individual is expected to possess skills to work collaboratively and individually in planning and directing the work of others, be skilled at public speaking and writing, be able to supervise, train, and evaluate staff, and be able to manage a complex budget. These tasks require the individual to understand and work with theories of management, organizational dynamics, and the complexity of U.S. laws—at the local, state, and federal levels. All of these responsibilities are compensated by a yearly salary of approximately $55,000, full insurance benefits, and a provided vehicle.

Source: American Jail Association, 1995. Adapted from job announcement for position of Executive Director.

efficient and cost-effective correctional goals. For example, several small (in terms of population) counties or cities combine their resources and operate one cooperatively administered jail.

Although it is a nationwide problem in our jails, overcrowding is not a universal problem. Many jails in our less populated communities typically house fewer than 2 dozen inmates.[17] This means that operating a jail with such a small inmate population is a relatively expensive endeavor. The expenses for personnel and basic operating/maintenance are present, regardless of whether a facility has 10, 20, or 200 inmates. Of course, costs will vary, but the baseline costs remain, making the expense of small jail operation comparatively higher than it is for medium or larger jails.

Cooperative jail administration arrangements may take one of several forms. First, several communities may decide to jointly fund the operations of a jail that already exists in one community. This would allow the other involved communities either to close an existing jail or to avoid building, renovating, or adding to a jail in their own community. Second, recognizing that none among them has an adequate facility, a collection of communities may close existing jails and build a new, regional jail. Third, communities that already have small jails may designate each of their jails for a particular population (those awaiting trial, convicted men, women, juveniles). Then, all jail inmates of that population, drawn from whichever of the cooperating communities, would be housed in the appropriate facility. This third model allows maximum use of existing resources, provides financial savings to communities, and maximizes security and classification efforts.

This is not to say there are no problems associated with cooperatively administered jails. First and foremost are the political issues involved. Deciding which community will have the jail may become a political battle as communities either fight for jobs or fight against having the facility "in their backyard." Also, practical obstacles may make cooperative administration of jails difficult. When the communities sharing one jail (or several specialized facilities) are distantly located, transportation problems, in terms of both time and financial costs, may become an issue. Therefore, communities may politically battle over how the transportation costs are to be shared (or not shared). Should all communities' transportation costs be considered a part of the overall budget, or should each community absorb the costs of transporting those inmates for whom they are responsible? These and numerous other, similar issues must be carefully planned before initiating a cooperative administration plan.

Cooperative jail administration
Agreements among several governmental bodies to jointly build, manage, and operate local facilities; purpose is to allow small or economically pressed communities access to local correctional facilities.

Private Corrections

The newest and apparently most promising alternative form of jail administration is operation of facilities by private, for-profit corporations. The movement toward privatization in corrections will be examined in greater depth in Chapter 14. However, at this point we will briefly explore the advantages and disadvantages of private businesses assuming responsibility for local corrections.

First of all, a government may *delegate* responsibilities for day-to-day jail operations to an outside body. However, this does not mean that the governmental body can *relinquish* its ultimate responsibilities for overseeing the care, safety, and security of inmates.[18] Therefore, privately administered jails operate on a contract basis whereby they agree to provide specified "services" in exchange for a set payment. Typically, payments are based on a set daily fee per inmate.

The private jail's goal is to operate at an efficiency level that allows the daily per-inmate fee not only to cover the costs of incarceration, but also to provide a profit margin. This leads to the criticisms that private facilities, especially jails—which usually hold people for short periods of time—cut corners and provide low-quality service, use undertrained and underpaid staff, and have overcrowded and poorly maintained facilities. Not all aspects of a jail need to be privatized, however. Some jails (like some prisons) have contracted portions of their operations—food service, laundry, physical plant maintenance, programming, and so on—yet have retained overall control and responsibility for operations.

Privatization Movement to transfer administrative and operational responsibilities for correctional facilities to private companies or charitable organizations.

Regardless of whether one likes the idea of **privatization,** private facilities are becoming increasingly common. Numerous states have entered into literally hundreds of contractual relationships for private corporations to deliver correctional services, which are often for juvenile correctional facilities. However, as communities find themselves unable and, on occasion, unwilling to provide the legally required services and types of facilities, the option of contracting some or all jail operation functions and administration becomes increasingly attractive.

Problematic Aspects of Jails

For a variety of reasons, some of which have been previously discussed, local correctional facilities have numerous problems. While many of these same problems also plague prisons, the inmates' special nature and the conditions of their incarceration make these situations more difficult to manage in the jail setting. Perhaps the primary difficulties arise from the highly transitory jail population. Literally every day the population of jails changes. Newly arrested people are brought in, people are released on bond or their own recognizance, and others are transferred to prisons or other local facilities. This constant turnover gives local correctional facilities little or no opportunity to establish a sense of stability in their programming or in the inmates' social organization. The constant arrival of new inmates presents jail administrators and staff with many problems. The full range of problems that people have on the streets accompanies them to jail. Brought into a setting where anxieties run high, these problems can consequently be exaggerated and aggravated.

In this section we will explore four major problem areas that make living and working in jails difficult: 1) substandard physical facilities, 2) minimum programming opportunities, 3) staffing deficiencies, and 4) health status of inmates. Remember what we have already discussed about the characteristics of jail inmates and the history of U.S. jails. These four major problem areas are not unique to the 1990s. Rather, these same problem areas have faced local correctional facilities for many decades and have yet to be fully resolved.

Substandard Physical Facilities

The most obvious problem facing contemporary jails is the poor condition of their physical structures, internal equipment, and furnishings. Because they handle such large numbers of typically transitory people, jails get very hard use. The maintenance required for jail facilities can be enormous, and often is so great that most jails cannot fulfill the time and financial requirements imposed.

That many U.S. jails have substandard facilities is not a new problem. As early as 1870, U.S. jails were known for their poor conjditions.[19] The substandard conditions in today's jails, however, can be attributed to the age of jail facilities. Very old facilities are especially likely to be found in rural areas.

FYI

Many U.S. jails are in poor condition not because of overcrowding or vandalism, but because they are old and maintenance costs are too high.

Our oldest jails are usually those that have the widest range of outdated facilities or those that have few facilities. A common problem in many jails is lighting. Because windows have traditionally been a security threat, most older jails have no natural light, meaning that lighting fixtures must be installed and maintained. Furthermore, a small number of our most outdated jails cannot invest money to renovate (or even install) modern plumbing systems, and their toilet facilities consist of nothing more than the "honey bucket" system. That is, a bucket, emptied once or twice a day, serves as the toilet. More common are those facilities that have toilets located in dayrooms with no or very little privacy accorded for their use.

Old jails remain in use because most rural areas have relatively low jail populations. Therefore, they do not contend with the overcrowding problems that many urban jurisdictions face. As a result, pressures to renovate or replace jail facilities are not present. Also, the financial commitment required to renovate or replace a jail is often too great for jurisdictions with a small tax base. Finally, even when financial resources are available or obtainable, spending significant monies to "improve" the conditions provided to "criminals, deviants, and generally bad people" may be a volatile political issue. Many politicians believe that advocating increased spending of tax dollars

A small number of jails remain unrenovated with little or no privacy afforded to inmates.

on corrections is a politically bad move. With all these factors in place, it is not surprising that many jail facilities, especially in small towns and rural areas, remain in use even when they are quite old and/or run-down.

The problems with old facilities are not just that "modern" construction and design plans have not been incorporated, but also that the required level—and cost—of maintenance can be quite high. One research team reported in 1992 that of 308 surveyed U.S. jails in counties with more than 50,000 residents, 31.8 percent of facilities were over 25 years old and 4 percent of operating jails were over 100 years old![20] The impact of U.S. jails' aging structures is further seen in the 1992 survey of jail administrators. Eighty-one percent reported that their facilities would need either to be replaced or expanded.[21]

Even in larger communities, substandard jail conditions are a problem. As recently as 1991, more than one-quarter (28.8%) of jail administrators in counties with more than 50,000 residents reported that their most serious institutional problems were related to physical and environmental conditions.[22] Similarly, both jail managers and social service providers agree that among the major problems facing jails are overcrowding and deteriorating physical structures.

The problems of substandard conditions are wide-reaching. Not only do we need to assess the actual physical structures, but we must also consider the social conditions these physical surroundings create. Perhaps the most common problem regarding jails' physical conditions is a lack of sufficient space. Overcrowding of jails creates numerous problems for both inmates and staff. Overcrowding also has a direct connection to the problems of limited programming opportunities, inmate adjustment problems, staff deficiencies, and poor health of inmates.

Because of their substandard conditions, many, if not most, jails do not have adequate or even necessary facilities to properly care for and manage inmates. Fewer than 1 in 6 U.S. jails has an on-site infirmary. This means sick and injured inmates are transferred to local hospitals or clinics, and additional financial resources and hours of employees' time are required. In addition, the National Sheriff's Association has reported that fewer than one-third of our nation's jails have space for counseling or educational programming, outdoor recreation, indoor recreation, contact visits, or library services. Fewer than 1 in 5 jails has space for dining, and fewer than 1 in 14 jails has space for vocational programming. This contributes directly to a lack of programming opportunities and to inmates' adjustment difficulties and health problems.

Dense jail populations are associated with inmates' negative psychological reactions. However, the **social density** (number of people in a housing unit) is more important and influential than the actual **spatial density** (space allocation per person). In addition to psychological reactions, inmates in more dense housing units also show elevated blood pressure rates, which impact their health and, consequently, increase the costs of jail confinement.[23]

Minimal Programming Opportunities

Because jail populations are highly transitory and because jails have space and financial restrictions, most jails offer inmates few, if any, structured program opportunities. Some jurisdictions may have doctors or nurses, mental health workers, social workers, or recreation therapists on staff. However, these people are typically available to deal with problems as they arise, rather than to organize and administer structured, ongoing groups and programs for inmates. Some citizens may conduct on-site self-help group meetings (Alcoholics Anonymous, Narcotics Anonymous, sexual abuse counseling, etc.). However, these are far from common and must contend with the rapid turnover issues as well.

Perhaps the most common, easiest to implement form of programming for jail inmates is work assignments. Generally speaking, work assignments involve inmate labor to provide basic maintenance and service functions within the facility. Such work programs are common in prisons, but they are more difficult to implement and supervise in many local correctional facilities. The inmate population rapidly turns over, and a limited range of work assignments is available for inmates.

Approximately one-half of all inmates in local correctional facilities have work assignments. Males are more likely than females to have work assignments, especially off-site. For example, males are nearly three times more likely than females to have off-site work assignments.[24] In addition, male inmates spend more time on work assignments. Males report spending a daily average of 5.9 hours on work assignments; females, a daily average of 4.2 hours. Consequently, women also report spending a greater portion of their time without activities, or an average of 16.8 hours. In contrast, men report only 14.6 hours per day spent in their cells or dormitory rooms.[25]

Approximately one-half of all inmates in local correctional facilities have work assignments.

A common alternative to on-site work assignments is **work-release** programs. That is, inmates are allowed to leave the facility to attend jobs on the outside. Work-release programs allow inmates to maintain community involvement while they are incarcerated. These programs have recently been identified as potential ways for local correctional facilities to offset some of the costs incurred in incarcerating inmates. In 1993 the average daily cost of incarcerating a jail inmate was $40.18.[26]

Staffing Deficiencies

More than 165,500 people are employed in our nation's jails.[27] This number represents an increase of more than 150 percent during the last decade. The majority (71%) of these staff positions are custodial. Since the personnel who work in jails are among the most transient of all correctional workers, staff turnover is a major problem. Working for only short periods of time, jail staff move on to higher-paying jobs or to jobs that offer more attractive hours, working conditions, or other advantages. The most frequently cited problems related to recruiting and retaining jail personnel are the low salaries, poor image of jail work, and limited range of career advancement opportunities.[28]

Recruitment and Retention   Because of the relatively poor pay they offer, many counties have difficulty recruiting and keeping jail staff. Jail officers earn an average of more than $3,000 less than prison correctional officers.[29] Furthermore, in those counties where the sheriff's office administers the jail, staff assignment to jail duty is usually a form of "punishment" that the sheriff uses to discipline deputies who violate departmental rules or regulations. All these factors

Work-release Programs whereby inmates are allowed to leave a correctional facility to attend jobs on the outside.

combine to create an environment in which 70 percent of U.S. jail managers report significant shortages of correctional officers.[30]

Recruitment procedures are often highly informal for jobs in jails. Because most sheriffs' offices are political, many deputy jobs are doled out as political favors or payments. This means that people working in jails often have little or no training in corrections. Of course, as elected officials, the same can also be said of sheriffs. However, recognizing that problems can be created or aggravated by a low-quality personnel pool, some larger jails in the country have formalized their recruitment and hiring procedures and have placed greater emphasis on behavioral factors rather than on physical attributes. Many jails have only a few, if any, qualifications that applicants must meet for employment. A few states require a high school diploma or GED, but most have no educational requirements. When individuals show interest, most jails are very lenient in using psychological, physical, and aptitude screening of prospective employees.[31]

One solution is becoming increasingly popular across the country: New police recruits or newly hired sheriffs' deputies are required to work in jails. Because a large number of people apply for each opening, most police departments always have an available pool of people from which to draw. This procedure can work in one of two ways.

A variety of jobs is available in local corrections, including academic teachers.

First, some sheriffs' departments require the most recently hired deputies to start in the jail and to stay there until a patrol (or other) position opens. Second, in some cities, such as Cincinnati, newly hired law enforcement officers must work a specified period (such as two years) in jails before being transferred to "real" police positions. This solution has a major problem: Jails are staffed by people who may prefer not to work there. Since these employees have invested little, if anything, into their jobs, they may have little, if any, incentive to do their jobs well.

Training   After new staff are recruited and hired, many jails have only the barest minimum of training programs. Most jails usually rely on current staff to "show the ropes" to newly hired staff. Jail managers generally recognize their staffs' needs for additional training in areas of crisis intervention skills, interpersonal relations skills, legal liability issues, management of problem inmates, and stress management. In fact, more than 60 percent of jail managers have identified these five training areas as seriously needed in their facilities.[32] However, the practicalities of financial and personnel restraints often prohibit these needs from being met.

Many jurisdictions have hired individuals who have more education and who presumably would understand better the formal and informal requirements of work in a jail. In addition, many believe that people who are more highly educated will contribute to a more professional, ethical, and easily managed staff. (See Figure 10–4.) However, these efforts have met with mixed results. More highly educated officers report more dissatisfaction with their jobs.[33] Jail work is not especially challenging intellectually and can include periods of extreme monotony. The boredom and tediousness of jail work, therefore, can lead to high levels of burnout among staff.

Staff Turnover   One important organizational problem concerning jail staff deficiencies is the high rate of turnover. Staff leave their jobs for a number of reasons, including dissatisfaction with work conditions, frustration from contact with inmates, and feelings of isolation and neglect originating from interactions with supervisors. Relationships, as evidenced by forms and frequencies of communications, between correctional officers and supervisors are critical to the officers' satisfaction level and, therefore, are important in determining how long they remain at their jobs.[34]

The undesirable conditions and poor pay that characterize many jail positions directly contribute to a generally low morale and high

Figure 10–4 American Jail Association Code of Ethics for Jail Officers.

As an officer employed in a detention/correctional capacity, I swear (or affirm) to be a good citizen and a credit to my community, state, and nation at all times. I will abstain from all questionable behavior which might bring disrepute to the agency for which I work, my family, my community, and my associates. My lifestyle will be above and beyond reproach and I will constantly strive to set an example of a professional who performs his/her duties according to the laws of our country, state, and community and the policies, procedures, written and verbal orders, and regulations of the agency for which I work.

On the job I promise to:

Keep	The institution secure so as to safeguard my community and the lives of the staff, inmates, and visitors on the premises.
Work	With each individual firmly and fairly without regard to rank, status, or condition.
Maintain	A positive demeanor when confronted with stressful situations of scorn, ridicule, danger, and/or chaos.
Report	Either in writing or by word of mouth to the proper authorities those things which should be reported, and keep silent about matters which are to remain confidential according to the laws and rules of the agency and government.
Manage	And supervise the inmates in an evenhanded and courteous manner.
Refrain	At all times from becoming personally involved in the lives of the inmates and their families.
Treat	All visitors to the jail with politeness and respect and do my utmost to ensure that they observe the jail regulations.
Take	Advantage of all education and training opportunities designed to assist me to become a more competent officer.
Communicate	With people in or outside of the jail, whether by phone, written word, or word of mouth, in such a way so as not to reflect in a negative manner upon my agency.
Contribute	To a jail environment which will keep the inmate involved in activities designed to improve his/her attitude and character.
Support	All activities of a professional nature through membership and participation that will continue to elevate the status of those who operate our nation's jails.

Do my best through word and deed to present an image to the public at large of a jail professional, committed to progress for an improved and enlightened criminal justice system.

The American Jail Association's Board of Directors has approved the AJA Code of Ethics as part of an integral program to achieve a high standard of professional conduct among those officers employed in our nation's jails.

Source: American Jail Association, November 10, 1991.

turnover rate among staff. Raising morale can be difficult because jails usually do not have many of the traditional opportunities that improve staff morale. For instance, the transitory inmates do not give staff many opportunities to see "success" in their work with individuals. Also, because most correctional facilities have strict security requirements, staff have only minimal opportunities to suggest changes or improvements in their work environment.

As previously discussed, in recruiting jail personnel, some jurisdictions prefer more highly educated people. The impact of higher education has been most noticeable in the small segment (fewer than 25) of exclusively women's jails. According to researchers, the staffs of these few facilities are relatively young, inexperienced, predominantly female, and well-educated.[35] This suggests that more sophisticated interpersonal management skills would be used and that staff would have a greater range of career opportunities open to them. In turn, this means that the undesirable aspects of jail employment would need to be addressed to control staff turnover.

Insufficient numbers of qualified, trained staff affect the range of other problems our jails face. When they have staff shortages, facilities cannot offer many programming opportunities for inmates, even if space and financial resources are available. Staff shortages are also connected with inmates' adjustment difficulties. When only a few staff are available, inmates may feel even more isolated and may be more successful in suicide attempts.

Health Status of Inmates

Health problems among jail inmates pose significant challenges for jail staff and administrators. Sick, injured, or disturbed inmates require special forms of staff attention. This attention, plus the costs for treatment, supervision, and care, can be extremely expensive. Consequently, the generally poor health status of our nation's jail inmates presents difficulties both at the individual level and at the organizational, institutional level.

Inmates of both urban and rural jails have significant health problems. The first major issue related to inmates' special health care needs centers on the fact that most U.S. jails have substandard facilities and are not equipped or prepared to deal with anything except the most minor medical problems. The National Institute of Justice reported in 1980 that 77 percent of U.S. jails had no medical facilities; 70 percent did not give inmates medical examinations upon admission to the jail; and only 15 percent provided medical examinations for inmates who were obviously ill.[36] Also in 1980, of the more than 3,000 U.S. jails, only 67 were **accredited** by the American Medical Association. This means that less than 0.3 percent of all jails met the minimum health care standards that the nation's leading medical association established.

Infectious diseases pose serious threats to modern jails' orderly management and daily functions. Because most jails have cramped and less-than-sanitary conditions and because inmates have more physical problems than does the general population, controlling the spread of infectious and contagious diseases is an important challenge for jail administrators.[37] Especially of concern today are outbreaks of serious diseases such as tuberculosis and hepatitis, and HIV infection. However, controlling the spread of "traditional" forms of disease is not the most significant threat to effective jail management and administration. On a day-to-day basis, the problems of substance abuse, suicide, and mental illness are of greater significance.

Substance Abuse   Alcoholism and illegal drug use and abuse are major health problems in jails. Alcohol law violations (primarily public

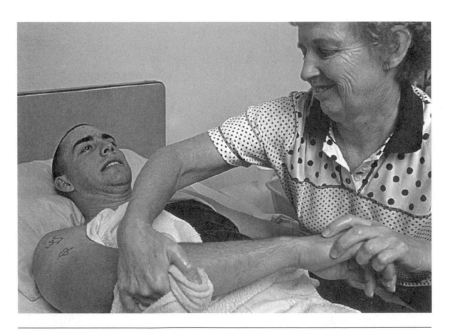

Significant health care problems among inmates are a serious concern for jail administrators.

intoxication) are the most common reason for arrest in the United States. Statistics from the Uniform Crime Reports suggest that between 20 and 40 percent of inmates are incarcerated for public intoxication. When those incarcerated for intoxication are actually alcoholics, they will go through withdrawal symptoms. Alcoholics have medical problems that affect the institution's organizational and managerial operations. Also, intoxication at the time of arrest is a major risk factor involved in inmates' suicides.

Alcohol users and abusers in jails also have a high rate of other health problems. In one large-scale study of New York individuals arrested for public drunkenness, many of those arrested had one or more health problems. Fifty percent arrived at jail with wounds, cuts, or burns; 25 percent had some types of seizures; 20 percent had broken bones; 20 percent had severe brain damage; 20 percent had internal bleeding; 20 percent reported hallucinations; and 14 percent reported cardiac problems.[38]

Large majorities of jail inmates are known to have used or to regularly use illegal drugs. According to the Bureau of Justice Statistics, in 1989 more than two-thirds of convicted inmates reported having at least once previously used illegal drugs, while well over one-half reported regular use. Convicted women, rather than men, more frequently reported illegal drug use. In fact, women are more likely to report having ever used "hard drugs,"[39] using hard drugs regularly, and having been under their influence at the time of their offenses.

The National Institute of Justice began its Drug Use Forecasting Program to estimate the prevalence of drug use among arrested individuals. In 1993, 23 cities were included as data collection sites. The range of males testing positive for any drug at the time of arrest ranged from a low of 54 percent in Omaha and San Jose to a high of 81 percent in Chicago. Female arrestees had positive drug test rates ranging from a low of 42 percent in San Antonio to a high of 83 percent in New York City.[40] The most common drug identified in testing adult arrestees was cocaine. Marijuana use has steadily decreased in prevalence among adult arrestees since the inception of the Drug Use Forecasting Program.

One study of jail inmates referred to substance abuse treatment programs reported that prior to their arrival, inmates had been drinking alcohol for an average of 8½ years and had been using cocaine for nearly 4½ years.[41] Not only had these inmates been using alcohol and drugs for a number of years, but they also frequently reported a history of unsuccessful attempts to complete substance abuse treatment programs. This suggests that many individuals will interrupt their alcohol or drug use while in jail but will need long-term follow-up and treatment programs after their release.

While large numbers of jail inmates report using illegal drugs, many of these individuals are not in jail for drug offenses. According to the U.S. Department of Justice, in 1993 "only" about one-fifth of all U.S. jail inmates were incarcerated for drug offenses.[42]

Suicide   Any discussion of inmates' health status must address the ultimate health problem: death. Some jail inmates do die while in jail, just as prison inmates do. During 1993 a total of 647 jail inmate deaths were reported. The reported causes of these deaths are diverse, although most are from natural causes. Approximately 50 percent of all jail deaths result from natural causes; approximately 10 percent of deaths are attributed to AIDS; and about 30 percent are due to suicide.

In terms of public outcry, deaths due to suicide are the most problematic issue confronting jail administrators. As inmates' most obvious indicator of problems adjusting to the jail setting, suicide attempts focus attention on jails' physical facilities, staff, and daily management. With approximately 200-400 completed suicides every year in U.S. jails, these problems obviously need to be addressed. The suicide rate among jail inmates is approximately 9 times higher than it is for the general population.[43] This rate is even higher among juveniles held in adult jails.[44] However, according to some observers, jail suicides remain a statistically rare event. David Lester and Bruce Danto argue that if viewed solely over a 24-hour period, only 2 out of about 1.2 million inmates behind bars will kill themselves on any given day.[45]

The characteristics of suicide attempts and of those who attempt suicide generally remain stable over time. Lindsay Hayes compared the characteristics of successful jail suicides in 1986 with those of the previous six years. She reported that, except for minor variations, most key characteristics of such events, including the individuals' offenses, states of intoxication, and methods and length of incarceration, remained constant.[46] Most notable among the "risk factors" associated with jail suicides are:

1. Inmates who come to the jail intoxicated.

2. Inmates who are physically and socially isolated in jail.

3. Inmates within their first 24 hours of detention.[47]

Some researchers have shown that fewer suicides occur in larger jails and in those where the staff/inmate ratio is lower. These studies emphasize the importance of inmate isolation and the role suicide plays as an "adjustment tool."[48]

Also important here are those instances in which inmates engage in generally non-life-threatening self-mutilation. Self-mutilation, commonly in the form of cutting and stabbing, accounts for nearly one-half of the "crisis situations" to which jail staff must respond.[49] In the 1990s legal liabilities and the potential for transmitting blood-borne diseases, such as HIV and hepatitis, add to the stress of such situations. These issues make clear the necessity for additional staff training in both emergency medical responses and organizational protective measures.

Mental Health   Also significant in the area of inmates' health problems is mental health. It is generally agreed that mental illness is a major health concern for jail inmates. However, the estimates of mental illness prevalence in this population are widely diverse. One 1983 study reported that 1 in 5 people admitted to U.S. jails was mentally ill or developmentally disabled.[50] Others have suggested that more than one-fifth of jail inmates can be diagnosed as psychotic and that nearly one-fourth of jail inmates have histories of long-term or multiple mental health hospitalizations.[51] Similarly, studies of older jail inmates, those over age 50, have shown that 15 percent are schizophrenic; 15 percent, neurotic depressives; 79 percent, personality disorders; and 61 percent, alcoholic.[52] Many of those studied had multiple diagnoses.

Somewhat surprisingly, those jail inmates diagnosed with the most serious mental health problems are four times more likely than non-psychotic inmates to be incarcerated for less serious offenses.[53] As suggested by numerous contemporary critics, the jails of the 1980s and 1990s have reverted to the roles filled by their predecessors centuries earlier. They have become depositories for society's undesirables and "different" members, not necessarily places reserved for criminals.

Summary

Jails and other local correctional facilities are often confused with prisons. However, some very important differences exist between the types of facilities. The inmates in each type of facility also differ in personal traits and legal standing. Operations among jails also vary.

Jail administration is of four basic forms: by local government, state government, regional cooperative agreements, and private operation. While local (usually county or city) government administration is by far the most common, regional cooperative arrangements and private operations are becoming more popular. Changes in jail operations are largely due to problems and financial difficulties.

Jails are a large, problem-plagued part of the criminal justice system. Many problems that hinder jail operations are difficult to overcome, however, because they arise from the institutions' basic purpose and daily operations. However, the one pervasive problem is the lack of money to correct other problems. This is similar to other aspects of corrections, however. Jails have few funds; they are often overcrowded and in poor physical condition; they house large numbers of inmates with a variety of problems; and they have difficulties recruiting and maintaining high-quality staffs.

The future for local correctional facilities promises changes. These changes will most probably result from crises and immediate needs, not from administrators' "luxury" of planning for changes to improve conditions.

QUESTIONS FOR REVIEW

1. How have the goals and procedures of local correctional efforts evolved?

2. How many people are housed in U.S. jails? Why are U.S. jails overcrowded?

3. What types of people (in terms of social statuses) are most likely to be in jail?

4. How are jails managed? Who has responsibility for overseeing the day-to-day responsibilities of jails?

5. What alternative models of jail administration are currently being used? What are the advantages and disadvantages of these models of administration?

6. What are the major problems in the administration and operation of jails?

7. What types of problems are typically found in jails' physical facilities, and why do these problems exist?

8. What types of programming opportunities are available for jail inmates?

9. What types of people are typically working in jails? What problems do jail administrators face in having high-quality staffs?

10. In what ways do inmates' generally poor health status impact the correctional facility's daily functioning?

ACTIVITIES

1. Contact your local jail and arrange for a tour of the facility.

2. Locate an individual in your community who has previously served time in prison. Talk with this individual about the differences between the time spent in prison and the time spent in jail.

3. Talk to your family and friends about whether they would be willing to work in a jail. What would they see as the attractions to such a job? What would they see as the negative aspects of such a job?

ENDNOTES

1. Michael Welch, "How Are Jails Depicted by Corrections Textbooks? A Content Analysis Provides a Closer Look," *American Jails: The Magazine of the American Jail Association,* July–August 1992, pp. 28–34.

2. Craig Perkins, James J. Stephan, and Allen J. Beck, *Jails and Jail Inmates, 1993–94* (Washington, D.C.: Bureau of Justice Statistics, 1995).

3. H. Burns, *Corrections: Organization and Administration* (St. Paul: West Publishing Co., 1995), p. 149.

4. Linda Zupan, *Jails: Reform and the New Generation Philosophy* (Cincinnati: Anderson Publishing Co., 1991), p. 15.

5. Burns, *op. cit.*, p. 153; Zupan, *loc. cit.*

6. W. R. Nelson and M. O'Toole, *New Generation Jails* (Boulder, CO: Library Information Specialists, Inc., 1983).

7. Dale Sechrest, *Correctional Facility Design and Construction Management* (Washington, D.C.: National Institute of Justice, 1985), pp. 96–99.

8. *Ibid.*

9. Randall Guynes, *Nation's Jail Managers Assess Their Problems* (Washington, D.C.: National Institute of Justice, 1988).

10. Perkins, et al., *op. cit.*

11. *Ibid.*

12. *Ibid.*

13. Tracy L. Snell, *Women in Jail, 1989* (Washington, D.C.: Bureau of Justice Statistics, 1992).

14. G. Larry Mays and Joel A. Thompson, "Mayberry Revisited: The Characteristics and Operations of America's Small Jails," *Justice Quarterly,* Vol. 5, No. 3, 1988, pp. 421–440.

15. *Statistical Abstract of the United States: 1992* (112th ed.) (Washington, D.C.: Bureau of the Census, 1992), pp. 22–23.

16. G. Larry Mays and Joel A. Thompson, "The Political and Organizational Context of American Jails," in Joel A. Thompson and G. Larry Mays (eds.), *American Jails: Public Policy Issues* (Chicago: Nelson-Hall, 1991).

17. U.S. Department of Justice, *Report to the Nation on Crime and Justice* (Washington, D.C.: Bureau of Justice Statistics, 1983); G. Larry Mays and Joel A. Thompson, "Mayberry Revisited."

18. Charles H. Logan, "The Propriety of Proprietary Prisons," *Federal Probation,* Vol. 51, No. 3, 1987, pp. 35–50.

19. Michael T. Charles, Sesha Kethineni, and Jeffrey L. Thompson, "The State of Jails in America," *Federal Probation,* Vol. 56, No. 2, 1992, pp. 56–62.

20. *Ibid.*

21. *Ibid.*

22. *Ibid.*

23. Paul B. Paulus and Garvin McCain, "Crowding in Jails," *Basic and Applied Social Psychology,* Vol. 4, No. 2, 1983, pp. 89–107; Richard E. Wener and Christopher Keys, "The Effects of Changes in Jail Population Densities on Crowding, Sick Call, and Spatial

Behavior," *Journal of Applied Social Psychology,* Vol. 18, No. 10, 1988, pp. 852–866.

24. Louis W. Jankowski, *Jail Inmates, 1991* (Washington, D.C.: Bureau of Justice Statistics, 1992), p. 8.

25. *Ibid.*

26. Perkins, et al., *op. cit.*

27. Perkins, et al., *op. cit.*

28. Guynes, *op. cit.,* p. 4.

29. Thomas R. Barry, "Jail Security: A Unique Challenge," *Corrections Today,* Vol. 49, 1987, pp. 16–18; "Survey: Correctional Officers," *Corrections Compendium,* Vol. 8, 1984, pp. 1–4.

30. Guynes, *op. cit.,* p. 4.

31. *The State of Our Nation's Jails, 1982* (Washington, D.C.: National Sheriff's Association, 1982).

32. Guynes, *op. cit.,* p. 5.

33. Francis Cullen, Bruce G. Link, Nancy T. Wolfe, and James Frank, "The Social Dimensions of Correctional Officer Stress," *Justice Quarterly,* Vol. 2, 1985, pp. 505–533; Susan Philliber, "Thy Brother's Keeper: A Review of the Literature on Correctional Officers," *Justice Quarterly,* Vol. 4, 1987, pp. 9–37.

34. Jeffrey D. Senese, "Communications and Inmate Management: Interactions Among Jail Employees," *Journal of Criminal Justice,* Vol. 19, No. 2, 1991, pp. 151–163.

35. G. Larry Mays and Mary K. Stohr, "Personal Characteristics and Training of Staff in Exclusively Women's Jails: A Descriptive Analysis," paper presented at the annual meeting of the Academy of Criminal Justice Sciences, Kansas City, MO, 1993.

36. U.S. Department of Justice, National Institute of Justice, Office of Research Programs, *American Prisons and Jails, Vol. III: Conditions and Costs of Confinement* (Washington, D.C.: U.S. Government Printing Office, 1980).

37. Paulus and McCain, *op. cit.;* Wener and Keys, *op. cit.*

38. *Jails in America: An Overview of Issues* (College Park, MD: American Correctional Association, 1985).

39. Hard drugs in this instance include cocaine, heroin, PCP, LSD, and methadone.

40. U.S. Department of Justice, *Drug Use Forecasting: 1993 Annual Report on Arrestees* (Washington, D.C.: National Institute of Justice, 1994).

41. Perkins, et al., *op. cit.*

42. U.S. Department of Justice, *Drugs and Crime Facts, 1991* (Washington, D.C.: Bureau of Justice Statistics, 1992).

43. Lindsay Hayes, "National Study of Jail Suicides: Seven Years Later," *Psychiatric Quarterly,* Vol. 60, No. 1, 1989, pp. 7–29.

44. Michael Flaherty, "The National Incidence of Juvenile Suicide in Adult Jails and Juvenile Detention Centers," *Suicide and Life-Threatening Behavior,* Vol. 13, No. 2, 1983, pp. 85–94.

45. David Lester and Bruce L. Danto, *Suicide Behind Bars: Prediction and Prevention* (Philadelphia: The Charles Press, 1993).

46. Hayes, *op. cit.*

47. Flaherty, *op. cit.;* Hayes, *op. cit.;* Gregory Winkler, "Assessing and Responding to Suicidal Jail Inmates," *Community Mental Health*

Journal, Vol. 28, No. 4, 1992, pp. 317–326.

48. John Wooldredge and Thomas Winfree, "An Aggregate-Level Study of Inmate Suicides and Deaths Due to Natural Causes in U.S. Jails," *Journal of Research in Crime and Delinquency,* Vol. 29, No. 4, 1992, pp. 466–479.

49. R. Johnson, "Ameliorating Prison Stress: Some Helping Roles for Custodial Personnel," *Prison Ecology for Correctional Managers,* unpublished report, 1976.

50. Katharine H. Briar, "Jails: Neglected Asylums," *Social Casework,* Vol. 64, No. 7, 1983, pp. 387–393.

51. Glenn E. Swank and Darryl Winer, "Occurrence of Psychiatric Disorder in a County Jail Population," *American Journal of Psychiatry*, Vol. 133, No. 11, 1976, pp. 1331–1333.

52. Patricia A. Washington, "Mature Mentally Ill Offenders in California Jails," *Journal of Offender Counseling, Services and Rehabilitation*, Vol. 13, No. 2, 1989, pp. 161–173.

53. Edwin V. Valdiserri, Kenneth R. Carroll, and Alan J. Hartl, "A Study of Offenses Committed by Psychotic Inmates in a County Jail," *Hospital and Community Psychiatry*, Vol. 37, No. 2, 1986, pp. 163–166.

CHAPTER 11

Community Corrections

CHAPTER OBJECTIVES

In the last chapter we examined the structure and processes of local correctional institutions and compared them with prisons. In this chapter we examine community corrections. After reading this chapter, you will be able to:

1. Discuss the arguments for and against the use of community-based correctional programs.

2. Identify the historical basis of probation.

3. Compare the historical precedents of community correctional programs with the modern versions.

4. Understand the social and political reasons for which U.S. versions of community corrections were founded and the reasons for its growth.

5. Explain the major varieties of community correctional programs used in our society.

6. Discuss home incarceration programs and explain why they are commonly used.

7. Identify and compare those serving sentences in community corrections with those serving sentences in institutions.

8. Discuss the legal foundation for using probation as a criminal sentence.

9. Understand the range of legal restrictions that can be imposed on probationers.

10. Explain the process for and legal restrictions on revocation of probation.

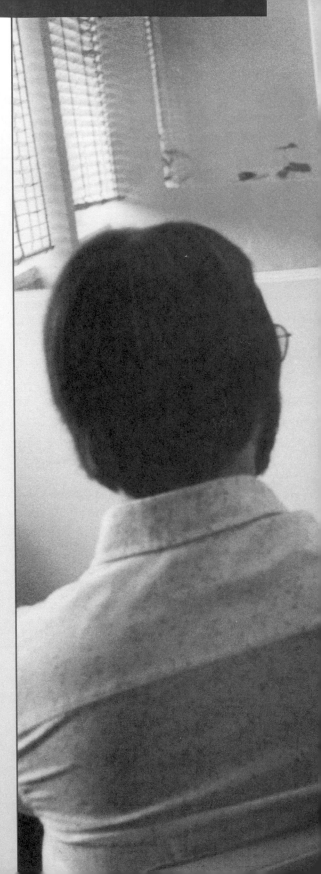

KEY TERMS

community corrections
suspended sentence
release on one's own
  recognizance (ROR)
probation
intensive supervision
  probation (ISP)
diversion centers
home incarceration
electronic monitoring
passive monitoring
  system

active monitoring
  system
revocation of
  probation
due process
restitution
community service
technical violations
due process rights
hearing

CHAPTER OUTLINE

One aspect of probation is client counseling.

Community Corrections Versus Institutional Corrections

As popularly thought, corrections usually involves some form of incarceration. However, incarceration is not the only or even most common form of corrections in our society. A majority of convicted offenders are sentenced to forms of corrections that keep them in their communities but impose upon them some degree of supervision and programming. These programs are called **community corrections** and include probation, home incarceration, and diversion programs.

More offenders are in community correctional programs than in prison and jail combined. However, many still strongly debate whether using community corrections is wise, appropriate, and safe. Our reliance on community corrections (especially probation) is based on both practical concerns and beliefs in specific correctional ideologies. Ideologies, of course, cause some people to believe we should incarcerate more (or all) offenders, rather than place them in community-based correctional programs.

The practical concerns that fuel debates about community corrections include overcrowding, financial costs

Community corrections Programs that allow offenders to remain in their home communities but impose upon them some degree of supervision and programming.

> # FYI
> **P**robation is the most common criminal sentence used in the United States. In most states offenders are eligible for probation for a large majority of crimes, including violent felonies.

of corrections, and concerns about recidivism. In terms of correctional ideologies, those who argue for using such programs commonly hold to some combination of rehabilitation, reintegration, and deterrence. On the other hand, those who argue against community corrections commonly hold to some combination of retribution, incapacitation, and deterrence. One's view of community corrections largely depends on what one believes the purpose of corrections is and how effective both options are in reducing crime.

Arguments in Favor of Incarceration

There are two primary arguments against community corrections and in favor of incarceration. First is the argument that convicted criminals should be punished (retribution) because they have broken the law. To be allowed to remain in their home communities rather than being sent to prison is not a right.[1] Some observers deem it inappropriate to grant convicted offenders privileges that include community corrections (probation and other forms of community-based programming). If the criminal justice system's purpose is to punish offenders and to protect citizens from offenders, then it should remove privileges from offenders.

The second argument against community corrections centers on rehabilitation. Although rehabilitation possibilities are among the strongest reasons for *not* placing offenders into an institutional setting, opponents of community corrections believe that offenders allowed to remain in their home communities will likely commit crime again. That is, offenders are less likely to be either rehabilitated, deterred, or incapacitated from future criminal activity unless they are locked up. Therefore, incarceration is necessary to remove the "bad influences" and to rebuild offenders into law-abiding people.

Opponents who believe community corrections is an ineffective rehabilitation method worry about offenders' recidivism. That is, if offenders remain in the community, they are likely to commit more crimes. Unless offenders are incarcerated so they do not want to commit crimes (deterrence) or are unable to commit crimes (incapacitation), recidivism rates are predicted to be rather high. These issues can be directly measured by comparing probationers with offenders who are sentenced to prison or jail. These measures do support the argument that community corrections may be associated with high rates of recidivism.

The work of Petersilia, et al. supports the argument that offenders sentenced to community-based programs often repeat crimes.[2] This study followed a sample of convicted felons sentenced to probation in California for a period of 40 months. At the end of the follow-up period, the researchers reported that approximately two-thirds of the offenders were rearrested at least once. Obviously, these individuals had not been incapacitated, deterred, or successfully rehabilitated. This is not the only research to support the claim that offenders serving sentences in community correctional programs continue to commit crimes. In fact, reviews of probation "success" and "failure" rates have traditionally shown that anywhere from 16 percent to 55 percent of felons on probation "fail."[3] Failure on probation can mean anything from being rearrested (on any charges) to removing the "privilege" of serving a sentence in the community instead of in prison and, hence, returning the individual to prison for the same crime.

So, in summary, critics of community corrections present some logical arguments that have evidence to support them. This position has support from "common sense," ideological beliefs, and research designed to measure the success of such programs. However, these same sources of support against community corrections also provide support for community corrections. We move next to these arguments.

Arguments in Favor of Keeping Offenders in the Community

Probation emerged in the United States during an era of many social changes. These changes concerned both the way our society was structured and the philosophical basis of what could and should be done with criminal offenders. A by-product of the Enlightenment period, the classical school of criminology called for eliminating harsh punishments and basing criminal justice on a system of citizenship rights. Along with this set of ideas was a focus on humanitarianism and a belief that people could be steered from inappropriate choices

Probationers often perform maintenance tasks as part of their community service obligations.

of behavior. No longer did we believe criminal offenders were inherently evil; instead, they were people who chose to behave in socially inappropriate ways. The way to teach appropriate social behavior, then, is to work with offenders while still in their communities.

Today, we continue to rely heavily on probation as a way of dealing with offenders. We want to "correct" offenders' behavior, but we rely on probation for other practical, necessary reasons. First, overcrowding in our prisons makes alternative sentences necessary, and this is a financially, politically driven argument in favor of probation. If we do not use probation, then we must either do nothing with, for, or to offenders (which is simply unacceptable to most people) or incarcerate many more people. The latter alternative is not feasible in much of our world today. The financial costs of building, staffing, and maintaining an ever-increasing number of prisons is simply too great.

These facts have led to the U.S. public's rather widespread support of community corrections. According to a recent national survey, 80 percent of Americans favor sentencing nondangerous offenders to programs outside prisons.[4] People are most favorable toward keeping offenders in the community when they believe that such will both assist the individual offenders (through requiring them to hold a job and to receive counseling) and make a positive contribution to the community (through community service and restitution to victims).

Generally speaking, though, the objectives of probation are not to benefit the corrections system, but to benefit offenders. The general objectives of probation are to:[5]

1. Reintegrate amenable offenders.
2. Protect the community from further antisocial behavior.
3. Further the goals of justice.
4. Provide probation conditions (and services) necessary to change offenders and to achieve the above objectives.

If we argue in favor of probation for convicted offenders, we must show that probation programs successfully achieve these objectives. The primary way to evaluate these objectives is to examine the rates at which offenders on probation return to criminal activity.

While the political argument in favor of probation is often criticized for being "soft on crime," the research on recidivism suggests that such criticisms are not completely correct. One major argument discussed earlier in favor of incarceration is that offenders on probation have high rates of recidivism. However, this is not a universal conclusion of recidivism research. Some research shows that probationers do not have high recidivism rates. Two state-level studies, one in Kentucky and one in Missouri, found that felons on probation for periods of 36 and 40 months had a recidivism rate of only 22 percent.[6] Moreover, in a comprehensive review of the research literature on the success or failure of probation as a criminal sentence, Kathryn Morgan has concluded that

FYI

Public support for community correctional programs varies according to the characteristics of individuals and communities. For instance:

- Support is highest in the West and lowest in the South.
- Support is higher among those who identify themselves as very liberal and lowest among those who consider themselves very conservative. (But even here, over two-thirds support community corrections.)
- Support is highest among nonwhite Americans.
- Opposition is highest among those older than 65.

Source: "Community Corrections Survey: Public Indicates Strong Support," *Corrections Today,* December 1991, p. 134.

"probation is effective as a correctional alternative."[7] Furthermore, the Rand Institute study discussed earlier, which reported approximately two-thirds of probationers recidivating, was reexamined by the same researchers to see how offenders on probation compared with offenders sent to prison. Much to the surprise of many critics of probation, the offenders on probation actually had lower rates of recidivism.[8]

However, it would be irresponsible to suggest that probation is the sentence of choice for all, or for all varieties of, offenders. Rather, we need first to identify what types of offenders would benefit more from probation. In an effort to do exactly this, one team of researchers has examined both the presentence investigations and postsentencing behavior of first-time offenders. It discovered that, as many other researchers have suggested, the factors related with "success" while on probation are as follows:

1. The most significant predictor of probation success is age. Older offenders are more likely than younger offenders to remain crime-free while on probation.

2. Employment is also important. Full-time employed *and* financially stable offenders are more likely to succeed while on probation.

3. Married offenders and those with military backgrounds are most likely to stay crime-free.

4. Offenders who have spent the least (if any) time in jail prior to their convictions are most likely to successfully complete probation.[9]

One factor related to probation success, however, makes the picture a bit cloudy and difficult. Offenders who are most likely to recidivate while on probation are those convicted of theft-related offenses, not personal or violent crime.[10] The difficulty here, as we will see in the following sections, is that the public views probation as an "easy" or "soft" sentence and, therefore, appropriate only for nonviolent offenders. However, these are precisely the type of offenders who are most likely to repeat their crimes if on probation.

History of Probation

Probation, as a recognized formal process, did not develop until the mid-nineteenth century. However, prior to that time judicial and quasi-judicial forerunners of probation existed. Included in the primary forerunners of probation are: benefit of clergy, judicial reprieve, recognizance, bail, and filing of cases. Each procedure will be discussed briefly to understand the developmental process that led to what today we call probation.

Benefit of Clergy

Although its origin is unknown, benefit of clergy began in the thirteenth century, when clerics who were convicted of crimes could have their cases transferred to church tribunals for sentencing. Whereas in modern times church law mainly governs its members' religious affairs and pertains to a particular denomination, in medieval Europe canon or ecclesiastical law was as important as civil law.

Benefit of clergy indirectly resulted from the monarchy's increasing power. Henry II insisted that clerics who violated the secular laws be tried in the civil courts. Benefit of clergy was a compromise and, of course, actually a benefit to the offender. Though the bishop could impose severe penance, his disposition was much more tolerable than hanging. Practiced centuries later in the American colonies, benefit of clergy was stopped shortly after the Revolution.

Judicial Reprieve

A basic element of probation is the suspension of a sentence. Historians have traced suspension of sentence to the judicial reprieve that English courts used. A **suspended sentence** is simply withholding imposition of a sentence for a period of time. Judicial reprieve was a temporary suspension that permitted the defendant to petition the Crown for full or partial pardon. In simple terms, this was a way of appealing one's conviction and allowing the offender not to suffer the pains of punishment while pursuing this option. Judicial reprieve first involved only a postponement of a sentence, but soon developed to the point where many suspended sentences were not reimposed. Basically, judicial reprieve is a reliance on the court's discretionary power.

Suspended sentence A punishment that is withheld but can be reimposed if the offender violates court-imposed conditions.

Recognizance

Release on one's own recognizance (ROR) is release from custody without bail while awaiting trial. People who are "ROR'd" are released on their honor and obligated to appear in court on the scheduled date.

Practiced in England for centuries, recognizance has sometimes involved posting a surety or bond to guarantee appearance in court. It is thus more similar to bail than is the present system of recognizance, which does not involve bail. The first recorded use of recognizance in the United States was in the case of *Commonwealth v. Chase,* an 1830 Boston municipal court case. Both England and New England practiced recognizance for much of the nineteenth century as a common way of dealing with nonserious crimes of youthful offenders.

Release on one's own recognizance (ROR) Release from custody without bail while awaiting trial.

Bail

The concept of bail is more familiar than the preceding forerunners of probation. Recognizance developed as a way of avoiding overly harsh punishments, but bail is a practical way of ensuring the defendant's appearance in court. In paying the bail and accepting custody of the bailed person, the bailor supervised the defendant to some degree. Without this supervision aspect, early bail systems would not be considered predecessors of probation.

Filing of Cases

Massachusetts developed an unusual form of reprieve: A sentence could be suspended and the case "filed." Filing a case required both the defendant's and prosecutor's consent, and the judge could set conditions to which the defendant was subject. The primary objective of this practice was to lessen the penalty, which reflected the courts' willingness to recognize extenuating circumstances. The suspension of a sentence, conditional release, and the imposition of conditions are also characteristic of today's versions of probation. However, unlike probation, no court-appointed official supervises the offender.

John Augustus

The American pioneer of probation, John Augustus was 57 and a very successful Boston bootmaker when he became interested in court activities in 1841. Since major changes were also taking place in the British courts, evolution was occurring simultaneously on both sides of the Atlantic. Seeing a bedraggled man appear for sentencing on a common drunk charge, Augustus was drawn to the unfortunate man. Augustus talked with the offender for a few moments and was so impressed that he asked the court to release the man to his care rather than sentencing him to the House of Correction. In describing this experience, Augustus first used the word "probation."[11] Therefore, Augustus is known as the "father of probation."

Extending his labors, Augustus became almost a fixture in the Boston lower courts. By 1858 he had bailed out 1,152 men and boys, and 794 women and girls, and he had also helped 3,000 neglected women. Of the first 1,100 on whom Augustus kept records, only one forfeited bond. His work was remarkable, and his compassion was desperately needed, for the times were heavily oriented toward punishment. Among the people Augustus helped were a 10-year-old who had been charged with highway robbery for keeping 6 cents that belonged to a friend and a 7-year-old child who had been charged with rape. However, even though today we regard John Augustus favorably, this was not necessarily the way he was viewed during his lifetime. The press's initial coverage of his actions and the public's reaction were not favorable. Augustus was criticized for being too easy on criminals and for preventing them from being properly punished.

John Augustus died in 1859, leaving a legacy that would have a lasting impact on the course of U.S. corrections. However, he did not see his work become a permanent part of the U.S. criminal justice system. Not until 1878 did Massachusetts pass the first state probation law, which began the slow spread of probation.

In fact, not until the development of the juvenile court system in 1899 did probation become popular in the United States. The new juvenile court system emphasized reforming offenders. Many people recognized the importance of keeping juvenile offenders with their families; and the way to accomplish this, while also providing an active role for the courts and criminal justice system, was to use probation. After probation became relatively common for juveniles, the process slowly spread into adult corrections. Not until 1956 did all the states have adult probation programs in place.

Forms of Probation

So, what exactly is probation? So far in this chapter we have assumed that the reader knows precisely what is meant by this term. We all have at least a general idea of the practice. However, even professionals in the criminal justice and corrections systems cannot concur on an interpretation of "probation." First, as we should know, probation means having been convicted of a criminal offense but being allowed to stay in the community as long as certain restrictions are followed. Traditionally, probation has been treated as a court sentence. Actually, only for a little over a decade have the courts sentenced offenders directly to probation. When federal and state courts placed convicted offenders on probation, this really meant that offenders' "real" sentences were terms in prison or jail but, as a privilege, those sentences were suspended. Instead, convicted offenders were placed on probation *in place of* being incarcerated. However, as a result of the Sentencing Reform Act of 1984, federal law now explicitly recognizes probation as a sentence in and of itself.[12]

Probation services, unlike incarceration programs, are administered by different agencies and segments of the government in different states. The state government has responsibility—just as with prisons—in 32 states. Twelve states have probation based at the county government level, and 6 states have a mixture of state and local authorities working together to administer community corrections.

For a formal definition of **probation,** we can review one that a set of renowned researchers has offered. Probation is:

> . . . a sentence which establishes the defendant's legal status under which his [or her] freedom in the community is continued or only briefly interrupted, subjected to supervision by a "probation organization" and subject to conditions imposed by the court. The sentencing court retains the authority to modify the conditions of the sentence or resentence the offender if he [or she] violates the conditions.[13]

Simply because a particular sentence and form of supervision is called "probation" certainly does not mean that we can know precisely what is being done with, for, and to individual offenders. Probation, as we saw in the previous section, evolved from several different (and sometimes competing) areas of thought. Sometimes probation is dominated by a social work perspective, which seeks to "help" offenders. Sometimes probation is dominated by a religious perspective, which seeks to "save" offenders. Sometimes probation is dominated by a punishment perspective, which seeks to "control" offenders. At other times some combination of these ideals may dominate a "probation" program.[14] Figure 11–1 demonstrates that probation takes on varying forms even within the same jurisdiction.

Figure 11–1 The four forms of probation under Florida statutes.

1. *Administrative probation* is a form of noncontact supervision in which an offender who presents a low risk of harm to the community may, upon satisfactory completion of half the term of probation, be placed by the Department of Corrections on nonreporting status until expiration of the term of supervision. The department is authorized to collect an initial processing fee of up to $50 for each probationer reduced to administrative probation.

2. *Community control* means a form of intensive, supervised custody in the community, including surveillance on weekends and holidays, administered by officers with restricted caseloads. Community control is an individualized program in which the freedom of an offender is restricted within the community, home, or noninstitutional residential placement and specific sanctions are imposed and enforced.

3. *Drug offender probation* means a form of intensive supervision which emphasizes treatment of drug offenders in accordance with individualized treatment plans administered by officers with restricted caseloads. Caseloads should be restricted to a maximum of 50 cases per officer in order to ensure an adequate level of staffing.

4. *Probation* means a form of community supervision requiring specified contacts with parole and probation officers and other terms and conditions as provided.

Source: Florida Revised Statutes, § 948.001 to 948.01, 1993.

New models of probation have become increasingly popular throughout the 1980s and 1990s. Including both more intensive and less intensive forms of supervision than have traditionally been associated with probation, these new models intend to maximize routing individual offenders into law-abiding behavior. Consequently, some offenders will need more contact and individualized direction, while others may need fewer resources devoted to their particular cases.

Intensive Supervision Probation (ISP)

Among the first modifications made to probation, **intensive supervision probation (ISP)** requires officers to make more frequent checks (scheduled and unscheduled) on probationers. ISP officers usually have smaller caseloads (10 to 50 probationers) than officers working standard probation cases. Also, in some states (such as Georgia) ISP officers may work in teams of two. This allows them to supervise their clients more closely and to check on several clients at the same time.

Generally, intensive supervision probation includes conditions such as a curfew, regular alcohol and drug testing, community service, requirements to hold (or be looking for) a full-time job, and no travel out of the county. Also, probation officers will regularly visit the probationers' employers, homes, or other typical locations to see what offenders are doing and to administer alcohol or drug screenings. While there is no set model for how they should function, nearly all intensive supervision programs have four central elements:

1. Multiple weekly contacts with a supervising probation officer.

2. Random and unannounced drug tests.

3. Strict enforcement of probation conditions, including more stringent conditions than those applied to offenders on standard probation.

4. Required participation in treatment, education, work and/ or community service programs.

Many offenders consider intensive supervision probation very restrictive. In some states about 10 percent of offenders choose instead to serve jail sentences. For those who serve sentences on intensive supervision probation, offenders are subject to sanctions when they

Intensive supervision probation (ISP) A form of community corrections supervision in which probation officers check on a smaller caseload of offenders more frequently, often unannounced.

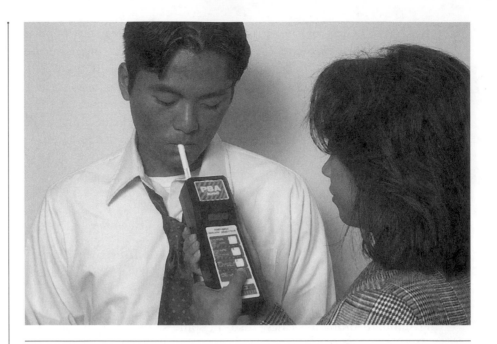

Under intensive supervision, probation officers may administer regular drug and/or alcohol tests.

violate a condition (such as having a positive Breathalyzer or urine test). The "punishments" given in response to violations are increasingly severe as the number and seriousness of violations increase. These range from having yet more contact with the probation officer to extra community service to removal from probation in favor of incarceration.

Diversion Centers

Diversion centers A form of intermediate sanction where offenders live in a facility for a few months and are supervised 24 hours per day, but can leave for work and other forms of necessary activity.

Another alternative form of probation is **diversion centers,** which attempt to find a middle ground between incarceration and supervision while free in the community. Offenders live in diversion centers and are supervised 24 hours a day. To be eligible for diversion center placements, offenders must hold jobs, and they can leave the centers only to perform their jobs. In addition to their regular jobs, diversion center residents regularly perform community service projects. The usual stay in diversion centers is relatively short, usually around 6 months. After leaving diversion centers, offenders are placed on regular probation. Diversion centers allow offenders to keep ties to their communities, yet provide them close supervision to guide them to law-abiding behavior.

Home Incarceration

Finally, the newest alternative to standard probation is **home incarceration.** Offenders who need something more than standard probation, who do not need round-the-clock, direct supervision, and who have an established life in the community may be sentenced to remain at home. In some ways, home incarceration is similar to when parents "ground" their children for punishment. That is, they must stay at home, except for specific functions such as school, work, or scheduled trips to the grocery store. The idea behind home incarceration is incapacitating offenders from committing future crimes because they have no access to victims.

Just as when parents (here, the legal system) ground their children (here, the offenders), parents cannot always be present to make sure their children remain at home. **Electronic monitoring** systems have answered this problem. Activating signals to the supervising probation department when individuals stray too far from home, electronic devices are semi-permanently attached to offenders.

Electronic monitoring is done in one of two ways: passive and active. Using a **passive monitoring system,** offenders wear electronic devices that emit continuous signals to receivers attached to offenders' home telephones. If the signals are broken, the receivers communicate with a computer at the local probation department that prints a notice that the offenders have violated their conditions of home incarceration. Offenders may leave home, but only during prearranged times to go to work, school, doctors, or other approved programs. A second form of monitoring is done with an **active monitoring system.** With an active system, offenders wear devices that, rather than constantly emitting signals, emit signals when plugged into devices attached to the offenders' home telephones. A computer program at the probation office randomly dials home telephone numbers of all home incarceration offenders several times a day. When offenders receive calls, they must answer their telephones within a specified number of rings. Then, when greeted by the computer voice, offenders must plug their bracelets into the devices. At this time, signals are generated and identify offenders to the computer. Because the computer must reach

Home incarceration Sentence where individuals are required to remain in their homes, except for special reasons (work, school, medical care); purpose is to incapacitate offenders from recommitting their offenses.

Electronic monitoring Use of special devices to signal supervising probation departments when offenders on home incarceration leave their premises, thereby violating the conditions of their sentence.

Passive monitoring system A form of electronic monitoring where devices emit constant signals to receivers attached to offenders' telephones; if the constant signals are broken, the devices automatically alert the probation department that offenders are in violation of the conditions of home incarceration.

Active monitoring system A form of electronic monitoring where offenders wear devices that, when activated, will respond to telephone requests to show that offenders are remaining at home.

Probation officers must have many different skills. Perhaps most important among these skills are the abilities to manage many tasks at one time, to be flexible, and to manage time and energies very well. Probation officers work with offenders to rehabilitate them, to supervise their activities, to serve as counselors and sources of referral, and in most states to conduct presentence reports on convicted offenders prior to their sentencing.

The overall goal of probation officers is both to protect the community by closely supervising offenders and to assist offenders to live law-abiding lives. Many probation officers find that much of their time is spent in helping people find jobs, finish school, find child-care, find a place to live, and become involved in support groups or other treatment programs. Much of probation officers' work requires the combined skills of social workers and law enforcement officers.

In most jurisdictions, probation officers are responsible for more than 100 individual cases. The average number of cases for which probation officers are responsible has been increasing in recent years. In 1994 the average caseload for probation officers was 124 cases. This is a 10 percent increase over one year earlier. Even with today's increased emphasis on incarceration, the caseloads of probation officers are expected only to increase.

In almost all cases, the minimum requirements for probation officers include a bachelor's degree, with preference given to applicants whose degree is in some social science. Usually the hiring process includes some form of testing (usually written) and several interviews. When applicants have experience working directly with clients in addition to their education, they have an advantage.

Probation officers are usually paid at a slightly higher rate than correctional officers. The median starting salary for entry-level probation officers is about $23,000. With a few years' experience and perhaps promotions, the pay of probation officers can be fairly good, going as high as $65,000 for officers who move into administrative positions.

Source: U.S. Department of Labor, Bureau of Labor Statistics, *Occupational Outlook Handbook,* 1994–95 ed., p. 296.

offenders at any and all times, most departments restrict people on home incarceration to telephone calls of no more than five minutes. If offenders are unable to respond to the random calls, then a printout is generated in the probation department, and offenders are considered to have violated conditions of home incarceration.

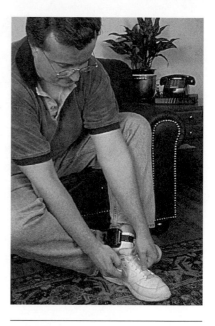

Probationers are often required to wear an electronic monitoring device during home incarceration.

Profile of Offenders in Community Corrections

Community corrections, the name for the collection of correctional programs in which offenders remain in free-society communities, is used increasingly in the United States. At the end of 1994 more than 2.9 million U.S. adults were on some form of probation.[15] This represents approximately 60 percent of all people being served by U.S. corrections. There are more than twice as many people on probation as there are in prison in the United States. The characteristics and statuses of these offenders, just as with all statistics in corrections, are not a representative cross-section of the U.S. population.

As expected, based on crime statistics and incarceration rates, definite patterns form in the representation of the sexes and races in the ranks of probationers. Of course, a majority of probationers are male. Although more women are represented here, these figures are similar to those previously seen for prison inmates. (See Table 11–1.) Women are more likely than men to receive sentences of probation (whether due to sex discrimination or to the fact that they commit "less serious" offenses). However, where the statistics on probationers differ significantly from those on prison inmates are in regard to the race of adults on probation. As shown in Table 11–1, 58 percent of probationers are white. While African-Americans are more than one-half the number (about 32%) of whites on probation, we need to remember that the percentage of African-Americans on probation is still an overrepresentation when considering they number only about 12.5 percent of the U.S. population.

Also somewhat surprising, the offenses for which adults are placed on probation do not follow expectations. As also shown in Table 11–1, nearly one-half of all probationers have committed felonies. This suggests that it is not necessarily just "minor" offenses for

Table 11–1	Characteristics of Adults on Probation	
Characteristic		**Percent of Adult Probationers**
Sex		
Male		79
Female		21
Race		
White		58
African-American		32
All others		10
Offense		
Felony		48
Misdemeanor		30
DWI/DUI		21
All others		1

Source: U.S. Department of Justice, *Probation and Parole, 1994* (Washington, D.C.: Bureau of Justice Statistics, 1995).

which probation is used. This can also be attributed to the fact that probation is used increasingly as an alternative to a sentence of incarceration to control the size of prison populations.

Statutory law in the individual state (or federal) jurisdiction determines the types of offenses for which probation is a legal option at the point of sentencing. Many states' legislatures have written their laws to exclude from consideration for probation those offenders convicted of particular offenses. However, even with such guidelines, decisions about which offenders receive sentences of probation are highly individualized. However, in most instances, all sentencing operates in this manner.

All forms of community corrections have been increasingly imposed in the past several decades. This increased use of probation can be due to changes in ideologies of political and correctional policymakers. However, more appropriately, we can attribute these large increases to the sheer numbers of offenders with whom our legal system must deal. As the number of people convicted of crimes continues to increase, it becomes impossible (and, as seen earlier, very expensive) to imprison all offenders. Therefore, with very few exceptions, the number of probationers has increased dramatically in all states. As shown in Table 11–2, today nearly 3 million U.S. adults

Table 11–2 — Adult Probation Populations, 1977, 1983, 1989, 1994

Jurisdiction	1977	1983	1989	1994
Total	812,485	1,502,247	2,520,479	2,962,166
Northeast				
Maine	2,348	3,495	6,851	8,669
New Hampshire	1,891	2,229	2,991	4,323
Vermont	2,476	4,264	5,399	8,676
Massachusetts	98,661	24,573	88,529	46,672
Rhode Island	4,080	6,495	12,231	18,179
Connecticut	17,136	40,571	42,842	53,453
New York	51,801	82,867	128,707	164,569
New Jersey	31,981	41,740	66,753	106,921
Pennsylvania	47,751	63,684	89,491	99,524
North Central				
Ohio	3,554	36,225	78,223	105,953
Indiana	14,155	NA	61,861	82,804
Illinois	51,258	58,512	93,944	79,466
Michigan	NA	31,120	121,436	143,478
Wisconsin	16,788	21,029	30,160	45,901
Minnesota	NA	27,745	58,648	81,972
Iowa	7,911	11,366	13,722	15,502
Missouri	10,611	22,575	45,251	36,295
North Dakota	704	1,367	1,652	2,006
South Dakota	NA	1,528	2,716	3,410
Nebraska	6,077	10,935	12,627	17,554
Kansas	7,833	14,576	21,675	24,102
South				
Delaware	3,507	5,419	9,701	15,507
Maryland	28,736	61,481	84,456	76,940
Dist. of Columbia	4,965	9,602	10,351	8,325
Virginia	NA	16,204	19,085	24,089
West Virginia	NA	2,798	4,963	5,950
North Carolina	33,450	45,863	72,325	89,889
South Carolina	18,167	16,568	29,652	40,456

continues on next page

Table 11–2 *continued*

Jurisdiction	1977	1983	1989	1994
Georgia	34,979	91,183	125,441	140,684
Florida	34,342	61,647	192,495	239,108
Kentucky	NA	14,999	8,062	11,417
Tennessee	5,858	11,979	30,906	35,727
Alabama	10,404	15,763	26,475	36,024
Mississippi	3,485	6,293	7,333	9,041
Arkansas	545	3,653	15,552	18,598
Louisiana	11,104	24,494	32,295	33,604
Oklahoma	12,776	16,012	24,240	26,484
Texas	NA	217,350	291,156	394,578
West				
Montana	1,772	2,471	3,459	5,641
Idaho	2,831	3,163	4,025	5,153
Wyoming	1,762	1,495	3,060	3,382
Colorado	10,571	15,563	28,037	36,430
New Mexico	NA	4,050	5,660	8,670
Arizona	NA	15,563	27,340	36,916
Utah	5,189	8,035	5,524	7,638
Nevada	2,722	5,095	7,065	9,410
Washington	12,560	62,475	74,918	111,450
Oregon	NA	19,873	31,878	38,086
California	149,587	176,555	285,018	285,105
Alaska	846	1,791	3,335	3,173
Hawaii	2,686	6,092	11,377	12,515

Sources: U.S. Department of Justice, *Historical Corrections Statistics in the United States, 1850–1984* (Washington, D.C.: Bureau of Justice Statistics, 1986), Table 7–12; Louis Jankowski, *Probation and Parole, 1989* (Washington, D.C.: U.S. Department of Justice, 1990), p. 2; U.S. Department of Justice, *Probation and Parole, 1994* (Washington, D.C.: Bureau of Justice Statistics, 1995). All statistics are for end of year listed.

are under probation supervision. This means that since 1977, the number of offenders on probation has increased 328.5 percent. During that same time period, the U.S. prison population increased "only" 261 percent. Obviously, the number of offenders in our correctional system has skyrocketed, with a greater increase in the ranks of community corrections.

The increase in offenders on probation is an ongoing problem for which correctional systems must quickly find solutions. In the 1-year period from 1989 to 1990, the total number of U.S. probationers increased 5.9 percent. Of course, the problem is more acute in some jurisdictions than others. This can be approached in two different ways, though. For some states, such as those shown in Table 11–3, the sheer volume of numbers can be overpowering. On the other hand, in states that show rapid increases in their number of probationers, increasing the size of the "system" can be a serious problem. Take, for example, the state of Arkansas. While having a comparatively small number of probationers in 1990, 15,983 (30th among the 50 states), this is a 437.5 percent increase since 1983 and a 2,933 percent increase since 1977! Even with a small number of offenders to serve, increases such as these present huge problems.

The tremendous growth in the number of offenders in community correctional programs is due to the general population increase in the correctional system as a whole, not due to jurisdictions being "soft" on criminals. This is further shown in Table 11–3. As seen in this list of the 10 states with the largest probation and prison populations, 8 states appear on both lists. This tells us that these states have overburdened prison systems and also have needed to place a large number of offenders into community correctional programs.

Table 11–3		States With the Highest Probation and Prison Populations, 1994	
Probation		**Prison**	
State	**Population**	**State**	**Population**
Texas	394,578	California	124,813
California	285,105	Texas	100,136
Florida	239,108	New York	65,962
New York	164,569	Florida	56,052
Michigan	143,178	Ohio	41,156
Georgia	140,684	Michigan	40,220
Washington	111,450	Illinois	35,614
New Jersey	106,921	Georgia	30,292
Ohio	105,953	Pennsylvania	27,071
Pennsylvania	99,524	Virginia	24,822

Sources: U.S. Department of Justice, *Probation and Parole, 1994* (Washington, D.C.: Bureau of Justice Statistics, 1995); U.S. Department of Justice, *Prisoners in 1994* (Washington, D.C.: Bureau of Justice Statistics, 1995).

The point is this: Community corrections is a necessity for practical reasons. Whether we believe it is "right" may not be as important as the necessity of placing ever-increasing numbers of offenders in community correctional programs.

Legal Rights of Probationers

Revocation of probation The process of removing offenders from probation programs and returning them to correctional facilities to serve the remaining time on their suspended sentences.

Due process The legally required steps that the legal system must follow in any action to fully protect the rights of citizens, including convicted criminal offenders.

Probationers' legal rights focus on three primary areas. First, the law regulates actual conditions of supervision that can be imposed on probationers. Second are the rights surrounding **revocation of probation,** those laws and rights that govern when and how probationers can be removed from probation supervision and placed in prison or jail. Finally, offenders have a number of rights regarding **due process,** or the steps that the legal system must follow to fully protect probationers' citizenship rights.

A state legislature (or the federal government) creates in its statutory law the basic structure and operation of a probation system. Some states also have their legislatures establish the range of conditions that may be imposed on offenders. Other states establish the range of possible conditions in administrative law. Within these boundaries individual probation departments and officers operate when selecting the conditions for specific individuals. A third variety of law, case law, is involved when some condition or some action of a probation official is challenged and ruled upon by a court. Finally, constitutional law, as our fourth form of law, is involved. That is, all other laws—whether related to probation or any other matter—must be within the legal boundaries of acceptability that both the federal and state constitutions establish. So, constitutions of the jurisdictions involved establish the framework for all government actions. Within this scope, legislatures have created a structure and process for operating a probation system. Once this is established, individual actors within the system put into operation individual case plans for offenders (administrative law) that may be challenged in court for rulings (case law) about whether they fit within the overall constitutional framework. So, all four varieties of law are involved in a discussion of probationers' rights.

Conditions of Probation

In placing offenders on probation, a tailored set of conditions must be created to best meet the offenders' needs and to best protect society as a whole. This means that from the broad statutes that establish probation, a fair amount of freedom must be exercised to select sets of conditions for individual offenders. Specifics are often found only in the form of mandatory conditions for all probationers. The most commonly required conditions include:

1. Offenders must not violate any laws.
2. Offenders must support their dependents.
3. Offenders must stay in the jurisdiction.
4. Offenders must report at assigned times and dates to their probation officers.

In the 1980s and 1990s two common conditions of probation have been restitution and community service. **Restitution** is court-ordered repayment of losses or expenses to the victims of offenders' crimes. This often includes payment of medical expenses or payments to (at least partially) replace damaged, destroyed, or stolen property. **Community service** requires offenders to participate in volunteer work to repay the community as a whole. Community service projects often involve manual labor such as picking up trash, cutting grass, or painting in public parks. These projects may also involve working with a social service agency and helping with children's organizations, stuffing envelopes, or completing other menial or semi-skilled tasks.

Restitution Court-ordered repayment of losses or expenses to the victims of offenders' crimes.

FYI

Probationers' activities are restricted by specific conditions of their probation sentences. Probation officers monitor offenders' activities and assist them in being law-abiding and meeting the specific conditions of their sentences. However, probation officers have limited authority to decide what probationers can and cannot do.

Some conditions imposed on probationers have been challenged in court and have been declared illegal. The general rule in determining the legality of a particular condition of probation is to ask whether the condition is reasonable and relevant to the offender's offense. A condition is invalid[16] if:

1. It has no relationship to the crime for which the offender was convicted.
2. It relates to noncriminal conduct.
3. It relates to actions not reasonably related to potential future criminality.

Community service A form of community corrections, usually accompanying other forms of sentences, in which offenders are required to participate in volunteer work to repay some of the harm/costs they imposed on society.

LEGAL BRIEF:

Permissible Conditions of Probation

The courts have historically viewed the specific conditions that can be placed on probationers as ways that support correctional officials' broad discretion. The guiding principle in determining the legality of particular probation conditions is whether the conditions are reasonably related to the goals of public safety, supervision of offenders, and prevention of further criminal activity. A sampling of court cases challenging specific conditions of probation emphasizes the breadth of conditions that are permissible.

State v. Morgan *(La.Sup.Ct. 1980, 28 Cr. L. 2260) Morgan was convicted of attempted prostitution in the French Quarter of New Orleans and sentenced to a period of probation. One condition of her probation was that she not be in the French Quarter. Morgan challenged this condition as a violation of her rights. The Louisiana Supreme Court ruled that the restriction was valid because of the high rate of prostitution in the French Quarter and the likelihood that Morgan would once again engage in criminal activities there.*

State v. Cooper *(N.C. Ct. App. 1981, 29 Cr.L. 2125) Cooper was convicted of unlawful use of credit cards and was sentenced to probation. As one of the conditions of his probation, Cooper was prohibited from driving a car between the hours of midnight and 5:30 A.M. Cooper challenged this condition as unreasonable and a violation of his rights. However, the North Carolina Court of Appeals ruled against him, citing several ways that his ability to drive could be related to his past criminal activities.*

United States v. Stine *(675 F.2d 69, 3d Cir. 1982, 31 Cr.L. 2081) One condition of probation imposed on Stine was mandatory participation in a psychological counseling program. Stine contested this condition, arguing that this violated his rights to privacy. However, the U.S. Circuit Court of Appeals ruled that the condition was valid, as it could be reasonably seen to work to prevent further criminal activities.*

In re Mannino *(92 Cal.Rptr. 880, Ct. App. Cal. 1971) In this California case a juvenile was convicted of attacking (kicking) a policeman during a protest demonstration and, subsequently, was sentenced to probation. As a condition of Mannino's probation, he was prohibited from speaking at and participating in future demonstrations. When this was challenged in court as a violation of Mannino's First Amendment free speech rights, the court found that because of the probationer's explosive temperament, it was reasonable to assume that his future attendance at such events would lead to additional criminal activities. Therefore, the prohibition on attendance was upheld. However, the court did find the additional condition prohibiting him from writing and distributing materials related to his cause to be unrelated to the offense and, therefore, a violation of the First Amendment.*

Also, the court-imposed conditions must be able to be completed during the probation period. For instance, for a one-year probation sentence, a court may not impose the condition that an offender earn a college degree during this time.[17] The conditions of probation also must be reasonable. Here, we have to remember that probation is a sentence, or "punishment," given to convicted offenders. Therefore, the conditions of probation must not violate the Eighth Amendment guarantee against cruel and unusual punishment.

Conditions that have been found unreasonable include: banishment from the state for 5 years,[18] requirement that an offender move out of his neighborhood,[19] requirement to make a $1,000 donation to a specific charity,[20] to "live honorably,"[21] condition ordering a male probationer "not [to] father any children during probation,"[22] and a requirement for an offender to perform 6,200 hours of community service work over a 3-year probation period (averaging more than 5½ hours per day!).[23] However, finding a pattern in the conditions of probation that have or have not been found permissible is quite difficult. Among the conditions that have been ruled as legal are: requirement that a probationer avoid all contact with bars,[24] not enter a particular county,[25] and not participate in antiabortion protests.[26]

Revocation of Probation

Remember that probation is a privilege. If offenders violate the conditions of probation, this privilege can be taken away, or revoked.

Probationers may be arrested for violating conditions of probation.

Probation can be revoked for one of two general reasons. First, if probationers commit new crimes (recidivate), it is appropriate, and some would say necessary, to revoke probation and to place them in jail or prison. Second, probation may be revoked for violating the specific conditions of the probation agreement. This is called revocation for **technical violations.** Except in the most extreme cases, though, revoking probation for technical violations requires offenders to commit a series of repeated infractions.

Only the court has authority to revoke offenders' probation. Recommendations for such actions come from probation officers and departments. However, as discussed in more detail in the next section, probation officers and departments can only advise judges about probationers' activities and obedience with conditions. The actual supervision of probationers remains the responsibility of the court that sentences them, although in practical terms this task can be delegated to probation departments and officers. However, when the court revokes probation, supervision and responsibility for offenders are transferred to the officials who oversee the new sentence (jail or prison).

While probation is a privilege extended to offenders, the court cannot simply decide to remove that privilege for no reason. Once placed on probation, offenders have both rights and responsibilities guiding their relationship with the court. Probationers agree to live within the conditions set by the court and probation department, and the legal system agrees to treat offenders fairly and to protect their basic constitutional rights. The most notable constitutional rights involved with probation are **due process rights.** These are the protections all citizens have from being treated unfairly and being punished without proper application of the legally required steps for removing their rights or freedoms.

Technical violations
Actions on the part of probationers or parolees that break the rules imposed by their sentences; these may serve as grounds for revoking probation/parole.

Due process rights
The protections all citizens hold against being treated unfairly and being punished without proper application of the legally required steps to ensure that only when necessary are their rights or freedoms removed or restricted.

Due Process Rights

Probationers' due process rights are based on the 1972 U.S. Supreme Court case *Morrissey v. Brewer.*[27] This case actually dealt with parolees' due process rights (and will be discussed further in Chapter 12), but these have since been interpreted to be applicable to probationers.[28] This case established that parolees (and, therefore, probationers) have basic due process rights. However, while the law recognizes that parole and probation revocation processes are bound by essentially the same legal requirements, the law does not require these to be identical processes. While offenders do have a significant privilege (liberty) to lose in revocation proceedings, the courts have held tightly to the idea that offenders are already convicted and, therefore, have more restricted rights than criminal defendants.

Morrissey v. Brewer (1972) passes down five specific due process requirements:

1. There must be written notices of offenders' alleged violations.

2. Offenders are to receive full disclosures of the evidence against them.

3. When facing possible revocation, offenders have the right to present their cases in person and to present witnesses on their behalf.

4. The decisions about whether to revoke offenders' probation are to be made by neutral and detached hearing bodies.

A probation revocation hearing is part of the due process procedure.

5. Once decisions are made, those making the decisions are to prepare and file written statements explaining the evidence on which they based their decisions and the specific reasons for deciding to revoke the offenders' probation.

In our criminal justice system, one central right is that to assistance and counsel of an attorney. Criminal defendants have a guaranteed right to assistance of an attorney in planning and presenting their defense at the time of a trial. However, this right is not as clearly established for offenders serving sentences in community correctional programs. The 1967 U.S. Supreme Court case *Mempa v. Rhay*[29] ruled that probationers facing revocation hearings are entitled to an attorney. The Court's ruling was based on its belief that a revocation hearing is a "critical phase" in the processing of a criminal case. Therefore, the process is subject to the due process protections established by the Fourteenth Amendment. When states revoke probation, they have removed offenders' liberty. In short, probationers facing revocation have essentially similar interests to protect as do defendants in criminal trials.

Probationers' due process rights are further specified and more firmly established in the U.S. Supreme Court case of *Gagnon v. Scarpelli* (1973). Here, the Supreme Court ruled that a two-stage hearing process is necessary when states seek to revoke offenders' probation. First, a required preliminary hearing is to establish whether there is probable cause to revoke probation. If probable cause is established, then a revocation hearing will be held. Additionally, *Gagnon v. Scarpelli* established that the state was responsible for providing an attorney for probationers who are unable to afford one on their own. Again, the similarities to criminal defendants' rights are clear.

When states attempt to remove their privilege of probation, probationers must be provided with attorneys to assist in their defense. They also must be provided with sufficient time to prepare their defense. Probationers facing revocation, as well as criminal defendants, must be provided with information about the charges against them and must have adequate time and resources to prepare their defense.[30] This means that offenders must be given notice of revocation hearings in a timely manner to allow them to prepare for the hearings. Probationers must also be provided with full information about the reasons for revocation.[31]

In simple terms, revocation of probation is done in a **hearing,** not a trial, that a judge conducts to make a decision about the procedures used with the offender. Technicalities of criminal trials, such as rules about the admissibility of evidence, formalities of procedures, and standards of proof, do not apply in hearings. Probationers facing revocation do not even have an absolute right to be present at their hearings. If probationers cannot be located or fail to appear at announced hearings, probation can be revoked in their absence. In such cases warrants will be issued for the offenders' arrest.

Hearing A procedure that a judge conducts to make a decision about the procedures used with an offender.

Summary

Keeping criminal offenders in the community, rather than putting them in jail or prison, is a practice that has become commonplace in contemporary society. Although debates still ensue about whether it is safe to supervise offenders in the community, a majority of people convicted of crimes in the United States receive sentences that allow them to remain in society.

Proponents and opponents make their arguments for and against community corrections. One argument against community corrections centers on the belief that people who are convicted of crimes deserve to punished, which can be done only via incarceration. A second argument is that offenders are unlikely to change their behaviors if the "only" punishment they receive is some form of community corrections. Concerns about recidivism highlight the arguments against the use of community corrections. However, the recidivism question is actually the core of arguments in favor of community corrections. Researchers have consistently found that recidivism rates are very similar, if not lower, for offenders who remain in the community. This argument is complemented by the practicalities and expenses of incarcerating ever-increasing numbers of people.

With our prisons as overcrowded as they are, if we sent all—or even most—offenders to prison, we would need at least twice the number of institutions that we now have. Financially, this is unrealistic.

Probation was not originally designed to deal with practical matters about prisons. Instead, probation (and hence all community correctional programs) was founded on the idea that prison was unnecessary for many offenders. By keeping them in the community, offenders could be rehabilitated and would maintain their family, work, and other important social ties. So, keeping offenders in the community was first centered on the idea of better serving the offenders' needs, not controlling prisons' costs or populations.

As the use of probation increased in the late-twentieth century, though, many people realized that a variety of programs were necessary to address offenders' diverse needs. People who serve sentences in community correctional programs are in many ways similar to the overall population of criminals. However, this group differs in some significant ways. While a majority of these people are male, a larger percentage of women is in community corrections than is in prison populations. Also, African-

Americans make up a smaller portion of this group than they do prison inmates. However, the one area where we might expect to find differences between prison inmates and community correctional offenders is in terms of their offenses. This is not really the case, though. Almost all crimes are eligible for sentences of probation, but this varies somewhat from state to state.

Recent variations in community correctional programs have increased the amount of supervision provided and have made the system more efficient. Intensive supervision probation and diversion centers impose stricter conditions on offenders and call for increased contact between officials and offenders. Home incarceration seeks to allow more people, especially those convicted of minor offenses, to be supervised but to require less commitment of an officer's time. Both these goals have become necessary as community corrections continues to increase in popularity in our society. Just as we turn to community-based programs instead of jails or prisons to save money, we are now modifying community correctional programs to increase the number of offenders who can be processed while saving the system money.

Offenders in community correctional programs maintain a variety of legal rights. These offenders' rights fall between those of free-society citizens and prison inmates. Statutory law is the basic legal foundation for community correctional programs, although case law and administrative law are also very important. The greatest differences may be in the area of revocation of probation. Because offenders are already convicted and under the state's supervision, due process rights involved at the time of revocation are less than those at the time of trial. However, probationers do have the right to challenge in a court of law either the conditions imposed on them or the process by which probation may be removed.

QUESTIONS FOR REVIEW

1. What do we mean when we talk about "community corrections"? What are the variety of programs included in this category?

2. What are the reasons for keeping convicted offenders in the community rather than incarcerating them?

3. What are the arguments for incarcerating convicted offenders? Or, what are the arguments cited by critics of community corrections?

4. How do recidivism rates for offenders sentenced to community correctional programs compare to recidivism rates for offenders sentenced to periods of incarceration?

5. How have community corrections developed in the United States? From where did these programs emerge?

6. What makes home incarceration unique from other forms of community corrections? Why have correctional authorities developed home incarceration programs? What are the goals of home incarceration?

7. How are offenders serving sentences to community correctional programs similar and different, in general, from offenders who are incarcerated?

8. What in the law makes a sentence to community corrections possible? In what ways have laws needed to be established and interpreted to allow convicted offenders to be sentenced to community programs instead of incarcerated?

9. What are the restrictions that can or must be imposed on people serving sentences in community correctional programs? What distinguishes legal and illegal restrictions on convicted offenders?

10. How does the process of revocation of probation work? What restrictions does the law put on the revocation process?

ACTIVITIES

1. Assume you are a newly hired intensive supervision probation (ISP) officer. You are expected to make one unannounced check on each of the 20 probationers you supervise. Make a schedule of when and where you will make these checks during your workweek.

2. Make a list of all the crimes that you believe would or would not be appropriate for a sentence of home incarceration. What are your reasons for making your decisions?

3. Working in groups of 3 or 4 students, debate the pros and cons of probation as the most common criminal sentence in the U.S. criminal justice system.

4. Obtain a list of conditions of probation that the probation department in your local community uses. Rank order the conditions according to importance. If for some reason you had to eliminate 5 of the conditions, which would they be? Why?

ENDNOTES

1. *Gagnon v. Scarpelli,* 411 US 778, 93 S.Ct. (1972).

2. Joan Petersilia, Susan Turner, James Kahan, and Joyce Peterson, "Executive Summary of Rand's Study, 'Granting Felons Probation: Public Risks and Alternatives,'" *Crime and Delinquency,* Vol. 31, 1985, pp. 379–392.

3. Harry E. Allen, Chris W. Eskridge, Edward J. Latessa, and Gennaro F. Vito, "Probation and Parole Effectiveness," in Harry E. Allen, Chris W. Eskridge, Edward J. Latessa, and Gennaro F. Vito (eds.), *Probation and Parole in America* (New York: Free Press 1985); also, see Michael R. Geerken and Hennessey D. Hayes, "Probation and Parole: Public Risk and the Future of Incarceration Alternatives," *Criminology,* Vol. 31, No. 4, 1993, pp. 549–564.

4. International Association of Residential and Community Alternatives, cited in "Community Corrections Survey: Public Indicates Strong Support," *Corrections Today,* December 1991, p. 134.

5. Allen, et al., *op. cit.*

6. Gennaro F. Vito, "Felony Probation and Recidivism: Replication and Response," *Federal Probation,* Vol. 50, 1986, pp. 17–25; Johnny McGaha, Michael Fichter, and Peter Hirschburg, "Felony Probation: A Re-examination of Public Risk," *American Journal of Criminal Justice,* Vol. 11, 1987, pp. 1–9.

7. Kathryn Morgan, "Factors Influencing Probation Outcome: A Review of the Literature," *Federal Probation,* Vol. 57, No. 2, 1993, p. 27.

8. Joan Petersilia, Susan Turner, with Joyce Peterson, *Prison Versus Probation in California: Implications for Crime and Offender Recidivism,* R-3323-NIJ (Santa Monica, CA: Rand Corporation, 1986).

9. Michael Liberton, Mitchell Silverman, and William R. Blount, "Predicting Probation Success for the First-Time Offender," *International Journal of Offender Therapy and Comparative Criminology,* Vol. 36, No. 4, 1992, pp. 335–347; Kathryn Morgan, "Factors Associated with Probation Outcome," *Journal of Criminal Justice,* Vol. 22, No. 4, 1994, pp. 341–353.

10. Liberton et al., *op. cit.*

11. John Augustus, *A Report of the Labors of John Augustus, for the Last*

Ten Years, In Aid of the Unfortunate (Boston: Wright & Hasty, 1852).

12. Toby D. Slawsky, "Revocation of Community Supervision: What the Courts Have Made of Congress' Ambiguous Language and Policies," *Federal Probation,* Vol. 56, No. 3, 1992, pp. 73–77.

13. Harry E. Allen, Eric Carlson, and Evalyn Parks, *Critical Issues in Probation: Summary Report* (Washington, D.C.: U.S. Department of Justice, 1979), pp. 12–13.

14. See Richard Gray, "Probation: An Exploration in Meaning," *Federal Probation,* Vol. 50, No. 4, 1986, pp. 26–31 for a discussion of the various meanings of "probation."

15. U.S. Department of Justice, *Probation and Parole, 1994* (Washington, D.C.: Bureau of Justice Statistics, 1995).

16. *People v. Dominguez,* 256 Cal.App.2d 623, 64 Cal.Rptr. 290 (1967).

17. *Ex parte Acosta,* 65 Cal.App.2d 63,149 P.2d 757 (1944).

18. *People v. Baum,* 251 Mich. 187, 231 NW 95 (1930).

19. *People v. Smith,* 252 Mich. 4, 232 NW 397 (1930).

20. *People v. Appel, People v. Sullivan,* 141 A.D.2d 374, 529 N.Y.S.2d 311 (1988).

21. *Norris v. State,* 383 So.2d 691 (Fla. Dist. Ct. App. 1980).

22. *Burchell v. State,* 419 So.2d 358 (Fla. Dist. Ct. App. 1982).

23. *Higdon v. United States,* 627 F.2d 893 (9th Cir. 1980).

24. *Brown v. State,* 406 So.2d 1262 (Fla. Dist. Ct. App. 1981).

25. *United States v. Cothran,* 855 F.2d 749 (US 11th Cir. (1988).

26. *Markley v. State,* 507 So.2d 1043 (Ala. Ct. Crim. App. 1987).

27. *Morrissey v. Brewer,* 408 US 471, 92S.Ct.2593,33L.Ed.2d 484 (1972).

28. *People v. Vickers,* 25 Cal.App. 3d 1080: 102 Cal.Rptr. 418 (1972).

29. *Mempa v. Rhay,* 398 U.S.128 (1967).

30. *Kuenstler v. State,* 486 S.W.2d 367 (Tex. 1972). *Burkett v. State,* 485 S.W.2d 578 (Tex. 1972).

31. *Burkett v. State,* 485 S.W.2d 578 (Tex. 1972).

CHAPTER 12

Parole

CHAPTER OBJECTIVES

In the previous chapter we learned that offenders could be sentenced to community correctional programs. In this chapter we will examine the structure and processes involved in parole, a form of community-based corrections that comes after, not in place of, incarceration. After reading this chapter, you will be able to:

1. Distinguish among the processes involved in parole, pardon, and probation.

2. Explain the historical development and implementation of parole in the United States.

3. Discuss the reasons for using parole in the U.S. criminal justice system.

4. Understand the arguments for and against parole.

5. Compare and contrast the characteristics of parolees to those of prison inmates.

6. Understand how states determine when offenders are eligible for parole and who are likely candidates.

7. Identify the similarities and differences between the supervision and conditions of probation and parole.

8. Explain the reasons for and process of parole revocation.

9. Discuss the due process requirements for revoking parole.

10. Understand the reasons for and processes involved in shock incarceration programs.

Parole boards are under the authority of a state's corrections department.

Paroles, Pardons, and Probation

People who are not familiar with the operations of the correctional system commonly confuse parole, pardon, and probation. Although these three concepts share some characteristics (all are concerned with placement of offenders in the community), they are really more different than they are similar. **Parole** is release from prison prior to the expiration of offenders' sentences. In contrast, a governor or the President grants a **pardon,** which legally clears offenders from the consequences of their convictions for criminal offenses. Then, as we saw in Chapter 11, *probation* is a judge's sentence that allows convicted offenders to live in the community with restrictions on their activities and with supervision. Furthermore, the type and amount of required, applied supervision differs with each concept. Parole officers, who are similar to probation officers, supervise parolees and assist offenders to reintegrate into the community. However, the amount of supervision that parolees receive is typically rather minimal. People who are pardoned receive no supervision at all; by receiving pardons, offenders are excused from serving any further time under supervision of any sort. In contrast, probationers may be intensively supervised or may have to serve time in home incarceration programs.

Not only is each concept different in form, but also each originates in a separate branch of government. A parole usually comes from authorities in the correctional system. A pardon, by definition, is granted by the politically elected leader of the government's executive branch. Probation, as a sentence, comes from the judicial branch of government. So, each concept is wholly different in its goal, process, and point of origin.

The goal of parole is to transform the actual substance of the sentence that a trial court hands down. When supervisory authority over offenders is passed from the judicial system to the correctional system, correctional officials not only have responsibility to supervise offenders, but also the responsibility for carrying out the courts' sentences. However, in those states where parole exists, statutory law gives correctional officials the authority to modify, within certain limits, the length of the sentence. Correctional officials may, therefore, change the conditions by which convicted offenders are supervised. This means that inmates may be released from prison to be supervised either in the community or in an outside facility (halfway house or prerelease center).

Parole Release from prison prior to the expiration of the full sentence with supervision while in the community.

Pardon An executive act that legally clears an offender from the consequences of conviction for a criminal offense.

Greenholtz v. Inmates of the Nebraska Penal and Correctional Complex, 442 U.S. 1 (1979).

According to Nebraska statutory law, prison inmates can be considered for parole after having served the minimum of their indeterminate sentences, minus earned good-time credits. At this time, the Board of Parole will review inmates' records for the periods both during and prior to imprisonment and determine whether inmates are good risks for release.

This legal challenge, concluded in 1979, was brought by the inmates of the Nebraska Penal and Correctional Complex, who argued that the Nebraska Board of Parole violated their constitutionally guaranteed civil rights by unfairly denying parole. The inmates' lawsuit focused on the fact that one section of the Nebraska statutes read:

> "Whenever the Board of Parole considers the release of a committed offender who is eligible for release on parole, it shall order his release."

If the Board found one of four specific reasons present, it delayed the inmate's release. The inmates keyed on the word shall, claiming that this language in the statute provided them with the expectation—and, in fact, the legal right to expect—to be released. In legal terms, the inmates who challenged their denial of release on parole argued that they were denied due process and that the language of the statute provided them with a protected conditional liberty interest.

While the federal trial court ruled in favor of the inmates and the Court of Appeals for the Eighth Circuit upheld the District Court ruling in part, the U.S. Supreme Court ruled that the inmates did not have a protected liberty interest. As the Court stated,

> "A state may, as Nebraska has, establish a parole system, but it has no duty to do so."

In other words, prison inmates do not have a guarantee of being released on parole. In fact, there is not even a right to be considered for release on parole. As the opinion of the Court concluded, "That the state holds out the possibility of parole provides no more than a mere hope that the benefit will be obtained."

Origins of Parole

Parole has been a part of the U.S. criminal justice system since the late-1870s. What we know as parole in today's world, though, is not what our founders originally envisioned. In all likelihood, what we know as parole today will not be the same in another decade. As Paul Herman, the chief state supervisor for the Missouri Board of Probation and Parole says, "The one constant in parole is change."[1] However, the practice of modifying or lessening the sentences given to criminals has a long history in Western civilization.

Sixteenth and seventeenth century England was concerned about dealing with the overcrowded conditions in its jails and prisons. The galley ships that it used for centuries had lost their popularity, largely because of the terrible conditions on the ships. After the American colonies declared their independence in 1776, the British could no longer banish criminals to the colonies and had to seek other solutions to their problem. Shortly after the American Revolution, the British started to transport convicts to Australia, which had been discovered by Captain Cook in 1770.

Alexander Maconochie

The conditions in the Australian penal colonies were never considered very good. Because of the awful conditions, the penal colony residents were often very brutal and difficult to control and discipline. One innovative method was developed to control these convicts. The **ticket of leave,** originally used at the Norfolk Island penal colony, allowed the governor to excuse convicts from work assignments and to live relatively independent lives. However, while convicts were permitted freedom of movement and allowed to establish their own homes, they were restricted to particular geographic areas for their residence and movements. Alexander Maconochie, who became governor of the Norfolk Island penal colony in 1840, modified how tickets of leave were used. (He did not first develop the idea.[2])

Maconochie is best known for developing and practicing a five-stage program that included the ticket of leave and a **marks system.** The use of marks is similar to the accumulation of points for earning (or losing) privileges. The goal of the marks system was to ease convicts' transition from closely supervised custody to freedom. Prisoners earned marks by fulfilling their work assignments or doing good

Ticket of leave A concept that allowed a government official to excuse offenders from the legal consequences of their criminal convictions and to return to their communities to live independently; an early forerunner of parole.

Marks system An early approach to structuring how convicts could earn early release from incarceration; offenders earned points (marks) based on their behavior while incarcerated; different levels of earned marks meant that convicts gained privileges and eventually time off their sentences.

Alexander Maconochie, governor of the Norfolk Island penal colony in 1840.

deeds, which could be used to cut time off from the end of their sentences.

However, when offenders were released on tickets of leave, they did have to abide by three general conditions. First, the ticket of leave was a conditional privilege. This meant that if offenders were found to have engaged in any form of misconduct, their tickets of leave could either be revoked or the specific conditions of the ticket could be made stricter. Second, not only did offenders have the constant threat of losing their privileges, but they also had to prove, throughout the period of their leaves, that they were deserving. This condition reminded offenders that their tickets of leave were never to be considered permanent. Rather, they were something constantly to be earned. Third and finally, revocation of their tickets of leave did not require convictions for new crimes. All the authorities had to do was to show that individuals were leading lives likely to lead to crime. Such discretionary revocation powers meant that if the supervising authorities believed the offenders were not supporting themselves or were associating with "bad characters," they could simply pull the offenders back into custody.

Sir Walter Crofton

The head of the Irish prison system, Sir Walter Crofton, was perhaps even more influential in the development of parole. Crofton's system, which became known as the "Irish system," had a strong influence on American correctional authorities and was the actual foundation on which parole was developed in the United States.

Crofton's system was possible because of two related developments. Australian citizens, like the American colonists, became increasingly resentful of the English for dumping unwanted criminals in their country. By threatening to revolt against England, the Australians finally brought an end in 1857 to the British practice of **transportation.** When England no longer had a place to send their criminal convicts, it needed to develop a new way to handle the large number of convicts whom the courts sentenced.

Crofton's "intermediate system" helped with this problem. A notable innovation, the intermediate system involved the community and used an official parole officer to supervise offenders released to the community. The first parole officer was James P. Organ, inspector of released prisoners. Inspector Organ's official duties were to supervise

Transportation
Early correctional practice of moving convicted criminals to different societies; convicts were transported (usually across seas/oceans) to colonies as punishments for crimes.

released inmates, help them find jobs, and assist them in adjusting to life in the community.

Parole in the United States

Some historians believe that indenture, putting a person in the service of a master for a specified period of time (similar to contracting with someone to be a slave for a particular length of time), was a forerunner of parole. Usually indentured servants entered into such agreements to learn trades or sets of skills. Some believe indenture was a predecessor of parole because the activities of indentured individuals were very restricted, and their social and recreational activities as well as their work habits were regulated.

The English felons transported to the American colonies were indentured as servants. The original design of indenture was not to be a correctional device. However, this is what indenture eventually became, and it was a common way to shorten the time juveniles spent in correctional institutions. Before the nineteenth century, adult felons were given sentences of fixed length. This meant that convicts knew exactly how long they would serve in detention when sentenced by the court. A three-year sentence meant that offenders would spend exactly three years incarcerated.

An important forerunner of parole was **good-time laws.** First used in 1817 in the state of New York, good-time laws were statutes that gave prison officials the power to shorten individual inmates' sentences in exchange for good behavior. However, when inmates were released and left prisons, they were not supervised in any way. Lack of continuing supervision and full discretionary power of wardens and other officials (with no rules or limits on their power) are what distinguishes good-time release from the modern practice of parole.

The contemporary U.S. version of parole is based on three concepts:

1. Reducing the length of incarceration as a reward for good conduct.

2. Supervising offenders released from custody.

3. Using indeterminate sentences.

Several key elements to organizational success for parole agencies are listed in Figure 12–1.

The **indeterminate sentence** is the critical event in the development of parole. An indeterminate sentence is one that has a

Good-time laws A forerunner of parole, these statutes gave prison administrators the power to release inmates prior to the expiration of their sentences based on the administrator's judgment that the inmate had shown good behavior and thereby deserved early release.

Indeterminate sentence Sentence that imposes a minimum and maximum period of time that an offender will serve in a correctional program; the actual length of the sentence is determined by the offender's behavior and rehabilitative progress.

Figure 12–1 Keys to organizational success for parole agencies.

1. *Remember that parole officers are not therapists.* This means that parole officers do not implement models to "cure" or "fix" people; the role of the parole agency and officer is to work *with* people to assist them in becoming law-abiding citizens.

2. *Embrace new protocols and strategies.* In all areas of contemporary life, technology and strategies for working with problems and problem people are constantly changing. In order to achieve the maximum amount of success possible, policymakers in parole agencies need to be willing and able to adopt new ideas and new ways of working with offenders. Although this may mean an increased amount of work at times, we need to remember what the purpose of parole is: to work with and help people.

3. *Publicize successes.* Most people hear about parole (and in fact all of the criminal justice system) only when something fails to work as we believe it should. We need to let the public know what parole officers and agencies do and why we use this approach with offenders. With the two top priorities on the public's mind being controlling crime and controlling the national economy, we need to show people how parole is important in pursuing both of these goals.

4. *Research.* Adopting new protocols and strategies to work with offenders is fine, but becomes truly important only when we conduct research to evaluate how well these new approaches work. For those approaches that do show improvements over older approaches, we need to publicize this information. Research on crime and criminal justice issues is not very well supported financially, however. The United States spends nearly $33 per citizen on health research, but less than 25 cents per citizen on criminal justice research.

Source: Paul Herman, "Changing Role of Today's Probation and Parole Officer," workshop presented at the American Correctional Association Winter Conference, Orlando, Florida, 1994.

minimum and a maximum length, and the court transfers authority to the correctional system to determine exactly how much of the maximum sentence length each individual offender needs to serve. Therefore, the United States had to enact statutory laws that allowed indeterminate sentencing before parole could become a reality. In 1869 our first indeterminate sentence statutes were enacted in Michigan and New York. However, the Michigan statute was challenged in court and found to be in violation of the state constitution. This considerably slowed the development and spread of parole.

The New York statute allowed Zebulon Brockway, the warden at the new Elmira Reformatory, to discontinue the good-time laws and instead to give inmates specific criteria that he would use in determining when they would be released during the span of their sentences. Under Brockway's system, inmates were graded on their overall conduct, performance at work assignments, progress in a mandatory education program, and personal adjustment. In this way, Brockway borrowed the earlier idea of marks, which placed the responsibility of earning release directly on the individual offenders.

Specific legal and institutional developments preceded parole, but the actual origin of parole in the United States is found in two basic prison reform movements. First was the belief that good conduct in prison should be rewarded by a reduction in the length of a sentence. That release could be revoked if offenders did not continue their good behavior once they were returned to the community. The second major influential movement was the development of volunteer prisoner aid societies.[3] Prisoner aid societies were originally developed to provide food, fuel, and clothing to colonial jail inmates who had no family or friends to provide them with supplies. When jails and prisons began providing the basic necessities to inmates, prisoner aid societies slowly turned their attentions to assisting released inmates. Courts assigned volunteers to supervise offenders released from prison. For several decades supervision of offenders in the community relied exclusively on volunteers. Not until 1845 was the first publicly paid employee hired in Massachusetts to assist released offenders in readjusting to the community.

Supposedly, the guiding ideology for using parole is rehabilitation. Under indeterminate sentencing, inmates are presumed to want to work to achieve release. The way to achieve this privilege is to actively participate in treatment programs and to change one's ways. This may be the ideal. In reality, parole (in fact, all forms of early release) today has become a way to control overcrowding and financial problems in prisons. While the rehabilitation focus has not been abandoned, it is no longer the only driving force behind parole. However, even though the reasons for using such forms of release may have changed, parole has been an increasingly common practice in the United States. (See Table 12–1.)

Parole is not the only way that inmates are released from prison before the end of their sentences. Today, more common than parole are **mandatory early release programs.** Such programs are focused

Zebulon Brockway, warden of the Elmira Reformatory in New York, helped develop the modern concept of parole in the late-1800s.

Mandatory early release programs
Procedures in correctional systems that require inmates to be released prior to the expiration of their sentences to maintain legal limits on institutional populations.

	Table 12–1	Rate of Parole Use in the United States, 1976–1994	
	Year	**Total Number of Adults on Parole**	**Rate per 100,000 Population**
	1976	168,000	78
	1979	199,600	92
	1981	225,539	98
	1983	251,708	147
	1990	531,407	213
	1994	690,000	400

Sources: U.S. Department of Justice, *Historical Corrections Statistics in the United States, 1850–1984* (Washington, D.C.: Bureau of Justice Statistics, 1986), Table 7–12; Louis Jankowski, *Probation and Parole, 1989* (Washington, D.C.: Bureau of Justice Statistics, 1990), p. 2; Louis Jankowski, *Probation and Parole, 1990* (Washington, D.C.: Bureau of Justice Statistics, 1991), p. 2; U.S. Department of Justice, Press release, August 27, 1995. All statistics are for end of year listed.

on meeting the needs of prisons, not inmates and their rehabilitation. Early release programs are methods by which prisons and prison systems control the size of their inmate population to keep these populations within legally defined acceptable limits. Inmates are released when an institution's population reaches the facility's maximum capacity. The decision about who gets released is based on which inmates have served the greatest percentage of their sentences and which have had the least number of disciplinary problems. This does not mean that only those inmates with no disciplinary problems or those close to the end of their sentences are released. Instead, this simply means releasing the least dangerous of an often dangerous lot. Early releases of this variety are a mandatory practice, not a privilege. Overcrowding, then, has limited the use of parole but has increased the use of mandatory early release.

Characteristics of Offenders on Parole

Those offenders who are released on parole are very similar to those offenders found in prison. This is to be expected, though, as parolees must have been prison inmates. However, not all who are sent to prison are released on parole. Rather, inmates who are the most serious offenders (with life or death sentences) or who have disciplinary problems while incarcerated generally do not get paroled. Instead, these individuals either live out their lives in prison or are released only when they have served their maximum sentences.

As shown in Table 12–2, the parolee population is essentially the same in sex distribution as the prison population. However, the racial distribution is more heavily weighted with whites in the parolee population than in the prison population. Also shown in Table 12–2 is the distribution of conditions under which parolees leave parole supervision. Officially, exactly one-half of parolees serve their time and are released. The other one-half of parolees either are returned to prison or are transferred to the authority of other criminal justice agencies and officials.

Table 12–2	Characteristics of Adults on Parole, 1990
Characteristic	**Percent of Adults On Parole**
Sex	
Male	92
Female	8
Race	
White	52
African-American	47
Other	1
Current Status of Supervision	
Active supervision	82
Inactive supervision	6
Whereabouts unknown/absconded	6
Supervised out of state	6
Conditions of Leaving Parole	
Successful completion	50
Terminated due to absconding	1
Discharged to other warrants	1
Returned to prison/jail	46
Transferred to different state	1
Death	1

Source: U.S. Department of Justice, *Correctional Populations in the United States, 1990* (Washington, D.C.: Bureau of Justice Statistics, 1991), p. 116.

The Parole Process

As is the case with probation, parole is a privilege, not a right. Remember that parolees are technically still in the state's custody. They are not "free"; they are merely granted the privilege of living in the community, not prison.

Granting Parole

Not all inmates are released on parole; deciding which inmates will be paroled is a combination of scientific and political decisions. The scientific input includes research on the likelihood of recidivism for offenders convicted of particular offenses or of particular statuses. Using guidelines and a point system, science also predicts the likelihood of an individual inmate succeeding or failing while on parole. Points are assigned to an inmate's case for aspects such as the severity of offense, history of alcohol and/or drug abuse, disciplinary problems while incarcerated, number of times previously arrested, convicted, and incarcerated, and any previous supervision on parole. An inmate's total point score is used as one factor in the parole board's decision. The political input concerns overcrowding in an institution and the community's possible reactions, if and when a particular inmate is paroled.

Inmates have their **parole eligibility date,** the first date on which they may be considered for release. The state's statutory law determines the parole eligibility date and specifies how much of a sentence the offender must serve before being considered for release. Generally, statutory laws establish equations that are used to subtract time from the end of sentences to determine when we would *expect* an inmate to be *possibly* prepared for release. Modern versions of "good-time laws" call for cutting an amount of days off the end of one's sentence for every set number of days the inmate serves without any disciplinary problems. The parole eligibility date, then, is set by subtracting the maximum number of good-time days an inmate could earn from the end date of the actual sentence. For example, consider an inmate who is sentenced to a 3-year sentence on January 1. If the state statutory law calls for 1 day of good-time credit for every 5 days served, the inmate will be credited with a total of 219 days of good time. This means that the inmate would have a parole eligibility date on May 26 of the third year served.

Parole eligibility date The first date on which an inmate may be considered for release; this date is determined by statutory law.

$$365 \text{ days} \times 3 = 1{,}095 \text{ days}$$
$$1{,}095 \text{ days} \div 5 = 219 \text{ days}$$
$$1{,}095 \text{ days} - 219 \text{ days} = 876 \text{ days}$$
$$876 \text{ days} = 2 \text{ years} + 146 \text{ days}$$

Statutory laws guide the decision about whether to grant parole to offenders. Usually these laws instruct parole boards to base their decisions on one (or more) of four considerations. These considerations are:

1. The likelihood of recidivism.

2. The welfare of society.

3. The inmates' conduct while in prison.

4. The quality of the plans the inmates have developed for their parole period.

These guidelines allow a great degree of discretionary decision making. Discretion is considered very important in parole decisions, as it is nearly impossible to specify all the factors that are likely to affect individuals' likelihood of successfully readjusting to the community. Of course, remember that offenders' performance on parole is also influenced by the conditions imposed upon them and their willingness and ability to behave within these rules.

Conditions of Parole

The conditions under which parolees must live their lives are very similar in form and structure to the conditions that accompany probation. Remember that parole is basically a contract between the government and the individual offender. This contract calls for the government to grant the offender release from prison, while the offender agrees, in return, to live within the particular rules (conditions) as defined by the government, in this case the parole agency.

When parole is granted to them, offenders are expected to remain within the jurisdictions they are assigned, to live within the law, and to report to their assigned parole officers for a specified period of time. The actual length of paroles (the time during which parolees must continue to report to parole officers) varies by jurisdictions and by individuals. Generally speaking, paroles last between two and seven years.[4] In some states parolees who show no problems adjusting to

JOB FOCUS: PAROLE OFFICER

Parole officers are responsible for both supervising the activities of released inmates and working with offenders to assist them in making successful returns to the community. To be effective, parole officers must be able to juggle two sometimes competing types of tasks, surveillance and social work. Parole officers must also be able to work with a large number of people simultaneously and be able to handle situations on a spur-of-the-moment basis.

Perhaps the most important skills required are interpersonal communication skills. Parole officers need to establish rapport with a number of very different people. They must also be able to command authority, while at the same time be able to work with people in a way that makes them want to cooperate.

In a large majority of the states, parole officers are required to have a bachelor's degree, preferably in a field such as criminal justice, social work, psychology, or some other behavioral science. The future for parole officers appears to be fairly bright. As overcrowding problems continue to plague correctional systems, an increasing number of people must be released from prison prior to the expiration of their complete sentences. This means that in many jurisdictions, parole officers are overseeing increasingly large caseloads, and the need for additional officers is becoming very clear today.

Parole officers are generally fairly well paid in the criminal justice field. Median salaries for entry-level parole officers are over $22,000, up from only $18,000 to $19,000 in the mid-1980s. As one moves up the ladder in a parole agency, the pay also increases. Those who manage parole offices can expect to earn, on average, approximately $15,000 more per year than entry-level parole officers.

Sources: Harold E. Williamson, *The Corrections Profession* (Newbury Park, CA: Sage Publications, 1990), p. 202; J. Scott Harr and Karen M. Hess, *Seeking Employment in Law Enforcement, Private Security, and Related Fields* (St. Paul: West Publishing, 1992), p. 38.

Parolees are required to meet with their assigned parole officers for a specified period of time.

the community and who are considered very low risks for recidivism may receive a final release from parole in very short time periods (perhaps a matter of months).

The conditions imposed on parolees are designed both to assist offenders in making successful readjustments to the community and to ensure that offenders are only minimal risks to the community. Because parolees are generally considered more dangerous than probationers (as evidenced by their harsher original sentence), conditions of parole are generally required to be stricter than the conditions of probation. When challenged in court, stricter conditions for parolees than for probationers are typically upheld as legal. Among the most common conditions imposed on parolees are, of course, to obey all laws, to report to parole officers, not to possess firearms or other dangerous weapons (without special permission), to remain within the jurisdiction, to allow parole officers to enter their homes or places of work, and to be employed. Figure 12–2 lists the federal guidelines regarding parole conditions.

Generally speaking, the courts have upheld as legal most conditions of parole, unless they require parolees to commit some illegal or immoral action or are impossible to abide by. For instance, requiring an offender who is an alcoholic to completely abstain from

Figure 12–2 Federal guidelines regarding parole conditions.

1. You shall go directly to the district showing on this CERTIFICATE OF PAROLE (unless released to the custody of other authorities). Within three days after your arrival you shall report to your parole advisor if you have one, and to the United States Probation Officer whose name appears on this certificate. If in any emergency you are unable to get in touch with your parole advisor, or your probation officer or his office, you shall communicate with the United States Board of Parole, Department of Justice, Washington, D.C. 20537.

2. If you are released to the custody of other authorities, and after your release from physical custody of such authorities, you are unable to report to the United States Probation Officer to whom you are assigned within three days, you shall report instead to the nearest United States Probation Officer.

3. You shall not leave the limits of this CERTIFICATE OF PAROLE without written permission from the probation officer.

4. You shall notify your probation officer immediately of any change in your place of residence.

5. You shall make a complete and truthful written report (on a form provided for that purpose) to your probation officer between the first and third day of each month, and on the final day of parole. You shall also report to your probation officer at other times as he [or she] directs.

6. You shall not violate any law. Nor shall you associate with persons engaged in criminal activity. You shall get in touch immediately with your probation officer or his [or her] office if you are arrested or questioned by a law-enforcement officer.

7. You shall not enter into any agreement to act as an "informer" or special agent for any law-enforcement agency.

8. You shall work regularly, unless excused by your probation officer, and support your legal dependents, if any, to the best of your ability. You shall report immediately to your probation officer any change in employment.

9. You shall not drink alcoholic beverages to excess. You shall not purchase, possess, use, or administer marijuana or narcotic or other habit-forming or dangerous drugs, unless prescribed or advised by a physician. You shall not frequent places where such drugs are illegally sold, dispensed, used, or given away.

10. You shall not associate with persons who have a criminal record unless you have the permission of your probation officer.

11. You shall not have firearms (or other dangerous weapons) in your possession without the written permission of your probation officer, following prior approval of the United States Board of Parole.

12. You shall, if ordered by the Board pursuant to Section 4203, Title 18, U.S.C., as amended October 1970, reside in and/or participate in a treatment program of a Community Treatment Center operated by the Bureau of Prisons, for a period not to exceed 120 days.

Source: United States Board of Parole, U.S. Department of Justice, Washington, D.C.

alcohol may be a condition impossible to abide by and may be declared invalid.[5]

Many parolees take issue with conditions they believe invade their right to privacy. However, parole is viewed as a privilege, not a right. By agreeing to be supervised on parole (rather than to remain in prison), offenders must also agree to be supervised. This means that parole officers have the legal right—and, in fact, responsibility—to oversee parolees' actions and living conditions. Parole officers also have the responsibility to work with offenders to assist them in returning to society as law-abiding citizens. In this vein, requiring offenders to participate in counseling programs as a condition of parole has been ruled as legal (or, not an invasion of privacy).[6]

The area of parolees' basic constitutional rights is more difficult to interpret. Most notable here are our First Amendment rights, which the courts have traditionally viewed as above other personal rights. These rights—freedom of speech, peaceable assembly, religion, and petitioning of the government—are, therefore, held to higher standards of review when concerning their exercise by parolees.

Freedom of speech shows how restrictive conditions are held to higher standards when concerning parolees. In the 1960s the state of California required parolees to obtain the permission of their parole officers before they could make any public speech. The federal court struck down this condition in 1970, saying that the restriction presented "an unwarranted chilling effect on the exercise . . . of his undisputed rights."[7] Similarly, in 1971 a New York parole condition that denied parolees the right to make public speeches against the Vietnam War was declared invalid.[8] However, in certain circumstances it remains permissible to restrict certain objectionable forms of speech, including speech likely to lead to violent reactions, disruptions of institutional activities, or criminal actions. However, to have such a condition upheld, the state must show that the restriction is necessary for the particular offender and circumstances.

Revocation and Return to Prison

Just as with probation, the state could revoke parole and force offenders to return to prison. In 1990 almost one-half of parolees were returned to prison. This simple statistic leads many critics to proclaim that parole is a bad idea and is generally a failure. However, this same statistic could be viewed from the other perspective: More than one-

To control the problem of overcrowding in many of our prisons and to ensure that parolees know they must obey the conditions of their parole, some states and cities have developed a new way to deal with parole violators. Programs that remove offenders from the community and place them for a limited time in a structured, often treatment-based environment are considered *halfway back* to prison.

Most common among halfway-back facilities are those operated by private contractors and which specialize in the treatment of substance abuse. Many proponents believe halfway-back facilities are an important step forward. They fulfill the supervision function of parole, and they also actively work with offenders to assist them in overcoming their problems and readjusting to their home communities. A final advantage of halfway-back facilities is that they are less expensive than prison.

half of parolees are *not* returned to prison. Therefore, one-half of parole cases are successful. In addition, we could argue that the time the returned parolees spent in their communities may be beneficial to their eventual, successful return. At least their first attempt to return to the community included some supervision. That is, they were not simply released from prison with no supervision whatsoever.

Parole can be revoked in two basic ways. As with probation, technical violations are instances in which offenders fail to abide by the conditions of their parole, leading to disciplinary actions by parole officers (which may include initiating the process to return offenders to prison). Parole can also be revoked if offenders are found to have committed new criminal offenses such as alcohol abuse, drug abuse, escape (disappearing from supervision), possession of weapons, problems with parole officers, and traffic violations.[9]

Whether offenders fail to obey conditions or commit new crimes, legally mandated procedures must be followed to revoke parole. All parolees today are entitled to hearings to determine whether there is sufficient cause to remove them from parole. However, hearings were rare events prior to the 1970s. During the 1970s, a decade when prison inmates earned numerous rights through their legal challenges to conditions of confinement, parolees also made significant strides in the legal arena. Prior to this time, the words of parole officers were sufficient reason to return offenders to prison. Hearings were merely formalities in which officers informed the proper authorities of needed action.

However, starting in the 1970s and resulting from the 1967 Supreme Court decision in *Mempa v. Rhay*,[10] state probationers were entitled to hearings and legal counsel when facing the possibility of having probation revoked. A number of courts subsequently interpreted the decision in *Mempa* as applying to parole revocation as well as to probation. This interpretation was somewhat clarified five years

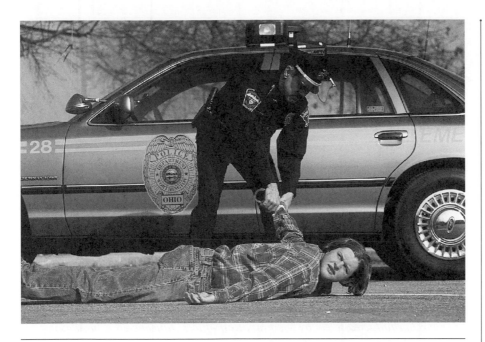

One frequent reason for parole revocation is the parolee's arrest for a criminal offense.

later with the Supreme Court's decision in the 1972 case of *Morrissey v. Brewer*.[11] This case provided the basic foundation on which parolees' due process rights and, hence, the due process requirements for states to follow were established. Specifically, *Morrissey v. Brewer* established these requirements:

1. To return parolees to prison, two hearings must be held. The first is a preliminary hearing for the purpose of determining whether there is probable cause to believe parolees have violated specific conditions of parole. The second hearing is to determine whether the violation of parole conditions should actually result in a return to prison.

2. Parolees must be provided with written notice of the date, time, and place of the hearings to determine whether to return them to prison.

3. Parolees must be provided with information about their alleged violations of parole conditions and with the evidence that is being used against them.

4. Unless there is good reason not to, parolees must be allowed the opportunity to confront and cross-examine witnesses against them in revocation proceedings.

Revocation and Return to Prison   **371**

Griffin v. Wisconsin, 482 U.S. 868 (1987).

Joseph Griffin was convicted in 1980 of resisting arrest, disorderly conduct, and obstructing an officer in the state of Wisconsin. Griffin was sentenced to probation and, therefore, required to abide by all conditions of probation. In April 1983 the Beloit, Wisconsin, police department informed the probation department that there were, or might be, guns present in Griffin's apartment. Unable to locate the officer assigned to supervise Griffin, the probation officer's supervisor (along with a second probation officer and three plainclothes police officers) went to Griffin's apartment. The supervisor introduced all the parties and told Griffin he was going to search the apartment. The search, conducted solely by the probation officers, uncovered a handgun, and Griffin was arrested.

When he came to trial charged with possession of a firearm by a convicted felon, Griffin tried to suppress the evidence. He argued that the handgun was obtained without a warrant and was, therefore, a violation of the Fourth Amendment. However, the trial court pointed out that Wisconsin statutory law allows for searches without warrants by probation (and hence parole) officers as long as they obtain permission for the search from their supervisors and there are "reasonable grounds" to believe contraband is within the area to be searched.

The appeals procedure of Griffin's conviction finally reached the United States Supreme Court in 1987. The Supreme Court ruled that the search of Griffin's apartment, done within the boundaries of Wisconsin's law, was in fact reasonable and legal. According to the Court, supervision of probationers and parolees presents a "special need" on the state's part. In meeting the special needs of supervising such offenders, it is necessary for officers to conduct searches without a warrant. Therefore, states may enact statutes to allow homes, cars, and personal possessions of probationers or parolees to be searched by supervising officers without a search warrant under conditions constituting "reasonable grounds."

5. When parole is revoked, written statements of the reasons for revocation must be provided.

6. The facts in revocation proceedings are to be judged by detached, neutral hearing committees.

The Supreme Court addressed the issue of whether parolees facing possible revocation were entitled to legal assistance one year later when it ruled in the case of *Gagnon v. Scarpelli.* This case specifically dealt with revocation of probation, but the ruling has been applied to revocation proceedings for both probation and parole. Here, the court ruled that allowing parolees (or probationers) the assistance of legal counsel should be determined on a case-by-case basis. The state authority responsible for administering the parole (or probation) system should make the decision. So, there is no hard and fast rule that allows (or provides at no cost) legal counsel to paroled offenders facing possible revocation. This is a case-by-case decision that the paroling authority makes.

Shock Incarceration

Parole supervision can be used as a follow-up period of supervision to a short term of incarceration. **Shock incarceration,** also referred to as shock parole, is where offenders are sentenced to short (perhaps 90 days) terms in prison *and* periods of time on community supervision. Such practices, also known as *split sentences* or *combination sentences,* were first begun in 1965 in Ohio with its enactment of a "shock probation" statute. Here, it is interesting to note that even among lawmakers and criminal justice practitioners, confusion exists about the distinction between probation and parole. In the case of shock incarceration, the community supervision period can be referred to as either probation (because it is a sentence from the court) or as parole (because it is a form of community supervision that follows offenders' releases from prison, which are earlier than they might have otherwise been).

Shock incarceration Sentencing offenders to short periods of time in prison with following periods of time on community supervision; the idea is to make offenders realize what prison is like and to avoid their future return to prison.

The actual way that shock incarceration works, however, varies by jurisdictions. For instance, the initial sentences from the trial judge may call for the combinations of incarceration and community supervision. Or, the original sentences may be for standard prison sentences, but may give offenders opportunities to petition the court for shock parole. Such petitions must convince the court that offenders do not really need the full terms in prison, but that short exposures to prison will achieve deterrent effects (by administering shocks) on offenders.

As expected, shock incarceration programs are reserved for only those inmates who are considered low risks for recidivism. Shock incarceration is almost always used only for first-time offenders. Typically, such sentences are also for people who, aside from their present offenses, lead very law-abiding lives and are "respectable" citizens. Shock incarceration also reinforces the ideology behind such programs: They are primarily for deterrence, although reintegration is also a goal. By not removing offenders from their home communities for extended periods of time, these sentences are intended to help people (through community supervision) live law-abiding lives. The rehabilitative ideal is also included in shock incarceration. Since these offenders are not "hardened criminals," the amount and type of rehabilitation they need can be provided relatively easily while on community supervision.

Split sentences, where offenders are sentenced to both a term of incarceration and a following period of community supervision, accounted for 7.4 percent of federal probationers in 1992.[12] These statistics suggest that such sentences continue to be relatively popular alternatives to less extreme sentences of probation or more extreme sentences of lengthy prison terms.

Many people believe that shock incarceration is an "easy" sentence for offenders, who spend relatively short times in prison. Other observers believe such sentences are "hard" since many people so sentenced would have otherwise been placed only on probation. Instead, they now have to serve time in prison. The true value of shock incarceration, as with any criminal justice policy, is the degree to which it can be shown to lower or control crime rates. However, the true value of shock incarceration programs is not yet known. Research evaluating the effectiveness of such programs has produced very mixed results.

Many critics fear these programs will be used in a **net-widening** effort. That is, programs or sanctions are used for people who otherwise would not have had such strict sentences. Specifically, critics

---

Split sentences Criminal sentences that include both time in an institution and a period of time on community corrections.

Net-widening Correctional programs or practices that are applied to people who otherwise would not have received such harsh sentences had the programs or practices not existed.

fear that offenders who would have otherwise been placed on probation will be given split sentences simply because the harsher alternative is available, not because it is any more advantageous for the offender. As seen by Gennaro Vito, a leading authority on shock incarceration:

> If shock (incarceration) is utilized, it should be used with a select group of offenders who cannot be considered as good candidates for regular probation. The period of incarceration must be short in order to achieve the maximum deterrent effect while reducing the fiscal cost of incarceration. . . . (S)hock (incarceration) has the potential to become a way to reduce institutional overcrowding, which is consistent with the objective of reintegration and public safety.[13]

Summary

Parole is one of the most politically controversial aspects of the U.S. correctional system. Parole is commonly viewed as being soft on offenders and allowing them to have their sentences reduced. However, as philosophically and practically developed in our nation, parole is actually a process designed to achieve positive effects for both individual offenders and the correctional system. Parole encourages inmates to work toward change in prison programs and also provides institutions with an incentive for enticing or controlling inmates. Parole, a privilege for inmates who earn the opportunity to return to the community, is used only after they have served their minimum sentences.

Parole can exist only with indeterminate sentencing. When determinate sentences are used, fixing specific amounts of time offenders must serve, parole is not theoretically possible. In both instances of determinate sentencing, as well as with some indeterminate sentencing approaches, other forms of early release can be used. Today many correctional systems release inmates early because their facilities' conditions and population sizes violate constitutional minimum standards.

Parole is very similar to probation in terms of the processes' actual functioning. In fact, in many states and communities, the same sets of individuals supervise probation and parole offenders. The range of conditions that can be legally imposed on probationers and parolees differs. Generally speaking, the conditions that are legally permissible for parolees but not for probationers are those that focus on stricter control of offenders. The assumption here is that parolees should be monitored more closely because their original sentences (prison instead of probation) indicate a need for higher-level security.

Parolees are, naturally, very similar to prison inmates. Their differences are typically relatively minor. Parolees are similar to probationers in that many do not successfully complete their periods of supervision and must be returned to incarceration. Just as with probationers, parolees can have their privilege of parole revoked because of either violating the conditions of their parole or committing new criminal offenses.

One modern variation of parole is shock incarceration. These programs provide at the time of sentencing specified periods of time to be served in a prison or jail, followed with short periods of time in community corrections. Shock incarceration can be viewed as a hybrid of probation and parole, but it is conceptually linked with parole because the period of supervision follows release from incarceration. Shock incarceration programs have received very positive evaluations, and some believe they are very promising options for mediating the popular and political disputes about the use of both probation and parole.

QUESTIONS FOR REVIEW

1. What are the major differences between parole and probation? How do both these concepts differ from pardons?

2. From where did the early American efforts at developing parole come? What is the historical basis upon which parole is based?

3. What are the goals of parole as a method of dealing with offenders? What are the purposes for parole?

4. What benefits does parole offer to offenders, the criminal justice system, and society in general?

5. How are parolees similar to and different from prison inmates?

6. How is a prison inmate determined eligible for release on parole? What factors are included in a decision about whether to grant parole to a particular individual?

7. What are the similarities and differences between the typical conditions of parole and probation? Why do these differences exist?

8. How does the process of parole revocation work? What are the legal requirements for this process?

9. What is shock incarceration?

10. What benefits do shock incarceration programs offer to offenders, the criminal justice system, and society in general?

ACTIVITIES

1. Talk with a parole officer about what he or she sees as the most common violations that parolees commit. How does the officer usually handle these violations? In what ways does the officer learn about

a client's violations? Does the manner in which this information is learned influence his or her reaction to the violation?

2. Ask two groups consisting of five students each to list all the restrictions they think should be placed on parolees. Gather these lists, and compile one master list for each group. Compare the lists from each group. How do the lists differ? Ask each group to explain any differences.

ENDNOTES

1. Paul Herman, "The Changing Role of Today's Probation and Parole Officer," presentation at the Winter Conference of the American Correctional Association, Orlando, Florida, 1994.

2. David Dressler, *Practice and Theory of Probation and Parole,* 2d ed. (New York: Columbia University Press, 1969), p. 61.

3. Vernon C. Branham and Samuel B. Kutash (eds.), *Encyclopedia of Criminology* (New York: Philosophical Library, 1949), p. 285.

4. Harry E. Allen, Chris W. Eskridge, Edward J. Latessa, and

Gennaro F. Vito, *Probation and Parole in America* (New York: The Free Press, 1985).

5. *Sweeney v. United States,* 353 F.2d 10 (7th Cir. 1965).

6. *United States v. Stine,* 675 F.2d 69 (3d Cir. 1982), 31 Cr.L2081.

7. *Hyland v. Procunier,* 311 F. Supp (N.D.Cal. 1970) at 750.

8. *Sobell v. Reed,* 327 F. Supp. 1294 (S.D.N.Y. 1971).

9. James Boudouris, *The Revocation Process in Iowa* (Des Moines: Department of Corrections, Bureau of Data, Research, and Planning, 1985); *Alternative to Prison Revocation Study* (Madison, WI: Wisconsin Department of Health and Social Services, 1985); Rebecca Zwetchkenbaum-Segal, *Case Preparation Aid Follow-Up Study: Major Findings* (Boston: Planning, Research, and Program Development Unit, Massachusetts Parole Board, 1984).

10. *Mempa v. Rhay,* 389 US 128, 88 S.Ct. 254, 19 L.Ed.2d 336 (1967).

11. *Morrissey v. Brewer,* 408 US 471, 92 S.Ct. 2593, 33 L.Ed.2d (1972).

12. U.S. Department of Justice, Compendium of Federal Justice Statistics, 1992 (Washington, D.C.: Bureau of Justice Statistics, 1995), pp. 45–46.

13. Gennaro F. Vito, "Developments in Shock Probation: A Review of Research Findings and Policy Implications," *Federal Probation,* Vol. 48, 1984, pp. 26–27.

CHAPTER 13

Juvenile Justice

CHAPTER OBJECTIVES

Throughout the first 12 chapters we have discussed how the U.S. criminal justice system operates and have placed special emphasis on the corrections component. Our focus has been exclusively on processing adult offenders. Here, we will examine the U.S. juvenile justice system. As you will see, a number of similarities, yet some very important differences, exist between the two systems. After reading this chapter, you will be able to:

1. Discuss the historical development and initiation of the U.S. juvenile justice system.

2. Distinguish between traditional and contemporary approaches to juvenile justice.

3. Explain the emergence and rationale for the U.S. juvenile justice system.

4. Compare and contrast criminal and status offenses by juveniles.

5. Understand the ideologies of our current approaches to juvenile corrections.

6. Discuss the similarities and differences between corrections for adults and for juveniles.

7. Explain the structure and functions of probation for juveniles.

8. Distinguish between the major types and typical functions of institutions for juveniles.

9. Contrast community correctional alternatives for juveniles with those for adult offenders.

10. Predict the future trends and developments in juvenile corrections.

Our juvenile justice system is based on the goal of protecting and rehabilitating young offenders.

History of Juvenile Crime and Justice

Youth and crime is not a new problem in our world. Since the beginning of history some children have been involved in "crime." Perhaps those crimes have not always been as serious and frequent as they are in the 1990s, but youths have always been involved in crime in one form or another.

If this is an age-old problem, why, then, have we not solved it? Good question, but then we also need to ask why we have not solved the crime problem in general. Juvenile crime probably has more similarities than differences to adult crime. Basically, the only real difference between a juvenile and an adult who commits crime is the age of the offender. Of course, a variety of social factors are associated with leading individuals into crime. But, these are largely *individual* differences, not differences based on whether offenders are old enough to be held legally responsible for their actions.

This says nothing, though, about how societies have reacted to crime by the young. Throughout most of known history, youthful offenders were seen as either unable to be responsible for their actions or as simply smaller (and younger) versions of adult criminals. A separate system to handle crimes by juveniles is a relatively modern idea. Only during the past one hundred years have modern societies established a system for young offenders. Traditionally, society has handled such individuals as if they were no different from older offenders.

Traditional Responses to Juvenile Offenders

Juvenile offenders have historically been viewed as essentially smaller (and obviously younger) versions of adult offenders. The ideas that "children" are less capable of intentionally committing a wrong or that they break the law for different reasons than do adults, have not traditionally been a part of criminal justice systems' ideology. However, this is not to say that juveniles have always been treated exactly as their adult counterparts. The differences in how we respond to and legally process juveniles has been based largely on individual exceptions to the supposed "rule."

Development of the American Model

The "American model" of juvenile justice is a **systematic approach** to process juvenile offenders through a separate, but similar, system

Systematic approach Viewing a process as a set of interrelated parts; viewing actions as part of a larger process, not simply as unconnected acts; recognition that the actions of one agency or person will affect other people or agencies.

of courts and corrections as that used with adult offenders. However, the guiding ideology behind the juvenile system is very different from the ideologies that structure our adult system. As we have repeatedly seen, the five basic ideologies have guided the actions of the adult correctional system at different times and in different situations. In juvenile justice, we strongly believe that juveniles are to be treated and "rehabilitated" rather than simply punished. Obviously, however, punishment may seem more appropriate for some juvenile offenders, and in some cases this is exactly what our system does. But, for the most part, our juvenile justice (especially corrections) system is based on the goal of working to protect, change, or "save" juveniles from the forces believed to lead or push them into criminal activities.

U.S. juvenile justice began with a primary goal of attempting to keep children out of the criminal justice system. This remains as one goal of today's juvenile system and can be seen in Figure 13–1, which shows the various points at which juvenile offenders can be filtered from the "system."

With a special court for juveniles, separate institutions, and a broad range of available community correctional options, the American model of juvenile justice developed in the 1890s. This was the same time that sociological theories of crime and delinquency led criminologists and politicians to examine the culture and organization of urban communities, the breakdown of the family, and the rapid "evolution" in both technological and moral culture as the probable causes of criminal behavior. Many people believed that adult criminals were largely lost to the strength of these social forces. However, they also believed that juveniles could be "rescued" from the destructive nature of these forces if trained experts intervened on their behalf and before the damage juveniles suffered became permanent.

Based on this idea of rescuing juveniles from their environments and due to the efforts of upper-class women, the first juvenile court was developed in Cook County (Chicago), Illinois, in 1899. On January 1, 1899, the Illinois legislature unanimously passed the bill creating the court. The idea of juvenile court spread across the country relatively quickly. By 1925 all but 2 of the 48 states had juvenile courts in place.[1]

The goals of these new courts were to assist in separating juvenile offenders from the factors that led to their downfall and to provide for the children's best interests. Said somewhat differently, the original juvenile court was not designed to be a criminal court for children. Rather, it was designed to be a social service agency, one that would serve as the central component for an entire child welfare system. On

Figure 13–1 Juvenile justice process.

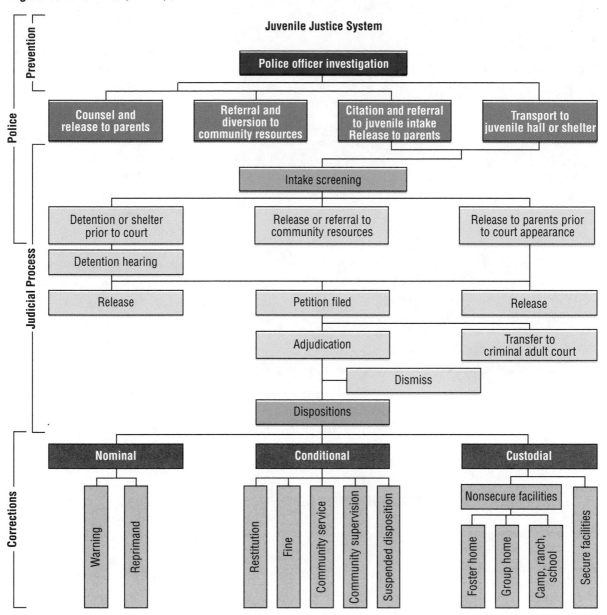

Source: National Advisory Committee on Criminal Justice Standards and Goals, *Juvenile Justice and Delinquency Prevention: Report of the Task Force on Juvenile Justice and Delinquency Prevention* (Washington, D.C.: U.S. Government Printing Office, 1976), p. 9.

Adjudicated The process of legally determining that a juvenile has committed an act that, if done by an adult, would/could lead to a criminal conviction.

Status offenses Acts of conduct that are illegal for juveniles but not for adults; activities that are illegal only because the individual involved has the status of a juvenile.

Incorrigible Being unmanageable or uncontrollable.

the surface these goals seem very logical and sensible. However, the developments of the twentieth century would quickly show us that these goals are often highly incompatible. Regardless, these two goals remain as the foundation for today's juvenile justice system.

The different approach our society takes toward juvenile offenders is evident in an actual court case involving juveniles. When processed through juvenile court for criminal actions and if found to have committed the acts, juveniles are not found "guilty," but are instead **adjudicated** as delinquent. "Adjudication" simply means that a court matter is brought to a final resolution. When adults are declared guilty of crimes, they are denounced as "bad people" and have permanent stigmas attached to them. In contrast, adjudication as a delinquent avoids such labeling. In most instances, juvenile court records are not accessible to those beyond the actual case, and no permanent consequences are supposed to accompany individuals.

Status Offenses　In the American model of juvenile justice, juveniles have an additional set of legal obligations that do not apply to adults. This is perhaps the most important difference between the adult and the juvenile justice systems. While all people in our society must abide by criminal law, juveniles must also abide by special laws that apply only to them. Failure to obey these special laws results in a **status offense,** which is "an act of conduct which is declared by statute to be an offense, but only when committed or engaged in by a juvenile, and which can be adjudicated only by a juvenile court."[2] Status offenses include a wide range of forbidden activities such as being truant from school, running away from home, possessing and/or using alcoholic beverages, and being **incorrigible.** A child who is incorrigible is unmanageable and uncontrollable. When parents or guardians are unable to control their children's behavior, they or a juvenile court may have the youths declared incorrigible and, therefore, have them become wards of the state.

Commonly filtered from the official processing stream, status offenses are instead handled on an informal level by individual law enforcement officials. However, according to the Uniform Crime Reports, status offenses continue to account for nearly 1 in 9 arrests of juveniles.[3] Reflecting this difference in approach, various states refer to such juveniles as Persons In Need of Supervision (PINS), Minors

LEGAL BRIEF:

In re Michael G., 243 Cal. Rptr. 224 (Cal. 1988).

In 1984 Michael G., a minor in Fresno, California, was adjudicated as a ward of the Fresno County Superior Court, Juvenile Division, and placed on probation. As one of the conditions of his probation, Michael G. was ordered to attend school regularly and not be either tardy or absent from school. However, Michael G. did not abide by this condition of his probation; and after two hearings, the juvenile court determined that Michael G. had willfully disobeyed the conditions of his probation. As a result, the court ordered him to be held in custody for 48 hours (6 P.M. Friday until 6 P.M. Sunday). However, the court delayed the imposition of the custody time to allow Michael G.'s attorney to ask for a review of the decision by an appeals court. In turn, Michael G.'s attorney filed a writ of habeas corpus, requesting the court to either show valid reason and justification for the detainment of Michael G. or to order his release.

When it reviewed this case, the supreme court of California ruled that the juvenile court does indeed have the authority to hold juvenile status offenders in contempt of court for failing to abide by court orders (including conditions of probation). Also, the court ruled that so long as the court of jurisdiction takes into consideration the possibility of applying less restrictive alternatives and so long as the detainment of the juvenile status offender does not bring the status offender into contact with juveniles adjudicated delinquent, the practice of institutionalization is permissible. Consequently, it is legal (within certain boundaries) for a juvenile court to commit a juvenile status offender to a period of institutionalization.

In Need of Supervision (MINS), Children In Need of Supervision (CHINS), or Juveniles In Need of Supervision (JINS).

Criminal Offenses Just like all other members of society, juveniles must abide by our criminal statutes. When juveniles commit acts that would be considered crimes if committed by adults, these acts are considered criminal for juveniles as well. Although the majority of juvenile crime falls into the status offense category,[4] the increasing number and increasing concern about criminal acts (especially violent crimes) by juveniles garner most of our media, official, and daily attention.

Throughout history people have almost always been concerned with the "juvenile crime problem."[5] Most societies and most historical periods have assumed that the problems with juvenile crime are the worst they have ever been and that they are the first to address such problems. This is simply not true. Officials in ancient Greece and Rome were concerned about crimes by youth.[6]

Knowing that juvenile crime has always been a concern, though, does little to ease our fears about its consequences. Also, based on our apparent inability to learn from history, this knowledge contributes little to our present efforts to eliminate or reduce such forms of crime. The problem remains, but many Americans are relatively unaware of its scope. What most of us know about the "juvenile crime wave" is what we see on television news or read in newspaper and magazine headlines. Therefore, before studying how our society attempts to "correct" juvenile offenders, we need first to examine the amount of juvenile crime in our society.

Those who study and work in corrections commonly speak of juvenile justice as a "cycle." This cycle refers to the historical swings in ideas and practices that characterize how societies react to juvenile offenders.[7] The system swings back and forth between a heavy emphasis on punishing juveniles and a heavy emphasis on trying to help juveniles.

The cycle begins with a belief that juvenile crime is at a very high level. This high rate of juvenile crime is responded to with very harsh punishments and few, if any, forms of treatment available. This forces officials to choose between applying severe punishments to youths or not doing anything at all with them. This means that many nonserious juvenile offenders avoid punishment because the punishments available are too severe. Also, if we apply severe punishments, minor offenders will be pushed deeper into crime and will be essentially more dangerous and more criminal. So, in this situation we commonly do nothing with minor offenders.

However, in not doing anything with offenders, officials soon realize that their choices offer little diversity. This brings about a movement for treatments, which are perceived not as punishments but as lenient measures, to help youthful offenders. This change in responses to juvenile offenders often has no change in the rate (or, at least, the *perceived* rate) of juvenile crime. As the rate of juvenile crime increases, the leniency of the juvenile justice system is blamed. As a result, society calls for punishing juveniles more harshly, supposedly as a deterrent.

As the emphasis changes from "lenient" treatment approaches to increasingly harsh punishments, we find ourselves right back where we started. We have a high rate of juvenile crime, and we once again have officials faced with deciding whether the available ways to respond to juvenile crime are too severe and potentially harmful. The cycle is complete and ready to begin again.

In today's society, crime is a serious problem among youthful offenders. As shown in Table 13–1, in 1993 a total of 710,916 people under age 18 were arrested for index offenses. The distribution of arrests for index offenses among juvenile offenders is similar to the distribution of these arrests for adult offenders. The differences are found in the offenses of burglary, motor vehicle theft, and especially larceny-theft, which account for greater proportions of juvenile arrests than for adult arrests. Furthermore, juveniles account for approximately 1 in 6 arrests in the United States.[8] In statistical terms, this percentage does not appear extreme, as approximately 1 in 4 Americans is under the age of 18. However, we need to remember that

FYI

Although increasing numbers of juveniles are becoming involved in crime, children are not destined to be criminals. Not even all children who grow up around the factors that are believed to lead to crime (drugs, poverty, weak family structures, etc.) will become criminals. **High-risk youths,** those juveniles whose situational and personal factors make them most likely to become delinquent, do not always become involved in delinquency or crime. This fact was made clear in a 1994 report from the Office of Juvenile Justice and Delinquency Prevention, titled *Urban Delinquency and Substance Abuse.*

While many adolescents are at high risk for delinquency, not all of them actually become delinquent. Some of them—**resilient youths**— manage to avoid the risk. . . . Among the family factors, parental supervision, attachment to parents, and consistency of discipline appear to be the most important. Commitment to school and especially avoidance of delinquent and drug-using peers also appear to be major protective factors. In sum, youths at risk who have more conventional lifestyles at home, at school, and with friends appear much better able to avoid the negative consequences of residing in high-risk, high-crime neighborhoods.

Source: U.S. Department of Justice, *Urban Delinquency and Substance Abuse: Initial Findings* (Washington, D.C.: Office of Juvenile Justice and Delinquency Prevention, 1994).

High-risk youths Juveniles who are believed, because of their environments, to be significantly more likely than others to become involved in delinquency.

Resilient youths Juveniles who, despite being subjected to numerous factors believed to lead to juvenile delinquency, remain free from delinquency and crime.

Table 13–1 Arrests of People Under Age 18 for Index Offenses

Offense	Number of Arrests	Percent of Juvenile Arrests*	Percent of Adult Arrests*
Murder	3,284	0.4	0.8
Forcible rape	5,303	0.7	1.3
Robbery	43,340	6.0	6.0
Aggravated assault	67,751	9.5	18.2
Burglary	116,024	16.3	14.1
Larceny-theft	391,950	55.1	51.8
Motor vehicle theft	75,315	10.6	6.9
Arson	7,949	1.1	0.7

*Percentages do not equal 100% due to rounding.

Source: Federal Bureau of Investigation, *Crime in the United States, 1993* (Washington, D.C.: U.S. Department of Justice, 1994).

many of the under-18 population are the very young, those who would be very unlikely to be arrested. Even the youngest juveniles, though, will sometimes be involved in crime and will be arrested. In 1993 the Uniform Crime Reports indicated that 35,572 juveniles under the age of 10 were arrested.[9]

While property crimes account for more arrests among juveniles than among adults, the major concerns in society today are focused on violent crimes by juveniles. This is especially true concerning juveniles who commit crimes using firearms. Table 13–2 shows the results of one study that asked both institutionalized and inner-city public high school students about their weaponry. As the results clearly show, significant percentages of institutionalized juveniles have owned guns, and nearly one-quarter of inner-city high school students admit owning a gun. Obviously, the potential for these guns to be used in criminal activity is fairly high.

Juvenile Corrections Today

Based on the original ideology of juvenile justice—that youthful offenders need more treatment and fewer harsh punishments—our present-day correctional efforts with juveniles reflect ideas of working with offenders, not simply punishing them. This, of course, is not always how individual cases appear to be handled; and there is a definite swing in attitudes today toward harsher punishments. However, the

Table 13-2	Gun Ownership Among Juveniles	
Type of Gun	Percent of Institutionalized Juveniles	Percent of Inner-City High School Students
Any gun	83	22
Hunting rifle	22	8
Shotgun	39	10
Sawed-off shotgun	51	9
Automatic or semi-automatic handgun	55	18
Homemade (zip) gun	6	4
Three or more guns	65	15

Source: Joseph F. Sheley and James D. Wright, *Gun Acquisition and Possession in Selected Juvenile Samples* (Washington, D.C.: Office of Juvenile Justice and Delinquency Prevention, 1993).

way we respond to juvenile criminals remains—and will probably always remain—different from how we respond to adult offenders.

As with adult offenders, a variety of correctional efforts are used with juvenile offenders. Although they are essentially the same for adults, these options are often administered in different ways for juveniles. The basic correctional efforts used for juvenile offenders are probation, institutionalization (what we would call "incarceration" with adults), parole, and community corrections. This section will examine how each of these efforts is performed, highlighting both the similarities and differences with the adult systems we have already examined.

Before studying how each correctional effort is actually conducted, we need to review the patterns of how each form of corrections is applied to juvenile offenders. Just as with adult offenders, distinct patterns of **dispositions** are applied to juvenile offenders. Whereas adults who are found guilty of criminal offenses are sentenced, juveniles who are adjudicated as delinquent receive a disposition. This simply means that their cases have concluded in juvenile court. However, in some cases juvenile offenders (typically the most serious and/or most violent) will have their cases transferred to the jurisdiction of the adult courts. In these instances, when juveniles are tried as adults, any sentence received will also be in the jurisdiction of the adult correctional system. In 1990 just over 2,300 juveniles were serving sentences in adult prisons.[10]

As we see in Figures 13–2 through 13–5, there are easily identifiable patterns of dispositions for juvenile cases across sex, race, age,

Dispositions The various outcomes of court cases; the findings and rulings of judges or courts.

Figure 13–2 Juvenile court dispositions, overall and by sex.

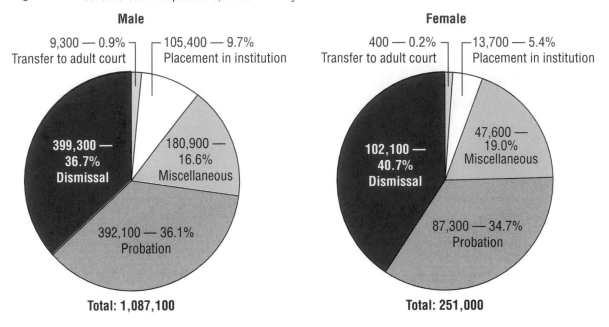

Male

9,300 — 0.9%
Transfer to adult court

105,400 — 9.7%
Placement in institution

399,300 — 36.7%
Dismissal

180,900 — 16.6%
Miscellaneous

392,100 — 36.1%
Probation

Total: 1,087,100

Female

400 — 0.2%
Transfer to adult court

13,700 — 5.4%
Placement in institution

102,100 — 40.7%
Dismissal

47,600 — 19.0%
Miscellaneous

87,300 — 34.7%
Probation

Total: 251,000

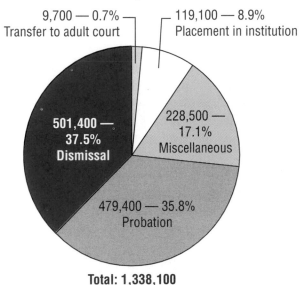

Overall Dispositions

9,700 — 0.7%
Transfer to adult court

119,100 — 8.9%
Placement in institution

501,400 — 37.5%
Dismissal

228,500 — 17.1%
Miscellaneous

479,400 — 35.8%
Probation

Total: 1,338,100

Source: Easy Access to Juvenile Court Statistics, 1991 (Pittsburgh, PA: National Center for Juvenile Court Statistics, 1993).

Figure 13–3 Juvenile court dispositions by race.

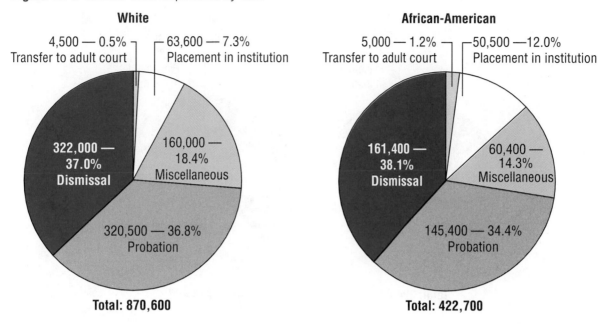

White

4,500 — 0.5%
Transfer to adult court

63,600 — 7.3%
Placement in institution

322,000 — 37.0% Dismissal

160,000 — 18.4% Miscellaneous

320,500 — 36.8% Probation

Total: 870,600

African-American

5,000 — 1.2%
Transfer to adult court

50,500 —12.0%
Placement in institution

161,400 — 38.1% Dismissal

60,400 — 14.3% Miscellaneous

145,400 — 34.4% Probation

Total: 422,700

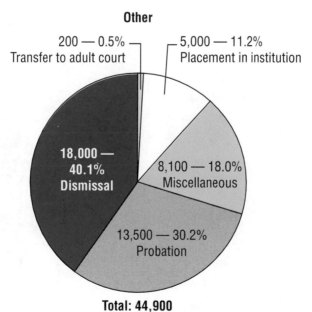

Other

200 — 0.5%
Transfer to adult court

5,000 — 11.2%
Placement in institution

18,000 — 40.1% Dismissal

8,100 — 18.0% Miscellaneous

13,500 — 30.2% Probation

Total: 44,900

Source: Easy Access to Juvenile Court Statistics, 1991 (Pittsburgh, PA: National Center for Juvenile Court Statistics, 1993).

Figure 13–4 Juvenile court dispositions by age.

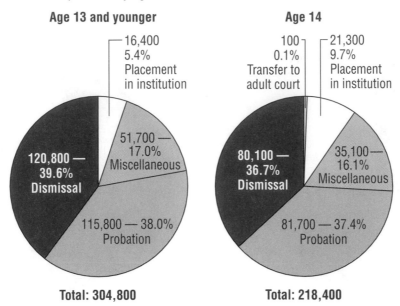

Age 13 and younger

16,400
5.4%
Placement
in institution

51,700 —
17.0%
Miscellaneous

**120,800 —
39.6%
Dismissal**

115,800 — 38.0%
Probation

Total: 304,800

Age 14

100
0.1%
Transfer to
adult court

21,300
9.7%
Placement
in institution

35,100 —
16.1%
Miscellaneous

**80,100 —
36.7%
Dismissal**

81,700 — 37.4%
Probation

Total: 218,400

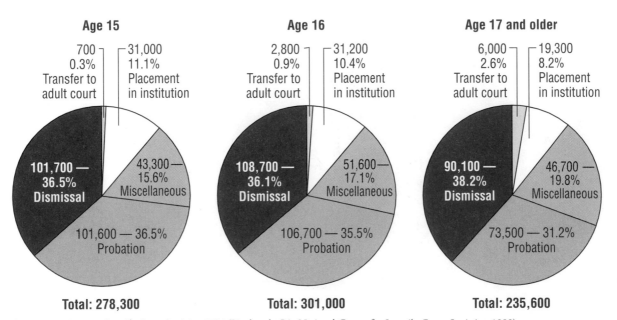

Age 15

700
0.3%
Transfer to
adult court

31,000
11.1%
Placement
in institution

43,300 —
15.6%
Miscellaneous

**101,700 —
36.5%
Dismissal**

101,600 — 36.5%
Probation

Total: 278,300

Age 16

2,800
0.9%
Transfer to
adult court

31,200
10.4%
Placement
in institution

51,600—
17.1%
Miscellaneous

**108,700 —
36.1%
Dismissal**

106,700 — 35.5%
Probation

Total: 301,000

Age 17 and older

6,000
2.6%
Transfer to
adult court

19,300
8.2%
Placement
in institution

46,700 —
19.8%
Miscellaneous

**90,100 —
38.2%
Dismissal**

73,500 — 31.2%
Probation

Total: 235,600

Source: Easy Access to Juvenile Court Statistics, 1991 (Pittsburgh, PA: National Center for Juvenile Court Statistics, 1993).

Figure 13–5 Juvenile court dispositions by offense.

Personal Offenses

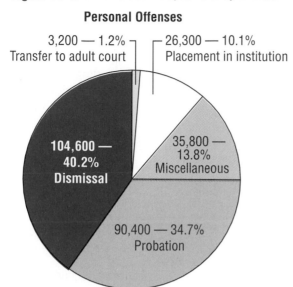

3,200 — 1.2%
Transfer to adult court

26,300 — 10.1%
Placement in institution

35,800 — 13.8%
Miscellaneous

104,600 — 40.2%
Dismissal

90,400 — 34.7%
Probation

Total: 260,300

Property Offenses

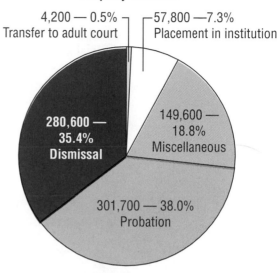

4,200 — 0.5%
Transfer to adult court

57,800 —7.3%
Placement in institution

149,600 — 18.8%
Miscellaneous

280,600 — 35.4%
Dismissal

301,700 — 38.0%
Probation

Total: 793,900

Drug Offenses

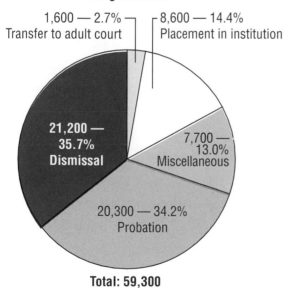

1,600 — 2.7%
Transfer to adult court

8,600 — 14.4%
Placement in institution

7,700 — 13.0%
Miscellaneous

21,200 — 35.7%
Dismissal

20,300 — 34.2%
Probation

Total: 59,300

Public Order Offenses

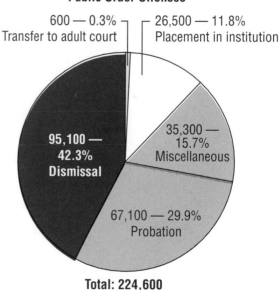

600 — 0.3%
Transfer to adult court

26,500 — 11.8%
Placement in institution

35,300 — 15.7%
Miscellaneous

95,100 — 42.3%
Dismissal

67,100 — 29.9%
Probation

Total: 224,600

Source: Easy Access to Juvenile Court Statistics, 1991 (Pittsburgh, PA: National Center for Juvenile Court Statistics, 1993).

and offense categories. As seen in Figure 13–2, the most common disposition for juveniles is probation or dismissal. Fewer than 1 in 10 (8.9%) of juvenile court cases result in placement in juvenile correctional facilities. Juvenile females are significantly less likely than juvenile males to receive the harshest dispositions (transfer to adult court or institutionalization) and significantly more likely to have their cases dismissed. In terms of distribution of case dispositions across racial categories, as shown in Figure 13–3, the only significant difference is that white juveniles are less likely to be institutionalized than non-white juveniles. Figure 13–4 shows the distribution of case dispositions by juveniles' age. As expected, the likelihood of being

JOB FOCUS: JUVENILE JUSTICE COUNSELOR

Because of the heavy emphasis on treatment in juvenile corrections, interested individuals may consider being counselors for juvenile offenders. Counselors work with the full range of juvenile offenders, from minor status offenders on probation to supposedly hardened adolescents who are institutionalized. The official goals of juvenile justice counselors are to promote the physical, emotional, and social well-being of juveniles in the state's care. In short, counselors are the primary rehabilitative agents, the individuals who personally conduct counseling and oversee juveniles' participation in other treatment programs.

To qualify for juvenile justice counselors, candidates must have a bachelor's degree in criminal justice, psychology, social work, or a directly related field. As always, hiring decisions give preference to applicants who have some experience either in the criminal justice system or in working with troubled youths. These are usually state government jobs. This means that civil service exams are also required. Salaries for juvenile justice counselors vary widely. In some states these positions have starting annual salaries of about $18,000, while in other states beginning salaries are about double that figure.

Source: Harold E. Williamson, *The Corrections Profession* (Thousand Oaks, CA: Sage Publications, 1990).

transferred to adult criminal court increases with age. However, no other significant trends are seen in the age distribution; there is not even a great increase in the number of juveniles processed across age categories.

Figure 13–5 shows juvenile court dispositions by offense. We see that not only are property offenses the large majority of offenses for which juveniles receive disposition, but we also see that they are the least likely to result in juveniles being sent to institutions. Drug

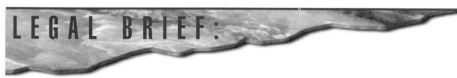

LEGAL BRIEF:

Stanford v. Kentucky, 109 S.Ct. 2969 (1989).

*O*ne controversial aspect of juvenile justice and corrections centers on the question of whether it is appropriate, moral, and constitutional to use the death penalty with juvenile offenders. The U.S. Supreme Court first faced this issue in the 1982 case of Eddings v. Oklahoma. The Court overturned the death sentence but did so because of a procedural error at the trial court. Eddings did not directly address the legality of death sentences for juveniles. In a second Oklahoma case in 1988, Thompson v. Oklahoma, the U.S. Supreme Court first prohibited the use of the death penalty for juveniles, but only for those below 16 years of age. These cases set the stage for the 1989 U.S. Supreme Court case of Stanford v. Kentucky.

In this case the Supreme Court was faced with the question: "At what age does the Eighth Amendment ban the death penalty as punishment no matter the crime?" The final ruling of the Court basically extended the logic of the earlier Thompson case. The Supreme Court ruled that capital punishment may be applied to those who commit murder at the ages of 16 or 17. In short, the conclusion of the Court in this case, as written by Justice Scalia, is: "We discern neither a historical nor a modern societal consensus forbidding the imposition of capital punishment on any person who murders at 16 or 17 years of age. Accordingly, we conclude that such punishment does not offend the Eighth Amendment's prohibition against cruel and unusual punishment." Therefore, statutes that create the possibility of applying the death penalty to 16- and 17-year-old juveniles are legal.

offenses show the harshest treatment of juveniles. Juveniles are most likely to be transferred to adult court or to be institutionalized for drug offenses.

Probation

As for adults, probation for juveniles is based on the idea that institutionalizing offenders, especially first-time and/or minor offenders, may be more negative than positive. Therefore, to avoid making matters worse, probation is widely used. As we have already seen when discussing adult offenders, probation is the most common sentence. The most common disposition for juveniles is also probation.[11] Both the general public and the judicial community consider probation as a form of leniency. While acknowledging that a more severe disposition could have been applied, probation is viewed as giving second chances to youthful offenders. Also, studies of the effects on public safety of institutionalizing youthful offenders versus placing them on probation have shown that institutionalization has no more effect than community placements, including probation.[12]

Probation for juveniles is so popular because our society and legal system believe that we should respond to juvenile offenders with the "least coercive dispositional alternative."[13] Probation accomplishes this. It allows juveniles to remain in the community (in fact, at home) and to attend school and/or work. Probation serves to work with the youths, not to pull them out of the community and to expose them to other, potentially negative influences. Especially in the cases of status offenders, research has demonstrated no public safety gains from institutionalization.[14] In simple terms, probation is a clear example of the philosophical doctrine of *parens patriae*—the idea that the government stands as a parent figure to children and other people who have some form of legal disability or restriction. In the case of juvenile probation, this means that the state assumes the role of setter and enforcer of rules. Through its probation officers, the state acts as a socialization agent and a guidance figure.

The juvenile probation officer acts as an enforcer of rules and serves as a guidance figure.

However, officials and departments that administer juvenile probation typically have very large caseloads. This is especially true in urban areas. Therefore, juvenile probation officers have relatively few opportunities to work with (that is, provide treatment to) the youths on their caseloads. Instead, juvenile probation officers (like adult probation officers) focus on verifying behaviors and make rare contacts with their clients.

In comparison with probation for adults, probation for juveniles is usually a possible disposition for any and all offenses. However, four states (Nevada, Washington, West Virginia, and Wisconsin) do not provide for the possibility of probation for juveniles. However, as shown in Figure 13–5, for all types of criminal offenses, the most common disposition for juveniles is probation.

Institutionalization

Juvenile justice has traditionally been based on helping and working with youthful offenders. However, one of the very first prison facilities in the world was designed for juveniles. The Hospice at San Michele in Rome was built in 1704 to treat "wayward youths." The facility's guiding principle was treatment; but the institution's guiding philosophy was one of **expiation.** That is, individuals were expected to make amends for their wrongs through suffering. Today, such philosophies have been officially discarded, although some critics of institutionalizing juveniles might argue otherwise.

When juvenile delinquents are considered dangerous to society, they may be placed in juvenile correctional institutions only until they reach the **age of majority.** When individuals' legal statuses change from those of juveniles to those of adults (with accompanying legal obligations), we say they have reached the age of majority. In other words, individuals are no longer minors but have entered the "majority." Age of majority is typically 18, although some jurisdictions may specify age 21 for some purposes.

Following the development of institutions for adult criminals, the first facility designed to institutionalize juvenile offenders opened in 1824 in New York City. Over the next 16 years, similar institutions opened in Boston, Philadelphia, Chicago, Cincinnati, Richmond, Mobile, and Bangor (Maine). The goal of these institutions, such as the House of Refuge in Philadelphia, was to provide "a good dose of institutionalization" and "shield [young offenders] from the temptations of a sinful world." This suggests that juveniles were seen as not

Expiation Making amends for wrongdoing by suffering; the process of suffering as a way of showing awareness of and responsibility for wrongdoing.

Age of majority The legal age at which individuals are no longer considered juveniles but adults; the age at which individuals can be held fully, legally responsible for their actions.

JOB FOCUS: JUVENILE PROBATION OFFICER

Juvenile probation officers, like their counterparts in the adult correctional system, provide a combination of supervision and assistance to offenders who are placed on probation by the court. However, in many instances juvenile probation officers work more closely with the court, in this case juvenile court, and attempt to work more closely with both the juveniles and the juveniles' families. Typically, juvenile probation officers handle caseloads of both status and criminal offenders who are age 16 or younger.

The primary responsibilities of juvenile probation officers are to conduct intake assessments (looking at the treatment needs, family, school and social backgrounds, and delinquency histories), to actively investigate the juveniles' backgrounds, and to supervise the youths and their participation in programs. While juvenile probation officers work to direct the youths away from further criminal or status offenses, much of their time is also spent in making referrals to community programs and agencies that can assist the youths in remaining law-abiding. Referrals are not directed only at the juveniles, but also include family services and services/assistance for other members of the juveniles' families. This is an important aspect of helping direct youths themselves from criminal and status offenses, as the situations in the juveniles' homes contribute to their delinquency.

To be qualified as juvenile probation officers, candidates must have a bachelor's degree in criminal justice, social work, psychology, or a related field and at least two years' experience in some type of counseling work. The qualities generally needed for jobs as juvenile probation officers are an ability to effectively manage a large caseload and skills to work with a manipulative, often hostile population. Also, a genuine concern for the welfare of juveniles is frequently considered a requirement for such a position. The starting salary for this type of position is usually between $23,000 and $28,000 annually.

Source: U.S. Department of Labor, Bureau of Labor Statistics, *Occupational Outlook Handbook,* 1994–95 ed., p. 137.

necessarily responsible for their actions. Rather, they were seen as being shaped by a world that was filled with negative and dangerous influences. Thus, to save youths from such a world and its bad influences, strict regimens of discipline, and close supervision and guidance were applied. In short, the earliest juvenile corrections institutions believed juvenile delinquents could be salvaged through strict and carefully structured routines.

An early facility to house juvenile offenders was The House of Refuge in Philadelphia.

Institutionalization of juveniles is typically accomplished today by placing individuals in one of three types of institutions: detention centers, training schools, or boot camps. (Each institution will be discussed in a later section.) We need to study not just the ideal forms of juvenile correctional facilities, but we also need to consider the actual living and treatment opportunities and conditions of such facilities. If the goal of juvenile corrections is to resocialize juveniles, then the environment and physical facilities in which this goal is pursued should allow staff and juvenile residents maximum opportunities to realize it.

When we consider institutionalization, we have to consider not only the effects the experience itself may have on juveniles, but also the actual conditions in which juveniles are confined. The Office of Juvenile Justice and Delinquency Prevention conducted a study in 1991 to determine the conditions of confinement in juvenile correctional facilities.[15] The review of nearly 1,100 facilities revealed some significant problems in the physical facilities. Most notably, these problems included very small amounts of actual living space per juvenile resident, inadequate health care, and insufficient security.[16] These problems were not restricted only to a few facilities or only to facilities of a certain type or in certain areas. Rather, these were widespread problems. Figure 13–6 addresses these problems and makes fifteen recommendations.

The institutionalization of juveniles has critics. As a result, several states have experimented with large-scale deinstitutionalization of juvenile offenders. These states include Massachusetts, Utah, Florida, and Maryland—a very diverse set of states, both politically and socially. Moving away from institutionalizing juvenile offenders and toward emphasizing community-based corrections for juveniles has been motivated by a combination of humanistic ideals stressing the ability of individuals to change and adapt to changing environments and the more pragmatic, financial and resource-based needs of government agencies. The difficulties that accompany such changes, though, include those predicted by the cycle of juvenile justice: As we remove them from institutional settings, juveniles often show high rates of recidivism (especially in the short run following the closing of institutions), and the juvenile justice system is perceived as being "soft on

---

Figure 13–6 Recommendations of the Office of Juvenile Justice and Delinquency Prevention concerning conditions for the confinement of juveniles.

Recommendation #1

We recommend that large dormitories be eliminated from juvenile facilities. No new facilities should be built that contain large dormitories. In existing facilities, large dormitories should be replaced as soon as possible.

Recommendation #2

We recommend that jurisdictions develop policies that regulate the use and duration of juvenile confinement and that guide future development of confinement and non-confinement placement options. To do this, states and localities should implement a planning process that identifies decisions that affect use of detention and confinement, that identifies characteristics of juveniles processed through the system, and that documents capacities of confinement and nonconfinement placement options.

Recommendation #3

We recommend that juvenile justice agencies conduct detailed comparative studies of facilities with low and high escape and injury rates to identify policies and practices that can materially improve safety and security. These studies should pay special attention to procedures used to classify juveniles and the ways in which classification is used.

Recommendation #4

We recommend that all juveniles be screened for risk of suicidal behavior immediately upon their admission to confinement facilities.

Recommendation #5

We recommend that suicidal juveniles be constantly monitored by staff. This means that suicidal youths should not be isolated or placed in a room by themselves. When suicidal juveniles are housed in single rooms, staff should be with them continuously. A mental health professional should assess suicidal youths as quickly as possible and, if they deem it necessary, the youths should be transferred to a medical or mental health facility that is staffed and equipped to deal with suicidal youths.

Recommendation #6

We recommend that agencies study the causes of high supervision staff turnover rates, develop strategies to reduce high turnover rates, and soften the effects of turnover by increased training.

Recommendation #7

We recommend that juvenile justice agencies act to ensure that initial health screenings are carried out promptly at admission and to ensure that health appraisals are completed or received within a week after admission. We also recommend that juvenile justice agencies take steps to develop and ensure the use of an adequate training program for nonmedical staff who conduct health screenings.

Recommendation #8

We recommend that existing public health surveillance systems be expanded to include and separately track confined juveniles. We also recommend a general review of the health needs of confined juveniles and the health services they receive, based on a review of medical records of a national sample of confined juveniles.

Recommendation #9

We recommend that federal agencies support funding of a study to document educational needs and problems of a national sample of confined juveniles and to evaluate the capacity of educational programs in confinement facilities to serve those needs and to address those problems.

Recommendation #10

We recommend that federal agencies support funding of a study to document the treatment needs of a national sample of confined juveniles and of the treatment services they receive.

Recommendation #11

We recommend that state and local fire codes for juvenile facilities be toughened and enforced more vigorously. In particular, we recommend that facilities be inspected more frequently, and that available enforcement authority be exercised more vigorously to correct violations. We also recommend that laws or regulations governing fire and life safety in juvenile facilities be as rigorous as those that apply to schools, hospitals, or other public buildings.

Recommendation #12

We recommend that juvenile facilities permit juveniles to receive as well as make telephone calls.

Recommendation #13

We recommend more extensive comparison of conditions in facilities with high and low rates of use of search, isolation, and restraints in order to identify and test the rationales and effects of these variations in practice.

Recommendation #14

We recommend that organizations that develop nationally recognized standards for juvenile facilities promulgate measurable performance standards that can serve both as goals for facilities to attain and as benchmarks against which their progress can be measured. Such standards are particularly important in areas of security, health care, education, mental health services, and treatment programming.

Recommendation #15

We recommend that a joint committee be created whose membership represents all national professional organizations with an interest in juvenile confinement. Over the next 4 years members of this joint committee should work to implement recommendations in this report and to coordinate activities within their respective organizations toward the common objective of improving conditions of juvenile confinement. Appropriate federal agencies should encourage and support the work of this joint committee.

Source: Office of Juvenile Justice and Delinquency Prevention, *Conditions of Confinement: Juvenile Detention and Corrections Facilities* (Washington, D.C.: U.S. Department of Justice, 1994).

crime." Consequently, an immediate outcry for the return to institutionalization of juvenile offenders should be expected.

Detention Centers

A **detention center** is an institution designed to hold juveniles for short periods of time. Juveniles may be placed in detention centers either before or after being adjudicated. The intent of such facilities is to provide a place to house and control juveniles who cannot, for whatever reason, be returned to the community. The 1990s detention center is the primary component of the juvenile correctional system.[17]

Detention centers typically serve three primary purposes. First, similar to adults placed in jail, juveniles may be placed in detention centers to ensure their appearance at court proceedings. Second, detention centers can house juveniles who cannot be returned to their homes. Third, detention centers allow the juvenile justice system to keep watch over individuals and to ensure they do not hurt themselves or disrupt the system's activities.

Usually only those youths believed to have committed the most serious offenses are held in custody. Remember: The juvenile justice system operates on what is "in the best interests of the child." "Best interests" is usually interpreted as remaining with one's family. However, some judges have used detention centers as post-adjudication facilities. In this way detention centers truly are mirror images of adult jails. Both offenders who have and who have not been processed by the court, and those who have and who have not been adjudicated are placed in detention centers.

Most juvenile detention centers were originally designed and constructed for some other purpose.[18] This means that many detention centers are not designed for effective and efficient security. Adding to this problem is the fact that most juvenile detention centers, similar to adult jails, are overcrowded. Also similar to jails, detention centers rely heavily on dormitory housing and offer few, if any, programs. Consequently, juveniles in detention centers have few constructive activities and spend most of their time idle and in the company of other idle juveniles. The potential for problems quickly becomes obvious.

Detention center A facility for the temporary placement of juvenile offenders and sometimes juvenile crime victims; a place where juveniles can be held and provided some forms of treatment.

Training Schools Usually considered the primary form of youth institution, the **training school** is typically a rather large residential facility that houses several hundred "students." Inside the training school, juveniles usually live in group settings, such as dormitories, and attend school. Since most jurisdictions require school attendance for juveniles, institutionalized youth must also attend school.

Most training schools are very similar to adult prisons. The residents/students of training schools are high-risk youths who have typically been adjudicated for serious and violent acts of delinquency. Training schools, therefore, are not the first or even early stops in juveniles' passage through the juvenile justice system. Most often training schools are places for repeat offenders. Juveniles usually must have committed a series of offenses and/or an especially serious offense to be placed in training schools.

Training schools do offer some treatment programs. However, similar to prisons for the most serious adult offenders, training schools' treatment programs are often minimal and rather ineffective. Because they house the "worst kids," such institutions often emphasize security instead of treatment. Even when they offer a number of high-quality treatment programs, training schools must balance these

Training school A facility that is designed to keep close supervision of juvenile offenders while it also encourages their continuation of education and other treatment programs; training schools are the juveniles' equivalent of the adult reformatory.

Repeat juvenile offenders are often placed in training schools.

against the requirements for security. As we know from adult prisons, security concerns override treatment concerns. Security concerns also make treatment programs more difficult to operate and less likely to function effectively and efficiently.

Boot Camps   When traditional forms of institutionalization are less than satisfactory but abandoning the idea entirely is unacceptable, the logical alternative is to alter or modify institutionalization. One popular alternative form of institutionalization today is the **boot camp,** where offenders are held in secure facilities and participate in programs similar to military basic training. The purpose of boot camps is to resocialize offenders and to instill in them discipline, routine, and obedience to orders. Although a form of institutionalization, boot camps are commonly thought of as an **intermediate sanction.** That is, boot camps are only "partway" to institutions; they are intermediate stops on the road to prison.

The guiding ideas behind boot camps are first, that many juvenile offenders will respond to a short but intensive period of confinement. In this way, boot camps serve as a form of shock incarceration. Second, many believe that these young offenders will benefit from the military-style atmosphere, which will help instill self-discipline and self-respect. Third, the intense nature of boot camps allows educational, vocational, and substance-abuse treatment programs to be intensively pursued. Finally, on a practical level, the shorter duration of boot camp programs, as compared to full institutionalization, saves money for the juvenile justice system.

Boot camps for both juveniles and young adult offenders are believed to break through the resistance such offenders commonly have to authority and traditional activities. By breaking down individuals (through physical labor and exercise) and by using psychological and social forces to force obedience, young offenders are then able to be resocialized to law-abiding behavior. This is the idea behind boot camps: Eliminate the old ways and rebuild individuals in the new, desirable manner.

Community Corrections

Community correctional programs for juveniles often resemble a cross between the traditional community correctional efforts for adults

Boot camp A development of the 1990s where juvenile offenders are housed in a military-style camp and subjected to strict discipline, work, and physical training; its purpose is to rehabilitate offenders through intensive program participation and strict discipline.

Intermediate sanction A correctional program that emphasizes supervision but is less intensive than incarceration; a program that falls between traditional probation and incarceration.

Juvenile boot camps serve as a form of shock incarceration for young offenders.

(probation, home incarceration, etc.) and institutionalization. One popular form of juvenile corrections is the **group home** program. Group homes are community facilities where juveniles live with other juvenile offenders and a staff who supervises them, provides for their basic needs, and attempts to resocialize them to law-abiding behaviors, norms, and values. As popular programs, group homes provide the public a sense of security and are an efficient and effective means of providing treatment to juveniles. In short, group homes are often perceived as a nice midpoint between being too harsh and being too soft on juvenile offenders. The relatively little research available suggests that group homes may be an effective way to reduce recidivism.[19] However, group homes are not necessarily the answer for all juveniles. Only for those juveniles with three or fewer offenses do group homes appear to significantly reduce their recidivism rates.[20]

In the continuing search for correctional programs that prove to successfully reduce crime, some jurisdictions use home incarceration

Group home A community correctional facility where a small group of juveniles live in a homelike setting with staff who provide for the juveniles' basic needs and attempt to socialize them with law-abiding norms, values, and behaviors.

for juvenile offenders. The disposition of home incarceration avoids the potential problems of institutionalizing an impressionable youngster with hardened juvenile offenders. Remember: The juvenile justice system works on what is in "the best interests of the child." Commonly believed to be for their best interests, juveniles are allowed to remain in their homes where their families can work with them. This view has led to the development of home incarceration programs for juveniles.

The available evaluations of such programs suggest that recidivism can be reduced. These programs report success rates of between 71 and 87 percent,[21] which is very high for correctional programs. One important reason for this success may be that early programs included rather close and intensive supervision, which is often associated with "success" in corrections. The key to continued success in juvenile home incarceration programs would appear, then, to be continued close and intensive supervision. This requires either a great deal of resources or a small number of juveniles in such programs. Both of these situations are highly susceptible to budget problems in corrections, however.

The monetary fine, a common adult sentence, is one disposition that today is being used more frequently. Traditionally, the idea of fining juvenile offenders did not make a great deal of sense. Juveniles were considered (usually correctly) simply not to have financial resources for paying fines. However, today this is not necessarily the case. Large numbers of adolescents hold jobs and, in fact, may be more able to pay a fine than some adults. Consequently, a number of states have changed their statutory laws to allow juvenile courts to impose fines on juvenile offenders. Just as with adults, juveniles are commonly fined in combination with probation.

One program that is most common with juvenile offenders is restitution. In this program, offenders are required to make payments of some form to the victims of their offenses to restore the victims to their pre-victimization status. Furthermore, to assist juvenile offenders in understanding the consequences of their actions, many programs require offenders to participate in face-to-face meetings with their victims. Generally speaking, most research has reported fairly high rates of successful restitution program completion. In the late 1970s the Institute of Policy Analysis reported that 86 percent of all juveniles referred to a restitution-type program fulfilled their assigned responsibilities.[22] Similar results have been reported in 1993 in Kentucky, Ohio, Idaho, Connecticut, Indiana, Michigan, Minnesota, and California.[23] More important, restitution programs appear to have a positive impact on reducing recidivism. Juveniles, especially first-time offenders, who complete a restitution program show significantly lower rates of recidivism than juvenile offenders who do not complete a restitution program.[24]

Summary

Juvenile justice, including the corrections component, is a system that has many similarities with the adult system of criminal justice. However, throughout the twentieth century a very different set of ideologies has guided juvenile justice. Rather than working on the basis of deterring or punishing youthful offenders, juvenile justice has been guided by the idea of rehabilitation, or "saving" children.

This has not always been how societies have responded to juveniles, however. Juveniles have historically been considered as simply smaller, younger versions of adult criminals or as children incapable of criminal intent. Thus, for most of recorded history a separate system and set of responses for offenders who were "children" did not exist. The development of such an approach is what we refer to as the *American model.*

However, at the end of the twentieth century we see a significant change in how society views juveniles and the likelihood of "saving" them. Today we are returning to the view that juvenile delinquents may simply be younger and sometimes smaller versions of adult criminals. Therefore, we are moving toward an approach where we work to deter and/or punish juvenile offenders rather than work to rehabilitate them. The idea of "the best interests of the child" may be replaced with the guiding idea behind adult corrections: "the best interests of society."

These slow changes in how we view juvenile offenders lead to changes in both the types of offenses we focus on—criminal rather than status—and how we process those adjudicated delinquent. Today's detention centers and training schools are very similar in both form and function to adult jails and prisons. Other dispositions are now borrowed directly from the list of sentences available for adult criminals: fines, home incarceration, and boot camps.

The future of juvenile corrections appears to be in a period of transition. However, as history has shown us, transition is to be expected. We need only to review our past to see our future.

QUESTIONS FOR REVIEW

1. What forces developed the U.S. juvenile justice system?

2. How are current juvenile justice practices different from their earlier forms?

3. What were the basic principles of the first juvenile justice efforts in the United States?

4. Define the term *status offense,* and give examples.

5. What ideologies guide current juvenile justice practices?

6. Explain the major difference between corrections for adults and corrections for juveniles.

7. List the major goals of juvenile probation programs.

8. What are the major types of juvenile correctional institutions?

9. Describe some major problems facing juvenile correctional institutions today.

10. What are the expected future developments in juvenile corrections?

ACTIVITIES

1. Contact a juvenile court judge in your community and ask if you can sit in on juvenile court. When you are in the courtroom, study the juveniles who come to court. Do you see any patterns or trends in those juveniles? Are there any patterns in how the court handles different types of juveniles? If you cannot get permission to sit in on court, try going to the local courthouse and sitting in the hallway outside the juvenile court to observe what goes on.

2. Make an appointment with the administrator of a juvenile detention center or other juvenile correctional institution. Ask to tour the facility and to talk to several of the juveniles being held there. Try to find out what the residents see as the good and bad points of the facility.

3. Visit a law library or your local courthouse to research what your community's status offenses are. Once you have a list of the status offenses, survey your friends and family to see what types of people are most likely to be status offenders. How many of the people who have violated these laws were caught? How many were processed through juvenile court or were sent to a juvenile correctional facility?

ENDNOTES

1. Robert M. Mennel, *Thorns and Thistles: Juvenile Delinquents in the United States, 1825–1940* (Hanover, NH: University Press of New England, 1973), p. 132.

2. George E. Rush, *The Dictionary of Criminal Justice*, 2d ed. (Guilford, CT: Dushkin Publishing, 1986), p. 229.

3. Federal Bureau of Investigation, *Crime in the United States, 1993.* (Washington, D.C.: U.S. Government Printing Office, 1994).

4. Clifford E. Simonsen, *Juvenile Justice in America,* 3d ed. (New York: Macmillan, 1991), pp. 231–233.

5. Thomas J. Bernard, *The Cycle of Juvenile Justice* (New York: Oxford University Press, 1992).

6. *Ibid.*

7. *Ibid.*

8. *Crime in the United States, 1993.*

9. *Ibid.*

10. U.S. Department of Justice, *Correctional Populations in the United States, 1990* (Washington, D.C.: Bureau of Justice Statistics, 1992).

11. As shown in Figure 13–2, probation is the most common disposition of cases, excluding cases that are dismissed. Therefore, when juvenile court cases are kept in the judicial system, the most common outcome for juveniles is probation.

12. Robert M. Regolli and John D. Hewitt, *Delinquency in Society: A Child-Centered Approach,* 2d ed. (New York: McGraw-Hill, 1992).

13. National Advisory Committee on Criminal Justice Standards and Goals, *Juvenile Justice and Delin-*

quency Prevention: Report of the Task Force on Juvenile Justice and Delinquency Prevention (Washington, D.C.: U.S. Department of Justice, 1976), pp. 673–674.

14. Barry Krisber, Ira Schwartz, Paul Litsky, and James Austin, "The Watershed of Juvenile Justice Reform," *Crime and Delinquency,* Vol. 32, 1986, pp. 5–38.

15. Office of Juvenile Justice and Delinquency Prevention, *Conditions of Confinement: Juvenile Detention and Corrections Facilities* (Washington, D.C.: U.S. Department of Justice, 1994).

16. *Ibid.*

17. Simonsen, *op. cit.*

18. *Ibid.*

19. Bahram Haghighk and Alma Lopez, "Success/Failure of Group Home Treatment Programs for Juveniles," *Federal Probation,* Vol. 57, No. 3, 1993, pp. 53–58.

20. *Ibid.*

21. Ronald Ball, Ronald Huff, and Robert Lilly, *House Arrest and Correctional Policy: Doing Time at Home* (Newbury Park, CA: Sage Publications, 1988), p. 60.

22. T. Armstrong, M. Hofford, D. Maloney, C. Remington, and D. Steenson, *Restitution: A Guidebook for Juvenile Justice Practitioners* (Reno, NV: National Council of Juvenile and Family Court Judges, 1983).

23. Sudipto Roy, "Two Types of Juvenile Restitution Program in Two Midwestern Counties: A Comparative Study," *Federal Probation,* Vol. 57, No. 4, 1993, pp. 48–53.

24. J. A. Butts and H. N. Snyder, "Restitution and Juvenile Recidivism," *Juvenile Justice Bulletin* (Washington, D.C.: Office of Juvenile Justice and Delinquency Prevention, 1982).

CHAPTER 14

Contemporary Issues in Corrections

CHAPTER OBJECTIVES

The goal of this final chapter is to examine two major issues of contemporary corrections (overcrowding and financial problems) and two possible solutions (private corrections and new construction). After reading this chapter, you will be able to:

1. Identify the problems of prison overcrowding.

2. Summarize the causes of prison overcrowding.

3. Distinguish among the proposed solutions for easing the problem of overcrowding.

4. Understand how financial problems affect the daily operations of correctional institutions and how they affect society in general.

5. Differentiate the organization and operations of government-run and privately run corrections.

6. State the advantages of private corrections.

7. Discuss the issues involved in debates about the location of new correctional facilities.

8. List the reasons communities may want to attract new correctional institutions.

9. List the reasons communities may want to ban new correctional institutions from their areas.

State legislators struggle to create legislation to address contemporary issues in corrections.

Current Challenges

In the 1990s U.S. corrections has the unenviable position of being faced with increasing internal problems, rapidly increasing numbers of inmates, budgets that do not keep pace with increases in expenses, and a political environment that calls for tougher and longer prison sentences for more and more offenders. These problems create tough situations for correctional professionals. Corrections is, frankly, in trouble. Many observers question whether our current system's structure and operations can meet the challenges that it faces today. Many believe that it cannot rise to the challenge. Regardless, corrections has very little choice. That is, even in the face of insurmountable challenges, the U.S. correctional system must meet its demands.

Rather than discussing whether our system can meet these challenges, we need to consider *how* corrections can meet them. Contemporary students, who will become the correctional professionals of tomorrow, need to study how to meet these evolving challenges. This study involves more than merely reviewing the daily job requirements; it means adapting our jobs and institutions to these increasing demands. In short, correctional professionals have to be **proactive** rather than **reactive.** That is, correctional professionals have to consider the future, anticipate changes and problems, and be prepared for what is coming. They cannot wait for problems to arise and then react to the immediate ones.

This chapter discusses four major, contemporary issues facing corrections in the 1990s. First, we will examine the effects of overcrowding in correctional facilities, looking at how overcrowding can lead to problems for institutional staff, administrators, and inmates. Second, the related issue of financial problems in corrections will be examined. These problems are escalated by shortfalls in corrections budgets and by a political environment that hesitates to spend resources on corrections. Our third and fourth topics in this chapter provide initial looks at two possible ways to address the problems of overcrowding and financial problems: privatization and new construction. Becoming more popular, privatization of correctional programs allows governments to control their expenses while also incarcerating increasing numbers of offenders. Finally, the location of new prisons and jails has been controversial in some communities. However, as the U.S. economic situation has changed over the past 15 years, so have we begun to see the attitudes of communities change.

Proactive Working to avoid problems; responding to potential problems before they actually develop.

Reactive Responding to problems after they develop; working to stop or reduce the effects of problems only after they occur.

Overcrowding

Overcrowding in prisons and jails is not a new problem in U.S. corrections. Since the very beginning, even at the Walnut Street Jail, our prisons and jails have had more inmates than they were either designed for or could reasonably hold in safe, secure environments. However, overcrowding was not considered an important issue for anyone other than the staff and administrators who had to ensure security.

This situation changed dramatically in 1979. In the 1979 case *Bell v. Wolfish,*[1] the U.S. Supreme Court ruled that the traditional "hands-off" policy toward corrections was no longer appropriate. The Supreme Court also ruled that putting two inmates in a cell originally designed for one inmate, which inmates argued violated their rights, was acceptable if the practice pursued an important correctional goal. This ruling allowed inmates to use the judicial system to investigate prison conditions and staff practices. Consequently, two years later in its 1981 case *Rhodes v. Chapman,*[2] the Supreme Court once again ruled that **double-celling,** making a one-person cell into a two-person cell, did not violate the Eighth Amendment protection against cruel and unusual punishment. The Supreme Court agreed that double-

Double-celling The practice of housing two inmates in a cell designed for only one inmate.

Overcrowding continues to be a problem for today's prisons.

celling might not be an ideal or even a standard practice, but if conditions outside the control of correctional officials made it necessary, then double-celling was legally acceptable.

There is a problem here, though. While we may have a good picture of what an overcrowded prison or jail looks like, these images are different for different people and at different times. What inmates may consider "overcrowded" may not look overcrowded to facility staff and administrators. Or, what correctional officers believe is an overcrowded dormitory or cellblock may be considered "normal" to a warden or sheriff. The term *overcrowded,* then, is a concept that needs a specific definition. To jail administrators who face the most severe overcrowding problems, **overcrowding** consists of the eight elements found in Figure 14–1.[3] Overcrowding in a jail is not only the number of inmates compared with the facility's capacity, but also involves issues of timing, flow of inmates, diversity of inmates, and effects on the jail's operations. Overcrowding, then, is more than simply a matter of numbers. More important, it involves how large populations of inmates influence the activities of jail operations.

While in many ways undesirable and problematic, overcrowding in correctional facilities is legal, up to a point. Numerous state and

Overcrowding The practice of housing more inmates in a facility that is not designed or legally approved to house more than a set maximum number of inmates.

Figure 14–1 Elements of overcrowding in jails.

Severity of Crowding =

Number of Inmates Compared With Facility Capacity
+
Timing (Day of Week, Time of Year)
+
Variations in Number of Incoming Inmates
+
Composition of Inmate Population
+
Architectural Design and Available Jail Facilities
+
Degree of Disruption of Normal Operations
+
Flexibility in Management of Staff
+
Abilities to Work Cooperatively With Other Criminal Justice Agencies

Source: Adapted from John M. Klofas, Stan Stojkovic, and David M. Kalinich, "The Meaning of Correctional Crowding: Steps Toward an Index of Severity," *Crime and Delinquency,* Vol. 38, No. 2, 1992, pp. 171–188.

federal courts have established cutoff points for maximum populations in prisons and jails. However, these decisions apply only to the specific facilities involved in the lawsuit or to a very restricted set of facilities. To determine the degree of legally tolerable overcrowding and what should be done to control or eliminate the problem when it becomes too severe, these factors are considered: reviews of specific conditions in facilities, reasons for the size of inmate population, previous efforts

JOB FOCUS: SPECIAL MASTER

Special masters Individuals appointed by courts to ensure that correctional administrators follow court orders.

Special masters, also sometimes called "monitors," "ombudsmen," or "compliance officers," are individuals who are appointed by courts to ensure that correctional institutions and systems implement court orders. Special masters actually work for the court, but spend a majority of time working in institutions or correctional administrators' offices. Special masters ensure that policies and procedures comply with court-ordered changes. Special masters represent a complete change in ideology from the "hands-off policy" years. That is, rather than leaving the operations of correctional facilities to the internal experts, the courts are now finding and appointing their own experts.

Special masters need to be experts in correctional operations. To be considered for special master positions, individuals usually need lengthy experience in administering a well-run institution (or correctional system) and an advanced education (usually a law degree, doctorate, or at least a specialized master's degree). Special masters are political jobs, working at the discretion of the court that appoints them. Some special masters are only parttime; these people commonly have other jobs such as university professors. The pay range for special masters can be rather high. Part-time positions often pay $30,000 or more annually, with full-time positions paying more than $70,000.

Source: Harold E. Williamson, *The Corrections Profession* (Thousand Oaks, CA: Sage Publications, 1990).

of officials to control the problem, and available resources for efforts to correct such problems.[4]

If U.S. courts consider some overcrowding acceptable, and if prison and jail officials can maintain their facilities in relatively calm manners, why is overcrowding considered an important problem? What is it about overcrowding that is the problem? These are the questions we will discuss next.

Negative Effects of Overcrowding

The negative effects of overcrowding in prisons and jails center on staff and administration concerns about maintaining control of large numbers of inmates. Other concerns focus on inmates' behavior and the extra demand such conditions impose on institutional staff and budgets.

Overcrowding is often a matter of perception. In any given correctional facility, regardless of the actual number of inmates, some inmates will perceive their environment as being overcrowded and some will not. Why is this important? Common sense dictates that as people perceive their surroundings as more restrictive and less private, they are likely to be defensive. Therefore, managing how inmates perceive an institution's overpopulation can be even more important than controlling the actual number of inmates. Not only the feeling of being crowded, but also the process by which an institution becomes crowded can be important. When the number of inmates in a facility rapidly increases, individuals have little time to adjust to differences, and the stress that results can be more extreme. A rapid increase in jail inmate population produces significant increases in perceptions of overcrowding, increased rates of sick calls among inmates, and less activity in public areas.[5]

The most apparent, effective way to manage how inmates perceive their environment is to alter the way inmates are housed. Inmates who live in single cells are allowed more privacy than inmates in multiple-person cells. Even less privacy is available to inmates in dormitories. This means that dormitory housing, the most common form of housing in U.S. prisons in the past several decades, leads to the greatest perception of overcrowding and also to the greatest number and degree of psychological and physical health changes in inmates.[6] The best-documented effect of dormitory housing is that these inmates report more health problems than inmates in either single or double cells.[7] This is not only a humanitarian problem; it also means an increase in health care costs for these inmates.

Social density Perceptions of overcrowding based on the number of people assigned to a given space.

What is more important, then, is not the actual density of people in a physical space, but the **social density** of a correctional facility. Social density refers to the feelings one has about the number of others with whom one *must* interact. As social density increases, so does an individual's stress, anxiety, and frustration. The research of David Lester clearly shows that state correctional systems with the fewest inmates in multiple-person cells and dormitories also have the lowest rates of inmate homicides and suicides.[8] When stress is controlled, so is most violence.

Research about how increased social density (that is, overcrowding) affects inmates' aggressive or violent behavior has mixed results. Some researchers have reported that as social density increases, so does the rate of violence and other forms of misconduct.[9] However, others[10] have reported that increases in social density are not related to increases in misconduct. Does overcrowding affect inmate behavior? The answer appears to be that overcrowding *can* have a negative effect, but this is most likely when other factors are present in the setting.

FYI

Overcrowding does not lead to lower recidivism rates. The costs of overcrowding, then, are not just the suffering of inmates. They also include increased health care costs as well as those costs associated with higher recidivism.

First, overcrowding likely leads to violations of institutional rules when a facility houses primarily young offenders.[11] Also, problems are most likely when an institution's social density increases rapidly. Other research[12] has shown that violence is most likely when inmates in an overcrowded prison have relatively high levels of racial tension. The degree of overcrowding in jails may not be directly related to violence (toward both other inmates and staff). Instead, the inappropriate uses of classification and inadequate levels of supervision of potentially violent inmates impact violence.[13] Finally—and this is a factor that correctional administrators cannot control—the weather appears to affect whether overcrowded prisons have increased rates of inmate violence and misconduct. A study of Canadian prisons positively related population size to the number of assaults between male inmates during summer months. As temperature increased, so did the rate of inmate misconduct. However, as weather conditions became windier (supposedly providing a cooling effect), rates of misconduct decreased.[14] This suggests rather strongly that overcrowding may certainly be related to violence among inmates, but it is not usually sufficient *by itself* to significantly influence behavior. Rather, overcrowding may be a factor that sets up a correctional institution for violence. With the presence of other (triggering) factors, violence becomes more likely.

While discussing the effects of overcrowding in corrections, we also need to address how overcrowding impacts the operations of prisons and jails for women. Research indicates that nearly all the effects linked to overcrowding in institutions for men can also be found in women's institutions. Female prison inmates show higher rates of misconduct, increased levels of stress, and higher rates of physical symptoms as their perceived social density increases.[15] Thus, the consequences of overcrowding are not gender-based or related to how individuals adapt to incarceration. Instead, the consequences for all inmates appear to be based on basic principles of social psychology.

When considering how overcrowding affects correctional policy, we need to review not only how overcrowding influences incarcerated inmates, but also whether these conditions have a lasting impact on behavior and whether institutional policies can be altered to ease the overcrowding problems. Most research on overcrowding has studied the effects of social density on inmates' health and behavior while incarcerated. The little research available on overcrowding and post-release behavior suggests that there is little, if any, relationship. Being incarcerated in an overcrowded jail or prison has not been shown to be associated with higher rates of recidivism.[16] Thus, the popular argument that housing offenders in overcrowded facilities will increase their frustrations and motivate them to seek revenge on society is not supported. Instead, overcrowded conditions could have a deterrent effect on inmates. Some observers thus believe that we *should* have crowded jails and prisons. That is, by making the conditions of incarceration "worse," we actively discourage offenders from recidivating. There are four problems with this argument, however. First, many consider such actions inhumane. Second, overcrowding can be illegal. Third, overcrowding puts extra stress on staff, often resulting in more turnover. Fourth, it contributes to inmates' unrest.

How, then, can we effectively and efficiently manage correctional systems and programs while we observe the boundaries of the law and also minimize the negative effects of overcrowding? Before deciding how to manage overcrowded correctional systems and institutions, we need first to study two areas of operations in corrections: the causes of overcrowding and our responses to overcrowding.

Causes of and Solutions to Overcrowding

Our jails and prisons are overcrowded for many reasons, which vary in importance to those who are affected. Many inmates believe that institutions are overcrowded because officials and the public (who influence how public monies are spent) are uncaring and perhaps enjoy seeing inmates suffer. Perhaps there is some truth to this, but a logical (and more humanistic) perspective would disagree.

More important than inmates' perceptions of overcrowding are those of correctional officials who must act to control the consequences of overcrowding. Figure 14–2 shows what correctional officials believe are the seven top causes for overcrowding. As is most obvious about this list, these are issues that are largely, if not entirely, beyond the control of those who work in corrections. Instead, they are political factors that cause the practical problem of overcrowding. This means that correctional officials have the responsibility of adapting their policies, procedures, and activities to cope with problems caused by outside forces. This clearly exemplifies the theme we have seen throughout this text: The social institution of corrections depends on both the political situation of a jurisdiction and the activities of the first two components of the criminal justice system.

What are the solutions to overcrowding, then? Most solutions have focused on modifying the internal workings of correctional systems and institutions. Again, because it depends on the activities of other agencies and forces, corrections cannot address the actual causes of overcrowding but must change itself to adapt to these outside influences. Sometimes the proposed "solutions" to overcrowding do not come from correctional officials. Instead, the judicial system mandates them after determining that an institution or system violates inmates'

Figure 14–2 Correctional officials' most commonly cited causes of overcrowding.

Reason #1	Public's desire for law and order.
Reason #2	Increased length of statutory minimum sentence length.
Reason #3	Decreased use of parole.
Reason #4	Availability of few alternatives to jail or prison sentences.
Reason #5	Necessity of holding increasing number of dangerous offenders.
Reason #6	Increasing use of mandatory sentences.
Reason #7	Changing demographics of society; effects of "baby boom" generation.

Source: Adapted from Fred Holbert and Jack E. Call, "The Perspective of State Correctional Officials on Prison Overcrowding: Causes, Court Orders, and Solutions," *Federal Probation,* Vol. 53, No. 1, 1989, pp. 25–32.

legal rights by being overcrowded. The proposed solutions to overcrowding that have come from court decisions are shown in Figure 14–3. All of these solutions can and will reduce or eliminate overcrowding. However, all of these "solutions" also come with high costs of their own. Some solutions, such as building new facilities or paying monetary fines, are so costly that they may cause even greater problems in the long run. Other solutions, such as releasing inmates or transferring "extra" inmates from jails to prisons (or vice versa), carry high social costs. Attempts to resolve one problem, then, can have ripple effects that lead to other problems.

Interestingly, most of these solutions are *not* what public opinion seems to support. Surveys of public opinion suggest that most Americans support using alternatives to incarceration (for instance, community correctional programs) to reduce overcrowding in prisons.[17] The public, however, sometimes very strongly opposes options such as shortened sentences, increased use of parole, and increased taxes for building and operating more prisons.

With the courts outlining one set of possible solutions and public opinion supporting very different approaches, what are the choices that correctional officials actually make? They have actually used many different methods to ease overcrowding, but they most frequently changed physical facilities, increased institutional personnel, and educated outside agencies whose actions contributed to overcrowding. Figure 14–4 shows the correctional systems' six most common responses to prison overcrowding.

Correctional officials have opted for a wide range of approaches to deal with the problems of overcrowding. Most notable are the

Figure 14–3 Judicial solutions to prison overcrowding.

Solution #1	Impose limits on the number of inmates that may be held in a particular institution.
Solution #2	Permit one-man cells to be converted to two-man cells.
Solution #3	Relocate convicted felons from local jails to state prisons.
Solution #4	Impose monetary fines on systems/institutions that fail to control the size of inmate populations.
Solution #5	Order construction of additional correctional facilities.
Solution #6	Retain oversight responsibilities of inmate populations. When maximum population figures are exceeded, inmates are ordered to be released to keep population within legal limits.

Source: Richard B. Cole and Jack E. Call, "When Courts Find Jail and Prison Overcrowding Unconstitutional," *Federal Probation,* Vol. 56, No. 1, pp. 29–39.

Figure 14–4 State correctional systems' most common responses to prison overcrowding.

Response #1	Hiring of additional correctional officers and other security staff.
Response #2	Converting one-man cells to two-man cells.
Response #3	Construction of new prison facilities.
Response #4	Education about overcrowding to courts sentencing felons.
Response #5	Hiring of additional counseling/treatment staff.
Response #6	Lobbying of parole authority for increased use of parole.

Source: Adapted from Fred Holbert and Jack E. Call, "The Perspective of State Correctional Officials on Prison Overcrowding: Causes, Court Orders, and Solutions," *Federal Probation,* Vol. 53, No. 1, pp. 25–32.

differences between correctional officials' responses and the courts' proposed solutions to overcrowding. Correctional officials report using means that attempt to cope with increased populations. The courts, on the other hand, have largely focused attention on ways to limit the number of inmates in an institution, not on how to effectively and efficiently manage a larger number of inmates. This is despite courts' sentencing increasing numbers of offenders to prison for longer and longer sentences. What we really have here, then, is a difference in how correctional officials and courts interpret "overcrowding." Recall, earlier in this chapter, that jail administrators' definition of "overcrowding" involved more than simply comparing the number of inmates to a facility's capacity. This focus is again seen in how correctional system administrators propose to respond to overcrowding in prisons. Simply addressing the number of inmates in an institution is not the most important factor. These attempts will likely be unsuccessful because our nation's political climate calls for increased use of incarceration. Therefore, effective and efficient responses need to examine other elements of overcrowded conditions and to direct energies there.

Financial Problems

As they work to manage the rapidly increasing costs of corrections, many government bodies are in difficult financial situations in the 1990s. Over the last three decades, corrections costs have increased dramatically. Of course, inflation has affected costs, but more important, the larger numbers of people entering corrections and the longer sentences have made corrections even more costly.

Significant public funds and significant portions of governmental budgets are spent on corrections. In 1992, the United States spent nearly $31.5 billion on corrections, representing one-third of the total expenses for our justice systems.[18] These expenses are not evenly distributed across governmental bodies, however. Over 90 percent of corrections expenses fall on state and local governments.[19] Another way to view this uneven distribution of corrections cost is to see that state governments (on average) spend 61.9 percent of their criminal justice budgets on corrections, while the federal government spends only 15 percent of its criminal justice funds on corrections.[20]

When discussing correctional budgets, the most important concept to address is that of *priorities*. The priorities of governments and correctional system officials determine budgets that, in turn, set the priorities for the administration of programs and institutions. When certain priorities, such as staff salaries and improvements to physical facilities, are in a particular year's budget, this means future years' budgets will need to prioritize other aspects (perhaps programs for inmates). Directing scarce resources for many needs is a long-term process that must consider how to cover all needs *effectively* and *efficiently*. The process is considered long-term because one year's budget affects future years' budgetary needs. Thus, budgets must be well developed and carefully planned. In an era when public dollars are increasingly difficult to come by, this means that many factors need to be considered. However, the problems that corrections faces in terms of finances result from many expenses that are not flexible. Rather, officials outside of corrections (legislators, governors, judges, etc.) set and determine most of corrections' expenses.

The cost of corrections has been rising dramatically in the past several decades. Between 1971 and 1990 the amount of money spent on corrections in all areas of the United States increased by 989.5 percent. This compares with the overall increase in criminal justice expenses of "only" 606 percent.[21] Obviously, when the costs of some necessary and unavoidable expense increases this much, significant problems will develop. Think of what might happen to your budget if over the next few years the amount of money you paid for food or for rent increased nearly 1,000 percent. Imagine what would happen to your other expenses if your income did not increase by nearly 1,000 percent!

As we have seen throughout our examination of corrections, how state systems administer corrections and respond to problems in correctional administration differs in many ways. Similarly, the portion of criminal justice budgets that each state devotes to corrections varies.

Table 14–1 shows the percentage of each state's criminal justice budget devoted to corrections. The figures vary widely, suggesting that different states have developed different ways to address the costs of corrections. Some states have developed ways to spend few funds while covering their expenses; others have chosen to divert monies into law enforcement and the courts. However, many corrections expenses are "set" by outside authorities and cannot be controlled.

The largest expense in corrections is not providing supplies such as food, clothing, and utilities to inmates. Rather, it is the salaries of employees. These are unavoidable expenses that likely will continue to increase. We have seen previously that people do not pursue careers

JOB FOCUS: BUDGET OFFICER

All correctional systems and many individual correctional institutions employ individuals who are responsible for overseeing budgets. These people are expected to monitor the expenses of the current budget period and to assist top officials in planning future budgets. This means that budget officers are key people in ensuring that correctional facilities can meet the needs of inmates, staff, and officials. Oftentimes budget officers are not very popular people in corrections, as they often have to say "no" to requests from inmates and staff.

Important players in correctional administration, budget officers are often high-ranking officials. Budget officers do not necessarily need experience working in other areas of corrections, although this can be helpful. Budget officer positions are really business positions. A background in accounting, economics, planning, and a thorough understanding of contracts and negotiating techniques are all important to the successful performance of this position. Because they are very important people, budget officers are well paid. Salaries generally range from $30,00 to $90,000. Budget officers' salaries are often very similar to those of wardens.

Source: Harold E. Williamson, *The Corrections Profession* (Thousand Oaks, CA: Sage Publications, 1990).

Table 14–1		Percentage of Criminal Justice Budgets Devoted to Corrections, by State	
State	Percent of Criminal Justice Budget	State	Percent of Criminal Justice Budget
Alabama	47.7	Nebraska	55.7
Alaska	53.3	Nevada	73.9
Arizona	65.5	New Hampshire	41.5
Arkansas	61.6	New Jersey	56.5
California	73.1	New Mexico	51.0
Colorado	62.4	New York	56.3
Connecticut	61.8	North Carolina	58.7
Delaware	57.5	North Dakota	39.5
Florida	60.7	Ohio	71.3
Georgia	79.6	Oklahoma	62.3
Hawaii	49.1	Oregon	46.1
Idaho	50.1	Pennsylvania	53.8
Illinois	59.9	Rhode Island	53.6
Indiana	68.5	South Carolina	71.0
Iowa	41.0	South Dakota	51.1
Kansas	60.8	Tennessee	68.7
Kentucky	44.5	Texas	64.5
Louisiana	56.6	Utah	52.7
Maine	50.6	Vermont	35.4
Maryland	60.9	Virginia	59.7
Massachusetts	54.2	Washington	77.3
Michigan	70.9	West Virginia	36.9
Minnesota	52.5	Wisconsin	62.1
Mississippi	59.2	Wyoming	40.3
Missouri	54.9		
Montana	45.9	Average per state	61.9

Source: U.S. Department of Justice, *Justice Expenditures and Employment, 1992* (Washington, D.C.: Bureau of Justice Statistics, 1995).

in corrections to get rich. In fact, correctional work is usually considered to be significantly underpaid. With this in mind, consider that more than 347,985 employees in state correctional systems in 1992 accounted for more than $843,000 in monthly payroll expenses.[22] This means that correctional employees, accounting for 33.6 percent of all criminal justice staff, received 31.6 percent of the payroll dollars. While this is not a large difference, it does suggest that correctional employees are underpaid relative to other criminal justice personnel. This does not, however, mean that correctional personnel are viewed as unimportant or of poor quality. Rather, this suggests that the rapid increase in correctional populations and expenses has made it very difficult to grant staff salary increases at levels similar to those provided to law enforcement and judicial personnel.

Private Corrections

Private prisons
Correctional institutions operated by private organizations or corporations; facilities that house inmates for governments and receive a per-inmate daily fee.

In response to overcrowding and financial problems facing correctional systems, many states and the federal system are turning to privately run correctional facilities. **Private prisons** are correctional institutions owned and operated by corporations that contract with government agencies to provide prison space. Private prisons house and provide programs for inmates in exchange for a flat fee payment. Usually fees are paid for each inmate for each day he or she is in the private prison's custody. So, although a private business owns and operates the correctional institution, it assumes the responsibilities usually thought to be the government's concern. Private prisons are becoming increasingly common because they remove many problems from the government's immediate realm of responsibility and because they are less expensive than state-run facilities.

The Private Corrections Project reported a total of 80 private prisons and jails operating in the United States at the end of 1994.[23] Fifteen different management companies had contracted with 12 different states and the federal government to operate these institutions. Since then, dozens of new private prisons have been contracted for, constructed, and opened. These numbers are for only prisons and jails and do not include community-based correctional centers. Hundreds of privately operated community correctional programs operate throughout the country. Among correctional institutions operated by

FYI

Private corrections corporations have demonstrated that efficient and innovative programming and management allows a prison or jail to be a profit-making business enterprise. Profits can be made while providing housing and programming comparable to those found in government-run prisons and jails.

private companies, the majority have primary contracts with state governments (See Figure 14–5.)

Privately run correctional facilities are usually lower level security institutions. Figure 14–6 shows that nearly one-half of all private correctional institutions are minimum security level. Only 1 in 25 (4%) of private facilities is a maximum security institution. There is good reason for this. Minimum security institutions are much less expensive to build and maintain and can be operated with fewer staff than higher level security institutions. These two reasons make it most attractive for a private corrections company (that has the goal of making a profit) to contract for a minimum security institution.

Private corrections have grown in number so rapidly because they save governments money. When a government pays a set daily fee per inmate to a private corrections company, its expenses are fully paid. Once a contract is signed, a private corrections company knows how much money it can expect to operate with and can plan its expenses accordingly. If the private facility is to be profitable, expenses must be less than planned income. Private corrections companies have consistently shown that they can plan, design, and construct a prison in a fraction of the time a bureaucratic government requires to bring a new prison into operation.[24]

Figure 14–5 Primary contractors with private correctional companies.

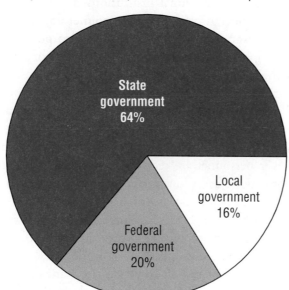

Source: Charles W. Thomas, *Private Adult Correctional Facility Census* (Gainesville, FL: University of Florida, Center for Studies in Criminology and Law, 1995).

Figure 14–6 Security levels of privately operated correctional facilities.

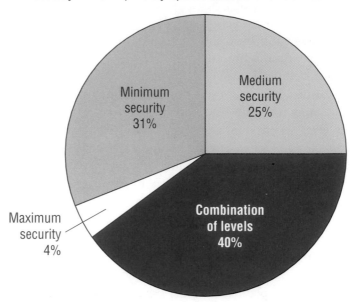

Source: Charles W. Thomas, *Private Adult Correctional Facility Census* (Gainesville, FL: University of Florida, Center for Studies in Criminology and Law, 1995).

The cost of personnel is one of the largest expenses any institution, including correctional institutions, faces. Private correctional facilities often operate with fewer personnel and pay their staff less than public prison or jail employees. Private corporations can also use part-time employees (so they save the expenses of benefits) and can establish their own (less expensive) retirement plans. This is not to say that private correctional facilities operate with too few staff or less qualified staff than does a state-run prison. Rather, private prisons and jails have developed management systems and housing facilities that allow fewer personnel to supervise larger numbers of inmates. In other words, fewer personnel are required to perform the same functions. Private corrections has a lower overall personnel cost for two reasons. First, private companies do not offer many of the costly benefits that government jobs have. Less vacation time, less sick time, and fewer "hidden" benefits are offered to private prison staff. Second, private prisons are very carefully placed in communities. As we will see in the following section, not all communities want prisons located near them. However, in some communities where the economy is poor and unemployment is high, a private prison can offer jobs but need not pay high wages. A state-run prison compensates staff on a state-based pay scale, and all state correctional officers begin at the same rate. This is not the case with private prisons. In this way both the correctional company and the community may benefit.

However, some people debate the appropriateness of delegating authority for holding and supervising citizens to a private group of people. Some critics of the privatization movement argue that it is simply wrong to take the government's central responsibility (protecting the people) and give it to a private company. This can be both a legal and an ethical issue. Legally, the question has been resolved— at least for now. The state can legally place offenders in a private facility's custody, as long as the state retains the ultimate authority over the inmates. In other words, if the state remains the actual body that restricted the inmates' freedom, it can delegate the day-to-day activities of enforcing these restrictions. In terms of ethics, this issue is still being debated.

The legal and ethical debates also raise questions about a private contractor's responsibility when inmates of its facility claim to have

Private prisons generally use fewer staff than state-run prisons to perform the same functions.

suffered violations of their constitutional rights. Individual officials of government agencies have **qualified immunity,** or protection against being held individually responsible, when the institution or agency they work for violates an individual's rights. This immunity is "qualified," however, and does not cover individuals' actions that are illegal or in violation of the agency's official policies and regulations. Since private correctional facilities are not government agencies, are their employees provided qualified immunity? According to one recent analysis of the law, this issue has not yet been fully settled. The federal courts have disagreed with one another, and there is no clear-cut answer at this time.[25]

Private corrections operate less expensively than government-operated corrections.[26] The lower costs of incarcerating individual offenders mean that additional public money is freed for other public functions (education, roads, public assistance, etc.) or that more offenders can be incarcerated. The fact that private corrections is less expensive does not mean that governments will spend less money on corrections. Rather, it means that governments can meet the political demand for increased incarceration rates and longer sentences while not spending more money. Simply stated, private corrections eases overcrowding in state institutions and allows either diversion of money to other needs or incarceration of more people.

FYI

While saving money for states, private prisons and jails are not inexpensive operations. In an April 1994 news release, the Wackenhut Corrections Corporation announced it had signed a contract with the Texas Board of Criminal Justice to build and manage two new prisons in Travis and Jack Counties. Texas agreed to pay Wackenhut $24 million a year for operating these two facilities. These two facilities brought the total number of Wackenhut facilities to 15 across the United States, Australia, and Britain.

Locations of New Correctional Facilities

As corrections expands, housing is obviously needed for the ever-increasing inmate population. This usually means building new, additional prisons (or, at least, new bedspace in existing prisons). This need necessarily draws corrections into public and political debates. Also, as we saw earlier, prison construction is an important political discussion because of the economic impacts it has on a state. Most obvious, building new prisons and prison bedspace is very expensive. For example, it can easily cost upwards of $100,000 to construct each and every prison bedspace. Political debates first focus on whether a

LEGAL BRIEF:

Medina v. O'Neill, 5890 F. Supp. 1928 (1984).

*A*t this time there have been no Supreme Court cases dealing specifically with the legality of or conditions of management involved in private corrections. In fact, there has been very little litigation concerning the use of private contractors in criminal justice and corrections. However, the case of Medina v. O'Neill *informs us of how we might expect the federal courts to respond to the privatization movement in corrections.*

This case concerned the detention of illegal aliens who were found as stowaways on ships. When found by the Immigration and Naturalization Service (INS), the illegal aliens were detained pending hearings for deportation. While detained in a privately operated facility, not one directly operated by the INS, the stowaways brought suit against the INS, claiming that they were being "punished" by their detention, not merely being held for processing. The argument held that this detention constituted punishment because of the poor quality of conditions in the private facility. The INS, the suit argued, was negligent for not overseeing their detention by having it contracted to a private firm.

The U.S. Supreme Court ruled that detention is a power reserved for the government. However, whereas Congress had granted the power to detain illegal aliens to the INS, the INS had in turn designated an entity to carry out detention. This was deemed acceptable with the qualification that detention facilities operated by both government bodies (here the INS) and government-designated, private contractors were bound by constitutional standards. Therefore, it appears that private corrections will withstand challenges claiming they do not have the right to detain people. However, it is more clear that private corrections will be held to the same standards as government-run correctional facilities.

New prison construction is a hotly debated issue.

Prison siting Processes of deciding where to locate new prisons.

Community development Actions and plans of communities to improve the economic and social conditions that affect residents.

state should build new prisons and, if so, where those prisons should be located.

In professional discussions these issues are referred to as debates over **prison siting.** Some communities have lobbied to have prisons built in or near them, and some state corrections departments have invited and supervised competitive bidding processes between communities.[27] However, communities more commonly work to ban prisons from them. Regardless of the controversy's specifics, when states begin to determine where to build new prisons, local residents express dissatisfaction and opposition.[28] In this final section we will examine this debate, looking specifically at the arguments in favor of and against building new correctional facilities in a particular community. We find that the arguments in favor of prison construction in a community are largely practical and focused on technical and measurable impacts. In contrast, the arguments against prison construction are heavily focused on social and emotional considerations.

Why Communities Do Want Facilities

Communities have several reasons for either actively working to attract new prisons or welcoming the idea of new prison construction. However, all of these reasons are focused on economic and **community development.** In simple terms, some communities view prisons as opportunities to expand their job and tax base. In the late twentieth century, these factors are very attractive to almost all communities. Economic difficulties are commonplace for American communities. Therefore, opportunities to expand an economic base are welcomed, even if this expansion includes something as undesirable as a prison.

Having a prison built in or near it has significant economic impacts on the community. Simply stated, prisons bring money into a community. This happens in several ways. Obviously, a number of jobs are created when a prison is being planned, built, and operated. Many of these jobs remain in the community. Being stable businesses, prisons rarely close or lay off employees. Prison jobs are also often considered relatively good, not because of the high pay scales but because of job security. The community's economies are also positively impacted by the increase in local business traffic and by the increased tax base. As a community offers jobs, more people both relocate in and travel through the community. These people will need goods and services, as will the inmates and institution itself. Thus, more businesses can conduct more business, and more business means more money collected in taxes. Therefore, both the community and its businesses benefit from the presence of a prison.

Not only does the actual community that houses a prison benefit economically, but the surrounding counties and nearby towns and cities also benefit. One study of the economic impact of a 500-bed, minimum security federal prison found that just over 50 percent of all the prison's business transactions were with businesses located within 25 miles of the institution.[29] Furthermore, nearly one-half of the institution's staff were hired from the local area. This means that the monies the prison generated remained in the community. This money, in turn, was spent to buy goods and services. What resulted was a cycle that stimulated local businesses and continually contributed to the community's tax base.

A prison's presence can also make a positive local impact through its **public service activities.** Nearly all prisons recognize that staff and inmates need to make a visible, positive impact on the community. Therefore, they complete a number of public service projects, which inmates usually do but which facility staff may also undertake. Community service projects include: inmates building local parks and recreation facilities (and then working to maintain those facilities), being involved in local youth sports programs (as referees, groundskeepers, etc.), and being mobilized in times of crisis to fight fires, build emergency flood walls, or help clean up after major storms. Perhaps these contributions may seem minor to some, but they accomplish much needed work at minimal (if any) cost. Obviously, such programs also are of value to inmates. They can assist in inmates' reintegration to communities, and they provide inmates with a sense of accomplishment and self-esteem.

Although research has yet to convincingly support this idea, the presence of a prison and the hundreds of correctional officers may serve to actually lower a community's crime rates. That is, crime rates in communities where prisons are built may be lowered because the prison's visibility and the increased presence and visibility of more peace officers have a deterrent effect. Here, the large number of correctional officers serves as a greater public policing presence. Therefore, crime will be less likely to occur.[30]

Public service activities Projects that prison inmates and staff engage in to make positive contributions to the communities in which prisons are located.

The arguments offered in support of bringing new prisons to communities are largely objective and concrete. The major argument centers on the anticipated economic development that a new, permanent, and most likely growing industry will bring to a community. These can be very convincing arguments, and many communities that face economic crises have found prisons to be their saving grace. However, for communities that do not see the economic aspect as important and for those that believe they can attract other forms of economic development, these arguments are often overshadowed by those in opposition to bringing a new prison to a community.

Why Communities Do Not Want Facilities

"Corrections officials are only too well aware that resident attitudes are frequently incongruent with what seem to be the largely beneficial effects of having a prison."[31] In simple terms, people's beliefs about the effects of a prison in their community often radically differ from what correctional officials believe those effects will be. This means conflict can be expected when a community is named as a possible site for a new prison.

The reasons for opposing construction of new prisons in particular communities are heavily focused on social and emotional issues. The arguments offered in support of prison construction are largely economic. However, economics are usually not a high priority when a community seeks to ban a prison. Instead, arguments center on issues of fear of crime and losses to community prestige and quality of life. Or, as explained by a former director of the California correctional system, Richard McGee, three types of factors lead community members to oppose prison construction: fear, economic anxieties, and civic pride.[32]

The arguments against constructing a prison in a community are not unique to opposition to correctional facilities. Prisons are simply in a class of undesirable forms of development, what politicians and community developers call **LULUs (locally unwanted land uses)**. Other LULUs include nuclear power plants, garbage dumps and processing facilities, public housing projects, interstate highways, airports, and mental hospitals. Obviously, having a prison in one's community is widely perceived as a stigmatizing element for both the community and its residents.

The strongest and most loudly expressed argument against construction of a prison in a community is fear of crime.[33] Communities that oppose prisons believe that crime will increase after the institution opens. They apparently believe that inmates who escape will commit crimes or that inmates who choose to settle in the community after their release will recidivate. However, several research projects have shown that communities that get new prisons generally do not show an increase in crime rates.[34] There are also some communities where crime rates, as well as social service utilization, have increased following prison construction.[35] Therefore, the debate about a new prison's effects on local crime rates does not appear to have a well-established answer.

Related to their concern about increased crime rates, many community members believe that prisons will attract inmates' families. They will come to visit, and perhaps they will relocate to the community to be close to the inmates (to maintain contact/visits). This, the community fears, will also lead to an increase in crime. One thing we do know about crime in our society is that when one family member is involved in crime, there is a good possibility that other family members will also be criminals. For instance, Fishman has shown that a large number of inmates' wives are involved in crime; so, many may assume that they will commit crimes in the prison community if they visit or relocate there.[36] However, numerous researchers have shown that an inmate's family rarely relocates close to the inmate's institution. This is to be expected, based on the background of most prison inmates. Most inmates have strained (if any) relationships with their families, and most inmates are from relatively poor, urban families. This means many inmates' families could not and probably would not want to relocate to the communities where a family member is incarcerated. Remember: A majority of prisons are in small towns and rural areas, not in or near cities.

A third concern in the argument against building a correctional facility in a community is the belief that property values will be negatively impacted. Actually, any LULU is generally believed (and some-

LULUs (locally unwanted land uses) Publicly perceived undesirable developments in communities; facilities and activities that are seen as detractions from the communities' quality of life and economic standing.

times supported by past experiences) to lower a community's property resale values, especially if that property is close to the LULU. For community members living close to the proposed prison, this is a very realistic and understandable concern. It is logical to expect that the value of one's property will decrease if a prison is built next door. However, this belief fails to consider some of the other consequences of prison construction in a community. Experience has shown that rather than lowering property values, construction of a new prison actually raises property values.[37] This suggests that the economic impacts that occur in a community where a new prison is built are either positive or, at the very least, not as negative as some people anticipate.

The main arguments in favor of prison constructions are economic. Those opposed to prisons question the supposed positive economic impact a new prison may bring. These observers believe that estimates and projections that officials offer overestimate the positive contributions that will accompany new prison construction. These same critics also express concerns about economic costs associated with the prison's operation. Additional law enforcement officers (due to the higher perceived risk of crime), fire protection, and other public services are expensive, and the taxes that the prison generates may not fully offset these costs. In short, many community residents are skep-

New prison construction creates strong community reaction.

tical about the promises a government or large corporation offer and fear that their communities will lose, rather than win, financially.

In addition to questioning economic gains, many people in small towns and rural areas believe prison construction is a detriment to their general quality of life. There are two reasons for this perception. First, such development changes a community's social structure, which affects the daily activities of community residents and, therefore, alters a community's culture. Also, if the community develops as correctional officials predict, then its physical environment will be significantly changed. What was once a "nice, small town" may have an influx of outsiders and "others." More housing will be needed, more businesses will need to be developed, and the community's entire physical layout will change to keep pace with the population and economic growth. People choose to live in small towns and rural communities because they find such cultural and physical environments attractive. Correctional institutions, according to those proposing their construction, will bring new residents and businesses, which many people in these communities do not desire. The reasons why some communities favor prison construction are the same reasons that others actively oppose such developments. Not all people perceive changes in the same way; what is progress to one may very well be the community's downfall to others.

A final argument offered against prison construction hinges on community members' fears that their community's prestige will be lowered. Here, remember that LULUs are not desirable in most communities. This means that facilities such as prisons are not prestigious. When a community's prestige is lowered, it may have negative impacts on long-term economic growth. However, also remember that many communities where construction is proposed are already low-status communities. Therefore, prisons are often planned for communities that are already stigmatized and suffer economic difficulties. Subsequently, these communities more likely see the positive economic developments promised as important and perhaps necessary.

The arguments in favor of and against construction of new prison facilities in communities are related to and build upon one another. Whether community members will support or oppose a prison comes down to their balancing the possible positive effects against the possible negative ones. A community rarely reaches consensus regarding a possible new prison. In the end, the question of whether a prison is good or bad for a community will always be answered tentatively. Similar to almost all aspects of U.S. corrections, there are no absolute answers, only relative ones.

Summary

Corrections in the United States is at a crossroads, facing some major obstacles to success. Largely as a consequence of our nation's political and legal cultures, the demands being made of correctional systems, institutions, programs, and staff are increasing rapidly. However, the resources allocated for meeting these needs have lagged far behind the increasing demands for services. If correctional programs are to meet their challenges—regardless of the ideology guiding corrections—new, innovative means must be developed to overcome these obstacles. This chapter has addressed four major issues—two problems and two potential solutions—facing corrections today.

As the number of people entering corrections has increased and as the sentences of incoming offenders have lengthened, a major problem of overcrowding has developed. Both jails and prisons are experiencing overcrowding. This situation leads to administrative/ management difficulties, increases in problematic behaviors among inmates, heightened staff stress, and, of course, significantly increased costs for operating correctional institutions and programs.

The second problem we examined is the financial crunch facing corrections. Costs are rising very rapidly. This is largely beyond the control of correctional administrators and staff. As more people enter the system, more costs are incurred. However, corrections is not a popular political issue. Consequently, few new resources have been added to corrections. This means that corrections consumes increasingly large portions of government budgets. As a result, other areas of public safety and criminal justice suffer economically, and other social programs and government functions are financially strained. When the financial cost of corrections increases, the funds must come from either new revenues, other areas of government, or savings within corrections.

One way that governments operate corrections more economically and efficiently is using private correctional companies. Private corrections has flourished in the 1990s.

Perhaps the most popular "solution" to the crime problem in our nation, though, is a "get tough" approach to crime and sentencing. This means that more people will be sentenced to prison, and more prisons will be needed. However, while it is politically popular to build more prisons, it is often politically unpopular to build new prisons in one's own community. Deciding where to locate new prisons can lead to bitter controversy, as many communities fight to halt new construction. However, the economic and development gains from prison construction lead some communities to actively lobby for the facility.

As we conclude our study, we see that corrections is a complex, often problem-ridden social institution. There are no easy answers regarding what to do with criminals. The challenges have been laid out for us. If we intend to maintain or improve our society's current quality of life, we must address the problems that face our contemporary correctional systems.

QUESTIONS FOR REVIEW

1. Describe the problems associated with prison overcrowding.
2. List the major causes of prison overcrowding.
3. What methods have been suggested to ease prison overcrowding?
4. How do financial problems impact the day-to-day activities of correctional institutions and programs, and how do they affect society in general?
5. What are the major differences between government-run and privately operated prisons and jails?
6. Why have private corrections been successful in the United States?
7. What are the major issues in the debate over prison siting?
8. Why do some communities actively seek to have prisons sited near them?
9. Why do some communities work to ban new prisons?

ACTIVITIES

1. Pick three classmates or acquaintances whom you do not know very well and lock yourself in a room with them for 24 hours. Your goal is to sense how it feels to be incarcerated. So, during your time locked up, you cannot have any contact with outsiders (no telephone, no visitors, no going out to eat). List things that you find

enjoyable about being locked up together and the things that you find annoying.

2. Make a list of all of the expenses involved in operating a prison. Begin with the daily costs of providing for one inmate's needs. Next, list all the expenses of operating the actual prison. Third, list the expenses for each necessary staff person. After you finish your list (with estimated costs), identify five specific places where you could cut back and save money.

3. Obtain a map of your community. If you were in charge of putting a new prison in your community, where would you put it? What would be the advantages of this location? What would be the disadvantages?

ENDNOTES

1. *Bell v. Wolfish,* 441 U.S. 520 (1979).

2. *Rhodes v. Chapman,* 452 U.S. 337 (1981).

3. John M. Klofas, Stan Stojkovic, and David A. Kalinich, "The Meaning of Correctional Crowding: Steps Toward an Index of Severity," *Crime and Delinquency,* Vol. 38, No. 2, 1992, pp. 171–188.

4. Richard B. Cole and Jack E. Call, "When Courts Find Jail and Prison Overcrowding Unconstitutional," *Federal Probation,* Vol. 56, No. 1, 1992, pp. 29–39.

5. Richard E. Wener and Christopher Keys, "The Effects of Changes in Jail Population Densities on Crowding, Sick Call, and Spatial Behavior," *Journal of Applied Social Psychology,* Vol. 18, No. 10, 1988, pp. 852–866.

6. Marc A. Schaeffer, Andrew Baum, Paul B. Paulus, and Gerald G. Gaes, "Architecturally Mediated Effects of Social Density in Prison," *Environment and Behavior,* Vol. 20, No. 1, 1988, pp. 3–19.

7. D. A. D'Atri, E. F. Fitzgerald, S. V. Kasl, and A. M. Ostfeld, "Crowding in Prison: The Relationship Between Changes in Housing Mode and Blood Pressure," *Journal of Psychosomatic Medicine,* Vol. 43, 1981, pp. 95–105; G. G. Gaes, "The Effects of Overcrowding in Prisons," in M. Tonry and N. Morris (eds.), *Crime and Justice: An Annual Review of Research,* Vol. 6 (Chicago: University of Chicago Press, 1985), pp. 95–106; G. McCain, V. C. Cox, and P. B. Paulus, *The Effect of Prison Crowding on Inmate Behavior* (Washington, D.C.: National Institute of Justice, 1980).

8. David Lester and Bruce L. Danto, *Suicide Behind Bars: Prediction and Prevention* (Philadelphia: The Charles Press, 1993).

9. V. C. Cox, P. B. Paulus, and G. McCain, "Prison Crowding

Research: The Relevance of Prison Housing Standards and a General Approach Regarding Crowding Phenomena," *American Psychologist,* Vol. 39, 1984, pp. 1148–1160; G. G. Gaes and W. J. McGuire, "Prison Violence: The Contribution of Crowding Versus Other Determinants of Prison Assault Rates," *Journal of Research in Crime and Delinquency,* Vol. 22, No. 1, 1985, pp. 41–65; L. G. Jan, "Overcrowding and Inmate Behavior," *Criminal Justice and Behavior,* Vol. 7, 1980, pp. 293–301; P. L. Nacci, H. E. Teitelbaum, and J. Prather, "Population Density and Inmate Misconduct Rates in Federal Prison System," *Federal Probation,* Vol. 41, 1977, pp. 26–31.

10. S. Ekland-Olson, D. M. Barrick, and L. E. Cohen, "Prison Overcrowding and Disciplinary Problems: An Analysis of the Texas Prison System," *Journal of Applied Behavioral Science,* Vol. 19, No. 2, 1983, pp. 163–176; *Population Density in State Prisons* (Washington, D.C.: Bureau of Justice Statistics, 1986); B. Pelissier, "The Effects of a Rapid Increase in a Prison Population," *Criminal Justice and Behavior,* Vol. 18, No. 4, 1991, pp. 427–447; R. B. Ruback and T. S. Carr, "Prison Crowding Over Time: The Relationship of Density and Changes in Density to Infraction Rates," *Criminal Justice and Behavior,* Vol. 20, No. 2, 1993, pp. 130–148.

11. Ruback and Carr, *op. cit.*

12. R. G. Leger, "Perception of Crowding, Racial Antagonism, and Aggression in a Custodial Prison," *Journal of Criminal Justice,* Vol. 16, 1988, pp. 167–181.

13. D. K. Sechrest, "The Effects of Density on Jail Assaults," *Journal of Criminal Justice,* Vol. 19, 1991, pp. 211–223.

14. O. Ganjavi, B. Schell, J. C. Cachon, and F. Porporino, "Geophysical Variables and Behavior: XXIX. Impact of Atmospheric Conditions on Occurrences of Individual Violence Among Canadian Penitentiary Populations," *Perceptual and Motor Skills,* Vol. 61, No. 1, 1985, pp. 259–275.

15. R. Barry Ruback and Timothy S. Carr, "Crowding in a Woman's Prison: Attitudinal and Behavioral Effects," *Journal of Applied Social Psychology,* Vol. 14, No. 1, 1984, pp. 57–68.

16. Obie Clayton and Tim Carr, "An Empirical Assessment of the Effects of Prison Crowding Upon Recidivism Utilizing Aggregate Level Data," *Journal of Criminal Justice,* Vol. 15, No. 2, 1987, pp. 201–210.

17. Robert T. Sigler and David Lamb, "Community-Based Alternatives to Prison: How the Public and Court Personnel View Them," *Federal Probation,* Vol. 59, No. 2, 1995, pp. 3–9; J. Sherwood Williams, Daniel M. Johnson, and John H. McGrath, "Is the Public Committed to the Imprisonment of Convicted Felons? Citizen Preferences for Reducing Prison Crowding," *Journal of Contemporary Criminal Justice,* Vol. 7, No. 2, 1991, pp. 86–94.

18. U.S. Department of Justice, *Justice Expenditure and Employment, 1992*

(Washington, D.C.: Bureau of Justice Statistics, 1995), Table 2.

19. *Ibid.*

20. *Ibid.*

21. *Ibid.*

22. *Ibid.*

23. Charles W. Thomas, "Private Adult Correctional Facility Census" (Gainesville, FL: University of Florida Center for Studies in Criminology and Law, 1995).

24. Byron R. Johnson and Paul P. Ross, "The Privatization of Correctional Management: A Review," *Journal of Criminal Justice,* Vol. 18, 1990, pp. 351–358.

25. Charles W. Thomas, "Resolving the Problem of Qualified Immunity for Private Defendants in Section 1983 and *Bivens* Damage Suits," *Louisiana Law Review,* Vol. 53, No. 2, 1992, pp. 449–493.

26. Martin P. Sellers, "The History and Development of Private Pris-

ons in the United States," unpublished doctoral dissertation, Temple University, Philadelphia, PA, 1988; Commonwealth of Kentucky, *Privatization Review of Intermediate Care Facilities/Mental Retardation Institutions and Minimum Security Correctional Facilities* (Frankfort, KY: Auditor of Public Accounts, 1994).

27. Faye A. Silas, "Not in My Neighborhood," *LawScope, ABA Journal,* Vol. 70, 1984, pp. 27–29; Kevin M. Travis and Francis J. Sheridan, "Community Involvement in Prison Siting," *Corrections Today,* Vol. 45, 1983, pp. 14–15.

28. Alan L. Greico, "New Prisons: Characteristics and Community Reception," *Quarterly Journal of Corrections,* Vol. 2, 1978, pp. 55–60; Richard A. McGee, *Prisons and Politics* (Lexington, MA: Lexington Books, 1981).

29. George O. Rogers and Marshall Haimes, "Local Impact of a

Low-Security Federal Correctional Institution," *Federal Probation,* Vol. 51, No. 3, 1987, pp. 28–34.

30. David Shichor, "Myths and Realities in Prison Siting," *Crime and Delinquency,* Vol. 28, No. 1, 1992, pp. 70–87.

31. Katherine A. Carlson, "Doing Good and Looking Bad: A Case Study of Prison/Community Relations," *Crime and Delinquency,* Vol. 38, No. 1, 1993, pp. 56–69.

32. Richard McGee, *Prisons and Politics* (Lexington, MA: D.C. Heath, 1981).

33. Silas, *op. cit.*; Rogers and Haimes, *op. cit.*

34. Kathleen Abrams and Arnick T. Martin, "Prisons as LULUs: A Sequel," *Florida Environmental and Urban Issues,* Vol. 14, 1987, pp. 18–21; Dale K. Sechrest, "Locating Prisons: Open Versus Closed Approaches to Siting," *Crime and Delinquency,* Vol. 38, No. 1, 1992, pp. 88–104; John O. Smykla, Carl E. Ferguson, Jr., David C. Cheng, Carolyn Trent, Barbara French, and Annette Waters, "Effects of a Prison Facility on the Regional Economy," *Journal of Criminal Justice,* Vol. 12, 1984, pp. 521–539.

35. Katherine A. Carlson, "Prison Escapes and Community Consequences: Results of a Case Study," *Federal Probation,* Vol. 44, 1990, pp. 36–42; Carlson, "Doing Good and Looking Bad."

36. Laura Fishman, *Women at the Wall: A Study of Prisoners' Wives Doing Time on the Outside* (Albany: State University of New York Press, 1980).

37. Abrams and Martin, *op. cit.*; Smykla et al., *op. cit.*; Shichor, *op. cit.*

Appendix A: Finding a Job

Planning Ahead

Perhaps the most important thing to remember about getting a job is that it is never too early to start planning or working toward that first or next job. As you read this section of the text, as you sit in class, and as you live your daily life, if you get an idea about how to apply for that job, act on it!

Know Whether You Meet the Job Requirements

Before you even begin looking for a particular job, you need to know whether you are qualified. A couple of requirements for correctional jobs can immediately eliminate you from the pool of potential employees. Some requirements are beyond your control, and you will simply have to accept that. Some requirements you can control and, therefore, can adapt yourself to meet them.

First, all correctional systems have age requirements. These vary by systems but usually require job applicants to be either 18 or 21 years old. If you are 19 in a state that requires you to be 21, you will not get hired for at least 2 more years. There is no changing this. Some systems also have a limit on how old you can be and still be hired. For instance, the Federal Bureau of Prisons will not hire correctional officers who are 37 or older.

Some systems require U.S. citizenship. Some states require a high school diploma or GED. Some systems require you to hold a driver's license, and some systems require you to have one or two years' work experience. Almost all systems will not hire you if you have a felony conviction on your record.

Finally, almost all correctional jobs require you to pass a physical agility test. The test will require you to meet certain standards for strength, flexibility, running speed, and stamina. You might want to consider getting into shape (or better shape) before applying for a job in corrections.

The specific requirements for correctional jobs vary across systems. You should write to the personnel department of the system(s) or institution(s) you are interested in working for and request a copy of its requirements.

Locating Job Search Resources

As students you have a great wealth of resources available to you for getting a job. First of all, you have your school's placement office or other resources designed to help students and graduates. If nothing else, your school has places where it posts job notices. Do not overlook this resource. Although you might not find the dream job that pays top dollar posted on a bulletin board tomorrow, it does not hurt to check what is posted every now and then.

You also have your instructors at your disposal. Instructors not only know a great deal about the subject matter they teach, but many of them also have worked or even currently work in the field in which they teach. One of the most disappointing things to many instructors is the fact that students never ask for help. Because instructors are part of the "real world," they often know about open jobs or jobs that will be available soon, or they have friends and colleagues who make hiring decisions. If you are interested in a job in private security, let your instructor of private security know that you have this interest. The same goes for corrections. Remember: Your instructors cannot help you if they are unaware that you are interested in such things.

Just being a student is a valuable resource. This means you often have access to influential people, simply by asking them if you can talk to them about their jobs. This is really one of the simple forms of *networking*, getting to know people in the field you are interested in. Whether we like it or not, if there is a job opening, people are more likely to "help out" someone they know and like rather than take a chance on someone they know little or nothing about. The least productive way to get a job is to respond to want ads and/or to submit your résumé blindly. This is not to say that you should not submit your résumé, but it is not an approach you should count on.

Another good networking skill—but one that might require more courage to use—is to identify people in your field of interest who are graduates of your school. Once you can identify these people, contact them (it would be best to write a professional letter rather than to call), tell them that you are a student at their former school, and ask if they would be willing to meet with you to talk about the job market in their field. If you approach this correctly, you will make them feel that they are important and respected. Remember: Your goal in meeting and talking with these people is not to ask them for a job but to ask them for advice on where and how to look for a job in your field. Do not put these people on the spot. Ask for *general* help, but do not hesitate to ask about any specific jobs (including at their agency) that they discuss.

If your school offers an internship or co-op program, consider looking into it. Interns are those who work—usually without pay—in exchange for exposure to what "real cops" or "real probation officers" do on a daily basis. This is an easy way to get your foot in the door. By interning at a particular agency, you will not have a lock on any jobs that open, but you will have an inside track. You will have been around the offices, people will have had a chance to know you, and you will have had an opportunity to prove that you can be a good worker. The other advantage of an internship is that you could very easily discover whether this is a type of work you really want to do. What a relief this would be: to find out while you are still in school that you really do not want to be a police officer. This could save you years of misdirected schoolwork, training, and time on the job. Internships are good ways to get jobs, and they are also good ways to learn the real story about jobs.

If your school does not have an internship program or if for some reason you do not wish to participate in one, consider contacting an agency yourself and inquiring about volunteer opportunities. Do not believe that because there is no one at your school who is responsible for setting up such contacts that they cannot be made. Taking the initiative to make the contact yourself can sometimes be interpreted in a positive manner.

Finally, remember that today's college classroom has people of all ages and at all stages of their careers. Especially in the fields of criminal justice and corrections, many who are already working in the field are returning to college. Look around your classes, listen to what people say about where they work, and do not hesitate to talk to your peers. They might be able to direct you to a job possibility.

Remember: Finding a job is a job in itself. There will be times when you might believe that there is not much hope and that you will have to sell pencils on street corners for the rest of your life. It is normal to feel frustrated and discouraged. It is rare to find great jobs right off the bat. Most of us struggle and even make mistakes, but whatever you do, keep working at finding work!

Making Your First Contact

Generally speaking, you have two ways to make your first contact with potential employers: You can either write to them or speak with them (usually on the telephone). It is almost always best to make your first contact in writing. There are several good reasons for that approach.

Writing to a Potential Employer

First, when you write to someone, you can carefully plan what you want to say and how you want to say it. When you are speaking with someone, you have to get it right the first time—not an easy task, especially if you are unsure of yourself to begin with! By writing to someone, then, you give yourself a better chance to make a good impression.

Second, writing is better than calling because you can be more certain that you will make contact with the correct person. Quite frankly, if you call someone, your chances of getting through to the right person can be pretty slim. Therefore, you will end up leaving messages, calling back repeatedly, or leaving messages on voice-mail. Talk about pressure! You have 30 seconds to make a good impression, tell these people who you are, what you want, and how to get ahold of you, and to convince them that it is worth their time to call you back or wait to hear from you again. If you write, you can get all of this on paper, and your letter will be waiting for them on their desks. This also means your letter will not interrupt someone who is busy on another project, who is running to a meeting, or who is simply not in a good mood.

Third, by writing to someone, you make a more professional and polished impression. In the professional world, most communication is done in writing, not on the telephone. This is partly because everyone is so busy and partly because this allows us to have a better understanding of what someone is trying to convey. If you call someone, you are suggesting that you are not very professional and that you are not tuned in to "how things are done."

The Rules to Follow

When writing to someone whom you believe can or may be able to offer you a job, you must follow a few simple rules. While these rules may seem picky or bothersome, remember, if you do not follow them, others will. You want to stand out from the rest, but only in a good way!

1. Be direct in stating your purpose in writing. Make a specific request of what you want from the reader.

2. Address your letter to a specific person.

3. Say everything you have to say, but say it quickly and do not add unnecessary information.

4. Be honest in what you say.

5. Send only letters that are neat, grammatically correct, and as professional-looking as possible.

6. Inform the reader how to contact you.

7. Thank the reader for his or her time/effort/attention.

Be Direct in Stating Your Purpose   Begin your letter by introducing yourself. Immediately after introducing yourself, tell the reader why you are writing. For instance:

> My name is Bill Q. Jones, and I am a student in the correctional program at Central State Community College. I am writing to request an appointment, at your convenience, to discuss the possibility of my interning with your agency.

If you do not tell the reader what you want, he or she will have to guess. In most cases, the guess will be that you do not know what you want. In this case, your letter will probably end up in the trash.

Address Your Letter to a Specific Person   One of the all-time worst mistakes is to address a letter to the "Human Resources Director" or, even worse, "To Whom It May Concern." Your letter probably will not concern anyone, and you will have wasted your time and postage stamp. Write to a specific person whenever possible.

This may mean finding out the human resources director's name. If you do not know it, call the agency and ask. People do it all the time.

Also, make certain that you get the name right! Names are easily misspelled. No one likes to have his or her name mangled. It is not the way to make a good impression.

Say What You Have to Say, But Nothing More   When writing to potential employers, you may be tempted to tell them about every positive quality you have. Do not follow through on this temptation. No one wants to read a long, rambling letter from a stranger. Tell the readers your purpose in writing, tell them what you want from them, and tell them (briefly) why they should be interested in responding to you.

Do not tell the human resources director of the local jail about how you won the art contest in high school, or how you play tuba in the marching band, or that your great grandfather once worked in the jail in Cleveland. You may be very proud of your tuba playing, but unless this is directly related to the job you are interested in, do not offer this information.

Be Honest   This rule really needs no explanation. You want to work in the field of criminal justice; your honesty is assumed. If you lie, you have proven yourself less than trustworthy and unsuitable for working in the field.

Mail Only a Letter That Is Perfect   This is the rule that many job-seekers find so frustrating. If you have to type a letter 30 times to get it right, then do so. Do not send a letter with mistakes in it! Also, do not trust yourself to catch all of your mistakes. Ask someone else to proofread your letter. It is much easier to catch someone else's mistakes than it is to catch your own. Do not "correct" mistakes on a letter by typing over a typo or by using liquid correction fluid or any other form of "cover up" correction. Of course, your letter should be typed.

Make certain that your letter is well written. Poor grammar, incorrect words, passive voice, incorrect verb tenses, and all other forms of "bad writing" can only work against you. Remember: You are competing for jobs. The person who can present the best overall package is likely to win the job. Poor writing skills, a lack of attention to detail, or so little care that a sloppy letter is mailed—these are factors that will be strikes against you.

Inform the Reader of How to Contact You   If you have been successful in catching your readers' eyes and if they are now interested in providing you what you have requested, they will need to know how to contact you. Do not assume that they will look at the envelope for your return address. Be explicit and direct in how you can be contacted. If there is more than one way to reach you, say this. However, provide only "professional" types of contacts for yourself. This means you should provide your address and at least one telephone number. If you provide more than one telephone number, you should indicate if there are usual times of day that you are likely to be at these

123 Main Street
City, State 12345
January 1, 19XX

Mr. George Smith
Human Resources Director
Private Prison Systems
999 Broad Street
City, State 98765

Dear Mr. Smith:

I understand you need entry-level correctional officers in your prison facilities. I am very interested in a position as a correctional officer in one of the prisons that your corporation operates.

I recently graduated from Minnesota State University with a degree in criminal justice, completeing my education with a grade point average of 3.9 on a 4.0 scale. In addition to my studies, I have also worked part-time as a security officer at a private psychiatric hospital, and I am a volunteer with homeless, abused children in the community. Also, I was the 1995 recipient of the Minnesota Good Citizen Award. My enclosed résumé details my work and educational history.

At the present time I am seeking a position such as those you are looking to fill. I am available for an interview at your convenience. Please call or write if you are interested in speaking with me about an entry-level position.

Sincerely,

Bill Q. Jones

Bill Q. Jones
Enclosure: Résumé

locations. Do not give your beeper number or other contacts that might catch you when you are not prepared to be at your best. For instance, it would not be advisable to say:

> You can call me at 555-0000 during the day. Or, I do not mind if you beep me (555-0001), but you can probably find me most afternoons at Sal's Bar. They all know me there. The number at Sal's is in the phone book.

This person should probably not be counting on getting a return telephone call.

The Magic Words   Your mother probably taught you always to say "thank you." When writing to potential employers (or to someone who could help you find a job), you always should thank them. If nothing else, you are saying "thank you" to them for devoting a few minutes to read what you have to say. Frankly, it is impolite *not* to say "thank you."

Résumés

To apply for a job in corrections—in fact, for most jobs in today's market—you will need to prepare and submit a résumé. Many students worry about writing a proper résumé or about what to put on a résumé. Do not panic. Millions of others have been in your position before, and not all of them have been jobless their entire lives! Remember: You are a student and are not expected to have a résumé full of impressive credentials. You are applying for entry-level positions and you do not necessarily need a six-page résumé that lists everything from a perfect grade-point average to 20 years' experience filling the exact responsibilities as the job for which you are now applying. Keep your goal in mind. If you are a 24-year-old college student who has never worked in corrections and what you have to offer is a decent GPA and a few good references, you are probably not qualified to be a warden. However, you could easily qualify for a job as a correctional officer.

A résumé is a written summary of your qualifications for a particular position. Remember that your résumé should fulfill three specific roles. First, a résumé should attract an employer's attention and interest in interviewing you. Second, a résumé provides a thorough, yet succinct summary of your education, work experience, and relevant personal information. Third, once you have an interview, your résumé serves as a point of reference for the interviewer.

The first task is to have a résumé that attracts attention. Ideally, your résumé should attract attention because of your outstanding qualifications and credentials. However, for most job applicants, the content of their résumés will not be much different from those submitted by other applicants. Therefore, your résumé needs to be easy to read, positive, and attractive.

Content of a Résumé

When developing your résumé, you will actually be writing individual sections that are then put together into the whole package. All résumés must include at least four major sections: job objective, education, employment history, and personal data.

Job Objective The first entry needs to be a statement of the specific position for which you are submitting your résumé. You want the person reading your résumé to know immediately whether you are applying for the position of prison chaplain, recreation specialist, or correctional officer. Stating the specific job for which you are applying can be especially important when you are submitting résumés to employers whom you think may have a job, but you are not certain. Most employers will keep a file of résumés for a year or more, pulling them out when a position opens.

Remember to state your objective clearly and simply. Most people who read résumés do not sit and ponder what you say. What type of job you want must be something that a reader can know by simply glancing at your résumé.

Education The second section of your résumé is a summary of your educational history. This section includes not only your formal, school-based education (high school, college, etc.), but also should include any relevant training (either on the job or otherwise) that you have completed. Be sure to include any military training that you may have completed also.

When summarizing your education, include the dates of your attendance and graduation, the names and addresses of schools, the exact degrees or certificates that you earned, your major (and minor, in college), and anything noteworthy about your education (awards, class standing, extracurricular activities).

Employment History   When summarizing your employment history, you are trying to communicate two types of messages. First, you are showing a potential employer that you do have some experience in a work setting and that some of your experience is related or relevant to the type of work you are now seeking. Second, you want the reader of your résumé to see you as someone who has a *stable* work history and as someone who can be counted on to do a good job.

When presenting your work history, start with your most recent (or present) job and work backwards. For each job that you include, provide the dates of your employment, the name and address of the employer, your job title and responsibilities, and your reason for leaving the job.

Personal Data   You may wish to include personal information when telling a potential employer about yourself. You need to provide enough information to prove yourself as a well-rounded, real person, yet not someone who is conceited or who has interests that are too specialized for the type of work the employer has to offer.

It is usually best to include on your résumé only those pieces of personal information that could be relevant to the job for which you are applying. You will want to include the place of your birth, your social security number, and any special skills (word processing, martial arts training, languages spoken, etc.). Some people believe it is important to include your marital status and whether you have any children. Others believe this is not related to your job performance and could work against you. This is a decision for you to make.

Final Tips on Résumés

Remember: Your resume will be representing you, and it must make a good first impression. While the specific style and content of your résumé may vary, a few general rules of thumb apply.

First, résumés are summaries, so they should not be very long. Preferably you want a one-page résumé. At most, your résumé should be two pages. Second, the appearance of your résumé is very important. Use a paper that stands out but is still professional. (No, do not use neon orange paper for your résumé!) This also means, of course,

Bill Q. Jones
123 Main Street
City, State 12345
(101) 555-0000

Job Objective Entry-level employment as a correctional officer.

Education

August 1991 - May 1995
Minnesota State University, College Town
B.S. in Criminal Justice
Major: Criminal Justice; Minor: Speech
Graduated Magna Cum Laude
Member Phi Beta Kappa, Alpha Phi Sigma

Employment

September 1992 - Present
Northern Minnesota Hospital for the Criminally Insane
Coldspot, Minnesota 52121
    Security Officer - Responsible for monitoring all
        entering and exiting visitors, maintaining order
        on seven hospital wards, and recapturing
        escapees.
August 1991 - September 1992
Minnesota State University Bookstore
100 College Green
College Town, Minnesota 52345
    Sales Clerk - Responsible for selling merchandise,
        maintaining store stock, and scheduling part-
        time employees.
Reason for leaving: Opportunity to work in criminal
justice-related field.

Personal Data

Date of Birth: July 4, 1976, Washington, D.C.
Social Security Number: 123-45-6789
Special Skills: Fluent in Spanish, German, Russian, and
    Japanese; Brown belt in karate
Awards: 1995 Minnesota Good Citizen Award

that your résumé is typed (or printed on a letter-quality computer printer) and completely free of errors or mistakes.

Job Interviews

Once you have made a contact or even simply responded to a posted job announcement, your next hurdle will be the job interview. Job-seekers often view interviews as highly stressful "tests" of whether they can "cut it" on the job. Yes, some interviews may be designed this way. However, most job interviews are really chances for you to sell yourself as the right candidate for the job. It is important that you go into an interview with a positive attitude. Think of this as your chance to show employers just how good you are, not a time for them to discover all of your faults.

Job interviews usually last between 15 minutes and 1 hour. However, the successful job interview requires a greater amount of time. The job interview process is composed of five steps: preparation, initial meeting, sharing information, closing, and post-interview contact.

Preparation

Being well-prepared for an interview cannot be stressed too much. Preparation is the key to making a good impression. What is it that you need to prepare and to prepare for, however? First, you will want to find out who will interview you, where, and when. Make sure you know the location of the interview site. This may mean making a practice run, to be sure you are not late. You will also want to know some things about the agency with whom you are interviewing. What types of positions is it seeking to fill? Have there been any major problems in the organization recently? (Check newspapers, etc.) What is the general reputation of the agency, both for the services it provides and as an employer?

What to Expect When you arrive at the interview, be prepared to spend some time filling out personnel forms. This is a good reason to arrive at least fifteen minutes early. Many employers will also want to see some form of identification. Be sure to have a driver's license, state identification card, or your social security card with you. Also, take a few extra copies of your résumé with you.

Being prepared for the interview itself means having some idea of what you might be asked and what your answers will be. You will also want to have some questions prepared to ask the interviewer. Having questions shows that you have an interest in the job, that you are intelligent, and that you have a curiosity. An employer almost always sees these as very positive traits.

Personal Appearance   Finally, your appearance counts. One of the most harmful things you can do is not to dress and groom appropriately for an interview. Job interviews are times to look professional, not necessarily fashionable. You want to appear responsible, mature, and stable. Generally speaking, you should dress conservatively, not flashy or sexy. This means that men should wear a suit and tie (or slacks, sportcoat, and tie) and that women should wear business dresses or suits with low, not high heels. Be sure your entire outfit is appropriate. A business suit with athletic shoes (no matter how new or expensive!) simply will not do. Jewelry should be kept to a minimum, colors should be subdued, and accessories (purses, notebooks, pens, etc.) should be well-maintained.

Also—and this should go without saying—be sure you are clean and well-groomed. If your hair needs to be cut or styled, do this before your interview. If your fingernails have grease caked under them, clean them. If your suit has a stain on it, get it cleaned. Also, remember you want to present a "clean appearance," so do not go to an interview wearing a strong perfume or cologne. Even if it is your favorite scent and an expensive import from Paris, save it for another occasion.

If you are not used to dressing this way and it makes you uncomfortable, you need to literally practice dressing this way. The point is: When you go for an interview, you want to appear as though this type of attire is "normal" for you, not something you wore just for the interview (even if that is the case).

Initial Meeting

After arriving at the interview site and filling out personnel forms, you will finally meet the interviewer(s). In some agencies you may be interviewed by a panel, perhaps as many as four or five. When first introduced to the interviewer, you will want to greet him or her (using name and title) and to give a firm handshake. Again, this is the interviewer's very first sight of you, so present yourself positively and warmly.

From the very first, be sure you make and maintain eye contact with the interviewer. People who will not or cannot make eye contact are viewed with suspicion in our culture. You do not want the interviewer to wonder what you are trying to hide. Also, make yourself as comfortable as you can. You will probably be seated during the interview. Be comfortable, but calm. Try not to tap your feet, play with your clothing, or do any other distracting "nervous habits."

Finally, during this initial meeting phase, be prepared to engage in some small talk. Here, your goal is not to "say the right things" but to allow the interviewer to see you as a friendly, warm, nice person.

Sharing Information

The "real" interview is the time during which you will answer questions the interviewer asks. While this may seem like an oral examination, remember that the employer is trying to see if you will fit with its needs and goals. Also, you are discovering whether what the employer wants is something you are interested in providing. Answer questions in honest, positive ways. Play up your strengths, showing how you can be an asset to the employer.

Remember also that you will have the opportunity to ask questions during the interview. You definitely want to have some questions to ask. However, do not ask obvious or trivial questions. Think these through beforehand. Also, do not focus your questions on salary. Focus on the job, opportunities for advancement, work environment, and other central aspects of the work.

One unique aspect of a job interview in the field of corrections is that you will probably have the opportunity to tour the facility or to be in the presence of inmates/clients. When you take the tour, be interested, ask thoughtful questions, and remember that the interviewer is watching you to see if you are comfortable and confident in the setting where you would be working. If you show fear or seem offended by the language and behavior of inmates/clients, you probably will not get the job. But, then, you probably should think about whether this is the type of job you want anyway.

- What are your long-range career objectives?
- Why are you interested in working here?
- What has made you interested in working in corrections?
- What do you see yourself doing five years from now? Ten years?
- What do you consider as your greatest strengths and weaknesses?
- How do you think a friend or professor who knows you would describe you?
- In what ways do you think you can make a contribution to our organization?
- Describe the relationship that you believe should exist between a supervisor and those reporting to him or her.
- What do you believe the goals of corrections should be?
- What subjects did you like best and least in college? Why?
- Do you have any plans to continue with your education?
- How do you work under pressure?
- What are the two or three things about a job that are most important to you?
- What do you know about our organization/agency?
- Why should I hire you?

Closing

Once you have discussed yourself and the employment thoroughly, and once you and the interviewer have answered each other's questions, you are ready to close. You may also be informed that the interview is over, if there are time constraints, or if the interviewer believes that all of the relevant questions have been asked and answered. This is your last couple of minutes to make a positive impression on the interviewer. Use the time to your advantage.

If you have any unanswered questions, this is the time to raise them. You might want to inquire about when you could expect to hear from the employer again. (This can reduce your long-term stress a great deal.) You might want to summarize briefly your strengths for the interviewer. Also, if you find that you really do want this job, say so. Do not let something go unsaid if you think the interviewer should know it.

Finally, ask if anything more is expected from you. Does the interviewer want you to submit references? Do you have to fill out any additional forms? Will you need to return for a second interview? Also, as always, clearly express your appreciation for the interview. Remember: Those magic words can work wonders!

Post-Interview Contact

After returning home from the interview, you will want to write another letter to the interviewer. Your letter is first to thank the interviewer for his or her time and willingness to meet with you. Second, your letter serves the purpose of putting your name in front of the employer once again. This can help remind the interviewer of you as he or she pores through piles of applications. It can also trigger the interviewer to think about you for a few minutes more, a couple of days after having met you.

You need to write this letter and post it no more than 24 hours after your interview. You want this to arrive a day or two after you met the interviewer. So, do not postpone writing it!

Finally, even if the interview did not seem to go very well (or especially if it did not go very well), review the strengths and weaknesses of your interviewing skills. Everybody has interviews for jobs they do not get. The person most likely to eventually get the job he or she wants, though, is the one who learns from interviews, both the good and the bad ones. Use the experience to your benefit. Persistence is the name of the game!

Where to Contact for Correctional Jobs

Depending on the specific job you are interested in, you may contact the person responsible for employment decisions in one of several types of agencies. This means you must first think about what type of work you are interested in and where you are interested in working.

Government Agencies

When most people think of corrections, they think of the state level. Each state has a department of corrections (although the specific name may vary by state). The specific mailing address for the department changes on a fairly frequent basis in some states. So, to get the correct address, you can look in either the government section of your local telephone book or talk to the reference librarian at your college or local library.

On the local level, your county or city government is involved in corrections to some degree. Again, look in the government pages of the local telephone book or ask your reference librarian for help.

At the federal level, you may contact the human resource director directly at any of the U.S. Bureau of Prisons' correctional institutions, or you can write for information packets to:

Federal Bureau of Prisons
National Recruitment Office, Suite 460
320 First Street, N.W.
Washington, D.C. 20534
1-800-347-7744

Private Corrections

Finally, a growing number of private correctional companies and institutions are opening around the country. Private corrections is the fastest growing area of corrections in the nation. Because of the rapid growth, it is not possible to list names and addresses of private correctional companies here. However, once you identify a particular company, you can locate its address through any number of sources available at your college or local library. Your college placement office should also have a listing of these companies' addresses.

Civil Service Tests

Many government jobs require a passing score on a civil service test before you become eligible for employment. Most states administer the tests once or a few times each year and at only one or a few places. To get the specifics on when and where (and how to register) for the civil service tests, you will need to contact your state government (or federal, for federal government jobs) civil service office or the human resources office at the department of corrections.

Once you take (and pass) the civil service test, you will then be considered eligible for civil service jobs. This means that you can place your name (and qualifications) on a list to be reviewed by those people responsible for hiring for certain classes of jobs. If you are pursuing a civil service job, you must be patient, because the process can be time-consuming. You should begin gathering all the necessary information well in advance of the time you hope to be working. Do not wait until you graduate, go on vacation, or try other avenues of finding a job before you find out when and where your state's civil service exam is given.

Final Words of Advice

Job hunting can be a very stressful time of your life. However, it is something almost everyone has been through. Do not let the process or the jobs that get away get you down. The real key to finding the job that is right for you is persistence. This means persisting in all aspects: looking, networking, preparing, revising your résumé, and interviewing.

Once you begin the job search, always think how you can improve upon (or do differently) something you have already completed. Always be on the lookout for new contacts; keep rechecking the job postings and keep submitting your résumé. Do not despair. The one thing that will make the experience even more stressful (and less likely to be successful) is a poor attitude. You need to remind yourself that you are a good candidate and that the perfect job awaits you. All you have to do is keep working to find it. Perhaps the best advice on which to base your job search is the cliché: "Looking for a job is a job in itself." Keep at it; it will work out!

Appendix B: Selected Amendments to the Constitution of the United States

Bill of Rights (Amendments 1-10)

Amendment I
(Ratified December 15, 1791)

Congress shall make no law respecting an establishment of religion, or prohibiting the free exercise thereof; or abridging the freedom of speech, or of the press, or the right of the people peaceably to assemble, and to petition the Government for a redress of grievances.

Amendment II
(Ratified December 15, 1791)

A well regulated Militia, being necessary to the security of a free State, the right of the people to keep and bear Arms, shall not be infringed.

Amendment III
(Ratified December 15, 1791)

No soldier shall, in time of peace be quartered in any house, without the consent of the Owner, nor in time of war, but in a manner to be prescribed by law.

Amendment IV
(Ratified December 15, 1791)

The right of the people to be secure in their persons, houses, papers, and effects, against unreasonable searches and seizures, shall not be violated, and no Warrants shall issue, but upon probable cause, supported by Oath or affirmation, and particularly describing the place to be searched, and the persons or things to be seized.

Amendment V
(Ratified December 15, 1791)

No person shall be held to answer for a capital, or otherwise infamous crime, unless on a presentment or indictment of a Grand Jury, except in cases arising in the land or naval forces, or in the Militia, when in actual service in time of War or public danger; nor shall any person be subject for the same offence to be twice put in jeopardy of life or limb, nor shall be compelled in any criminal case to be a witness against himself, nor be deprived of life, liberty, or property, without due process of law; nor shall private property be taken for public use without just compensation.

Amendment VI
(Ratified December 15, 1791)

In all criminal prosecutions, the accused shall enjoy the right to a speedy and public trial, by an impartial jury of the State and district wherein the crime shall have been committed; which district shall have been previously ascertained by law, and to be informed of the nature and cause of the accusation; to be confronted with the witnesses against him, to have compulsory process for obtaining witnesses in his favor, and to have the assistance of counsel for his defence.

Amendment VII
(Ratified December 15, 1791)

In Suits at common law, where the value in controversy shall exceed twenty dollars, the right of trial by jury shall be preserved, and no fact tried by a jury shall be otherwise re-examined in any Court of the United States, than according to the rules of the common law.

Amendment VIII
(Ratified December 15, 1791)

Excessive bail shall not be required, nor excessive fines imposed, nor cruel and unusual punishments inflicted.

Amendment IX
(Ratified December 15, 1791)

The enumeration in the Constitution of certain rights shall not be construed to deny or disparage others retained by the people.

Amendment X
(Ratified December 15, 1791)

The powers not delegated to the United States by the Constitution, nor prohibited by it to the States, are reserved to the States respectively, or to the people.

Amendment XIII
(Ratified December 6, 1865)

Section 1: Neither slavery nor involuntary servitude, except as a punishment for crime whereof the party shall have been duly convicted, shall exist within the United States, or any place subject to their jurisdiction.

Section 2: Congress shall have power to enforce this article by appropriate legislation.

Amendment XIV
(Ratified July 9, 1868)

Section 1: All persons born or naturalized in the United States and subject to the jurisdiction thereof, are citizens of the United States and of the State wherein they reside. No State shall make or enforce any law which shall abridge the privileges or immunities of citizens of the United States; nor shall any State deprive any person of life, liberty, or property, without due process of law; nor deny to any person within its jurisdiction the equal protection of the laws.

Amendment XVI
(Ratified February 3, 1913)

The Congress shall have power to lay and collect taxes on incomes, from whatever source derived, without apportionment among the several States, and without regard to any census or enumeration.

Amendment XVIII
(Ratified January 16, 1919)

Section 1: After one year from the ratification of this article the manufacture, sale, or transportation of intoxicating liquors within, the importation thereof into, or the exportation thereof from the United States and all territory subject to the jurisdiction thereof for beverage purposes is hereby prohibited.

Amendment XXI
(Ratified December 5, 1933)

Section 1: The eighteenth article of amendment to the Constitution of the United States is hereby repealed.
Section 2: The transportation or importation into any State, Territory, or possession of the United States for delivery or use therein of intoxicating liquors, in violation of the laws thereof, is hereby prohibited.

Amendment XXVI
(Ratified July 1, 1971)

Section 1: The right of citizens of the United States, who are eighteen years of age or older, to vote shall not be denied or abridged by the United States or by any State on account of age.
Section 2: The Congress shall have power to enforce this article by appropriate legislation.

Glossary

Absolute deprivation The state of not having sufficient resources to survive.

Accreditation Process by which correctional institutions and programs are declared to meet a minimum set of professional standards; professional organizations create and enforce this process.

Accredited Status of having met the minimum standards established by relevant professional associations.

Acquittal Declaring a defendant not guilty of the charges against him or her.

Active monitoring system A form of electronic monitoring where offenders wear devices that, when activated, will respond to telephone requests to show that offenders are remaining at home.

Adjudicated The process of legally determining that a juvenile has committed an act that, if done by an adult, would/could lead to a criminal conviction.

Age of majority The legal age at which individuals are no longer considered juveniles but adults; the age at which individuals can be held fully, legally responsible for their actions.

Amnesty Protection against prosecution.

Auburn system Approach to corrections that emphasized silence but required collective work projects; developed to overcome problems associated with the Pennsylvania system.

Authority The recognized potential power of a person or an agency to use force.

Autocratic wardens Early form of prison administration; total power centered in the hands of the top-level administrator; individuals who held the authority to make any and all decisions about the operations, personnel, or inmates of a particular institution.

Banishment Being permanently removed from a group or a location; the practice of forcing someone to leave a particular location or jurisdiction.

Boot camp A development of the 1990s where juvenile offenders are housed in a military-style camp and subjected to strict discipline, work, and physical training; its purpose is to rehabilitate offenders through intensive program participation and strict discipline.

Bureaucratic model Form of correctional management that emerged following the World War II; calls for specialization of tasks and dispersion of responsibility among numerous staff members and multiple levels of administration.

Captain of the guard Commanding officer of the custodial staff in a correctional institution.

Career criminals Offenders who are in and out of corrections and who spend the majority of their lives involved in some type of criminal activity.

Case law Court decisions that regulate the outcome of all future, similar cases.

Civil death Practice of legally transforming a convicted criminal to a nonbeing; the civilly dead individual was stripped of all legal rights, private property, and claims to inheritance and relationships.

Civil service Part of the bureaucratic model of management where staff receive specialized forms of job protection as governmental workers.

Classical view Perspective on crime that believes people freely choose their behaviors; criminal actions are seen as voluntarily chosen.

Classification The practice of assessing inmates and assigning them to facilities and programs that suit their security and treatment needs.

Cocorrectional institution An institution that houses both male and female inmates in different units of the institution.

Collateral consequences Loss of privileges and rights that accompany a criminal conviction.

Collateral costs   The disruptions to the lives of those related to offenders and the economic impact on offenders and their families that result from being involved in the criminal justice system.

Collective bargaining   Process whereby a labor union (or other group representing a collection of individuals) negotiates a contract of wages, benefits, and working conditions for staff with an employer's administrative agents.

Community corrections   Programs that allow offenders to remain in their home communities but impose upon them some degree of supervision and programming.

Community development   Actions and plans of communities to improve the economic and social conditions that affect residents.

Community service   A form of community corrections, usually accompanying other forms of sentences, in which offenders are required to participate in volunteer work to repay some of the harm/costs they imposed on society.

Community treatment centers   Lower-level security institutions designed to house convicted offenders but to allow them interactions in free society.

Conditions of confinement   The prisons' actual physical conditions and the positive or negative impacts they have on inmates.

Congregate work   Practice of bringing inmates together to work in a common location on a common job.

Conjugal visits   Time that inmates are allowed to spend with family and spouses in private; usually thought of as opportunities for spouses to visit inmates and to engage in sexual activity.

Consensus model   A form of participatory management in which administrators met with inmate groups to discuss changes to institutional policies and programs.

Constitutions   The formal documents that create the structure and outline the basic procedures of a governmental body; the most powerful forms of law in our society.

Contact visits   Visiting in a setting where inmates and visitors are not separated by a partition.

Contraband   Forms of personal property that are not allowed in correctional institutions.

Conviction   Declaring a defendant guilty of, or a defendant pleading guilty to, the charges against him or her.

Cooperative jail administration   Agreements among several governmental bodies to jointly build, manage, and operate local facilities; purpose is to allow small or economically pressed communities access to local correctional facilities.

Corporal punishment   Physical forms of punishment such as whipping, stoning, or burning.

Correctional institutions   Facilities designed to hold and control convicted criminal offenders; include various types of prisons and jails.

Corrections   The set of interrelated organizations, agencies, and programs that hold, treat, and sometimes punish people known or strongly believed to have committed a crime.

Cottage system   A housing pattern most common for women and juveniles; inmates are housed in house-like buildings, in small groups, and with staff who stay in the building, acting as "parents" overseeing the inmates' activities.

Courtesy stigmas   Negative labels others apply to individuals whom they perceive as associated with known or suspected criminals.

Crime index   The measure of society's most serious crimes; the collection of statistics from the Uniform Crime Reports of the amount of murder, rape, robbery, assault, burglary, larceny-theft, motor vehicle theft, and arson; reported in terms of the number of these offenses per 100,000 people.

Criminology   The study of crime; the science whose goal is to develop principles to explain the processes of law, crime, and treatment.

Depersonalization   Result of living in a total institution where individuals lose their sense of individuality and identify themselves as simply members of a set of similar individuals.

Deputies Top-level assistants in an administrative structure; typically have daily responsibilities for particular areas of operation in a facility or program; also sometimes referred to as *assistant wardens.*

Detention center A facility for the temporary placement of juvenile offenders and sometimes juvenile crime victims; a place where juveniles can be held and provided some forms of treatment.

Determinate sentences Fixed periods of time that convicted offenders must serve in a correctional program.

Deterrence Belief that punishing criminal actions will reduce crime in the future.

Direct supervision Opportunities for jail or prison staff to continuously and directly monitor inmates' activities, made possible by technologies or new generation architecture.

Discipline An administrative goal for prisons; involves punishment for inmates or staff members who break a prison's rules.

Disenfranchisement Loss of the right to vote.

Dispositions The various outcomes of court cases; the findings and rulings of judges or courts.

Diversion centers A form of intermediate sanction where offenders live in a facility for a few months and are supervised 24 hours per day, but can leave for work and other forms of necessary activity.

Double-celling The practice of housing two inmates in a cell designed for only one inmate.

Double jeopardy Holding a person responsible for a criminal action more than one time; this is prohibited by the Fifth Amendment to the United States Constitution.

Due process The legally required steps that the legal system must follow in any action to fully protect the rights of citizens, including convicted criminal offenders.

Due process rights The protections all citizens hold against being treated unfairly and being punished without proper application of the legally required steps to ensure that only when necessary are their rights or freedoms removed or restricted.

Electronic monitoring Use of special devices to signal supervising probation departments when offenders on home incarceration leave their premises, thereby violating the conditions of their sentence.

Equality Viewing all similar people and acts as deserving the same punishments or rewards.

Equal protection Legal requirement from the Fourteenth Amendment that, regardless of sex or race, inmates of various groups must be treated similarly.

Equity Rewarding or punishing people for their actions based on their contributions to the outcome of their actions.

Executive clemency Special power granted to elected office holders that permits them to overrule some court decisions.

Expiation Making amends for wrongdoing by suffering; the process of suffering as a way of showing awareness of and responsibility for wrongdoing.

First generation jails Early correctional facilities in which all prisoners were held in one communal room or building.

Force The use of power to gain physical control over others.

Gaols Early forerunners of modern jails; first established in 1166 in England.

Gender Social roles based on presumed qualities associated with a person's sex.

General deterrence Belief that punishing criminals will prevent others who know of this punishment from commiting crimes.

Geriatric inmates Elderly inmates who present unique health and social needs.

Good-time laws A forerunner of parole, these statutes gave prison administrators the power to release inmates prior to the expiration of their sentences based on the administrator's judgment that the inmate had shown good behavior and thereby deserved early release.

Group home A community correctional facility where small groups of juveniles live in a homelike setting with staff who provide for the juveniles' basic needs and attempt to socialize them with law-abiding norms, values, and behaviors.

Hands-off policy Practice of the courts throughout U.S. history to avoid involvement in correctional matters.

Hearing A procedure that a judge conducts to make a decision about the procedures used with an offender.

High-risk youths Juveniles who are believed, because of their social environments, economic situations, and family structures, to be significantly more likely than other juveniles to become involved in delinquency.

Home incarceration Sentence where individuals are required to remain in their homes, except for special reasons (work, school, medical care); purpose is to incapacitate offenders from recommitting their offenses.

Household crimes Criminal offenses that victimize people by removing or destroying property.

Incapacitation Belief that criminal offenders should be removed from opportunities to commit future crimes.

Incarceration rates Number of people in prison per 100,000 population.

Incorrigible Being unmanageable or uncontrollable.

Indeterminate sentences Sentences that impose a minimum and maximum period of time that offenders will serve in a correctional program; the actual length of each sentence is determined by the offender's behavior and rehabilitative progress.

Index offense The eight crimes considered the most serious; the eight offenses (murder, rape, robbery, aggravated assault, burglary, larceny-theft, motor vehicle theft, and arson) that are combined to create the crime index.

Inmate code Set of norms and values that structure the informal patterns of life among inmates; these are the "rules" that inmates impose on their community.

Inmate council Groups of inmates whom administrators select to inform or to make decisions about areas of institutional life.

Intensive supervision probation (ISP) A form of community corrections supervision in which probation officers check on a smaller caseload of offenders more frequently, often unannounced.

Intermediate sanction A correctional program that emphasizes supervision but is less intensive than incarceration; a program that falls between traditional probation and incarceration.

Intermittent supervision Periodic, not constant, supervision of inmates.

Iron law of oligarchy Idea that people in positions of power strive to maintain their power through giving somewhat powerful subordinate positions to loyal followers.

Jailhouse lawyers Inmates who are knowledgeable about the law and how to work in the judicial system; inmates who use their skills and knowledge to assist other inmates in preparing and submitting legal paperwork.

Jails Local correctional institutions designed to hold both convicted misdemeanants and people charged with crimes and awaiting judicial processing.

Judicial intervention Actions of the courts to determine whether the actions of correctional officials are legal and within constitutional boundaries.

Judicial review The process whereby an appellate court reviews a trial court decision and determines whether the decision is within the legal boundaries established by the Constitution.

Just deserts model Belief that criminal offenders should receive punishments in amounts equal to the degree of harm they caused to other individuals and society.

Labeling theory Belief that the names and terms used to identify people shape the identities and behaviors of such people.

Law A rule of conduct that an authority formally recognizes and enforces; the statements in society that tell people what is expected of them and what they can expect from others.

Leasing system Early form of prison industries where inmates were rented to individuals who put them to work and who assumed responsibility for providing necessities and security to inmates.

Life skills Basic tools for adequate social functioning in society; includes such things as household management, simple financial management, communication skills, and parenting skills.

Line officers Those who directly supervise the inmates of a correctional institution; also referred to as *correctional officers.*

Lockstep Practice of requiring inmates to walk/march in unison while holding the shoulder of the inmate in front of them.

Lockup A holding center for people who have not been detained long enough to be fully processed into jail.

Long-term incarceration Serving more than 7 or 8 years in a correctional institution.

LULUs (locally unwanted land uses) Publicly perceived undesirable developments in communities; facilities and activities that are seen as detractions from the communities' quality of life and economic standing.

Mala in se Early category of crimes; those offenses that are considered intrinsically wrong.

Mala prohibitum Early category of crimes; those offenses that are considered wrong only because society has prohibited them.

Mandatory early release programs Procedures in correctional systems that require inmates to be released prior to the expiration of their sentences to maintain legal limits on institutional populations.

Marks system An early approach to structuring how convicts could earn early release from incarceration; offenders earned points (marks) based on their behavior while incarcerated; different levels of earned marks meant that convicts gained privileges and eventually time off their sentences.

National Crime Victimization Survey (NCVS) The Bureau of the Census' annual national study that gathers data from U.S. citizens about the amount of crime they experienced; the main alternative source of crime statistics to the Uniform Crime Reports.

Natural law Belief that some actions are intrinsically wrong and that people do not really make decisions about right and wrong; restrictions on behavior come not from social groups, but from higher moral powers.

Net-widening Correctional programs or practices that are applied to people who otherwise would not have received such harsh sentences had the programs or practices not existed.

Neurotics Individuals with milder forms of mental illness and whose extreme forms of anxiety interfere with their abilities to effectively cope with daily life.

New generation jails Modern design of local correctional facilities; individual cells/rooms are placed around the outside of a large room with officers' stations in the middle of the facility, allowing constant observation of all cells/rooms; includes common areas in the building's open spaces where inmates spend most of their time.

Obligations The actions that society may legitimately expect from us, based on our roles and statuses.

Organized disturbances Planned and coordinated uprisings that have only minimal disruptive and damaging effects.

Overcrowding The practice of housing more inmates in a facility that is not designed or legally approved to house more than a set maximum number of inmates.

Pardon An executive act that legally clears an offender from the consequences of conviction for a criminal offense.

Parens patriae Legal doctrine that says the state must provide parental-like protections to those who are unable to care for themselves; applied to convicts when popular ideology holds that criminals have shown themselves unable to act like adults.

Parole Release from prison prior to the expiration of the full sentence with supervision while in the community.

Parole eligibility date The first date on which an inmate may be considered for release; this date is determined by statutory law.

Participatory management Management model where both correctional staff and inmates are included in decision-making processes.

Passive monitoring system A form of electronic monitoring where devices emit constant signals to receivers attached to offenders' telephones; if the constant signals are broken, the devices automatically alert the probation department that offenders are in violation of the conditions of home incarceration.

Penalty An imposed cost for the consequences of one's actions; usually considered a negative experience.

Penitentiary First form of American prisons; institutions designed to encourage criminals to contemplate their actions and the consequences of them.

Pennsylvania system Approach to correctional institutions that included silence and complete separation of inmates.

Personal theft The crime of stealing money or property directly from a person.

Physical coercion The use of force to make someone follow orders.

Plantation system Form of prison industry based on agriculture; inmates are housed and work on large farms where they produce food and other agricultural products for consumption in the correctional system.

Positivistic view Perspective that believes something causes or pushes people to commit crime; belief that something in biology, psychology, or social structures leads to criminal behavior.

Post-modernism A perspective that criticizes the positivistic view and argues that social science should question the supposed causes of crime; also known as *post-structuralism*.

Post-structuralism See *post-modernism*.

Precipitating factors Circumstances that trigger actions.

Predisposing factors Circumstances in an institution that make people willing to take action to change conditions.

Presentence investigation (PSI) A report, usually prepared by a probation department, that informs a sentencing court about the social, criminal, economic, and educational background of a convicted offender; PSIs recommend sentences for offenders, and courts use them as one source of information in deciding sentences.

Price-piece system Form of prison industry where private contractors supply prison officials with raw materials and tools that inmates use to produce finished goods; contractors pay a specific per-unit price to the institution for goods produced.

Prison argot A language that is unique to a prison.

Prison gangs Groups of inmates, usually organized along racial or ethnic lines, who victimize other inmates to improve the gang members' quality of life.

Prison industries Vocational training offered to inmates through employment in manufacturing jobs provided in the prison.

Prisonization Process where inmates internalize the institution's norms, values, and activity patterns.

Prison siting Processes of deciding where to locate new prisons.

Private prisons Correctional institutions operated by private organizations or corporations; facilities that house inmates for governments and receive a per-inmate daily fee.

Privatization Movement to transfer administrative and operational responsibilities for correctional facilities to private companies or charitable organizations.

Proactive Working to avoid problems; responding to potential problems before they actually develop.

Probation A sentence that allows convicted offenders to remain in the community, with restrictions on their activities and with assigned officers to supervise and assist them.

Procedural laws The rules governing how laws are made, interpreted, and enforced.

Professionalization The process through which an occupation changes status to a profession.

Protective custody Highly restrictive, special housing units where inmates who require extra protection are placed.

Pseudofamilies A social phenomenon in women's prisons where inmates assume statuses and roles that create family-like situations; developed to offset the emotional and psychological differences between life in prison and on the outside.

Psychotics Seriously disturbed, mentally ill people who experience reality differently than do individuals who are not mentally ill.

Public service activities Projects that prison inmates and staff engage in to make positive contributions to the communities in which prisons are located.

Punishment The process of causing others pain for the purpose of making them suffer.

Qualified immunity Legal protection of government officials that restricts the individuals' responsibilities when they or the agencies they work for violate inmates' legal rights.

Reactive Responding to problems after they develop; working to stop or reduce the effects of problems only after they occur.

Recidivism The recurrence of crime by an individual known to have previously committed a crime.

Reformation The idea that when people commit crimes, society should work to change the people so that they do not repeat their crimes.

Reformatory Correctional institution designed for younger, less-serious offenders; its purpose is to provide rehabilitative opportunities to offenders.

Rehabilitation Belief that criminal offenders should receive treatment to change the aspect that led the individuals to commit crime.

Reintegration Belief that criminal offenders should receive treatment to assist them in returning to society in ways that will allow them to fit in better (and commit less crime) than they experienced previously.

Relative deprivation The state of having less than others in the same environment with whom individuals compare themselves.

Release on one's own recognizance (ROR) Release from custody without bail while awaiting trial.

Resilient youths Juveniles who, despite being subjected to numerous factors believed to lead to juvenile delinquency, remain free from delinquency and crime; youths who do not become delinquents, although their social environments would lead to predictions that they would be delinquent.

Responsibility model A form of participatory management that attempted to encourage a sense of community among inmates by imposing minimum restraints on daily life.

Restitution Court-ordered repayment of losses or expenses to the victims of offenders' crimes.

Retaliation Responding to people with actions similar to their crimes because they deserve to suffer similar harms.

Retribution The idea that a crime (or any wrongdoing) is reacted to with a punishment because the individual who commits a wrong deserves to be punished.

Revocation of probation The process of removing offenders from probation programs and returning them to correctional facilities to serve the remaining time on their suspended sentences.

Rights The actions we may legitimately expect from others in society.

Riot An incident when authorities lose control of a significant number of prisoners in a significant area of the prison for a significant amount of time.

Routine activities theory People's usual, daily activities that place them in contact with others who have opportunities to victimize them.

Second generation jails Correctional facilities operated by local governments and designed with rows of side-by-side cells with offices located at one end of the building.

Security An administrative goal of maintaining order; the top priority in any correctional institution; includes preventing escapes, preventing intrusions from unwanted outsiders, and keeping order among inmates.

Segregation An administrative goal for prisons; involves classifying (segregating and separating) various types of prisoners to protect them from other inmates and to protect the prison's internal and external security.

Sentence The official, required punishment or course of treatment that a court imposes on a convicted offender.

Sexual violence Using sexual activity to bring harm to another person; in prison this comes in forcible rape, coerced sex, and coerced prostitution.

Shock incarceration Sentencing offenders to short periods of time in prison with following periods of time on community supervision; the idea is to make offenders realize what prison is like and to avoid their future return to prison.

Snitches Inmates who inform on other inmates to institutional officials; lowest of the low in the inmate social hierarchy.

Social density Perceptions of overcrowding based on the number of people assigned to a given space.

Spatial density Number of people per particular sized spaces; used to compare the degree of overcrowding in various locations.

Special masters Individuals appointed by courts to ensure that correctional administrators follow court orders.

Special needs inmates Inmates who require special programming, housing, or health services.

Specific deterrence Belief that punishing criminals will reduce the likelihood of their recommitting crimes.

Split sentences Criminal sentences that include both time in an institution and a period of time on community corrections.

Stare decisis The principle that when courts decide cases, decisions are based on precedents; the idea that laws are accumulated to provide predictability in court decisions.

State use system Form of prison industry where inmates produce goods that, rather than being sold on the open market, are used by state agencies.

Status degradation ceremony Procedures where individuals are officially declared no longer to occupy particular social roles and statuses and are symbolically and officially placed into a less valued social position.

Status offenses Acts of conduct that are illegal for juveniles but not for adults; activities that are illegal only because the individuals involved have the status of juveniles.

Statutes The laws that legislatures make; most commonly these are substantive laws.

Statutory codes The organized collection of statutes that regulate a particular jurisdiction.

Statutory laws Laws that elected representatives make; also known as *legislative law.*

Substantive law The set of rules that tell us what behaviors are allowed and required from people; the official rules of society that regulate what people must or must not and may or may not do.

Suspended sentence A punishment that is withheld but can be reimposed if the offender violates court-imposed conditions.

Systematic approach Viewing a process as a set of interrelated parts; viewing actions as part of a larger process, not simply as unconnected acts; recognition that the actions of one agency or person will affect other people or agencies.

Taboos Actions that are considered unthinkable in a culture.

Technical violations Actions on the part of probationers or parolees that break the rules imposed by their sentences; these may serve as grounds for revoking probation/parole.

Texas control model A form of participatory management where strong and powerful inmates were given authority to maintain order and security among segments of the inmate population; declared unconstitutional in 1982 by the Supreme Court in *Ruiz v. Estelle.*

Ticket of leave   A concept that allowed a government official to excuse offenders from the legal consequences of their criminal convictions and to return to their communities to live independently; an early forerunner of parole.

Total institution   An approach where others regulate and control all aspects of an individual's life and activities.

Totality of conditions   An institution's complete set of physical and social circumstances; during the prisoners' rights movement, this was the focus of lawsuits claiming that prisons/jails were in violation of minimum constitutional standards.

Training school   A facility that is designed to keep close supervision of juvenile offenders while it also encourages their continuation of education and other treatment programs; training schools are the juveniles' equivalent of the adult reformatory.

Transportation   Early correctional practice of moving convicted criminals to different societies; convicts were transported (usually across seas/oceans) to colonies as punishments for crimes.

Treatment   An administrative goal for prisons; involves psychological and substance-abuse counseling, basic and advanced education, and behavioral modification and job-training programs.

Treatment modalities   General approaches to providing rehabilitation and/or reintegration programming for inmates.

Two-track system   In women's corrections, the historical development of prisons and reformatories; both types of institutions were used for several decades, had different goals, and were designed to serve different types of inmates.

Uniform Crime Reports (UCR)   Official crime statistics that the FBI gathers; the collection of all criminal offenses reported to law enforcement agencies.

Violent crime   Criminal offenses that either directly cause or threaten physical harm to a person.

Walnut Street Jail   The first U.S. correctional institution that opened in 1790 in Philadelphia.

Warden   Top-level administrator who manages an individual correctional institution; also sometimes referred to as a *superintendent.*

Work-release   Programs whereby inmates are allowed to leave a correctional facility to attend jobs on the outside.

Index

Case Index

Name Index

Subject Index

Retaliation, as reaction to crime, 14
Retention, of jail staff, 301–303
Retribution, as reaction to crime, 14
Retribution ideology, 59, 60
Revocation of parole, 369–373
Revocation of probation, hearings
    and, 345
Rights, 26
    of prisoners. *See* Prisoner's rights
    of probationers. *See* Probationer's
        rights
Riots, 215–216, 223–237
    at Atlanta, 230–232
    at Attica, 224–226
    explanations for, 232–237
    at Oakdale, Louisiana, 230–232
    at Santa Fe, 226–230
Rising expectations/relative
    deprivation model, of riots,
    237
ROR (release on one's own
    recognizance), 325
Routine activities theory, of violence,
    206

San Quentin, 82
Santa Fe Penitentiary, riot at, 226–
    230
Schools, training, for juvenile
    offenders, 405–406
Second generation jails, 283–284
Security, as administrative goal, 109
Segregation, as administrative goal,
    109
Selection, of prison staff, 120–124
Self-inflicted violence, 212–213
Sentences, 36–37
    death. *See* Death sentence
    determinate, 51
    indeterminate, 51, 359–360
    reducing, 73
    split (combination), 373–375
    suspended, 325
Sentencing Reform Act of 1984,
    327
Sexual violence, 210–212
Shock incarceration, 373–375
Sing Sing Prison, 81
Snitches, 229

Social control model, of riots, 236–
    237
Social density, 422
    in jails, 300
Social functions of criminal justice,
    25–33. *See also* Laws; Sources
    of law
Societies
    law's role in, 25–26
    primitive, punishment in, 52–53
Society's reaction to crime, 12–15
    banishment as, 14
    prevention as, 15–16
    reformation as, 15
    retaliation as, 14
    retribution as, 14
Sources of law, 28–33
    administrative law as, 32–33
    case law as, 30, 32
    constitutions as, 28–29
    legislatures as, 29–30
Spatial density, in jails, 300
Special master, job as, 420
Special needs inmates, 142
Specific deterrence, 61
Split sentences, 373, 374
Spontaneity model, of riots, 234–
    235
Staff, 113–115
    inmate violence against, 207–208
    professionalization of, 124–128
    selection and training of, 120–
        124
    as "the other prisoners," 120
    unionization of, 128–130
    violence on inmates by, 208–210
Stare decisis, 32
State government jail administration,
    292–293
State institutions, for women, 259–
    261
The State of Prisons (Howard), 68
State use system, 162
Status degradation ceremony, 148
Status offenses
    of juveniles, 386–388
    of women, 249
Statutes, 29
Statutory codes, 29
Statutory laws, 28

Subculture. *See* Culture of prisons
Substance abuse, among jail inmates,
    306–308
Substantive law, 27
Suicide, among jail inmates, 308–
    309
Suspended sentences, 325
Systematic approach, to juvenile
    justice, 383–386

Taboos, 52
Target hardening, 15
Technical violations, of probation,
    342
Terre Haute Penitentiary, 98
Tests, civil service, 465–466
Texas control model, 118
Thefts, personal, 5
Thirteenth Amendment, 179
Ticket of leave, 357
Total institution, 137
Totality of conditions, 185
Training. *See also* Education;
        Programming
    of jail staff, 303
    parenting, for women inmates,
        265
    of prison staff, 120–124
Training schools, for juvenile
    offenders, 405–406
Transportation, 358
Treatment. *See* Programming
Turnover, of jail staff, 303, 305
Two-track system, 254

Underreporting of crimes, 10–12
Uniform Crime Reports (UCR), 6–
    8, 9–10
Uniforms, 89
Unionization, 128–130
United States, profile of crime in, 4–
    12
Utilitarian view of crime. *See*
        Positivistic view of crime

Vengeance, methods of, 53–54
Vengeance ideology, 59, 60

Photo Credits